AUGUSTUS TO NERO :
A SOURCE BOOK ON ROMAN HISTORY,
31 BC – AD 68

AUGUSTUS TO NERO:
A Sourcebook on Roman History
31 BC-AD 68

DAVID C. BRAUND

BARNES AND NOBLE BOOKS
Totowa, New Jersey

© 1985 David Braund
First published in the USA in 1985 by
Barnes & Noble Books, 81 Adams Drive,
Totowa, New Jersey, 07512

Library of Congress Cataloging in Publication Data

Braund, David, 1957-
   Augustus to Nero.

   Bibiography: p.
   Includes indexes..
   1. Rome — History — Augustus, 30-B.C.-14 A.D. — Sources.
2. Rome — History — The five Julii, 30 B.C.-68 A.D. — Sources.
I. Title.
DG277.5.B73 1985   937'.07   84-20368
ISBN 0-389-20536-2

Printed and bound in Great Britain.

CONTENTS

74836

PREFACE

Many of the most important sources for the years 31 BC to AD 68 are inaccessible, because they are buried in obscure publications and/or simply because they are in Greek or Latin. This is particularly the case with more recent discoveries. In selecting the sources collected in this book I have sought to unearth these obscurities and to make them available to a much wider public by translating them, often for the first time; in making these translations I have made accuracy, not elegance, my main objective. This book is therefore a tool, designed to facilitate in-depth study of a central period in Roman history. But it must be stressed that it is a sourcebook, not a course-book: as such, it is meant to be used in conjunction with other books in the context of teaching or private study. The reader should not be led to forget this by the fact that I have included some explanatory notes, references to the likes of Tacitus and Suetonius and references to widely-available textbooks. Reference to more obscure material is occasionally made in order to account for provenance or new readings.

I have deliberately omitted from this selection the works of Tacitus, Suetonius and Cassius Dio. Any one of these, let alone all three, would have dominated the whole collection, but they can be safely omitted since the first two are readily available to all, as will soon be the third, also. Instead, I have concentrated upon the documentary sources — inscriptions, coins and papyri — and relatively inaccessible literary sources of various types, from epigrams to legal tracts. Of course, it is not implied and it should not for one moment be supposed that the value of a source bears any relationship to its obscurity.

Collections of the sources for this period have been made before. Two stand out: Victor Ehrenberg and A.H.M. Jones *Documents Illustrating the Reigns of Augustus and Tiberius* (reprinted with additions, 1976) and E. Mary Smallwood *Documents Illustrating the Principates of Gaius, Claudius and Nero* (1967). Both are excellent, but they contain no translations and little literary evidence, as their titles suggest. Recent researches have also rendered them both a little out of date. For all that, their abiding value is such that I have found it necessary to include, in translation, most of the texts they contain.

References are given to assist the reader who wishes to compare the Latin and Greek texts conveniently available in those two collections. To this end I have also arranged the sources in this book along lines broadly similar to those laid down by my distinguished predecessors: it may be helpful to detail the main differences of arrangement. My first section, 'The Imperial Family', includes much of what my predecessors would have classified as 'Historical Events' and 'Imperial Cult'. Sources relating to the cult of a member of the imperial family are, for the most part, gathered towards the end of the sources relating to that person; it has seemed best, however, to keep together evidence for the imperial cult under Augustus and Tiberius – this is gathered towards the end of the material on Tiberius. Sources which my predecessors would have classified under 'Roads', 'Public Works', 'Other Religion' and 'Varia' mostly appear in my final section, 'Society and Economy'. Sources on kings, towns and cities have been collected into the same section, since they are best seen together.

It should be noted that all dates are AD unless otherwise stated. Also, that the term 'Bilingual' means that the document concerned was originally written in both Greek and Latin with no significant differences between the two versions, unless specifically stated. Uncertainties in the texts have been mentioned only where important: in some cases particularly questionable restorations have been omitted. In citing publications of the original Greek or Latin text, I have had almost as much regard for availability as for recentness, unless improved readings dictated otherwise. Little of this will concern those for whom this book is primarily intended. But all should note that all texts included are to be understood to be inscriptions unless the contrary is obvious or stated.

In any selection of this sort there will always be texts which might have been included but were not; that is the nature of selection. In this book I have tried to please everybody – obviously impossible – by including not only my own choice of texts, but also texts frequently mentioned and discussed by others, whether or not I personally consider them to be particularly important. It is my hope that by keeping my own preferences in check to this extent, I have made this book more useful to more people.

A few words on methodology and areas of difficulty seem appropriate. First, the texts included have been loosely grouped under section headings of a deliberately vague nature; needless to say, many texts could have been included under several different headings – the reader is invited to make extensive use of the index. Second, sourcebooks seldom give anything like sufficient prominence to representational art and archaeological evidence in general: this book is no exception to this rule, not least because illustrations of the most important evidence of that sort for our period are already available – for example, in the Plates of the *Cambridge Ancient History*. Third, although the subject of this book is a neatly defined, fixed period of history and although it is convenient and practical to divide history into such periods for the purposes of study, it should not be forgotten that history is a continuum: to divide it up into periods is an essentially artificial and misleading procedure, as becomes most apparent in the study of social and economic history – themselves rather arbitrary categories. Fourth and probably most important, it must be recognised that the sources are not self-explanatory in any way: contrary to popular belief, they do not and cannot 'speak for themselves', for they are silent until we read and interpret them. In the introduction to this book I have set about the hazardous task of explaining and seeking to deal with this complex problem in a few pages.

In conclusion to this preface it is a great pleasure to offer my thanks to friends who have helped and fortified me in the writing of this book. I must first thank Richard Stoneman, Humanities Editor at Croom Helm, who had both the vision to appreciate the need for books of this sort and the confidence to entrust this book to me. Joyce Reynolds, who supervised my doctoral dissertation, has taken an interest in this book from the very first, providing encouragement and advice on one or two points of detail; in addition, her surveys of epigraphical work, compiled with the help of others, which have appeared in the *Journal of Roman Studies* at intervals over the past 20 years and more, have been of outstanding assistance to me. Peter Wiseman has somehow found time to cast a critical eye over my introduction at short notice, despite heavy commitments of his own. And my wife, Su, has once again helped me enormously, in ways small and large, in the writing of this book. Of course, it must be understood that these generous people are in no way responsible for what I have made of their help and advice.

BIBLIOGRAPHICAL NOTE

The purpose of this note is to suggest further complementary reading; as stated in the Preface, this book is not designed to be used in a vacuum.

Easily the best introduction to the whole period with which we are concerned is Peter Garnsey and Richard Saller, *The Early Principate: Augustus to Trajan* (Greece and Rome: new surveys in the Classics no. 15, 1982); it is up-to-date, pithy, reliable and reasonably priced.

The rise of Augustus, in particular, and the development of Republic into Principate is treated in masterly fashion in Sir Ronald Syme's classic *The Roman Revolution* (1939). An accessible biography of Augustus is A.H.M. Jones, *Augustus* (1970); still valuable on the same subject is T. Rice Holmes, *The Architect of the Roman Empire* (2 vols., 1928-31) who gives very full references to the original sources in the course of a sensitive and perceptive narrative.

The period AD 14-68 is covered in A. Garzetti, *From Tiberius to the Antonines* (trans. 1974), a solid narrative with extensive bibliography. The emperors from Tiberius to Nero have also been treated in scholarly biographies: B.M. Levick, *Tiberius the Politician* (1976) and R. Seager, *Tiberius* (1972), J.P.V.D. Balsdon, *The Emperor Gaius* (1934), A.D. Momigliano *Claudius: the Emperor and his Achievement* (2nd edn, 1961) and V.M. Scramuzza, *The Emperor Claudius* (1940), B.H. Warmington *Nero: Reality and Legend* (2nd edn, 1983).

The role of the emperor is explored at length in F. Millar, *The Emperor in the Roman World* (1977). M.T. Griffin, *Seneca: a Philosopher in Politics* (1976) is an excellent case-study of one member of the imperial elite, full of insights into the period as a whole. J.A. Crook, *Law and Life of Rome* (1967) and, now, K. Hopkins, *Death and Renewal* (1983) are useful starting-points for the study of imperial society, while A.H.M. Jones, *The Roman Economy* (ed. P.A. Brunt, 1974) contains useful general essays on aspects of its subject; these may be supplemented with R.P. Duncan-Jones, *The Economy of the Roman Empire: Quantitative Studies* (2nd edn., 1982) and M.I. Finley, *The Ancient Economy* (1973). P.A. Brunt's monumental *Italian Manpower, 225 BC to AD 14* (1971) contains much of importance for the society and economy of the Augustan age.

I have tried to provide a simple discussion of the sources for our period in the introduction to this book: my own comments may be supplemented most usefully by R.H. Martin, *Tacitus* (1981), who does not confine his considerations to Tacitus alone. See now also M.H. Crawford (ed.), *Sources for Ancient History* (1983).

The tenth volume of the *Cambridge Ancient History* (1934) is still widely used, for it provides a convenient treatment of the years 44 BC to AD 70. Though outdated, it is not without value; a second edition of the entire *Cambridge Ancient History* is now in progress.

Finally, let me stress the highly selective nature of this note. The works mentioned are very far indeed from being the only good books on our period; I have deliberately omitted any reference to articles in learned periodicals. The reader is encouraged to explore the bibliographies to be found in most of the works mentioned and to form his own opinions.

ABBREVIATIONS

AE	*L'Année épigraphique*
AntAfr	*Antiquités africaines*
BICS	*Bulletin of the Institute of Classical Studies*
CAH	*Cambridge Ancient History*
CIL	*Corpus Inscriptionum Latinarum*
CIRB	*Corpus Inscriptionum Regni Bosporani*
EJ	V. Ehrenberg and A.H.M. Jones, *Documents Illustrating the Reigns of Augustus and Tiberius*, repr. with additions (1976)
ERW	F. Millar, *The Emperor in the Roman World* (1977)
FIRA	*Fontes Iuris Romani Anteiustiniani*, ed. S. Riccobono *et al.*, 2nd edn (1940-3)
IGRR	*Inscriptiones Graecae ad Res Romanas Pertinentes*
ILS	*Inscriptiones Latinae Selectae*
IRT	*Inscriptions of Roman Tripolitania*
JRS	*Journal of Roman Studies*
LibAnt	*Libya Antiqua*
MGR	*Miscellanea Greca e Romana. Roma.*
OGIS	*Orientis Graecae Inscriptiones Selectae*
PCPhS	*Proceedings of the Cambridge Philological Society*
POxy	*Oxyrhynchus Papyri*, ed. B.P. Grenfell *et al.* (1898-)
PP	*Parola del Passato*
PRyl	*Catalogue of the Greek Papyri in the John Rylands Library at Manchester*, ed. A.S. Hunt *et al.* (1911-38)
QAL	*Quaderni di Archeologia della Libia*
RDGE	*Roman Documents from the Greek East*, ed. R.K. Sherk (1969)
REG	*Revue des Études Grecques*
RendNap	*Rendiconti dell'Accademia di Archeologia, Lettere e Belle Arti di Napoli*
RG	*Res Gestae divi Augusti*
RSA	*Rivista storica dell'Antichità*
SA	*Sovietskaya Archeologija*
SelPap	*Select Papyri*, ed. C.C. Edgar and A.S. Hunt (1932-4, Loeb)

Small   E.M. Smallwood, *Documents Illustrating the Principates of Gaius, Claudius and Nero* (1967)
Syll³   *Sylloge Inscriptionum Graecarum*, 3rd edn
ZPE   *Zeitschrift für Papyrologie und Epigraphik*

INTRODUCTION

The purpose of this introduction is not to offer a potted account of the years 31 BC to AD 68. This period is far too rich and well documented to permit a brief summary of any value. Moreover, a great deal has already been written and is widely available. Instead, it has seemed better to devote these few pages to a consideration of the historical sources selected and collected in this book. What good are they? How is the historian of antiquity to use literature, inscriptions, coins and papyri? For all the apparent simplicity of these questions, they are in the last resort the most fundamental questions that an ancient historian can ask. And as with most important questions, there are no easy answers: the sources must be approached with great care and sensitivity. The purpose of this short introduction is to offer some general indications of the problems and pitfalls to be negotiated when one uses the ancient sources — to suggest some working rules of thumb.

The first principle that must be grasped is that we have only scraps. Of the vast literary output of antiquity in general and the Julio-Claudian period in particular only a small percentage has survived to the present day; most has been preserved on manuscripts copied from other manuscripts, which were themselves copies of copies. What survives is essentially what appealed to people — most importantly scholarly monks — between the first and twentieth centuries AD. It is only thus that we have such mainstays as Tacitus, Suetonius and the rest, whose existence we tend casually to take for granted. As for inscriptions, coins and papyri, their discovery or loss is an essentially random matter of chance — it was even more so before the development of more stringent archaeological methods in quite recent years. For these reasons the historian of antiquity always finds himself short of source material. He has only fragments with which he must do his best. Herein lies a sharp distinction between the ancient historian and the historian of modern times, who more usually has quite the opposite problem, for he can be embarrassed by the sheer amount and quality of source material with which he must cope.

We are here touching upon the very heart of the subject: how does

1

one set about writing ancient history — indeed, any history?

This is a complex matter which raises passions to a height commensurate with its importance. In an introduction of this sort a few words may suffice. It has long been the fashion to write ancient history by painstakingly reading all the relevant sources, sifting out the passages deemed significant and then trying to fit them together as far as they permit. This method has produced results: much has been achieved by such careful researches. However, in recent years many ancient historians have taken a rather different, more structured approach. They have started with hypotheses and proceeded to test them against the evidence of the sources. If the hypothesis proves wholly correct, all well and good; in most cases the hypothesis requires modification or complete abandonment in the light of the sources. Properly applied, this approach can supply insights which the more traditional methodology would probably not have permitted. Of course, for the experienced historian, hypothesis and source become intimately intertwined, so that it becomes impossible to say which comes first, since hypotheses are developed around and by notions generated by previous experience in the subject: there is a persistent, on-going dialogue between hypothesis and source — at least, there should be.

We may now look more closely at individual types of source; for all the sparsity of our sources there is a considerable variety. Our literary sources may conveniently be considered in two groups: namely, prose and poetry, though there are those who would prefer to stress a distinction between those sources which set out to provide evidence and those sources which provide it in passing — I am not sure whether, still less where, this distinction can be drawn.

The most obviously relevant type of prose literature is historiography. In assessing the value of evidence supplied by, say, Tacitus, we must first fix his date and his milieu, as far as possible: how does our source know what he is telling us? Did he himself take part in the events he describes or is he looking back over several centuries or just a few decades? Were the sources available to him reliable ones in any sense?

Every historian (modern as well as ancient) writes under the dominating influence of his own interests and preoccupations. The 'open mind' is a mirage: the only truly open mind is an empty one. Thus, for example, in writing history Tacitus was profoundly influenced by the fact that he was a Roman senator living in an imperial regime.

The fact that an historian may, like Tacitus at the beginning of his *Annals*, claim to be giving an impartial account is neither here nor there. As early as the mid-first century AD a satirist, probably Seneca, showed such claims up for what they are by parodying what had evidently already become a cliché: his satire upon the deification of Claudius, the *Apocolocyntosis* ('Pumpkinification'), begins: 'I want to record for posterity proceedings in heaven on October 13th, last year, at the beginning of the most blessed age. There will be no malice or favour. This is the actual truth.' He proceeds to recount his grossly farcical tale, very much in a spirit of malice towards Claudius and favour for Nero.

The preconceptions and allegiances of some ancient authors are rather more clear than are those of Tacitus: for example, Velleius Paterculus, a keen supporter of Tiberius' regime in general and of Sejanus in particular, and Josephus, a similarly ardent supporter of the Jewish cause in the context of Jewish compliance with Roman rule. It is instructive to compare Tacitus' sketch of Sejanus with that of Velleius and with what Josephus has to say about him (Tac. *Ann*. 4.1; nos. **95** and **97**). It would be quite wrong to suppose that any of these writers have deliberately set out with the intention of deceiving us: there is no reason to doubt that they are telling us the 'truth' — but it is the 'truth' as they saw it. Many would contend, myself included, that the 'truth' is always no more than the 'truth' as we variously perceive it, that there is no 'objective truth'. It is the job of the historian to consider why we have such different pictures of the same man, not to condemn our sources as liars.

At the same time, we must seek to appreciate the nature of historiography in antiquity. The main point is that Tacitus and the others were concerned to produce not only history but history which was also literature. They were not just dry recorders of events or of events as they saw them. They were artists, quite prepared at least to elaborate upon events. Tacitus and the rest should not be treated as hunting-grounds where facts may be found and excised without regard for art and context: that is one reason why extracts from such historians seldom appear in this book.

Biography had (and still has) concerns some way removed from those of history. The importance of Suetonius, the biographer, for students of the Julio-Claudian period makes it particularly important to recognise the distinction. The Greek biographer, Plutarch, a rough contemporary of Suetonius, describes the distinction as he saw it in order to defend any omissions in his account of the lives of Alexander the Great and Julius Caesar:

> You see, I am not writing histories but lives. Even in the most out-
> standing deeds there is not invariably a sign of virtue or vice. On
> the contrary, a small thing or word or joke more often gives an
> indication of character than battles where thousands died or the
> greatest formations or city-sieges. So, just as painters catch like-
> nesses from the face and the set of the eyes, where character shows
> itself, and all but ignore the rest of the body, I too must be per-
> mitted to devote myself to insights into the soul and to depict
> in that way the life of my subject, leaving great affairs and conflicts
> to others. (Plut. *Alex*.1.2-3)

The concerns of the biographer are clearly different from those of the
historian.

There are also the antiquarians and polymaths, such as Dionysius of
Halicarnassus, Pliny the Elder and Aulus Gellius. In their different
ways each provides us with useful evidence. Dionysius, concerned
principally with the early history of Rome, occasionally refers to the
Augustan age in which he wrote. In fact, as with Livy, Dionysius'
very concern with early Rome is itself some indication of the mood
of his times. The same may be said, albeit in a rather different way,
for Gellius, writing in the second century AD, when his brand of
dilettante scholarship was in vogue. The *Natural History* of Pliny
the Elder, who died in the eruption of Vesuvius in AD 79, is a diffuse
collection of material collected from a great many sources and collated
under various headings; as might be expected from such a quantity of
material, amounting to 37 books, there are many interesting snippets.

Geographers, especially Strabo, who completed his work under
Tiberius, provide a wealth of information, particularly on the provinces. Agricultural writers are of obvious value for the historian of
the ancient economy; in particular, Columella, who seems to have
written under Nero, provides some interesting general remarks upon
the economic situation in his period, remarks which are doubtless
coloured by his wish to justify the publication of his work.

Some occasional monographs, as they may be called, are also significant. Philo's contemporary evidence on the position of the Jews of
Alexandria in the reign of Gaius is of special value, despite (more
accurately, because of) its manifest partiality for the cause of the
Alexandrian Jews, of whom he was a leading personality. Very different, but at least as important, as Seneca's essay *On Clemency*, which

is addressed to Nero; it is one of the very few extant works of Roman political philosophy and provides invaluable insights into the ideology of the Principate. Seneca's letters are also of use: they provide vivid evidence on Roman society in his day. For all that, it must be remembered that they are not ordinary, everyday correspondence, but letters of a literary nature: to take them as straightforward evidence of Roman life is therefore almost as dangerous as using satirists like Juvenal in that manner.

Finally, there is the legal evidence, scraps of laws mentioned in passing in later legal works. Most important are the collections of legal material compiled in the sixth century AD under the aegis of Justinian, above all the *Digest*. This contains numerous important passages quoted from earlier legal authorities: how faithful these quotations are we cannot always tell. Our earliest extant legal treatise is the *Institutes* of Gaius, a distinguished jurist of the second century AD: written in four books, the bulk of which survives, Gaius' *Institutes* helps us to 'control' the *Digest*, where it is often quoted, and helps us fill out our incomplete knowledge of Julio-Claudian legislation. Our very fragmented knowledge of this legislation will be apparent from the passages included in this selection (nos. **694-719**).

At first glance, poetry may seem to be a rather curious source for the historian, but it can tell him much; hence the amount of poetry in this selection. Once again, caution must be our watchword. The historian must first seek to understand the literary nature and purpose of the poem under study. This can be an awesome and consuming task: for example, Virgil's *Aeneid* (written under Augustus, of course) and Lucan's *Pharsalia* (written under Nero) have each been regarded by some scholars as slavish propaganda for the imperial regime and by others as subversive literature. Others still have sought to chart some sort of middle course. Unfortunately for the historian, there is much to be said for each of these two conflicting assessments, for all their extremity.

However, the tone of many other poems is rather easier to assess, in general terms at least. Most of the poetry included in this selection is broadly propagandist. That is, it praises and presents as praiseworthy individuals and regimes. For example, Calpurnius Siculus (probably writing towards the beginning of Nero's reign) goes out of his way to glorify the regime of Nero in the course of his pastoral poems (no. **238**); he does so particularly through comparison with the preceding reign of

Claudius, which is implicitly criticised. Calpurnius harps on Nero's clemency, particularly towards his more elevated subjects, the senators, which he allusively contrasts with Claudius' supposed bloodthirstiness. How far Calpurnius sincerely believed in this view is unanswerable, largely unimportant and quite irrelevant: what really matters is that he could state it, evidently in expectation of finding favour with Nero and his court. Calpurnius' statements become all the more interesting when brought together with the other literature of the period, particularly Seneca's *On Clemency* and the *Apocolocyntosis*, which are built around a very similar view. In this way, poetry can provide very valuable insight into the ideas and concerns in particular circles at particular times. The poetry of the Augustan age is regularly used in this manner. In one case, that of Horace's *Secular Hymn*, the historian can exploit the fact that the poem is set in a very particular context – that of the Augustan marriage legislation of 18 BC and the Secular Games of 17 BC, for which the poem was written and where, as the inscriptional record explicitly states, it was performed. It is a poetic prayer for and, essentially, a confident announcement of the rebirth of Rome in a new golden age under Augustus (nos. **768-72**).

Rather different, but also of value, is poetry avowedly written for a particular specialised purpose, which may touch on the contemporary world at various points. Ovid's *Fasti*, a poetic treatment of the Roman religious year, has much to say of contemporary issues and concerns. In his poem on astronomy, Manilius can take the opportunity to praise Tiberius (no. **79**), while Phaedrus, writer of moralistic fables, tells us of a conflict with Sejanus (no. **103**).

Poetry helps our understanding of what was seen as particularly important at certain times. The poems in this selection on Claudius' invasion of Britain are very much a case in point, for they tell us much about the way in which the invasion could be presented; they also dovetail neatly with our other sources on the subject, such as Claudius' own allusions in the Lyons tablet (no. **212; 570**). Poetry can even provide hard information. Our fullest account of the career of an individual imperial freedman is that provided by the Flavian poet Statius, who traces – albeit grandiloquently – the career of the father of Claudius Etruscus (no. **350**).

There is also what may be called negative propaganda, such as the *Octavia*. This play is written after the style of Seneca, but was probably composed some decades after his· death. It portrays Nero's wife Octavia as a heroine; Nero himself is depicted as a murderous tyrant with no regard for the imperial virtues, such as clemency. This contrasts strikingly with the propagandist literature of Nero's early years (as may well have been intended) and tells us something about the view of Nero's reign taken by someone who was probably a rough contemporary of Tacitus. Moreover, just like positive propaganda, negative propaganda helps us to appreciate what was regarded as praiseworthy and what reprehensible. Therefore, propaganda-poetry is an important source for imperial ideology and, more broadly, the ideology of the Roman nobility, for it is not only members of the imperial family who are praised in poetry. Perhaps the first principle to be grasped when we seek to use poetry in this way is the simple fact that the Roman elite was intimately concerned with poetry and its composition and performance — even with writing it themselves.

Epigraphy, the study of inscriptions on stone and other materials, is the most important source of documentary evidence for historians of antiquity. For example, it should never be forgotten that the *Res Gestae* itself, so important for the study of the Augustan age, though now readily available in printed form, was actually an inscription cut and erected at focal points in the Roman empire (no. 1). The value of this document and other 'official' public documents is evident. Epigraphy provides us with the very words of edicts and decrees of the authorities of the Roman empire: they tell us much directly of laws made and decisions taken and they tell us still more when we can, particularly with the help of other related sources, read between the lines and set their evidence in a broader context. They can also be used to 'control' other sources: when the epigraphic version of Claudius' speech to the Senate on the admission of Gauls to the Senate, the Lyons tablet (no. 570), is compared with the version of Tacitus, we learn as much about Tacitus as about Claudius' speech. Inscriptions such as this, the official record, are clearly more reliable than a literary source such as Tacitus, to the extent that the official record is much more likely to be an accurate account of what was actually said: to this extent, as is often stated, inscriptions do not lie.

But they can and do mislead the unwary. The fact that, for example, the Senate issued a particular decree on a particular matter need not mean that it did not, shortly afterwards, issue another decree amending the first; such a second decree may not have survived. More important, inscriptions cannot be assumed to provide straightforwardly factual and 'true' accounts. The *Res Gestae* is a case in point; it sets out the achievements of Augustus very much as Augustus wanted them presented — it is Augustus' version of events. The *Res Gestae* depicts Augustus as a zealous champion of the Roman state against the forces of chaos, whereas a more sober estimate might describe him as the victor in bloody civil warfare.

Similarly, the numerous honorific inscriptions, carved, often with a statue or some other monument, in honour of a particular individual, invariably laud their subjects to the skies. It would be rash to presume that the sentiments expressed in such inscriptions were really those of all or any of those who had the inscription cut: the popularity of an emperor or a governor is not at all to be gauged from the number or contents of such inscriptions. We should remember the case of Claudius Timarchus of Crete, which casts uncomfortable light upon just this (Tac. *Ann.* 15.20-2). When dealing with honorific inscriptions we must expect what is to us gross flattery and overstatement — though hardly complete invention, for the inscription was open to all to see and criticise, if they could read it — and estimate it accordingly.

Apart from the decrees, edicts, speeches and letters of state, lists of magistrates, calendars and the rest, epigraphy has preserved the careers and brief details of countless individuals, mostly in the form of tombstones. Many of those so recorded are relatively humble folk in whom our literary sources take little interest. Of course, tombstones still cost money: graffiti, which cost nothing but a little time and effort, allowed even the complete pauper to record something. The wealthy could afford grand monuments. The tombstones of many important, wealthy individuals have survived; a significant number of those most familiar to us from the literary sources are represented on tombstones and other inscriptions, which have come down to us. Quite apart from the light such records cast on the lives of important individuals, we can also learn much from inscriptions about the career structures of the elite which ran the empire — members of the imperial family, imperial slaves and freedmen and, especially, senators and equites. By amassing data we can also make calculations that tell us a great deal about Roman society: for example, we can make calculations about the age at which a Roman might expect to die, about age at marriage, about the length of military service, about the sources of recruitment for the Roman army and much else.

Should we be tempted to sneer at the bombast evident in many inscriptions, not only honorific texts, we should remember that this very bombast is itself an indication of ancient ideology. In particular, we can usefully observe the sorts of achievements and conduct that are regarded as praiseworthy for particular sorts of person: for example, inscriptions show clearly the importance of military achievements for the men of the Roman elite (no. **378** is a particularly striking case) and the importance of obedience and 'domestic virtues', such as wool-making, for women (e.g. no. **720**). In fact, the very existence of many inscriptions and associated monuments is the direct result of the Roman concern (sometimes expressed in the texts themselves) to display in public places, often in a striking fashion and in particularly frequented locations, not only documents of state, but also accounts of the glorious achievements of private persons. This was display to contemporaries and display to future generations, including ourselves. It is therefore hardly an exaggeration to say that what we consider bombast and egotism is what ultimately created many of our most important inscriptions. If the Roman elite had not been disposed to — not to say obsessed with — self-glorification, we would possibly not have the *Res Gestae*. How many were literate enough to read these texts is a problem to which we shall return in the context of the evidence provided by coins.

Coins are regularly used as historical sources: they figure prominently in this collection. Yet we know little about conceptions of coinage in antiquity. We know that coins circulated within the empire and beyond, bearing depictions and legends, but we do not know who precisely it was that decided upon particular presentations under the Principate. Nor do we know how far these were intended to be understood by the people who used these coins, still less how far they were actually understood. As to the economic role of ancient coinage, it is generally agreed that the main impetus for the production of coinage was the need to meet state expenses, particularly to pay the army. When the father of Claudius Etruscus calculated the amount of coinage needed (no. **350**), he probably did so particularly with this in mind. But, for all that, we have little idea as to how far the Roman authorities thought about, let alone understood, the role of coinage and the money supply in the Roman economy.

These fundamental questions await conclusive answers which may never come. But we know enough to be able to lay down some general guidelines. It is clear enough that some part of the Roman administration concocted the depictions (or 'types') and legends that appear on Roman coinage. Even if the emperor was never directly or personally involved, it may reasonably be supposed that his views, concerns and aspirations were in broad terms those of his administration, part of which produced the coinage. It is also clear enough that the imperial coinage had a propagandist function, a function which it inherited from the coinage of the Republic. It published to the world at large allusions, in pictorial or literary form, to achievements and events which redounded to the credit of the Roman authorities in general and the emperor in particular: an obvious example is the coinage that proclaimed Augustus' successful dealings with Parthia (nos. **29-30**). In fact, we can only explain the evident Roman interest in changing coin-types by supposing a recognised propagandist function: it would have been easier to keep issuing coins bearing the same depiction and legend.

The historian must then inquire as to the impact these coins made on those who used them. In theory, at least, this could have been massive in a world without mass media. But coinage stayed in circulation for a long time: thus, new coinage must have been swallowed up to some extent by the mass of other coins in circulation and the impact will have been diminished correspondingly. Except, that is, in circumstances where people received coin fresh from the government. It therefore becomes tempting to wonder if coin propaganda was directed primarily at the soldiers who received their pay from the government. At the same time, it must be true that any propaganda message on different denominations of coin will have had something of a different audience: propaganda on an aureus will have had little impact on the poorer in society who seldom possessed such a coin. Still more important, many inhabitants of the Roman empire were illiterate and must have had difficulty in reading even the simplest of legends; many more did not even speak Latin, for in the eastern half of the empire Greek was the dominant language, while local languages, such as Punic and Syriac, flourished throughout. This situation was no doubt aggravated by the extensive use of abbreviations so as to allow a long legend to be crammed on to the small surface-area of a coin: many such abbreviations are obvious and standard, but quite a few are all but undecipherable. Of course, these difficulties will have been relieved to some extent by the pictorial representations on coins, which sometimes say it all, though many mean nothing without the accompanying legend. It is perhaps worth remembering that soldiers in the Roman army, again, needed a modicum of Latin to understand their orders.

Therefore, if coin-propaganda did impinge upon the inhabitants of the empire, it probably affected in particular the army and those literate in Latin, who were by and large the more wealthy and powerful city-dwellers. This is precisely the public which the imperial government would have most wanted to impress. But the most basic question remains: did anyone really bother to look at the depictions and legends on their coins? There is remarkably little evidence that they did, yet there is enough to suggest that coin-propaganda was not completely ignored. Indeed, if it had been, the imperial government would hardly have continued to change coin-types. The imperial head seems to have attracted most attention, or so our sources tend to suggest. In the second century AD, Epictetus advised that coins bearing Nero's head should be rejected as being therefore 'rotten', whereas coins of Trajan, the archetypal 'good emperor', should be accepted (Arrian, *Discourses of Epictetus*, 4.5.17). Pliny the Elder tells us of a freedman, one Annius Plocamus, collector of taxes in the Red Sea area, who was carried to Ceylon in a storm. The king of Ceylon is said to have been impressed by the fact that the denarii in the freedman's possession, though the heads on them showed that they had been minted by different emperors, were of the same weight; taking this to be a sign of Roman honesty, we are told, he despatched an embassy to visit the Roman emperor, then Claudius (Pliny the Elder, *Natural History*, 6.84-6; cf. no. **735**). More famous is Christ's advice to render unto Caesar that which is Caesar's, where attention is drawn to the likeness and titles of the emperor (Matt.22.21; Mark 12.17; Luke 20.25). There is a clear tendency to associate the emperor intimately with the coinage he issued. This may help to account for the tradition that Tiberius regarded it as a capital offence to take a coin bearing the image of Augustus into a brothel or lavatory (Suet.*Tib*.58; Philostratus, *Life of Apollonius* 1.15).

We must balance and bear in mind all these uncertainties and problems whenever we seek to use coinage as an historical source. The sad truth is that, on their own, coins can tell us little; they become really valuable only when they can be slotted into a broader picture constructed with the help of our other sources.

Papyri — with which are conventionally grouped inscriptions on pieces of terracotta called ostraca — catch the headlines every now and then with the discovery of some lost literary work, such as poetry of Gallus (no. **426**). This can be useful in its own right, but papyri are primarily of importance for the historian in that they provide our best evidence on the countryside in antiquity and on the 'ordinary people' who inhabited it: we hear in detail of peasant landholdings, livestock, disputes, thefts, acts of violence and more. Our other sources are by contrast notably urban. Thanks to papyri, the historian can construct a detailed (though still very incomplete) picture of the society and economy of the countryside which would have been quite lost to us otherwise, despite the help that archaeology provides.

However, there is again a problem. The overwhelming bulk of papyri come from Egypt (particularly Egypt south of Alexandria): the countryside they illuminate is therefore the Egyptian country-side. The crucial question immediately arises: how far can we generalise from the evidence of Egypt to the rest of the empire? Certainly nothing like as much as we might wish. The Pharaonic and Ptolemaic pre-decessors of the Romans in Egypt had evolved a highly complex and specialised system of administration which the Romans inherited. The economy of Egypt was almost entirely dependent upon the flood-ing of the Nile: it was the rich silt deposited by the floodwaters that provided a viable medium in which crops could not only grow, but actually give exceptionally high yields. The Egyptian countryside was thus essentially the Nile basin. We can easily understand why we so often find references to and concern for the flood of the Nile in the papyri and in our other sources from Egypt. Egypt was evidently special: just how special is still a matter of keen dispute among his-torians. The fact that we do not have comparable evidence from other areas does not help us.

But there are matters in the papyri from which we can plausibly generalise, particularly matters concerning the army. For example, there is no good reason to doubt that the sufferings of the civilian population at the hands of the military which are revealed by the papyri were markedly similar to sufferings elsewhere in the empire. Similarly, the organisation of the Roman army revealed in the papyri is presumably not special to Egypt (e.g. nos. **494**; **533**).

Papyri also provide quite exceptionally detailed accounts of dealings between Egypt — more properly Alexandria, usually considered to be a separate entity not in Egypt but 'by Egypt' — and the imperial government. Quite apart from valuable evidence on imperial estates in Egypt, papyri preserve what purport to be verbatim records of speeches, edicts and letters and, most interestingly, audiences before the emperor. Most striking is that of the encounter between Claudius and a Greek delegation from Alexandria (no. **575**). It has long been thought, quite probably rightly, that far from being an accurate account, this papyrus is the product of some writer whose intention was simply to glorify the Greeks involved as 'pagan martyrs', standing up for their rights against an emperor biased towards the Jews. This may be so, but the discovery of quite similar, but more sober accounts of other audiences (nos. **555-6**) have raised doubts in some minds.

The tone of this introduction has been rather negative. Deliberately so, because the positive benefits of the sources are all too easy to see, for the most part. It is hoped that the reader will now proceed to read the sources collected in this book not in a mood of depression, but in one of caution, forewarned and forearmed.

1 THE IMPERIAL FAMILY

[1] *EJ 1*
See P.A. Brunt and J.M. Moore (eds.), *Res Gestae Divi Augusti: the Achievements of the Divine Augustus* (1967)

Appended is a copy of the achievements of the divine Augustus, by which he subjected the world to the power of the Roman people, and of the expenditures which he made for the state and the Roman people, as engraved on two bronze columns set up at Rome.

1. At the age of nineteen I obtained an army at my personal initiative and personal expense, through which I restored the state, which was oppressed by the domination of a faction, to liberty. (2) On that account the Senate, with honorific decrees, took me into its order in the consulship of Gaius Pansa and Aulus Hirtius,[1] awarding me a consular place to express my opinion, and gave me *imperium*. (3) It instructed me, as propraetor, together with the consuls, to ensure that the state suffered no harm. (4) And in the same year the people appointed me consul, since both consuls had fallen in battle, and triumvir for the organization of the state.

2. Those who butchered my father I drove into exile, exacting vengeance for their crime through lawful courts; and subsequently, when they made war upon the state, I defeated them twice in pitched battle.

3. I often waged war by land and sea, wars civil and foreign, all over the world, and in my victory I spared all those citizens who sought pardon. (2) Foreign peoples who might safely be pardoned I preferred to preserve rather than destroy. (3) About 500,000 Roman citizens served under oath to me. Of these I settled in colonies or sent back to their municipalities rather more than 300,000 on completion of their service and to them all I assigned lands or gave money as a reward for their military service. (4) I captured 600 ships, quite apart from those which were smaller than triremes.

4. I have triumphed twice in ovations and three times in curule triumphs and have been called imperator 21 times; although the Senate decreed more triumphs for me, I declined them all. The laurel from

my *fasces* I deposited on the Capitol, having fulfilled all the vows I had sworn in each war. (2) For the successful achievements by land and sea of myself or my legates acting under my auspices, the Senate decreed on 55 occasions that thanksgivings be made to the immortal gods. And the days during which thanksgivings were made by decree of the Senate amounted to 890. (3) In my triumphs nine kings or children of kings were led before my chariot. (4) I have been consul 13 times at the time of writing and am in my 37th. year of tribunician power.[2]

5. The dictatorship, offered to me in my absence and presence by the people and Senate, I refused in the consulship of Marcus Marcellus and Lucius Arruntius.[3] (2) I did not decline, during a great poverty of grain, the supervision of the corn supply, which I administered in such a way that within a few days I freed the whole community through my expenditure and care from the fear and danger that was pressing. (3) The annual and perpetual consulship that was then also offered to me I refused.

6. In the consulship of Marcus Vinicius and Quintus Lucretius and then in that of Publius Lentulus and Gnaeus Lentulus and thirdly in that of Paullus Fabius Maximus and Quintus Tubero,[4] when the Senate and people of Rome agreed that I be appointed sole curator of laws and manners with the greatest power, I accepted no magistracy offered in contravention of ancestral tradition. (2) What the Senate then wanted me to do I did through my tribunician power, in which power I demanded and received a colleague five times, of my own volition.

7. I was triumvir for the organization of the state for ten consecutive years. (2) I have been *princeps senatus*, up to the day of writing, for 40 years. (3) I have been pontifex maximus, augur, one of the 15 for the performance of sacred rites, one of the 7 for feasts, Arval brother, Titian sodalis and fetial.

8. I increased the number of patricians in my fifth consulship by order of the Senate and people.[5] (2) I revised the roll of the Senate three times and in my sixth consulship[6] I performed a census of the people with Marcus Agrippa as my colleague. I carried out a *lustrum* after 42 years, in which 4,063,000 Roman citizens were registered. (3) Then for a second time with consular *imperium* I carried out a *lustrum* alone in the consulship of Gaius Censorinus and Gaius Asinius,[7] in which 4,233,000 Roman citizens were registered. (4) And for a third time with consular *imperium* I carried out a *lustrum*, my colleague being Tiberius Caesar, my son, in the consulship of Sextus Pompeius

and Sextus Appuleius,[8] in which *lustrum* 4,937,000 Roman citizens were registered. (5) Through new laws introduced on my initiative I restored many exemplary practices of our ancestors which were falling out of use now in our age and I have myself handed down to our descendants examples to be imitated in many areas.

9. The Senate decreed that vows be made for my health by the consuls and priests every fifth year. Due to these vows they have often staged games in my lifetime, sometimes the four greatest priestly colleges, sometimes the consuls. (2) Further, privately and by municipality, all citizens have unanimously and continuously prayed for my health at all the couches.

10. My name has been included by decree of the Senate in the Salian hymn and it has been laid down in law that I be sacrosanct in perpetuity and in my lifetime possess tribunician power. (2) So that I would not become pontifex maximus in place of my living colleague, I refused that priesthood when the people offered it to me because my father had held it. Some years later, when the incumbent, who had assumed the office at a time of civil unrest, had died, when a multitude of unprecedented size gathered from all Italy at my election, I accepted that priesthood in the consulship of Publius Sulpicius and Gaius Valgius.[9]

11. The Senate consecrated the altar of Fortuna Redux in front of the temples of Honour and Virtue at the Porta Capena in honour of my return; it instructed the priests and Vestal virgins to perform an annual sacrifice at this altar on the day on which, in the consulship of Quintus Lucretius and Marcus Vinicius, I returned to the city; and it named that day the Augustalia from my cognomen.[10]

12. By the authority of the Senate some of the praetors and tribunes of the plebs, together with the consul Quintus Lucretius and the leading men, were sent to Campania to meet me. (2) When I returned to Rome from Spain and Gaul after successful achievements in those provinces, in the consulship of Tiberius Nero and Publius Quinctilius,[11] the Senate decreed that the altar of Augustan Peace should be consecrated in the Campus Martius in honour of my return; it instructed the magistrates and priests and Vestal virgins to perform an annual sacrifice at that altar.

13. Janus Quirinus, which our ancestors had closed when peace had been won through victories throughout the empire of the Roman people by land and sea, the Senate decided to close three times in my principate, though history states that from the foundation of the city to my birth it was closed a total of two times.

14. My sons, whom Fortune snatched away from me in their prime, Gaius and Lucius Caesar, the Senate and people of Rome, in my honour, designated consuls at the age of 14, so that they would enter the Senate after five years; and the Senate decreed that they should take part in public affairs from the day on which they were introduced into the Forum. (2) And each of them was presented with silver shields and spears and called princeps of the youth by the equites.

15. To the Roman plebs I paid 300 sesterces per man under my father's will and in my own name, as consul for the fifth time,[12] and I gave 400 sesterces from war-booty; and for a second time, in my tenth consulship,[13] I paid out from my patrimony 400 sesterces per man in largesse; and in my eleventh consulship,[14] I distributed twelve rations of grain purchased at my personal expense; and in my twelfth year of tribunician power,[15] I gave 400 sesterces per man for the third time. My largesses were never distributed among less than 250,000. (2) In my eighteenth year of tribunician power, as consul for the twelfth time,[16] I gave 60 denarii per man to 320,000 of the urban plebs. (3) And to the colonists among my soldiers, in my fifth consulship,[17] I gave 1,000 sesterces per man from booty; about 120,000 men among the colonists received it as triumphal largesse. (4) In my thirteenth consulship,[18] I gave 60 denarii each to the plebs in receipt of public grain: that is, a little more than 200,000 men.

16. I paid money to the townsmen for the lands which I assigned to soldiers in my fourth consulship and later in the consulship of Marcus Crassus and Gnaeus Lentulus Augur.[19] The sum I paid for Italian lands amounted to about 600,000,000 sesterces, and I paid about 260,000,000 for provincial lands. I was the first and only one of all those who have settled colonies of soldiers in Italy or in the provinces to do this, as far as anyone today recalls. (2) And thereafter, in the consulship of Tiberius Nero and Gnaeus Piso and, likewise, in the consulship of Gaius Antistius and Decimus Laelius and in the consulship of Gaius Calvisius and Lucius Passienus and in the consulship of Lucius Lentulus and Marcus Messalla and in the consulship of Lucius Caninius and Quintus Fabricius,[20] I paid financial rewards to soldiers whom I settled in their home towns on the completion of their service, for which purpose I spent about 400,000,000 sesterces.

17. Four times I helped the treasury with my own money in that I paid 150,000,000 sesterces to those in charge of the treasury. (2) And in the consulship of Marcus Lepidus and Lucius Arruntius,[21] I paid 170,000,000 sesterces into the military treasury, which was established

on my initiative as a source of rewards for soldiers who have served for twenty years or more.

18. From the year in which Gnaeus and Publius Lentulus were consuls,[22] whenever the taxes proved insufficient, I gave grain and money, sometimes to 100,000 men, sometimes to more, from my own granary and patrimony.

19. I built the Senate House and the Chalcidicum adjacent to it and the temple of Apollo on the Palatine with its porticoes, the temple of the divine Julius, the Lupercal, the portico at the Circus Flaminius, which I allowed to be called by the name of the man who built its predecessor on the same site — the portico of Octavius — a couch at the Circus Maximus, (2) the temples on the Capitol of Jupiter Feretrius and Jupiter the Thunderer, the temple of Quirinus, the temples of Minerva and Juno the Queen and Jupiter Liberty on the Aventine, the temple of the Lares at the top of the Sacred Way, the temple of the Di Penates on the Velian, and the temple of Youth and the temple of the Great Mother on the Palatine.

20. I rebuilt the Capitol and the theatre of Pompey, each at considerable expense, adding no inscription of my name. (2) I rebuilt the channels of aqueducts which were collapsing with age in several places and I doubled the capacity of the aqueduct called the Marcia by sending a new spring into its channel. (3) I completed the Forum Julium and the basilica situated between the temple of Castor and the temple of Saturn, a project begun and largely finished by my father; and when that same basilica was consumed by fire I enlarged its site and started work on it in the name of my sons and, if I do not complete it in my lifetime, I have ordered its completion by my heirs. (4) In my sixth consulship,[23] on the authority of the Senate, I rebuilt 82 temples of the gods in the city, omitting none which should have been rebuilt at that time. (5) In my seventh consulship,[24] I rebuilt the Via Flaminia from the city to Ariminum and all the bridges, except the Mulvian and the Minucian.

21. On private ground I built the temple of Mars the Avenger and the Forum Augustum out of booty. I built the theatre by the temple of Apollo on ground largely bought from private persons, to bear the name of Marcus Marcellus, my son-in-law. (2) I consecrated offerings from booty on the Capitol and in the temple of the divine Julius and in the temple of Apollo and in the temple of Vesta and in the temple of Mars the Avenger, which cost me about 100,000,000 sesterces. (3) In my fifth consulship,[25] I returned 35,000 pounds of crown gold which the municipalities and colonies of Italy contributed to my

triumphs and thereafter, whenever I was called imperator, I did not accept crown gold, though the municipalities and colonies decreed it with as much good will as before.

22. I gave gladiatorial games three times in my own name and five times in the name of my sons or grandsons, at which games about 10,000 men fought. I showed the people a spectacle of athletes gathered from all parts, twice in my own name and three times in the name of my grandson. (2) I staged games four times in my own name and in place of other magistrates 23 times. For the college of 15, as master of the college, with my colleague Marcus Agrippa, I staged Secular Games in the consulship of Gaius Furnius and Gaius Silanus.[26] In my thirteenth consulship,[27] I was the first to stage games of Mars, which thereafter in subsequent years were staged by the consuls by decree of the Senate and by statute. (3) I gave the people beast-hunts with African beasts 26 times in my own name or in that of my sons and grandsons in the circus or in the Forum or in the amphitheatres, in which about 3,500 beasts were killed.

23. I gave the people the spectacle of a naval battle across the Tiber in the place where the grove of the Caesars now stands, after hollowing out the ground for 1,800 feet in length and 1,200 feet in breadth, in which thirty beaked ships, triremes or biremes, and more lesser vessels fought each other; in these fleets fought about 3,000 men, besides the rowers.

24. In the temples of all the communities of the province of Asia I replaced upon my victory the ornaments which my adversary had taken for himself after despoiling the temples. (2) About 80 silver statues of myself, on foot and on horseback and in chariots, stood in the city; these I removed and from the proceeds I placed offerings of gold in the temple of Apollo in my name and in the name of those who honoured me with the statues.

25. I made the sea peaceful, without pirates. About 30,000 slaves, who had fled from their masters and taken arms against the state, I captured and handed over to their masters for punishment. (2) The whole of Italy swore allegiance to me of its own volition and demanded that I be leader in the war I won at Actium; the provinces of Gaul, Spain, Africa, Sicily and Sardinia also swore allegiance. (3) There then served under my standards more than 700 senators, including 83 who became consuls either before or after up to the day of writing, and about 170 priests.

26. I advanced the boundaries of all those provinces of the Roman people bounded by peoples not obedient to our empire. (2) I pacified

the Gallic and Spanish provinces, likewise Germany, where Ocean is the boundary from Gades to the mouth of the River Elbe. (3) I pacified the Alps from the area closest to the Adriatic to the Tuscan Sea, waging war unjustly on no people. (4) My fleet sailed across Ocean from the mouth of the Rhine to the eastern region, as far as the borders of the Cimbri, where no Roman had previously gone by land or sea; and the Cimbri and the Charydes and the Semnones and other German peoples of the same tract sought through envoys my friendship and that of the Roman people. (5) By my order and under my auspices two armies were led at about the same time into Ethiopia and Arabia, which is called Eudaemon, and large hostile forces of both peoples were killed in battle and several towns were captured. They advanced into Ethiopia as far as the town of Nabata, near Meroe; the army marched into Arabia beyond the borders of the Sabaeans to the town of Mariba.

27. I added Egypt to the empire of the Roman people. (2) Although I could have made Greater Armenia a province upon the death of its king, Artaxes, I preferred to follow the practice of our ancestors and pass it to Tigranes, son of King Artavasdes and grandson of King Tigranes, through the agency of Tiberius Nero, who was then my stepson. And when that same people rose up and rebelled and was subdued by Gaius, my son, I passed it to King Ariobarzanes, son of the king of the Medes, Artabazus. Upon his death, I sent to that kingdom Tigranes, a member of the royal family of the Armenians. (3) I recovered all the provinces to the east of the Adriatic and Cyrene, which were then possessed for the most part by kings, and, before, Sicily and Sardinia, seized in the slave war.

28. I settled colonies of soldiers in Africa, Sicily, Macedonia, both Spains, Achaea, Asia, Syria, Gallia Narbonensis and Pisidia. (2) And Italy has 28 colonies settled by my authority, which in my lifetime have been most bustling and populous.

29. Several military standards lost by other generals I have taken back from conquered enemies, from Spain, from Gaul and from the Dalmatians. (2) I forced the Parthians to return to me the spoils and standards of three Roman armies and to seek the friendship of the Roman people as suppliants. And I have placed those standards in the inner sanctum of the temple of Mars the Avenger.

30. The Pannonian peoples, whom, before my principate, no army of the Roman people had reached, I subjected to the empire of the Roman people, when they had been conquered by Tiberius Nero, who was then my stepson and legate, and I advanced the borders

of Illyricum to the banks of the River Danube. (2) When a Dacian army crossed the river it was defeated and put to flight under my auspices and later my army was led across the Danube and forced the Dacian peoples to submit to the empire of the Roman people.

31. To me royal embassies from India have often been sent, not seen before that time with any Roman leader. (2) The Bastarnae and Scythians and the kings of the Sarmatians situated this side of the Tanais and beyond and the kings of the Albanians and Iberians and Medes have sought our friendship through envoys.

32. To me fled as suppliants the kings of the Parthians, Tiridates and, later, Phraates, son of King Phraates, of the Medes, Artavasdes, of the Adiabeni, Artaxares, of the Britons, Dumnobellaunus and Tincommius, of the Sugambri, Maelo, of the Marcomanni and Suebi . . . (2) To me the king of the Parthians, Phraates, son of Orodes, sent all his sons and grandsons, to Italy; he had not been conquered in war, but sought our friendship by pledging his children. (3) And very many other peoples have experienced the good faith of the Roman people in my principate, peoples with whom previously the Roman people had had no exchange of embassies and friendship.

33. From me the Parthian and Median peoples received the kings they requested, through envoys who were the leading men of those peoples: the Parthians, Vonones, son of King Phraates, grandson of King Orodes; the Medes, Ariobarzanes, son of King Artavasdes, grandson of King Ariobarzanes.

34. In my sixth and seventh consulships,[28] after I had extinguished civil wars, in charge of all affairs by universal consent, I transferred the state from my power to the control of the Senate and people of Rome. (2) For this, my service, I was called Augustus by decree of the Senate and the door-posts of my house were clothed with laurel by the state and a civic crown was fixed above my door and a golden shield was placed in the Curia Julia, given me by the Senate and people of Rome for my virtue and clemency and justice and piety, as testified by the inscription on that shield. (3) Thereafter, I excelled all in authority, but of power I have had no more than those others who have been my colleagues in each magistracy.

35. When I was holding my thirteenth consulship,[29] the Senate and the equestrian order and all the Roman people called me father of my country and decreed that the title be inscribed in the entrance of my house and in the Curia Julia and in the Forum Augustum beneath the chariot set up for me by decree of the Senate. (2) When I wrote this I was in my seventy sixth year.

Appendix

1. The total amount of money which he gave either to the treasury or to the Roman plebs or to discharged soldiers: 6,000,000 denarii.
2. As new buildings he built the temple of Mars, Jupiter the Thunderer and Feretrius, Apollo, the divine Julius, Quirinus, Minerva, Juno the Queen, Jupiter Liberty, the Lares, the Di Penates, Youth, the Great Mother, the Lupercal, the couch in the circus, the Senate House with the Chalcidicum, the Forum Augustum, the Basilica Julia, the theatre of Marcellus, the Octavian portico, the grove of the Caesars beyond the Tiber.
3. He rebuilt the Capitol and 82 sacred buildings, the theatre of Pompey, the channels of aqueducts and the Via Flaminia.
4. The amount he expended on theatrical spectacles and gladiatorial games and athletes and beast-hunts and the sea battle and the money given to colonies, municipalities and towns ravaged by earthquake and fire, or individually to friends and senators whose property qualification he made up, is beyond reckoning.

Notes

1. 40 BC.   2. AD 14.   3. 22 BC.   4. 19, 18 and 11 BC respectively.   5. 29 BC.
6. 28 BC.   7. 8 BC.   8. AD 14.   9. 12 BC.   10. 12th.Oct.19 BC.   11. 13 BC.
12. 29 BC.   13. 24 BC.   14. 23 BC.   15. 12/11 BC.   16. First half of 5 BC.
17. 29 BC.   18. 2 BC.   19. 30 and 14 BC.   20. 7,6,4,3 and 2 BC respectively.
21. AD 6.   22. 18 BC.   23. 28 BC.   24. 27 BC.   25. 28 BC.   26. 17 BC.
27. 2 BC.   28. 28 and 27 BC.   29. 2BC.

[2] *EJ 12* with J.M. Carter, *ZPE*, 24 (1977) pp. 227-30
29 BC, Nicopolis, dedication after Actium

To Neptune and Mars; Imperator Caesar, son of the divine Julius, having achieved victory by sea in the war which he waged for the state in this area, dedicated the camp from which he went out to attack the enemy, decorated with spoils. Consul for the fifth time, imperator seven times, peace having been obtained by land and sea.

[3] Philip, *Palatine Anthology*, 6.236
Probably from the reign of Gaius. Octavian dedicated beaks from the warships of Antony's fleet both at Actium (Dio 51.1.3) and at Rome (Dio 51.19.2)

We, beaks with brazen bite, voyage-loving naval armour,
Stand as monuments of the Actian war.
Look — bees' wax-fed gifts form a hive
Laden with a buzzing swarm all round;
Good is the grace of Caesar's orderly rule:
He has taught enemy weapons to bear the fruits of peace.

[4] Anonymous, *Palatine Anthology*, 9.553

On the foundation of Nicopolis, which means 'City of Victory'

Caesar founded me in place of Leucas and fertile Ambracia
And Thyrreum and Amphilochian Argos and all
The cities round about that War leapt upon, raging with his spear
And smashed.
He founded me, Nicopolis, divine city, which
Lord Phoebus receives in return for victory at Actium.

[5] Excerpts from the Calendars

(a) Passed in 30 BC (Dio 51.19.3)

14th January: evil day, by decree of the Senate: the birthday of Antony.

(b) 28 BC

9th October: to the public genius, to fortunate Felicity, to Venus the Victorious on the Capitol, to Apollo on the Palatine, games.

(c) 28 BC

9th October: games. Augustus dedicated the temple of Apollo.

(d) 30 BC

1st August: Egypt brought into the power of the Roman people. To Victory the Virgin on the Palatine. To Hope in the Forum Holitorium. Holiday by decree of the Senate, since on that day Imperator Caesar Augustus liberated the state from the most wretched peril.

[6] *EJ 14*

An inscription cut (identically) on two obelisks brought from Heliopolis in Egypt to Rome by Augustus in 10 BC. One, dating from the 7th century BC, was set up in the Campus Martius. It was of red granite, standing 21.79 m high. Augustus made it the centre of a large meridian (a sort of sundial), the rest of which was made up of a large marble pavement inlaid with metal strips showing midday at various seasons of the year.

The other obelisk, dating from 14th century BC and 23.70 m high, was erected in the Circus Maximus. On the Egyptian vogue at Rome, see A. Roullet *The Egyptian and Egyptianizing Monuments of Imperial Rome* (1972).

Imperator Caesar Augustus, son of a god, pontifex maximus, imperator 12 times, consul 11 times, in his 14th year of tribunician power, Egypt having been brought into the power of the Roman people, presented this to the Sun.

[7] *EJ 15*
Denarius, 28 BC

Obv. Head of Augustus. CAESAR CONSUL SIX TIMES.
Rev. Crocodile. EGYPT CAPTURED.

[8] *EJ 13*
Silver quinarius, 29-27 BC. Cf.D.Magie, *Roman Rule in Asia Minor* (1950) p. 442

Obv. Head of Augustus. CAESAR IMPERATOR SEVEN TIMES.
Rev. Victory on a mystic chest. ASIA RECOVERED.

[9] *EJ 16*
Denarius, 29-27 BC. Cf. *CAH*, X, p. 113

Obv. Victory on ship's prow, with wreath and palm.
Rev. Octavian in quadriga. IMPERATOR CAESAR.

[10] *EJ 17*
29 BC, Rome, in the Forum. Possibly inscribed on a triumphal arch dedicated to Augustus

The Senate and people of Rome to Imperator Caesar, son of the divine Julius, consul five times, consul designate for a sixth, imperator seven times, the state having been saved.

[11] *EJ 18*
Tetradrachm, 28 BC, Asia Minor, Cf. C. Wirszubski, *Libertas as a Political Idea at Rome* (1950) esp. pp. 100ff.

Obv. Head of Augustus. IMPERATOR CAESAR, SON OF A GOD, CONSUL SIX TIMES, CHAMPION OF THE LIBERTY OF THE ROMAN PEOPLE.

Rev. Peace with a mystic chest. PEACE.

[12] *EJ 19*
Sestertius, Rome. Cf. *RG* 34.2

Obv. Oak wreath. FOR CITIZENS SAVED.

Rev. BY DECREE OF THE SENATE. GNAEUS PISO, SON OF GNAEUS, TRIUMVIR FOR THE CASTING AND STRIKING OF GOLD, SILVER AND BRONZE.[1]

1. Cf.Tac. *Ann.* 2.55-71.

[13] *EJ 22*
27 BC, Arelate; cf. *RG*, 34.2

The Senate and people of Rome gave Imperator Caesar Augustus, son of a god, consul eight times, a shield of virtue, clemency, justice and piety towards the gods and the country.

[14] *EJ 23*
After 12 BC. Altar with Victory holding a shield, Rome

The Senate and people of Rome to Imperator Caesar Augustus, son of a god, pontifex maximus, imperator, consul, with tribunician power.

[15] *EJ 24*
Denarius, Spain

Obv. Head of Augustus.

Rev. Shield inscribed with the words SHIELD OF VIRTUE. THE SENATE AND PEOPLE OF ROME. CAESAR AUGUSTUS.

[16] *EJ 25*
Denarius, Rome

Obv. Head of Augustus. AUGUSTUS.

Rev. Augustus with a shield inscribed with the words SHIELD OF VIRTUE, placing a star on a statue of Agrippa. LUCIUS LENTULUS, FLAMEN OF MARS.

[17] *EJ 58*
23-22 BC (?), Tridentum; cf. *RG*, 6.2; 10.1

Imperator Caesar Augustus, son of a god, consul 11 times, with tribunician power, gave this; Marcus Appuleius, son of Sextus, legate, had it made by his order.

[18] *EJ 58a*
Copper as, Emerita

Obv. Head of Augustus. CAESAR AUGUSTUS, WITH TRIBUNI-
CIAN POWER
Rev. PUBLIUS CARISIUS, LEGATE OF AUGUSTUS[1]
1. In the twenties BC: cf. Dio 53.25.8; 54.5.1-3.

[19] *Excerpt from the Praenestine Calendar*; cf. *RG*, 35.1; Suet.*Aug*.58.2 BC

5th February: holiday, by decree of the Senate, because on that day Imperator Caesar Augustus, pontifex maximus, in his 21st year of tribunician power, consul 13 times, was called father of his country by the Senate and people of Rome.

[20] Ovid, *Fasti*, 2.127-30

O holy father of your country, to you the plebs, to you the Senate
Gave this name; we gave this name to you, the equites.
But history had already bestowed it: though late, you took
Your true titles: you had long been the father of the world.

[21] *EJ 60*
6-5 BC, Urgavo, Baetica; cf.*CAH*, X, p. 156

To Imperator Caesar Augustus, son of a god, pontifex maximus, in his 18th year of tribunician power, consul 11 times, father of his country.

[22] Crinagoras, *Palatine Anthology*, 9.545; cf.*RG*, 21.1; Tac.*Ann*.2.41; 6.50; Virg.*Aen*.6.860ff.; Prop.3.18

By Callimachus this poem was wrought;
He let out all the Muses' sails over it.
He sings of the hut of welcoming Hecale
And the labours set Theseus by Marathon.
May your hands, Marcellus, gain youthful strength
Like Theseus' — and the same renown for a glorious life.

[23] Crinagoras, *Palatine Anthology*, 6.161

From the western war returning to the borders
Of craggy Italy, Marcellus, bearing spoils,
First cut his auburn beard. As his country wanted:
To send him out a boy and welcome him home a man.

[24] *ILS 898*
Pompeii

To Marcus Claudius Marcellus, son of Gaius, patron.

[25] *Syll.*³ *774 A and B*

(a) Delphi
The city of the Delphians honoured Claudius Marcellus, its patron.

(b) Tanagra, Boeotia
The council and people honoured Marcus Claudius Marcellus, son of Gaius, for his virtue and good-will, their patron.

[26] Velleius Paterculus, 2.93

About three years before the plot of Egnatius erupted, around the time of the conspiracy of Murena and Caepio, fifty years ago, Marcus Marcellus, son of Augustus' sister, Octavia, died, still in his youth, after presenting a most magnificent spectacle as aedile. People thought that he would have succeeded to power if anything had happened to Caesar, though not without trouble with Marcus Agrippa. Indeed, as they say, he had the gentlemanly virtues and a cheerful mind and heart: he was fit for the destiny for which he was being groomed. After his death Agrippa returned from Asia, to where he had temporarily withdrawn, apparently on imperial business, but in fact, according to gossip, because of a secret rift with Marcellus; upon his return Agrippa married Julia, Caesar's daughter and Marcellus' widow, a woman whose progeny did no good either to the state or to herself.

[27] *AE* (1928) no. 88
Mausoleum of Augustus

Marcellus, son of Gaius, son-in-law of Augustus Caesar.
Octavia, daughter of Gaius, sister of Augustus Caesar.

[28] *EJ 61*
7-8, Pavia or Ticinum; cf. R. Seager, *Tiberius* (1972) pp. 46-7

(5) To Imperator Caesar Augustus, son of a god, pontifex maximus, father of his country, augur, one of the 15 for the performance of sacred rites, one of the 7 for feasts, consul 13 times, imperator 17 times, in his 30th year of tribunician power.

(6) To Livia, daughter of Drusus, wife of Caesar Augustus.

(7) To Gaius Caesar, son of Augustus, grandson of a god, priest, consul, imperator.

(8) To Lucius Caesar, son of Augustus, grandson of a god, augur, consul designate, princeps of the youth.

(4) To Tiberius Caesar, son of Augustus, grandson of a god, priest, consul twice, imperator three times, and augur, in his ninth year of tribunician power.

(3) To Germanicus Julius Caesar, son of Tiberius, grandson of Augustus, great-grandson of a god.

(2) To Drusus Julius Caesar, son of Tiberius, grandson of Augustus, great-grandson of a god, priest.

(1) To Nero Julius Caesar, son of Germanicus, great-grandson of Augustus.

(9) To Drusus Julius Germanicus, son of Germanicus, great-grandson of Augustus.

(10) To Tiberius Claudius Nero Germanicus, son of Drusus Germanicus.

[29] *EJ 26*
Denarius, Rome

Obv. Head of Liber. TURPILIANUS TRIUMVIR.
Rev. Kneeling Parthian, extending a standard. CAESAR AUGUSTUS, STANDARDS RECEIVED.

[30] *EJ 27*
Aureus

Obv. Head of Augustus. THE SENATE AND PEOPLE OF ROME TO IMPERATOR CAESAR AUGUSTUS, CONSUL 11 TIMES, IN HIS 6TH YEAR OF TRIBUNICIAN POWER.
Rev. Triumphal arch. CITIZENS AND MILITARY STANDARDS RECOVERED FROM THE PARTHIANS.

[31] *EJ 28*
Denarius, Rome

Obv. Head of Liber. TURPILIANUS TRIUMVIR.
Rev. Armenian king kneeling. CAESAR, SON OF A GOD, ARMENIA CAPTURED.

[32] Crinagoras *Planudean Anthology*, 61
The exploits of Tiberius, here called Nero; cf. *RG*, 27.2

> Sunrise and sunset are the measures of the world; and
> The deeds of Nero traversed both limits of the earth.
> The rising sun saw Armenia subjugated at his hands,
> And the setting sun Germany.
> Let his double military conquest be hymned: Araxes
> And Rhine know, as slave peoples drink their waters.

[33] *EJ 29*
Denarius, Rome

Obv. Busts of Fortune the Victorious and Fortune the Lucky. QUIN-TUS RUSTIUS, FOR FORTUNE OF ANTIUM.[1]
Rev. Altar inscribed. FOR FORTUNA REDUX,[2] FOR CAESAR AUGUSTUS, BY DECREE OF THE SENATE.

1. Cf. Hor. *Od*. 1.35 with Nisbet and Hubbard *ad loc*. 2. Lit. 'Fortune the Homebringer': cf. *RG*, 11.

[34] Excerpt from the Calendar
19 BC

12th October: holiday by decree of the Senate, since on that day Imperator Caesar Augustus, returning from overseas provinces, entered the city and an altar was established for Fortuna Redux.

[35] *EJ 34*
Denarius, 16 BC, Rome

Obv. Bust of Augustus on round shield. BY DECREE OF THE SENATE, FOR THE STATE PRESERVED WITH THE SAFETY OF IMPER-ATOR CAESAR AUGUSTUS.

Rev. Mars. THE SENATE AND PEOPLE OF ROME; PUBLIC VOWS MADE FOR THE SAFETY AND RETURN OF AUGUSTUS.

[36] *EJ 35*
Denarius, 16 BC, Rome

Obv. Oak-wreath. TO JUPITER OPTIMUS MAXIMUS, THE SENATE AND PEOPLE OF ROME, VOWS MADE FOR THE SAFETY OF IMPERATOR CAESAR, SINCE THROUGH HIM THE STATE STANDS MORE GREAT AND MORE PEACEFUL.

Rev. Cippus with inscription IMPERATOR CAESAR AUGUSTUS, BY CONSENSUS OF ALL. Outside the cippus, BY DECREE OF THE SENATE, LUCIUS MESCINIUS RUFUS, TRIUMVIR.

[37] *EJ 36*
13 BC, Rome; cf. *RG*, 12.2

Publius Quinctilius Varus, son of Sextus, priest, consul, presented votive games for the return of Imperator Caesar Augustus, son of a god, for Jupiter Optimus Maximus, with Tiberius Claudius Nero, his colleague, by decree of the Senate.

[38] *Excerpts from the Calendars*
(a) 13 BC
4th July: holiday, since on that day the Altar of Augustan Peace was erected in the Campus Martius, in the consulship of Nero and Varus.

(b) 9 BC
30th January: on that day the Altar of Augustan Peace was dedicated. A thanksgiving by order of Caesar Augustus, custodian of Roman citizens and of the world.

[39] Ovid, *Fasti*, 1.709-22

> My poem itself has brought me to the Altar of Peace.
> This will be the penultimate day of January.
> Come, Peace, your hair tied back and wreathed with Actian laurels
> And let your gentle being remain to pervade the whole world.
> While there are no enemies and no reason for a triumph,
> You will be a greater glory to our leaders than war.
> May the soldier take arms only to ward off attacks
> And may the fierce trumpet only ring out in ceremonial.
> May the world near and far dread the family of Aeneas;
> If there is any land fearing Rome too little, may it love her.
> Cast incense, priests, on the flames of peace
> And let a white victim fall, struck on the forehead,
> And ask the gods, who heed pious prayers, that that house,
> The champion of peace, may live with her forever.

[40] *EJ 37*
8 BC; Macrobius, 1.12.35

Since it was in the month of Sextilis that Imperator Caesar Augustus first entered the consulship and led three triumphs into the city and brought the legions down from the Janiculum to follow his auspices and good faith; and since it was also in this month that Egypt was brought into the power of the Roman people and in this month that an end was put to civil wars; and since, for these reasons, this month is and shall be most lucky for this empire, it is the will of the Senate that this month be called Augustus.

[41] *EJ 38*
8 BC, Rome

Gaius Marcius Censorinus, son of Lucius, augur, consul, presented votive games for the return of Imperator Caesar Augustus, son of a god, pontifex maximus, for Jupiter Optimus Maximus, with Gaius Asinius Gallus, his colleague, by decree of the Senate.

[42] *EJ 39*
7 BC, Rome; cf. Hor.*Od*.4.2.33ff.

Tiberius Claudius Nero, son of Tiberius, priest, consul twice, imperator twice, presented votive games for the return of Imperator Caesar Augustus, son of a god, pontifex maximus, for Jupiter Optimus Maximus, with Gnaeus Calpurnius Piso, his colleague,[1] by decree of the Senate.

1. Piso's name has been erased, presumably after his trial; cf. Tac. *Ann*. 3.16f.

[43] *EJ 40*
7-6 BC, Trophy of Augustus, Maritime Alps. Pliny the Elder, *Natural History*, 3.136-7. Cf. *RG*, 26.3

To Imperator Caesar Augustus, son of a god, pontifex maximus, imperator 14 times, in his 17th year of tribunician power, the Senate and people of Rome, because under his leadership and auspices all the Alpine peoples, from the upper sea to the lower, have been brought under the power of the Roman people.

Alpine peoples conquered: the Trumplini, Camunni, Venostes, Vennonetes, Isarci, Breuni, Genaunes, Focunates, 4 Vindelician peoples, the Consuanetes, Rucinates, Licates, Catenates, Ambisontes, Rugusci, Suanetes, Calucones, Brixenetes, Leponti, Uberi, Nantuates, Seduni, Varagri, Salassi, Acitavones, Medulli, Ucenni, Caturiges, Brigiani, Sogiontii, Brodiontii, Nemaloni, Edenates, Vesubiani, Veamini, Barbarous Gauls, the Ulatti, Ecdini, Vergunni, Egui, Turi, Nematuri, Oratelli, Nerusi, Velauni, and Suetri.

[44] *EJ 42*
Base of a golden statue of Augustus, Rome, Forum of Augustus, after 2 BC; cf. *RG*, 24.2

To Imperator Caesar Augustus, father of his country, Further Spain, Baetica, because through his beneficence and perpetual care, the province has been pacified. 100 pounds of gold.

[45] *EJ 43*
6-7, Lepcis Magna; cf. Suet. *Tib*. 31.2; Tac. *Ann*. 3.32 and 35; Dio 55.28.3-4

Dedicated to Mars Augustus; the state of Lepcis, liberated from the Gaetulian war under the auspices of Imperator Caesar Augustus, pontifex maximus, father of his country, and the leadership of Cossus Lentulus, consul, one of the 15 for the performance of sacred rites, proconsul of the province of Africa.

[46] *EJ 43a*
Near Tusculum; cf. *RG*, 30.2

Marcus Vinicius[1] ... consul, one of the 15 for the performance of sacred rites ... propraetorian legate of Augustus Caesar in Illyricum, was first[1] to cross the River Danube ... an army of ... and Bastarnae and routed the Cotini ... and Anartii ... of Augustus ...

1. Uncertain restorations.

[47] *EJ 43b*
Dalmatia; cf. J. J. Wilkes, *Dalmatia* (1969) pp. 205-6

Dedicated to Father Janus Augustus; Gaius Julius Aetor, son of Gaius, of the tribe Sergia, aedile, awarded the greater torc in the Dalmatian War by Tiberius Caesar Augustus, son of Augustus, erected this, together with his children, by virtue of his office as duumvir.

[48] *EJ 44*
Between 4 and 14, Bagacum Nerviorum, Gallia Belgica. Cf. R. Seager, *Tiberius* (1972) p. 145

To Tiberius Caesar, son of Augustus, grandson of a god. A dedication for his advent. Gnaeus Licinius Navos, son of Gaius, of the tribe Voltinia.

[49] *EJ 45*
Vetera, Lower Germany

(Relief of soldier)
To Marcus Caelius, son of Titus, of the tribe Lemonia, from Bononia, in the third rank of legion 18,[1] 53 years of age, fell in the Varian War. The bones of his freedmen may be buried here in future. Publius Caelius, son of Titus, of the tribe Lemonia, his brother, made this.
(Bust)
Marcus Caelius Privatus, freedman of Marcus.
(Bust)
Marcus Caelius Thiaminus, freedman of Marcus.

1. Legion 18 was destroyed in the Varian disaster of AD 9, very probably the occasion of Caelius's death.

[50] *EJ 46*
2, Cyrene. Beneath a relief of a reclining banqueter

Year 33. In the priesthood of Pausanias, son of Philiscus, born the son of Euphanes, when all had ceased sorrowing. Lucius Orbius, son of Lucius, gatekeeper, honours the war-ender:

> When ceased the din of Marmaric war,
> Greatly rejoiced the mortal city of Battus.
> Then carved a reclining banqueter
> Lucius and placed him by his road-side porch,
> holder of the gate-key. Dear Hours, where strong wine
> holds priest Pausanias, who has passed away.

[51] *EJ 47* with L. Gasperini, *QAL*, 5 (1967) pp. 53-64
Cyrene

(a) [Beginning is lost] . . . having exercised this care, worthy both of his ancestors and his country, having twice been priest of the divine Caesar with energy and enthusiasm, and having acted as envoy during the Marmaric War, in winter, putting himself in danger and bringing military aid which was most timely and sufficient for the safety of the city. And having assumed the crown of the founder of our city, Apollo, he carried out his duties towards the gods with energy and piety and his duties towards men with generosity and lavishness beyond his means.

It was decreed, in addition to the honours already conferred upon him, that the city should offer him public thanks and invite . . .

(b) . . . to erect statues in whichever public or sacred places he wishes and to set up in the temple of Apollo a statue of Parian marble and a gilded shield, bearing the inscription:

Phaos, son of Clearchus the Patriotic, for his virtue and good-will towards the city, the Cyrenians.

[52] *EJ 62*
4 BC, Pelusium, Egypt

On behalf of Imperator Caesar Augustus, son of a god, and Livia Augusta and Gaius Caesar and Lucius Caesar, the sons of the imperator, and Julia, the daughter of the imperator, and Gaius Turranius, prefect of Egypt; Quintus Corvius Flaccus, son of Quintus, having been epistrategus of the Thebaid, administrator of justice at Pelusium, dedicated the throne and altar, year 26 of Caesar, Tybi 13th.

[53] *EJ 63*
Eresus, Lesbos, bilingual

To Julia, daughter of Caesar, Venus Genetrix.

[54] *EJ 63a*
Rome; cf. *RG*, 14.1

The urban plebs resident in region 13 of the city[1] ... of wards ... to Gaius Caesar, son of Augustus, princeps of the youth, priest, consul designate, money collected.

1. Cf. Suet. *Aug*. 30; Dio 55.8.

[55] *EJ 64*
Athens, Theatre of Dionysus

The people honoured Gaius Caesar, son of Augustus, new Ares.

[56] *EJ 65*
3 BC, Rome; cf. *RG*, 14.1

To Lucius Caesar, son of Augustus, grandson of a god, princeps of the youth, consul designate at the age of 14, augur; the Senate.

[57] *EJ 66*
Aureus, Lyons

Obv. Head of Augustus. CAESAR AUGUSTUS, SON OF A GOD, FATHER OF HIS COUNTRY.

Rev. Gaius and Lucius Caesar, standing. GAIUS AND LUCIUS CAESAR, SONS OF AUGUSTUS, CONSULS DESIGNATE, PRINCIPES OF THE YOUTH.

[58] *EJ 67*
Mytilene

To Gaius Caesar and Lucius Caesar, the sons of Augustus, son of the divine Caesar, principes of the youth.

To Marcus Agrippa, saviour god and founder of the city, and to his son, Marcus Agrippa,[1] the grandson of Augustus.

1. = Agrippa Postumus

[59] Aulus Gellius, *Attic Nights*, 15.7.3

Letter of Augustus to Gaius in the East, quoted by Gellius from a book of such letters from Augustus to his son. Cf. Ovid, *Art of Love*, 1.594ff.

Greetings my dear Gaius, my favourite little donkey. By heaven, I always miss you when you're away from me! But I need to see my Gaius all the more on days like today. Wherever you are I trust you're in good spirits and well enough to celebrate my 64th birthday. As you see, I've climbed above the 63rd year on the ladder of life, the critical point for all old men. And I pray to the gods that you and I may pass the time remaining in good health with the state flourishing, while you exercise your virtue and succeed to my position.

[60] Antipater of Thessalonica, *Palatine Anthology*, 9.297

Go forth to the Euphrates, son of Zeus, for already
The Parthians are deserting to you on eastern feet.
Go forth, lord Caesar, and find their bows unstrung by terror;
Rule by your father's shining example and
Be first to set your seal, before the rising sun, on the fact that
Rome is bounded on all sides by Ocean.

[61] Velleius Paterculus 2.101.1-3

It was a little later when Gaius Caesar, after touring other provinces, was sent to Syria; he met Tiberius Nero en route and treated him with every honour as his senior. In Syria his behaviour was inconsistent, providing many grounds for praise and some for criticism. He met the Parthian king, a most distinguished young man,[1] on an island in the Euphrates, with an equal retinue on either side. This spectacle, of the Roman army standing on one side, the Parthian on the other, as two most eminent heads of empires and mankind met together, an exceedingly notable and memorable event, I happened to witness at the beginning of my service as a military tribune.

1. = Phraataces.

[62] *EJ 68*
2-3, Pisa. Cenotaph for Lucius Caesar

19th September, at Pisa, in the Augusteum in the forum, present at the drafting were Quintus Petillius, son of Quintus, Publius Rasinius Bassus, son of Lucius, Marcus Puppius, son of Marcus, Quintus Sertorius Pica, son of Quintus, Gnaeus Octavius Rufus, son of Gnaeus, and Aulus Albius Gutta, son of Aulus.

Since Gaius Canius Saturninus, son of Gaius, duumvir, presented a statement concerning increasing the honours paid to Lucius Caesar, son of Augustus Caesar, father of his country, pontifex maximus, in his 25th year of tribunician power, augur, consul designate, princeps of the youth, patron of our colony, and asked for a decision on that matter, on that matter the following was decreed:

Since the Senate of the Roman people, among the very many and very great other honours paid to Lucius Caesar, son of Augustus Caesar, father of his country, pontifex maximus, in his 25th year of tribunician power, augur, consul designate, by the consensus of all the orders, with the eagerness ... the responsibility having been given to Gaius Canius Saturninus and the ten leading men of seeing and choosing which of those two places seems suitable and of buying the place they prefer from its private owners with public money. And it was decreed that at that altar each year on August 20th offerings be made to his departed spirit by the magistrates or those in charge of the administration of justice there, dressed in dark togas in the case of those for whom it is right and proper to wear that garment on that day; and that a black bull and ram, garlanded with dusky head-bands, should be sacrificed to his departed spirit and those victims should be burnt at that place and over each of them an urn of milk, honey and oil should be poured; and that at this stage, any others wishing to make individual offerings to his departed spirit should be permitted to do so, though none should offer more than one taper or one torch or one crown, until those who have conducted the sacrifice, dressed in the Gabine manner, set fire to the pile of wood and tend it. And it was decreed that the area in front of that altar, where that pile is collected and constructed, should lie open for forty feet square and be fenced off with oak stakes and that a heap of wood should be put there each year for that purpose and that this decree, together with previous decrees relating to honours paid to him should be inscribed or carved on a great cippus set beside the altar; as for the other practices which they have decreed or shall decree as to be avoided or guarded against on that day, the decree of the Senate of the Roman people is to be followed in their regard. And it was decreed that envoys of our order should, at the very first opportunity, go to Imperator Caesar Augustus, father of his country, pontifex maximus, in his 25th year of tribunician power, and request that he permit the Julian colonists of the colony of Obsequens Julia Pisana to do and perform everything in accordance with this decree.

[63] *EJ 69*
4, Pisa. Cenotaph for Gaius Caesar

... at Pisa, in the Augusteum in the forum, present at the drafting were Quintus Sertorius Atilius Tacitus, son of Quintus, Publius Rasinius Bassus, son of Lucius, Lucius Lappius Gallus, son of Lucius, Quintus Sertorius Alpius Pica, son of Quintus, Gaius Vettius Virgula, son of Lucius, Marcus Herius Priscus, son of Marcus, Aulus Albius Gutta, son of Aulus, Tiberius Petronius Pollio, son of Tiberius, Lucius Fabius Bassus, son of Lucius, Sextus Aponius Creticus, son of Sextus, Gaius Canius Saturninus, son of Gaius, and Lucius Otacilius Panthera, son of Quintus.

Since statements were presented, since there were no magistrates in our colony because of disputes among the candidates and the following was done:

Since on April 2nd word was brought that Gaius Caesar, son of Augustus, father of his country, pontifex maximus, guardian of the Roman empire and protector of the whole world, grandson of a god, after the consulship which he held with good fortune, waging war beyond the farthest borders of the Roman people, when the state was successful and the greatest and most warlike peoples were conquered or received into good faith, had himself been snatched by cruel fate from the Roman people through wounds received in the service of the state, having already been designated a princeps most just and most in accord with the virtues of his father and the single defence of our colony. And that loss, at a time when mourning at the death of Lucius Caesar, his brother, consul designate, augur, our patron, princeps of the youth, undertaken by the whole colony, had not yet subsided, renewed and redoubled the sorrow of each and every one. For that reason all the decurions and colonists, since at that time there were no duumvirs or prefects in the colony, nor anyone in charge of the administration of justice, agreed amongst themselves, in the light of the size of so great and so unexpected a calamity, that, from the day on which news of his death arrived until the day when his bones were brought home and buried and rites were performed for his departed spirit, that everyone, dressed in mourning, with all the temples of the immortal gods and the public baths and taverns closed, should abstain from banquets and that the married women of our colony should mourn and that that day, the day on which Gaius Caesar died, 21st February, should be recorded as a day of mourning, like the day of the Allia, and be marked in the presence and by the command and wish of all and that care be taken lest any public sacrifice or offerings or weddings or public banquets is in future celebrated, planned or advertised for that day or on that day, 21st February, and lest any performances in theatre or circus be presented or watched on that day. And it was decreed that on that day each year that public offerings should be made to his departed spirit by the magistrates or those in charge of the administration of justice at Pisa in the same place and in the same manner as it has been fixed that offerings be made to Lucius Caesar. And it was decreed that an arch should be erected in the most frequented place in our colony, decorated with the spoils of those peoples conquered or received into good faith by him, and that on top of it should be placed a statue of him on foot in triumphal costume, with two gilded statues of Gaius and Lucius Caesar on horseback, flanking it. And it was decreed that, as soon as we can elect and have duumvirs under the law of the colony, those two men first elected should refer this, the will of the decurions and all the colonists, to the decurions and that, on receipt of their public endorsement, it should be legally enacted and at their instigation entered in the public records. Meanwhile, Titus Statulenus Juncus, flamen of Augustus, lesser priest of the public rites of the Roman people, should be asked, together with the envoys, to excuse the present straits of the colony and submit a deposition and inform Inperator Caesar Augustus, father of his country, pontifex maximus, in his 26th year of tribunician power, of this public devotion and the wish of all; and Titus Statulenus Juncus, princeps of our colony, flamen of Augustus, lesser priest of the public rites of the Roman people, submitted a deposition, as stated above, to Imperator Caesar Augustus, pontifex maximus, in his 26th year of tribunician power, father of his country, and did what was asked of him.

The decurions therefore decreed that everything done, performed and established by the common agreement of all the orders on 2nd April in the consulship of Sextus Aelius Catus and Gaius Sentius Saturninus,[1] should be so done, performed and kept and observed by Lucius Titius, son of Aulus, and by Titus Allius Rufus, son of Titus, the duumvirs, and by whoever shall be duumvirs, prefects or any other magistrates in our colony, and that it should all be done, performed, kept and observed in that way in perpetuity. And it was decreed that Lucius Titius, son of Aulus, and Titus Allius Rufus, son of Titus, the duumvirs, should ensure that everything written above, in accordance with our decree and in conjunction with the proquaestors, is entered into the public records by the public scribe at the very first opportunity. Passed.

1. AD 4.

[64] *EJ 70*
Denarius, Rome; cf. B. M. Levick, *Tiberius the Politician* (1976) p. 234 n. 35

Obv. Head of Augustus. CAESAR AUGUSTUS
Rev. Head of Agrippa. MARCUS AGRIPPA. PLATORINUS, TRIUM-
  VIR

[65] *EJ 71*
4-3 BC, Ephesus

To Imperator Caesar Augustus, son of a god, pontifex maximus, consul 12 times, in his 20th year of tribunician power, and to Livia, wife of Caesar Augustus.

To Marcus Agrippa, son of Lucius, consul three times, imperator, in his sixth year of tribunician power, and to Julia, daughter of Caesar Augustus.

Mazaeus and Mithridates to their patrons.
[and, in Greek]
Mazaeus and Mithridates to their patrons and to the people.

[66] *EJ 72*
Myra, Lycia

Divine Augustus Caesar, son of a god, imperator of land and sea, the benefactor and saviour of the whole world, the people of the Myrians.

Marcus Agrippa, the benefactor and saviour of the province, the people of the Myrians.

[67] *Syll.*[3] [cf. no. 25] *776*
Ilium

Marcus Agrippa, the kinsman[1] and patron of the city and its benefactor, for his piety towards the goddess[2] and for his good-will to the
people.

1. As husband of Julia, whose family claimed Trojan ancestry.
2. Minerva, patron goddess of Ilium.

[68] H. W. Pleket, *The Greek Inscriptions of the Rijks-
museum van Oudheden at Leyden* (1958) no. 5
Smyrna (?)

The members of the association of the friends of Agrippa set up this
monument for their own associate, Marion, also known as Mares,
citizen of Adana,[1] in his memory.

1. In Cilicia.

[69] *EJ 73*
Between 18 and 12 BC, Corinth

To Marcus Agrippa, consul three times, with tribunician power; the
tribe Vinicia made this dedication to its patron.

[70] *EJ 74*
16-15 BC, Emerita, in the theatre

To Marcus Agrippa, son of Lucius, consul three times, in his third
year of tribunician power.

[71] *EJ 75*
16-15 BC, Nemausus, so-called Maison carrée. Cf. B. M. Levick, *Tiberius
the Politician* (1976) p. 45

To Marcus Agrippa, son of Lucius, consul three times, imperator,
in his third year of tribunician power; given by Colonia Augusta
Nemausus.
    [Later replaced by]
To Gaius Caesar, son of Augustus, consul, and to Lucius Caesar, son of
Augustus, consul designate, principes of the youth.

[72] *EJ 76*
Between 17 and 12 BC, Thespiae

(a) The people honoured Agrippina, daughter of Marcus Agrippa. The people honoured Marcus Agrippa, son of Lucius. To the Muses.

(b) The people honoured Lucius Caesar.
The people honoured Gaius Caesar.
The people honoured Julia, daughter of Imperator Caesar Augustus, wife of Marcus Agrippa. To the Muses.
The people honoured Livia, wife of Imperator Caesar Augustus. To the Muses.

[73] *EJ 366*
L. Koenen, *ZPE*, 5 (1970) pp. 217-83; cf. A. K. Bowman, *JRS*, 66 (1976) pp. 153-4; B. M. Levick, *Tiberius the Politician* (1976) p. 233 n. 6
   The funeral oration spoken by Augustus over Marcus Agrippa. A Greek copy, preserved on a papyrus fragment from Egypt. 12 BC

[Beginning is lost] ... For tribunician power for five years was given to you by decree of the Senate, when the Lentuli were consuls.[1] And the same was given again for another Olympiad, when Tiberius Nero and Quinctilius Varus, your sons-in-law,[2] were consuls. And it was legally enacted that, to whichever province the Roman state might summon you, no one there would have power greater than yours[3] ... web and our ... with their own and ... of all men ...

1. 18 BC. They were Publius Cornelius Lentulus Marcellinus and Gnaeus Cornelius Lentulus.   2. Tiberius Claudius Nero, the future emperor, and Publius Quinctilius Varus, famous for the disaster of AD 9, were consuls in 13 BC. Tiberius's first wife, Vipsania, was Agrippa's daughter. The family connection between Varus and Agrippa is not otherwise known.   3. I.e. *imperium maius,* probably, though *imperium aequum* is also possible.

[74] *EJ 77*
Thasos

The people honoured Livia Drusilla, wife of Augustus Caesar, divine benefactress.
   The people honoured Julia, daughter of Caesar Augustus, benefactress by descent.
   The people honoured Julia, daughter of Marcus Agrippa.

[75] *EJ 77a*
Bronze coin, Asia Minor

Obv. Head of Augustus. OF THE DIVINE AUGUSTUS.
Rev. Agrippa Postumus, standing. AGRIPPA, SON OF AGRIPPA AND JULIA.

[76] *EJ 375*
Via Salaria, near Vicus Novus. Probably before AD 14

[Beginning is lost] ... camp-prefect for ... years under Tiberius Caesar, son of Augustus, likewise under Gaius Caesar, son of Augustus, in Spain, Illyricum and Armenia ... Agrippa[1] ...

1. = Agrippa Postumus?

[77] *ILS* 144
Tarraco

To Tiberius Claudius Nero, son of Tiberius, priest, praetor.

[78] *EJ 77b*
Between 6 BC and AD 2, Rhodes, Pythion

The people of the Rhodians, on behalf of Tiberius Claudius Nero.

[79] Manilius 4.763-6

     ... blessed by land and sea is
Rhodes, where stayed the future ruler of the world and princeps.
Then indeed was it the home of the Sun, patron god,
When it received the light of the great world in Caesar.

[80] Apollonides, *Palatine Anthology*, 9.287; cf. Suet. *Tib.* 14

I, the sacred bird, hitherto a stranger to the Rhodians,
I, the eagle, hitherto a story among the sons of Cercaphus,[1]
Came on soaring wing through the open sky,
When the island of the Sun was Nero's.
I stayed with him, tame to the hand of the ruler;
I did not flee from the future Zeus.

1. A legendary Rhodian.

[81] *EJ 78*
1, or earlier, Olympia

Tiberius Claudius Nero, son of Tiberius, victor at the Olympic Games with four-horse chariot ... Apollonius, son of Apollonius, the Elean, also known as Tiberius Claudius, honoured his patron and benefactor. To Olympian Zeus.

[82] *EJ 79*
2-4, Saepinum, Italy

Tiberius Claudius Nero, son of Tiberius, priest, consul twice, imperator twice, in his fifth year of tribunician power, and Nero Claudius Drusus Germanicus, son of Tiberius, augur, consul, imperator ... had built at their own expense the wall, gates and towers.

[83] *EJ 80*
Rome, Augustan Forum; cf. R. Seager, *Tiberius* (1972) p. 28

Nero Claudius Drusus Germanicus, son of Tiberius, consul, urban praetor, quaestor, augur, has been called imperator in Germany.

[84] *Excerpt from the Calendar of Amiternum*; cf. R. Seager, *Tiberius* (1972) p. 37
AD 4

26th June: holiday by decree of the Senate since on that day Imperator Augustus adopted Tiberius Caesar as his son, in the consulship of Aelius and Sentius.

[85] *EJ 81*
Aureus, Lugdunum, 13-14

Obv. Head of Augustus. CAESAR AUGUSTUS, SON OF A GOD, FATHER OF HIS COUNTRY
Rev. Head of Tiberius. TIBERIUS CAESAR, SON OF AUGUSTUS, IN HIS 15TH YEAR OF TRIBUNICIAN POWER

[86] *EJ 81a*

[Beginning is lost] ... legate of Imperator Caesar Augustus and Tiberius Caesar ...

[87] *EJ 82*

21, bridge near Ariminum

Imperator Caesar Augustus, son of a god, pontifex maximus, consul 13 times, imperator 20 times, in his 37th year of tribunician power, father of his country,[1] and Tiberius Caesar Augustus, son of the divine Augustus, grandson of the divine Julius, pontifex maximus, consul four times, imperator eight times, in his 22nd year of tribunician power, gave this.

1. These were Augustus's titles upon his death; he may have planned or ordered work on the bridge.

[88] *EJ 83*

Dupondius, 22-3, Rome

Obv. BY DECREE OF THE SENATE, TIBERIUS CAESAR AUGUSTUS, SON OF THE DIVINE AUGUSTUS, PONTIFEX MAXIMUS, IN HIS 23RD YEAR OF TRIBUNICIAN POWER
Rev. Female head. JUSTICE

[89] *EJ 84*

Dupondius, 22-3, Rome

Obv. BY DECREE OF THE SENATE, TIBERIUS CAESAR AUGUSTUS, SON OF THE DIVINE AUGUSTUS, PONTIFEX MAXIMUS, IN HIS 23RD YEAR OF TRIBUNICIAN POWER
Rev. Female head. AUGUSTAN SAFETY

[90] *EJ 48*

Bizye, Thrace; cf. Tac. *Ann.* 3.38

To holy highest god, on behalf of Rhoemetalces and Pythodoris, Gaius Julius Proclus, having prayed for and been granted safety from danger in the Coelaletic War; a thank-offering.

[91] *EJ 49*

Sestertius, AD 22-3, Rome; cf. D. Magie, *Roman Rule in Asia Minor* (1950) pp. 499-500

Obv. BY DECREE OF THE SENATE, TIBERIUS CAESAR AUGUSTUS, SON OF THE DIVINE AUGUSTUS, PONTIFEX MAXIMUS, IN HIS 24TH YEAR OF TRIBUNICIAN POWER
Rev. Tiberius seated on curule chair. THE STATES OF ASIA RESTORED.

[92] *EJ 50*

AD 30, later restored, Puteoli; cf. Tac. *Ann.* 4.13 with 2.47

To Tiberius Caesar Augustus, son of the divine Augustus, grandson of the divine Julius, pontifex maximus, consul four times, imperator eight times, in his 32nd year of tribunician power. Restored by the state.

[This text stands at the head of a huge block, on the four sides of which are sculpted representations of 14 cities of Asia, with their names inscribed beneath each one]

henia[1] Sardis *ulloron*[1] — Magnesia — Philadelphia — Tmolus — Cyme — Temnus — Cibyra — Myrina — Ephesus — Apollonis — Hyrcanis — Mostene — Aegae — Hierocaesarea

1. Meaning unknown.

[93] *ILS 8785*

31-2, Mostene, Asia. A response to Tiberius's help

Tiberius Caesar Augustus, son of the divine Augustus, grandson of the divine Julius, pontifex maximus, in his 33rd year of tribunician power, imperator eight times, consul four times, founder of twelve cities simultaneously, founded the city.

[94] *EJ 54*

As, under Tiberius, Rome: cf. R. Seager, *Tiberius* (1972) pp. 176-7

Obv. Head of Augustus. THE DIVINE AUGUSTUS, FATHER
Rev. Altar. BY DECREE OF THE SENATE, PROVIDENCE

[95] Velleius Paterculus 2.127.3-4; contrast Tac. *Ann.* 4.1

Tiberius has had, now and in the past, Aelius Sejanus as his special helper in bearing all the major burdens of state — the son of a father foremost in the equestrian order and, on his mother's side, embracing the most renowned, old and illustrious families, a man with brothers, cousins and an uncle who were consuls, a man endowed in his own right with outstanding energy and loyalty and physical fitness to match, a man of cheerful self-discipline and old-fashioned light-heartedness, always apparently at leisure, a man who claims nothing for himself and thus gains everything, who values himself beneath the valuation that others put upon him, a man who is relaxed in manner and lifestyle, but vigilant in mind.

[96] *EJ 50a*

31, Bilbilis, Tarraconensis; cf. Suet. *Tib.* 65; Tac. *Ann.* 6.8

Obv. Head of Tiberius. TIBERIUS CAESAR AUGUSTUS, SON OF THE DIVINE AUGUSTUS
Rev. Wreath. THE MUNICIPALITY OF AUGUSTA BILBILIS, IN THE CONSULSHIP OF TIBERIUS CAESAR, FOR THE FIFTH TIME, AND LUCIUS AELIUS SEJANUS

[97] Josephus, *Jewish Antiquities*, 18.181-2

Moreover, in her own right, Antonia had done Tiberius the greatest of favours. For a great plot had been hatched against him by Sejanus, his friend, a man who then held the greatest power as praetorian prefect and was supported by most senators and freedmen; the soldiers had been bribed. The conspiracy prospered and Sejanus would have achieved his ends if Antonia had not bravely outwitted the villain. For, when she discovered the plot against Tiberius, she wrote to him, setting out everything in careful detail, entrusted the letter to her most faithful slave, Pallas, and sent him to the emperor on Capri. Once informed, Tiberius executed Sejanus and his fellow conspirators. As for Antonia, whom he had always held in high regard, he thought even more of her and trusted her implicitly.

[98] *Excerpt from the Ostian Calendar* with G. V. Sumner, *Phoenix*, 19 (1965) pp. 134-45

18th October: Sejanus strangled.
24th October: Strabo, son of Sejanus, strangled.
26th October: Sejanus' Apicata committed suicide.
...December: Sejanus' Capito Aelianus and Junilla lay on the Gemonian Stairs.

[99] *EJ 51*

32, Interamna, Umbria

To perpetual Augustan safety and the public liberty of the Roman people.

    To the municipal genius in the 704th year from the foundation of Interamna to the consulship of Gnaeus Domitius Ahenobarbus and Lucius Arruntius Camillus Scribonianus.[1]

To the providence of Tiberius Caesar Augustus, born for the eternal endurance of the Roman name, upon the removal of the most pernicious enemy of the Roman people; Faustus Titius Liberalis sevir Augustalis for a second time, had this made at his own expense.

1. Name erased after his revolt in AD 42.

[100] *EJ 52*
Gortyn, Crete

To the divinity and providence of Tiberius Caesar Augustus and the Senate, in memory of that day, which was 18th October. Publius Viriasius Naso, proconsul for a third year, consecrated this at his own expense.

[101] *EJ 53* with B. M. Levick, *Tiberius the Politician* (1976) pp. 119-20; cf. R. Syme, *Roman Papers* (1979) pp. 305-14. On the tone, cf. Suet. *Tib*. 65.2
Rome. Tiberius speaking shortly after Sejanus's conspiracy was foiled.

[Beginning is lost] ... But now, since Sejanus' wicked incitement has broken the peace[1] of 60 years[1] and those evil assemblies have taken place on the Aventine, where Sejanus was made consul and I was made the feeble companion of a useless stick, so that I became a suppliant, I now call upon you, worthy fellow-tribesmen, if I have always seemed to you to be a worthy and useful tribesman, if I have never deserted my duty, nor ...

1. Uncertain restorations.

[102] Seneca, *Consolation to Marcia*, 22.4-7
Marcia was the daughter of Aulus Cremutius Cordus. Cf. Tac. *Ann*. 2.34-5; Suet.*Aug*. 35.2; *Tib*. 61.3; *Cal*. 16.1

Remember that time, most bitter for you, when Sejanus gave your father as a present to his client, Satrius Secundus. Sejanus was angry with your father because he was too outspoken once or twice, for he could not silently endure the fact that Sejanus had not only been set on our backs but had actually climbed there. Sejanus was decreed a statue which was to be placed in the theatre of Pompey, which Caesar was restoring after a fire; Cordus cried out, 'Now the theatre is really destroyed!' Should it not make one burst with rage that

Sejanus be set over the ashes of Gnaeus Pompeius, that a treacherous soldier be consecrated in the building of the greatest general? Consecrated too was his signature, and the ravening dogs, vicious to all, whom he kept as his personal pets by feeding them on human blood, began to bay all around Cordus, who was already trapped.

[103] Phaedrus, *Fables*, 3. prologue 33-44

I shall now tell briefly why the genre of fable
Was invented. The vulnerable slave
Dared not speak his mind and so
Changed his private feelings into fables and
Evaded calumny by humorous inventions.
Aesop's track I have made a highway
And have created additions to his legacy,
Favouring some additions which brought me calamity.
Yet if the prosecutor had been one other than Sejanus,
If the witness another, if indeed the judge had been one other
　　than he,
I would admit that I deserve troubles so great
And would not assuage my pain with cures such as these.

[104] *EJ 85*
32-3, Via Flaminia, near Capena

To Tiberius Caesar Augustus, son of the divine Augustus, pontifex maximus, consul five times, in his 34th year of tribunician power, best and most just princeps, saviour of his country, for his welfare and safety; Aulus Fabius Fortunatus, consular and praetorian messenger, first Augustalis, erected this in fulfilment of a vow.

[105] *EJ 86*
33, Oneum, Dalmatia

To Tiberius Caesar Augustus, son of the divine Augustus, grandson of the divine Julius, pontifex maximus, consul five times, imperator eight times, in his 35th year of tribunician power, augur, one of the 15 for the performance of sacred rites, one of the seven for feasts . . .

[106] *EJ 87*
Sestertius, 22-3, Rome; cf. R. Seager, *Tiberius* (1972) pp. 144-5

Obv. BY DECREE OF THE SENATE, TIBERIUS CAESAR AUGUS-
    TUS, SON OF THE DIVINE AUGUSTUS, PONTIFEX MAXIMUS,
    IN HIS 23RD YEAR OF TRIBUNICIAN POWER
Rev. Coach (a carpentum) with mules. THE SENATE AND PEOPLE
    OF ROME TO JULIA AUGUSTA

[107] *EJ 88*
Myra, Lycia

Tiberius Caesar, divine Augustus, son of the divine Augusti, imperator
of land and sea, the benefactor and saviour of the whole world, the
people of the Myrians.

[108] *EJ 89*
Athens, in the Agora, near the Council House

Julia Augusta Boulaea,[1] mother of Tiberius Augustus, the council of
the Areopagus.
1. = 'goddess of the council'.

[109] *EJ 90*
22-3, near Caudium

To Drusus Caesar, son of Tiberius Augustus, grandson of the divine
Augustus, great-grandson of the divine Julius, consul twice, in his
second year of tribunician power.

[110] *EJ 91*
As, 22-3, Rome; cf. Tac. *Ann.* 2.84; R. Seager, *Tiberius* (1972) p. 109.

Obv. BY DECREE OF THE SENATE, DRUSUS CAESAR, SON OF
    TIBERIUS AUGUSTUS, GRANDSON OF THE DIVINE AUGUS-
    TUS, PRIEST, IN HIS SECOND YEAR OF TRIBUNICIAN POWER
Rev. Winged caduceus between two horns of plenty, each with a bust
    of a small boy.

[111] *EJ 92*
23 or later, Rome; cf. R. Seager, *Tiberius* (1972) p. 120, esp. n.2

(a) The urban plebs of the 35 tribes to Drusus Caesar, son of Tiberius Augustus, grandson of the divine Augustus, great-grandson of the divine Julius, priest, augur, *sodalis Augustalis*, consul twice, in his second year of tribunician power; money collected.

(b) The urban plebs of the 35 tribes to Germanicus Caesar, son of Tiberius Augustus, grandson of the divine Augustus, augur, *flamen Augustalis*, consul twice, imperator twice; money collected.

[112] *EJ 93*
Ilium

Antonia, kinswoman of the divine Augustus, who has become the wife of Drusus Claudius, the brother of Imperator Tiberius Augustus, son of Augustus, and who has become the mother of Germanicus Caesar and Tiberius Claudius Germanicus and Livia, divine Aphrodite Anchisias, having provided the fullest and greatest beginnings of the divine family; Philo, son of Apollonius, honoured his goddess and benefactress at his own expense.

[113] *EJ 93a*
Bronze coin, Romula, Spain

Obv. Head of Germanicus. GERMANICUS CAESAR, SON OF TIBERIUS AUGUSTUS
Rev. Shield. BY PERMISSION OF AUGUSTUS, COLONIA ROMULA

[114] *EJ 94*
Eresus, Lesbos

Germanicus Claudius Caesar, son of Imperator Tiberius Caesar Augustus, grandson of Imperator Caesar, Olympian Augustus, his benefactor; Damarchus, son of Leon, high-priest.

[115] *EJ 94a*
Bill in honour of Germanicus, 19-20, Heba, Etruria. Sometimes called the Tabula Hebana. See F. Javier Lomas, *Habis*, 9 (1978) pp. 323-54 for text and discussion.

[Beginning is lost] ... And it was decreed that on the Palatine, in the portico by the temple of Apollo, in that temple in which the Senate is accustomed to meet, among the images of men of brilliant ability, should be set images of Germanicus Caesar and of Drusus Germanicus, his natural father and the brother of Tiberius Caesar Augustus, who has also shown himself a man of fruitful ability, above the capitals of the columns supporting the roof which covers the effigy of Apollo. And it was decreed that the Salian priests should include in their verses the name of Germanicus Caesar to honour his memory, the honour also enjoyed by Gaius and Lucius Caesar, brothers of Tiberius Caesar Augustus.

And it was decreed that, to the ten centuries of the Caesars which are accustomed to cast their votes in the election of praetors and consuls, five centuries should be added; and since the first ten are to be called to vote as the centuries of Gaius and Lucius Caesar, the following five should be called the centuries of Germanicus Caesar; and in all those centuries senators and equites of all the decuries established for the public courts at present or in future should cast their votes. Whichever magistrate shall call together the senators and those permitted to speak their opinion in the Senate in order to hold an election, likewise the equites, into the enclosure, in accordance with the law carried by the consuls Lucius Valerius Messalla Volesus and Gnaeus Cornelius Cinna Magnus,[1] that magistrate should ensure that, as the senators, so the equites of all the decuries established for the public courts, at present or in future, cast their votes, as far as possible, in the fifteen centuries. As for the casting of lots among the 900, or those called guards, which that law provides for and prescribes with regard to ten centuries, the man obliged to cast lots under that law or under this bill among the 900, or those called guards, should do so with regard to the fifteen centuries, as if he were obliged under that law to hold and conduct the casting of lots among the 900 or the guards with regard to fifteen centuries.

And it was decreed that on that day on which, under the law carried by the consuls Lucius Valerius Messalla Volesus and Gnaeus Cornelius Cinna Magnus or under this bill, the senators and equites must attend to cast their votes, the said person, in the presence of the praetors and the tribunes of the plebs, should order fifteen large wicker baskets to be set out in front of his tribunal, into which the voting tablets may be cast, and he should likewise order waxed tablets to be placed beside the baskets, as many as he deems necessary; likewise he should ensure that whitened placards, on which the names of the candidates may be written, are placed where they may most conveniently be read. Then, in the sight of all the magistrates and those about to cast their votes, sitting on benches — just as they used to sit when they voted in the ten centuries of the Caesars — the said person should order balls of as equal a size as possible to be thrown into a revolving urn, these representing the 33 tribes (Suburana and Esquilina being excepted), and the casting of lots to be proclaimed and lots to be cast as to which senators and equites should cast their votes into which basket, provided that in the case of the first centuries, which are called the centuries of Gaius and Lucius Caesar, lots be cast in such a way that two tribes are allotted to the first, second, third and fourth baskets, three tribes to the fifth basket, two to the sixth, seventh, eighth and ninth baskets, and three to the tenth, and then in the case of those called the centuries of Germanicus Caesar lots be cast in such a way that two tribes were allotted to the eleventh, twelfth, thirteenth and fourteenth baskets and three tribes to the fifteenth basket; so that, when he calls the tribe designated by lot to vote, he should call in order the senators and those permitted to speak their opinion in the Senate from that tribe and order them to approach the first basket and cast their votes; then, when they have cast their votes in this way and have returned to their benches, he should call from the same tribe the equites and order them to cast their votes in the same basket. Then he should choose by lot another tribe and another and call the senators and then the equites of all the individual tribes so that they may cast their votes in the baskets in which they are supposed to cast them, provided that, with regard to the votes of any members of the tribes Suburana or Esquilina or likewise of a tribe in which there is no senator or no eques and less than five senators, likewise with regard to the sealing of the baskets after voting has been completed and their handing to the praetors of the treasury, so that with the electoral votes they may be carried into the Saepta, and in the matter of verifying the seals and sorting the votes, the said person adheres to all the provisions in this regard . . . written and included in that law which the consuls Cinna and Volesus carried with regard to the ten centuries of the Caesars; and he should do and perform and have done and performed with regard to the fifteen centuries all the same things as he was obliged to do and perform with regard to the ten centuries under the law which the consuls Cinna and Volesus carried; what is thus done is to be lawful and valid.

Then, when the votes of the fifteen centuries of Gaius and Lucius Caesar and Germanicus Caesar electing the consuls and praetors have been counted, and when the ballot of that century which has been chosen by lot has been brought in, the person holding this election should read it out, just as he was obliged with the ten centuries of the Caesars to read that ballot chosen by lot from those centuries under the law which the consuls Lucius Valerius Messalla Volesus and Gnaeus Cornelius Magnus carried, provided that he ensures that the roll of each century of Gaius and Lucius Caesar, coming out by lot, is read under the name of Gaius and Lucius Caesar and that each of the candidates elected by that century is announced under their names, and provided that he ensures that the roll of each of those centuries named after Germanicus Caesar under this bill, coming out by lot, is read under the name of Germanicus Caesar and that each of the candidates elected by that century is likewise announced under his name. And the number of centuries added under this bill should be added to the number of the remaining centuries, just as, under the law which the consuls Cinna and Volesus carried, it is provided that the number of ten centuries to be added are added. Thus he who holds an election for the creation of consuls and praetors should ensure that a count is made of that number in the electoral assembly and that votes are thus cast. As to other details which are not specifically written into this bill, those should all be performed, done and complied with just as under the law which the consuls Cinna and Volesus carried.

And it was decreed that, at the Augustan Games, when the seats of the *sodales* are set out in the theatres, curule chairs of Germanicus Caesar should be placed among them with oak wreaths in memory of his priesthood; these chairs should be brought out from the temple of divine Augustus when that temple is finished and, in the meantime, should be kept in the temple of Mars Ultor and brought out from there, and whoever conducts the aforementioned games should ensure that the chairs are brought from the aforementioned temple and placed in the theatres and replaced in that temple when they are put away.

And it was decreed that on that day on which it is stipulated that the bones of Germanicus Caesar be conveyed to the tomb, the temples of the gods should be closed and those enrolled in the equestrian order but without the public horse who wish to play their part and are not prevented by their health or a death in the family should come to the Campus Martius dressed in the broad stripe, while those with the public horse should come wearing full dress.

And it was decreed that in memory of Germanicus Caesar the temples of the immortal gods situated, at present or in future, in the city of Rome or within a mile of the city of Rome should be closed each year on the day of his death and that those in charge of those temples, at present or in future, should ensure that this is done; and in his memory the masters of the *sodales Augustales* every year should ensure that offerings are made to the departed spirit of Germanicus on the same day in front of his tomb, or if one or more masters is unable to attend the sacrifice, those to be masters in the next year should perform it in place of those who cannot perform the ceremony . . .

1. AD 5.

[116] *EJ 94b*
Bill in honour of Drusus (?), 23-4 (?), Ilici, Spain

[Beginning is lost] . . . and he should likewise order waxed tablets to be placed beside the baskets, as many as he deems necessary; likewise, he should ensure that whitened placards, on which the names of candidates may be written, are placed where they may most conveniently be read. Then, in the sight of all the magistrates and those about to cast their votes, sitting on benches — just as they used to sit when they voted in the fifteen centuries of the Caesars and Germanicus Caesar — the said person should order balls of as equal a size as possible to be thrown into a revolving urn, these representing the 33 tribes (Suburana and Esquilina being excepted), and the casting of lots to be proclaimed and lots to be cast as to which senators and equites should cast their votes into which basket, provided that in the case of the first centuries which are named after Gaius and Lucius Caesar lots be cast . . . [several lines missing] . . . lots be cast . . . baskets; so that when he calls the tribe designated by the lot to vote, he should call in order the senators and those permitted to speak their opinion in the Senate from that tribe and order them to approach the first basket and cast their votes; then, when they have cast their votes in this way and have returned to their benches, he should call from the same tribe the equites and order them to cast their votes in the same urn. Then he should choose by lot another tribe and another and call the senators and then the equites of all the individual tribes so that they may cast their votes in the basket in which they are supposed to cast them . . .

[117] *EJ 95*
Mytilene

The people honoured Nero Julius Caesar, son of new god Germanicus Caesar and goddess, Aeolis, harvest-bringer, Agrippina.

[118] *EJ 96*
27-9 Rome; cf. Tac. *Ann.* 3.29

To Nero Caesar, son of Germanicus Caesar, grandson of Tiberius Caesar Augustus, great-grandson of the divine Augustus, *flamen Augustalis, sodalis Augustalis, sodalis Titius*, Arval brother, fetial, quaestor, by decree of the Senate.

[119] *EJ 96a*
Bronze coin, Tingis, Mauretania

Obv. Head of Nero, son of Germanicus. NERO, JULIA TINGIS
Rev. Head of Drusus, son of Germanicus. DRUSUS

[120] *EJ 97*
Between 33 and 37, Vienna, Gaul

To Gaius Caesar Germanicus, son of Germanicus, grandson of Tiberius Augustus, great-grandson of the divine Augustus, priest, quaestor.

[121] *ILS 164*
Rome

Bones of Tiberius Caesar Augustus, son of the divine Augustus, pontifex maximus, in his 38th year of tribunician power, imperator 8 times, consul 5 times.

[122] *EJ 98* with Sherk *RDGE* no. 65

A. Letter of Paullus Fabius Maximus, proconsul of Asia, probably 9 BC

[Beginning is lost] ... we have inherited from our predecessors ... of the gods ... well-disposed and ... whether the birthday of the most divine Caesar is more pleasant or more advantageous, the day which we might justly set on a par with the beginning of everything, in practical terms at least, in that he restored order when everything was disintegrating and falling into chaos and gave a new look to the whole world, a world which would have met destruction with the utmost pleasure if Caesar had not been born as a common blessing to all. For that reason one might justly take this to be the beginning of life and living, the end of regret at one's birth. And since one could take one's beginning from no day more propitious to the public and private benefit than that day which has been a benefit to all, and since entry into public office occurs at roughly the same time in the cities of Asia — a synchronism evidently pre-arranged in accordance with some divine wish, so that it might be a basis for honouring Augustus — and since it is hard to give appropriate thanks for the very great benefits bestowed by him, unless we devise some manner of repayment for each of these benefits, and since people would celebrate his birthday more joyfully, a day shared by all, if it coincided with some particular cause for celebration because of public office, it is my view that all the communities should have one and the same New Year's Day, the birthday of the most divine Caesar, and that on that day, 23rd September, all should enter their term of office, so that his birthday may be honoured more exceptionally and with more universal distinction through the addition of separate rites, a day which I think will prove most propitious to the province. A decree must be drafted by the league of Asia, encompassing all his virtues, so that our plan for the honouring of Augustus may abide forever. I shall order the decree to be inscribed on a pillar and erected in the temple, having instructed that the ordinance be inscribed in both Greek and Latin.

B. Decree of the League of Asia

Decreed by the Greeks of Asia, on the proposal of the high-priest Apollonius, son of Menophilus, of Aezani.

Since the providence that has divinely ordered our existence has applied her energy and zeal and has brought to life the most perfect good in Augustus, whom she filled with virtues for the benefit of mankind, bestowing him upon us and our descendants as a saviour — he who put an end to war and will order peace, Caesar, who by his epiphany exceeded the hopes of those who prophesied good tidings, not only outdoing benefactors of the past, but also allowing no hope of greater benefactions in the future; and since the birthday of the god first brought to the world the good tidings residing in him, and since Asia voted at Smyrna, in the proconsulship of Lucius Volcacius Tullus, when Papion, son of Diosierites, was secretary, that a crown should be awarded to whoever suggested the greatest honours for the god, and since Paullus Fabius Maximus, the proconsul and benefactor of the province, sent by the right hand and reason of the god, in addition to all the other benefits he has conferred on the province, benefits of a size to beggar description, has devised to honour Augustus something hitherto unknown to the Greeks: to begin time from his birthday. For that reason, with good fortune and safety, the Greeks of Asia have decided that the New Year in all the cities should begin on 23rd September, the birthday of Augustus; and that the Greek date should be used as well as the Roman date so as to ensure that the dates in the various cities correspond; and that the first month should be called Caesareius, as already decreed, beginning on 23rd September, the birthday of Caesar; and that the crown decreed for the man who devised the greatest honours for Caesar should be awarded to Maximus the proconsul and it should forever be proclaimed of him at the athletic festival of the Roman Augusti held at Pergamum that Asia crowns Paullus Fabius Maximus, the most pious deviser of honours for Caesar, and the same proclamation should be made at the city festivals of the Caesars; and that the letter of the proconsul and the decree of Asia should be inscribed on a pillar of white marble, which is to be placed in the sacred precinct of Rome and Augustus; and that the annual public advocates should ensure that the letter of Maximus and the decree of Asia are inscribed on pillars of white marble in the leading cities of the assize-districts and that these pillars are placed in the temples of Caesar.

The months are to be observed as follows: Caesareius, 31 days; Apellaeus, 30 days; Audnaeus, 31 days; Peritius, 31 days; Dystrus, 28 days; Xandicus, 31 days; Artemision, 30 days; Daesius, 31; Panemus, 30; Lous, 31; Gorpiaeus, 31; Hyperberetaeus, 30. In total, 365 days. In leap years Xandicus will last 32 days. So that the months and days may proceed in sequence from the present day, the present month of Peritius will continue until the 14th and on 24th January we will observe the first day of Dystrus, and in each month the first day will be seven days before the beginning of the Roman month. The day intercalated will always be the first day of the month of Xandicus, with an interval of two years.

C. Another decree of the League of Asia

Decreed by the Greeks of Asia, on the proposal of the high-priest Apollonius, son of Menophilus, of Aezani.

Since New Year's Day must always be the same in every case as the day of entry into public office, in accordance with both the edict of Paullus Fabius Maximus, the proconsul, and the decree of Asia, and since the arrangement of time is disrupted by the announcements of the elections of magistrates, it is decreed that electoral business should be conducted in the tenth month on the tenth day, as set down in the Cornelian law.

[123] *EJ 98a*
Halicarnassus

[Beginning is lost] . . . since the eternal and immortal nature of everything has bestowed upon mankind the greatest good with extraordinary benefactions by bringing Caesar Augustus in our blessed time the father of his own country, divine Rome, and ancestral Zeus, saviour of the common race of men, whose providence has not only fulfilled but actually exceeded the prayers of all. For land and sea are at peace and the cities flourish with good order, concord and prosperity − it is the prime crop of all good, as mankind, filled with high hopes for the future and high spirits for the present, with festivals, dedications, sacrifices and hymns . . . their . . . [about 25 lines missing] . . . and that a copy of this decree be inscribed and placed in the precinct of Rome and Augustus by the high-priest, Gaius Julius . . . friend of Caesar, and in the other cities by the magistrates, and that the altars [?] be dedicated on 25th November by the priests and magistrates . . . while people keep festival . . .

[124] *EJ 99* with Sherk, *RDGE* no. 68
5-2 BC, Sardis

The league of the Greeks of Asia and the people of the Sardians and the gerusia honoured Menogenes, son of Isidorus, son of Menogenes, as follows:

(1) Metrodorus, son of Conon, and Cleinias and Musaeus and Dionysius, the strategi, having made their reports. Since Gaius Julius Caesar, the oldest of the sons of Augustus, has taken off the purple-bordered toga and assumed the most prayed for, brilliant white toga in all its splendour and all mankind is rejoicing at the sight of their prayers on behalf of his children coming to fruition for Augustus; and since our city, at a time of such great good fortune, has adjudged the day when he came to manhood sacred, a day on which, every year, all should wear white and crowns on their heads and the annual strategi should sacrifice to the gods and should pray through the sacred heralds for his safety and should dedicate a statue of him, placing it in the temple of his father; and as for the day on which the city received the glad tidings and on which the decree was made, crowns should be worn on this day too and the most outstanding sacrifices made to the gods; and since our city has decided to send an embassy to Rome on these matters to

congratulate both him and Augustus, the council and the people
have decided to send envoys chosen from the best men to give him
the city's greetings and to deliver to him a copy of this decree, sealed
with the public seal, and to discuss with Augustus the state of Asia
and the city both. Chosen as envoys were Iollas, son of Metrodorus,
and Menogenes, son of Isidorus, son of Menogenes.

(2) Imperator Caesar Augustus, son of a god, pontifex maximus, in
his 19th year of tribunician power, to the magistrates and council
of the Sardians, greetings.

Your envoys, Iollas, son of Metrodorus, and Menogenes, son of
Isidorus, son of Menogenes, came before me in Rome and delivered
your decree, in which you display your measures for your city and
rejoice that my elder son has come to manhood. I therefore congratulate you for your zeal and for showing your gratitude towards me
and all mine for the benefactions you have received from me.

(Sections 3-6, here omitted, record similar honours to Menogenes
from the council, council and people, and gerusia respectively)

(7) Charinus, son of Charinus, of Pergamum, the high-priest of divine
Rome and of Imperator Caesar Augustus, son of a god, to the magistrates, council and people of the Sardians, greetings.

When the electoral assembly was convened and the 150 men from
the cities met, they unanimously decided to honour the annual public
advocate of the league of the Greeks of Asia, Menogenes, son of Isidorus, son of Menogenes, your citizen, for his evident good-will towards
Asia and for fulfilling his office honestly and expeditiously, with an
engraved statue, armoured and gilded, to be placed in whichever city
of Asia he chooses and to be inscribed, 'The Greeks of Asia honoured
Menogenes, son of Isidorus, son of Menogenes, of Sardis, public advocate, who fulfilled his office honestly and expeditiously for Asia.' On
account of this we have written to you about the honours conferred
upon him, so that you may know of them.

(Sections 8-12 are more documents covering much of the same ground:
the letter of another high-priest of Rome and Augustus, two decrees
of the Greeks of Asia, and two decrees of the council of Sardis
respectively.)

[125] *EJ 100*
12-3, Narbo. Re-engraved in the second century

A. In the consulship of Titus Statilius Taurus and Lucius Cassius Longinus, 22nd September, to the divinity of Augustus, a vow undertaken by the plebs of Narbo in perpetuity:

May it be good, fortunate and felicitous for Imperator Caesar Augustus, son of a god, father of his country, pontifex maximus, in his 34th year of tribunician power, and for his wife, children and family, and for the Senate and people of Rome and for the colonists and inhabitants of Colonia Julia Paterna of Narbo Martius, who have bound themselves to the worship of his divinity in perpetuity. The plebs of Narbo erected an altar at Narbo in the forum, at which each year on 23rd September, on which day the felicity of the generation (*saeculum*) brought him forth to guide the world, three Roman equites, chosen from the plebs, and three freedmen should each sacrifice a victim and should bestow upon the colonists and inhabitants on that day, at their own expense, incense and wine for the supplication of his divinity; and on 24th September they should likewise bestow incense and wine upon the colonists and inhabitants; on 1st January also they should also bestow incense and wine upon the colonists and inhabitants; also on 7th January, on which day he first entered upon the rule of the world, they should make supplication with incense and wine and each sacrifice a victim and on that day bestow upon the colonists and inhabitants incense and wine: and on 31st May, because on that day, in the consulship of Titus Statilius Taurus and Manius Aemilius Lepidus, he joined the courts of the plebs to the decurions, they should each sacrifice a victim and bestow upon the colonists and inhabitants incense and wine for the supplication of his divinity. And one of those three Roman equites or three freedmen . . .

B. The plebs of Narbo dedicated an altar of the divinity of Augustus . . . under the regulations set out below:

O divinity of Caesar Augustus, father of his country, when I give and dedicate this altar to you today, I shall give and dedicate it under those regulations and rules which I shall publicly proclaim to be the foundation of this altar and this inscription.

If anyone should wish to clean, adorn or repair it as a benefaction, let it be lawful and right. If anyone should dedicate a victim and not hold forth the entrails, let it be held to be properly done, nevertheless. If anyone should wish to make a gift to or to enhance this altar, let it be permitted and let the same regulation apply to that gift as applies to the altar. Let the other regulations applying to this altar and inscription be the same as those applying to the altar of Diana on the Aventine.

Under these regulations and rules, as I have stated, I give and dedicate this altar to you for Imperator Caesar Augustus, father of his country, pontifex maximus, in his 35th year of tribunician power, for his wife, children and family, for the Senate and people of Rome and for the colonists and inhabitants, who have bound themselves to the worship of his divinity in perpetuity, so that you may be well-disposed and propitious.

[126] *EJ 101*
18, Forum Clodii, Etruria

In the consulship of Tiberius Caesar, for the third time, and Germanicus Caesar, for the second time, when the duumvirs were Gnaeus Acceius Rufus Lutatius, son of Gnaeus, of the tribe Arnensis, and Titus Petillius, son of Publius, of the tribe Quirina, decreed:

The shrine and these statues and a victim for the dedication. For the birthday of Augustus, 24th September, two victims, which were usually sacrificed in perpetuity at the altar dedicated to Augustan divinity, should be sacrificed on 23rd and 24th September; likewise, on the birthday of Tiberius Caesar the decurions and people, to do so in perpetuity, should dine — an expense which Quintus Cascellius Labeo promises to pay in perpetuity, so that he should be thanked for his munificence — and that on that birthday a calf should be sacrificed each year. And that on the birthdays of Augustus and Tiberius Caesar, before the decurions go to eat, their geniuses should be invited to feast with incense and wine at the altar of Augustan divinity. We have had an altar built for Augustan divinity at our own expense; we have had games presented over six days from 13th August at our own expense. On the birthday of Augusta we gave honey-wine and a cakelet to the women of the community for Bona Dea at our own expense. Likewise, at the dedication of the statues of the Caesars and of Augusta we gave to the decurions and people honey-wine and cakelets at our own expense and we swore that we would give them in perpetuity on the day of that dedication; and so that that day may be more celebrated each year we shall keep it on 10th March, on which day Tiberius Caesar was most felicitously made pontifex maximus.

[127] *EJ 102*

Decree and letter of Tiberius, Gytheum, Laconia. Cf. Tac. *Ann.* 4.38

(a) [Beginning is lost] . . . let him place . . . on the first pedestal, of divine Augustus Caesar the father, and on the second from the right that of Julia Augusta, and on the third that of Imperator Tiberius Caesar Augustus, the city furnishing him with the statues. And let a table be set out by him in the middle of the theatre and let a censer be placed upon it and let the councillors and all the other magistrates make sacrifice before the performances begin, for the safety of the principes. And let him celebrate the first day as that of divine Caesar Augustus Saviour Liberator, son of a god, the second as that of Imperator Tiberius Caesar Augustus, father of his country, the third as that of Julia Augusta, the Fortune of the province and of our city, the fourth as that of Germanicus Caesar, Victory, the fifth as that of Drusus Caesar, Aphrodite, the sixth as that of Titus Quinctius Flamininus, and let him ensure the good order of those taking part. And, after the festival, let him submit to the city an account of all expenditure upon the performances and of the management of the sacred monies; and if, upon examination, he should be found guilty of embezzlement or of falsifying the accounts, let him hold no office in future and let his property be confiscated by the state. And, should any property ever be confiscated, let it be sacred property and let the annual magistrates draw upon it to provide additional adornments. And let it be permitted for any citizen of Gytheum who so wishes to bring an action over the sacred monies without liability. And, after the days of the gods and principes have been completed, let the agoranomus present two further days of theatrical performances, one in memory of Gaius Julius Eurycles, who was the benefactor of the province and of the city in many respects, and the second in honour of Gaius Julius Laco, who is the guardian of the security and safety of the province and our city. And let him celebrate festivities for as many days as he can after the day of the god. And, when he leaves office, let him hand over to his successor as agoranomus all the oracles bearing on the festival by means of a public document and let the city receive a written declaration from that successor. When the agoranomus celebrates the theatrical festivities, let him set off a procession from the temple of Asclepius and Health, consisting of the ephebes and the young men and the other citizens, garlanded with crowns of laurel and wearing white. And let the sacred maidens and the women join in the procession in sacred dress. And, when the procession reaches the temple of Caesar, let the ephors sacrifice a bull for the safety of the principes and gods and for the eternal endurance of their principate and, when they have sacrificed let them constrain the messes and the other magistrates to sacrifice in the market-place. And if they do not carry out the procession or do not sacrifice or sacrifice but fail to constrain the messes and the other magistrates to sacrifice in the market-place, let them pay a fine of 2,000 sacred drachmas to the gods. And let it be permitted for any citizen of Gytheum who so wishes to prosecute them.

Let the ephors in office when Chaeron was strategus and priest of divine Augustus Caesar, the colleagues of Terentius Biadas, contract out for three inscribed statues, of the divine Augustus, of Julia Augusta and of Tiberius Caesar Augustus, and, for the theatre, for a dancing-stage, four stage-doors and a place for the choir to stand. And let them erect a stone column, having had the sacred law inscribed upon it and let them deposit a copy of the sacred law in the public records office, in order that the law, on public show in the open air for all to see, may be evidence for all mankind of the everlasting gratitude of the people of Gytheum towards the principes. And if they fail to have this law inscribed or to erect the column in front of the temple or to have a copy made . . .

(b) Letter of Tiberius.
Tiberius Caesar Augustus, son of divine Augustus, pontifex maximus, in his 16th year of tribunician power, to the ephors and city of Gytheum, greetings.

The envoy you sent to myself and my mother, Decimus Turranius Nicanor, gave me your letter, in which were set out the measures you have taken to show piety towards my father and honour towards us. For this I commend you: I consider it fitting that all mankind in general and your city in particular should observe special honours, commensurate with the size of my father's benefactions to the whole world, honours fit for gods, but as for myself, I am satisfied with honours more modest and of a human sort. My mother will reply to you when she hears your decision about the honours to her.

[128] *EJ 103*
Altar with Lar, near Cosa, Etruria

To Imperator Caesar Augustus, son of a god, pontifex maximus: Quintus Lucretius Eros Murdianus and Lucius Volumnius Eros, master Augustales.

[129] *EJ 104*
13-12 BC, Nepet, Etruria

To Imperator Caesar Augustus, son of a god, pontifex maximus, consul 11 times, in his 11th year of tribunician power; the first master Augustales, Philippus, freedman of Augustus, Marcus Aebutius Secundus, Marcus Gallius Anchialus and Publius Fidustius Antigonus.

[130] *EJ 105*
Narbo, of uncertain date

[Beginning is lost] ... at Narbo ... when the flamen performs the rite and offers sacrifice, let the lictors who attend the magistrates attend him ... in accordance with the law and right of that province ... let him have the right to declare his opinion and to vote among the decurions or in the senate; likewise ... let him have the right to watch the public games of that province, seated among the decurions or senators on the first bench ... the wife of the flamen dressed in white or purple on festival days ... let her not swear an oath against her will nor touch the body of a dead man ... unless that man is a relative, and let her be permitted a place ... at the public spectacles of that province.

On the honours of an ex-flamen. If a man has been a flamen and has done nothing contrary to this law, let the incumbent flamen ensure ... under oath they should decide by ballot whether it is their wish that the ex-flamen be permitted to erect a statue for himself. When they have thus decided that a man be permitted to erect a statue and to have it inscribed with his name and that of his father and his place of origin and the year in which he was flamen, let that man have the right to erect the statue at Narbo within the confines of that temple, unless Imperator ... forbids it. Let this man also have the right to declare his opinion and to vote ... in his senate and at the council of Narbonensis among persons of his own order, in accordance with the law. Likewise, at any public spectacle that is presented in the province, let him have the right to sit among the decurions, wearing the praetexta, and on those days on which he offered sacrifice as flamen, let him have the right to wear in public that garment which he wore when offering sacrifice.

If the flamen should pass away. If the flamen should pass away and there is no appointed replacement, then whoever acts as flamen within three days of being informed and is able, let him perform

the religious ceremonies at Narbo and let him hold all the said ceremonies in accordance with this law for the rest of that year, in the
order in which they are held by the annual flamines; and if he holds
these for not less than 30 days, let him have the same duties, rights
and position as are to belong to the flamen Augustalis appointed
under this law.

With regard to the meeting-place of the council of the province.
Let those who meet in the council of the province at Narbo hold
it there. If anything is done at a council held outside Narbo or the
boundaries of the Narbonenses, let it be unlawful and invalid.

On money allocated for sacred rites. Let a man leaving the flaminate,
from the residue of the money allocated for sacred rites, dedicate
statues or images of Imperator Caesar ... within the same temple
under the guidance of the governor of the province in that year ...
and let him prove to the auditor of the accounts of the province that
he has done everything in this matter exactly as prescribed in this
law ... temple ...

[131] *EJ 105a*
11-12, Lepcis Magna

To the divinity of Imperator Caesar Augustus, son of a god, pontifex
maximus, imperator 20 times, consul 13 times, in his 34th year of
tribunician power, are dedicated the Chalcidicum and portico and
gate and road by the 15 ... of sacred rites.

[132] *EJ 105b*
8 BC, Lepcis Magna, in Latin and Neo-Punic

Imperator Caesar Augustus, son of a god, consul 11 times, imperator
14 times, in his 15th year of tribunician power, pontifex maximus,
Marcus Licinius Crassus Frugi, son of Marcus, being consul, augur,
proconsul, patron, the flamines of Augustus Caesar being Iddibal,
son of Aris, and Abdmelqart, son of Annobal ... the suffetes being
Muttun, son of Anno ...

Annobal Tapapius Rufus, son of Himilcho, suffete, flamen, prefect
of sacred rites had this made at his own expense and also dedicated
it.

[133] *EJ 106*
Thinissut, Africa

To Augustus the god; the Roman citizens who conduct business at Thinissut, under the supervision of Lucius Fabricius.

[134] *EJ 107*
Stobi, Macedonia, in the theatre

To divine Caesar Augustus, father of his country, and to the municipality of Stobi Nemesis Augusta: Sextus Cornelius Audoleo and Gaius Fulcinius Epictetus and Lucius Mettius Epictetus, Augustales, made this.

[135] *EJ 107a*
Bronze coin, Tarraco

Obv. Augustus on curule chair. TO DIVINE AUGUSTUS
Rev. Temple. OF AUGUSTAN ETERNITY; COLONIA VICTRIX
TRIUMPHALIS TARRACO

[136] *EJ 108*
Acanthus, Macedonia

To Imperator Caesar Augustus, god, son of a god; the city and the Roman businessmen and the resident aliens.

[137] *EJ 109*
Ancyra

(a) The Galatians who sacrificed to divine Augustus and divine Rome.
(b) ... son of King Brigatus, gave a public feast and provided olive oil for four months; he presented spectacles and thirty pairs of gladiators and gave a beast-hunt with bulls and wild beasts. Rufus gave a public feast and presented spectacles and a beast-hunt.

In the governorship of Metilius. Pylaemenes, son of King Amyntas, twice gave a public feast and twice presented spectacles and presented games with athletes, chariots and race-horses. Likewise a bull-fight and a beast-hunt. He gave oil to the city. He offered up young animals where the temple of Augustus is situated and the festival and horse-racing takes place. Albiorix, son of Ateporix, gave a public feast and dedicated two statues, of Caesar and of Julia Augusta. Amyntas, son of Gaezatodiastes, twice gave a public feast and sacrificed a hecatomb and presented spectacles and gave corn-rations at the rate of 5 modii ... of Diognetus. Albiorix, son of Ateporix, for the second time gave a public feast.

In the governorship of Fronto. Metrodorus, son of Menemachus and the natural son of Dorylaus, gave a public feast and provided olive oil for four months. Musaeus, son of Articnus, gave a public feast. ... son of Seleucus, gave a public feast and provided oil for four months. Pylaemenes, son of King Amyntas, gave a public feast for the three tribes[1] and at Ancyra sacrificed a hecatomb and presented spectacles and a procession; likewise, a bull-fight and bull-fighters and 50 pairs of gladiators. He provided oil for the three tribes for the whole year and presented a wild beast-fight.

1. The three tribes that made up the Galatians: the Tolistobogii, Tectosages and Trocmi.

[138] *EJ 110*
Puteoli

Lucius Calpurnius, son of Lucius, at his own expense built the temple for Augustus, with its adornments.

[139] *EJ 111*
Masculula, Africa

To divine Augustus, a dedication; the community of Roman citizens and Numidians who reside at Masculula.

[140] *EJ 113*
Corinth

To Callicratea, daughter of Philesus, priestess in perpetuity of Augustan Providence and Public Safety; the tribesmen of the tribe Agrippia to one who well deserves this.

[141] *EJ 114*
Alabanda, Caria

The people honoured with great honours, not for the first time, and dedicated this statue of Aristogenes, son of Meniscus, son of Aristogenes, priest by inheritance of the Health and Safety of Imperator Caesar and of the Sun, a man of magnanimity and outstanding piety and justice and a benefactor of the city, having been high-priest in his country of Rome and Augustus Caesar and having accomplished the greatest and most lavish acts of honourable ambition.

[142] *EJ 115*
Ammochostus, Cyprus

(a) Inscribed between 9 BC and AD 2, altered to (b) between 19 and 23.
To Imperator Caesar Augustus, god, son of a god, ... high-priest for life of him and his two sons Gaius and Lucius Caesar, gymnasiarch; to his benefactor. Year 24.[1]
(b) To Tiberius Caesar Augustus, god, son of a god, ... high-priest for life of him and the two sons of Drusus Caesar, Tiberius and Germanicus Caesar, gymnasiarch; to his benefactor. Year 24.[1]

1. Reading uncertain.

[143] *EJ 116*
AD 1, Tentyra, Egypt

On behalf of Imperator Caesar Zeus the Liberator Augustus, son of a god, when Publius Octavius was prefect and Marcus Claudius Postumus was epistrategus, Tryphon being strategus, the inhabitants of the metropolis and the nome dedicated the porch to Isis, the greatest goddess, and the divinities that share her temple. Year 31 of Caesar, Thoth 9th Augusta.

[144] *EJ 117*
37

[Beginning is lost] ... village-secretary ... of Eremus.

I swear by Tiberius Caesar, New Augustus, Imperator, son of divine Zeus the Liberator Augustus, so help me, that I know of no one in the aforementioned village who has suffered extortion at the hands of ... the soldier and his accomplices.

If my oath is true, may all go well with me, but if I have sworn falsely the opposite. Year 23 of Tiberius Caesar Augustus, Mecheir 17th.

[145] *EJ 118*
6 BC

Year 25 of Caesar, Hathyr 22nd, at the meeting held in the Paratomus of the Augustan synod of the divine Imperator Caesar, at which the convenor and president was Primus, slave of Caesar, the priest, Jucundus, slave of Caesar, the gymnasiarch, Alexander, the majority being present.

Since we have instructed the aforesaid priest Jucundus to draw, as he is empowered, upon the funds of the synod and pay . . ., slave of Caesar, on behalf of Syntrophus, member of the synod of Caesar, within one month of the present year, the 120 silver Ptolemaic drachmas that he owes him, it has been decided unanimously that Jucundus should pay in full, within the month of Hathyr, the 120 silver drachmas on behalf of Syntrophus, without interest, and that the members of the synod should credit Jucundus with these drachmas to the amount due to the synod, and that Jucundus should not be accountable with regard to this transaction nor liable for prosecution by anyone over this expenditure . . . nor . . . such . . . and that the subscription should confirm the duplicate copies, one of which . . . and the other . . .

[146] *EJ 119*
Sestertius, Lugdunum

Obv. Head of Augustus. CAESAR, PONTIFEX MAXIMUS
Rev. Altar at Lugdunum. ROME AND AUGUSTUS

[147] *EJ 120*
Divona Cadurcorum, Gaul; cf. Caesar, *Gallic War*, 7.5

To Marcus Lucterius Leo, son of Lucterius Senecianus, who has held all offices in his country, priest of the altar of Augustus at the confluence of the Arar and Rhone; the state of the Cadurci erected this at public expense to reward him.

[148] *EJ 121*
Tarracina, Italy, on a temple

To Rome and Augustus Caesar, son of a god; Aulus Aemilius, son of Aulus, had this made at his own expense.

[149] *EJ 122*
Tetradrachm, 19-18 BC, Pergamum

Obv. Head of Augustus. IMPERATOR 9 TIMES, IN HIS FIFTH YEAR
   OF TRIBUNICIAN POWER
Rev. Temple. ROME AND AUGUSTUS, THE LEAGUE OF ASIA.

[150] *EJ 123*
Anticaria, Baetica

To Julia Augusta, daughter of Drusus, wife of the divine Augustus,
mother of Tiberius Caesar Augustus, princeps and saviour, and of
Drusus Germanicus, mother of the world; Marcus Cornelius Proculus,
priest of the Caesars.

[151] *EJ 124*
Bronze coin, Romula, Baetica

Obv. Head of Augustus, radiate with star and thunderbolt. BY PER-
   MISSION OF DIVINE AUGUSTUS, COLONIA ROMULA
Rev. Head of Livia with crescent on globe. JULIA AUGUSTA, MOTHER
   OF THE WORLD

[152] *EJ 125*
Rome, tomb of freedmen and slaves of Livia

To the departed spirit ... Bathyllus, freedman of Augusta, sacristan
of the temple of divine Augustus and divine Augusta which is situated
on the Palatine, exempt and honoured.

[153] *EJ 126*
Gaulus, near Malta

To Ceres Julia Augusta, wife of divine Augustus, mother of Tiberius
Caesar Augustus; Lutatia, daughter of Gaius, priestess of Augusta in
perpetuity, wife of Marcus Livius Optatus, son of Marcus, of the tribe
Quirina, flamen on Gaulus of Julia Augusta in perpetuity, together
with her five children consecrated this at her own expense.

[154] *EJ 112*
Emerita

To divine Augustus; Albinus, son of Albuus, flamen of divine Augusta in the province of Lusitania.

[155] *AE (1966) 177*
48, Scallabis, Lusitania

To Lucius Pomponius Capito, son of Marcus, duumvir of Colonia Augusta Emerita, prefect of engineers, flamen of Colonia Augusta Emerita, flamen of the province of Lusitania of divine Augustus and divine Augusta. In the consulship of Aulus Vitellius, son of Lucius, and Vipstanus, by decree of the decurions.

[156] *EJ 127*
3, Africa

To Juno Livia, wife of Augustus, a dedication; with Lucius Passienus Rufus, imperator, in charge of Africa, Gnaeus Cornelius Rufus, son of Gnaeus, of the tribe Cornelia, and Maria Galla, daughter of Gaius, wife of Gnaeus, having been saved, fulfil their vows freely and with good cause.

[157] *EJ 128*
Athens

Julia divine Augusta Providence; the council of the Areopagus and the council of the 600 and the people; dedicated by Dionysius, son of Aulus, of Marathon, from his own resources, when the agoranomi were the same Dionysius, of Marathon, and Quintus Naevius Rufus, of Melite.

[158] *EJ 129*
Lampsacus

Julia Augusta Hestia, new Demeter; the gerusia; the cost of the statue, its base and its erection being borne, from his own resources, out of piety towards the crowns, by the priest of the Augusti, the stephanephorus of their whole house, the treasurer of the people for the second time, Dionysius, son of Apollonotimus.

[159] *EJ 130*
Corinth

To Diana Bringer of the Light of Peace Augusta, a dedication, for the safety of Tiberius Caesar Augustus; Publius Licinius ... freedman of Publius ... Philosebastus, had this made at his own expense.[1]
1. Or, 'their own expense'.

[160] *EJ 130a*
Bronze coin, Asia Minor; cf. Tac. *Ann.* 2.43; 4.44

Obv. Younger Drusus and Germanicus on curule chairs. DRUSUS AND GERMANICUS, NEW BROTHER-LOVING GODS
Rev. Wreath, containing OF THE LEAGUE OF ASIA. Outside: IN THE HIGH-PRIESTHOOD OF ALEXANDER, SON OF CLEON, OF SARDIS

[161] *EJ 131*
Olisipo, Lusitania

To Quintus Julius Plotus, son of Quintus, of the tribe Galeria, aedile, duumvir, flamen of Germanicus Caesar, flamen of Julia Augusta in perpetuity.

[162] *EJ 132*
Aquitania

To Jupiter Optimus Maximus[1] Tiberius Caesar Augustus, a dedication; ... Valerius Silvanus made this dedication at his own expense.
1. Reading not certain.

[163] *EJ 133*
27, Rome

To the genius of Tiberius Caesar Augustus, son of the divine Augustus; Gaius Fulvius Chryses, master of the lesser Amentine district, dedicated this on 28th May, in the consulship of Lucius Calpurnius Piso and Marcus Crassus Frugi.

[164] *EJ 134*
16th Nov. 29, Lapethus, Cyprus; cf. R. Seager, *Tiberius* (1972) p. 145

To Tiberius Caesar Augustus, god, son of divine Augustus, imperator, pontifex maximus, in his 31st year of tribunician power, when Lucius Axius Naso was proconsul and Marcus Etrilius Lupercus was legate and Gaius Flavius Figulus was quaestor, Adrastus Philocaesar, son of Adrastus, the hereditary priest of the temple and statue of Tiberius Caesar Augustus in the gymnasium, provided by him at his own expense, patriotic, all-virtuous, willing and eager gymnasiarch and priest of the gods in the gymnasium, provided the temple and the statue for his own god at his own expense, when the ephebarch was Dionysius, son of Dionysius, also the son of Apollodotus Philocaesar.

Adrastus Philocaesar, son of Adrastus, dedicated this, being joined in the dedication by his son, Adrastus Philocaesar, himself the willing and eager gymnasiarch of the boys, on the birthday of Tiberius. Year 16, Apogonicus 24th.

[165] *EJ 134a*
Bronze coin, Corinth

Obv. Head of Augustus, radiate. LUCIUS ARRIUS PEREGRINUS, DUUMVIR
Rev. Temple inscribed: TO THE JULIAN FAMILY. Round the edge: LUCIUS FURIUS LABEO, DUUMVIR. CORINTH.

[166] *EJ 135*
Altar, Byrsa, Carthage

To the Augustan family; Publius Perelius Hedulus, priest in perpetuity, built the temple on private land at his own expense, the first to do so.

[167] *EJ 136*
Athens

The council and the people honoured Drusus Caesar, son of a god, new god Ares.

[168] *EJ 137*
Nasium, Belgica

To Tiberius Caesar Augustus, son of Augustus, and for the perpetual safety of the divine house.

[169] *EJ 138*
Wall of inner enclosure of Herod's Temple in Jerusalem. Cf. E.M. Smallwood, *The Jews under Roman Rule* (1976) p. 93

No gentile is to pass within the balustrade and enclosure around the temple. Anyone caught will have himself to thank for his consequent death.

[170] *EJ 139*
Probably 7 BC, Rome. Cf. W. Liebeschuetz, *Continuity and Change in Roman Religion* (1979) pp. 70-1

To the Augustan Lares; the servants who, on 1st August, were the first to enter office: Antigonus, slave of Marcus Junius Eros, Anteros, slave of Decimus Poblicius Barna, Eros, slave of Aulus Poblicius Dama, and Jucundus, slave of Marcus Plotius Anteros.

[171] *EJ 140*
2 BC, Rome, cippus

To the Augustan Lares; the servants of year 6: Felix, slave of Lucius Crautanius, Florus, slave of Sextus Avienus, Eudoxus, slave of Gaius Caesius, Polyclitus, slave of Sextus Ancharius, in the consulship of Lucius Caninius Gallus and Gaius Fufius Geminus, 18th September.
   To the Augustan Lares of the ward of Stata Mater; the servants of year 6: ... Felix, slave of Gaius Crautanius Ptolemy, Eudoxus, slave of Gaius Caesius Niger, son of Lucius, Polyclitus, slave of Sextus Ancharius Faustus, in the consulship of Lucius Caninius Gallus and Gaius Fufius Geminus, 18th September.

[172] *EJ 141*
12, Rome

In the consulship of Germanicus Caesar and Gaius Fonteius Capito, 1st January, to Stata, Fortuna Augusta, a dedication; Sextus Fonteius

Trophimus, freedman of Gaia, and Gnaeus Pompeius Nicephorus, freedman of Gnaeus, masters of the ward of the cobblers, region 4,[1] of year 18, made this dedication.

1. Cf. Suet. *Aug.* 57.

[173] *EJ 142*
1, Rome

To Mercury,[1] eternal god Jupiter, Juno the Queen, Minerva, Sun, Moon, Apollo, Diana, Fortuna ... Ops, Isis, Piety ... divine Fates. May it go well, fortunately and felicitously for Imperator Caesar Augustus, his empire,[2] the Senate and people of Rome and the families, the ninth year entering felicitously, with Gaius Caesar and Lucius Paullus consuls. Lucius Lucretius Zethus, freedman of Lucius, by order of Jupiter, erected the Augustan altar. Semonian Safety. Victory of the People.[2]

1. Later addition.
2. Uncertain.

[174] *Small. 31*
AD 37-8, fragment of the Ostian Fasti

(37) Gnaeus Acerronius, Gaius Pontius,
1st July, Gaius Caesar, Tiberius Claudius Nero Germanicus. 1st Sept., Aulus Caecina Paetus, Gaius Caninius Rebilus. 16th March, Tiberius Caesar died at Misenum. 29th March, his body was carried into the city by soldiers. 3rd April, he was buried with a public funeral. 1st May, Antonia came to the end of her days. 1st June, largesse was distributed to the people, 75 denarii to each. 19th July, another 75. Duumvirs, Caecilius Montanus, Quintus Fabius Longus, for the third time.
(38) Marcus Aquila Iulianus, Publius Nonius Asprenas,
1st July, Servius Asinius Celer, Sextus Nonius Quintilianus. 10th June, Drusilla died. 21st Oct., fire of the Aemiliana.[1]

1. District of Rome situated outside the Servian wall in the south of the Campus Martius; cf. Suet. *Claud.* 18.

[175] *Small. 81*
Sestertius, 37-8, Rome

Obv. Head of Gaius, laureate. GAIUS CAESAR AUGUSTUS GERMANICUS, PONTIFEX MAXIMUS, WITH TRIBUNICIAN POWER

Rev. SENATE AND PEOPLE OF ROME within an oak-wreath. FATHER
OF HIS COUNTRY, FOR CITIZENS SAVED

[176] *Small. 82;* cf. Suet. *Cal.* 23.1

(a) Copper coin of Gaius, Germany (?)
Obv. Head of Gaius, bare. GAIUS CAESAR, SON OF GERMANICUS,
GRANDSON OF MARCUS AGRIPPA
Rev. GRANDSON OF THE DIVINE AUGUSTUS, AUGUSTUS GER-
MANICUS round PONTIFEX MAXIMUS, WITH TRIBUNICIAN
POWER, CONSUL

(b) As, probably Gaian
Obv. Head of Marcus Vipsanius Agrippa wearing a rostral crown.
MARCUS AGRIPPA, SON OF LUCIUS, THRICE CONSUL
Rev. Neptune holding a dolphin and a trident

[177] *Small. 83*; cf. Tac. *Ann.* 2.41; 56; no. 625

Gaian dupondius, Rome
Obv. Germanicus holding an eagle-tipped sceptre standing in a chariot.
GERMANICUS CAESAR (Countermarked APPROVED BY NERO
CAESAR AUGUSTUS)
Rev. Germanicus standing, holding a legionary eagle and raising his
right hand. STANDARDS RECEIVED, GERMANS CONQUERED
BY DECREE OF THE SENATE

[178] *Small. 84*

(a) Rome, probably in the mausoleum of Augustus
The bones of Agrippina, daughter of Marcus Agrippa, granddaughter
of the divine Augustus, wife of Germanicus Caesar, mother of Gaius
Caesar Augustus Germanicus, princeps.

(b) Gaian sestertius, Rome
Obv. Bust of the elder Agrippina. AGRIPPINA, DAUGHTER OF
MARCUS, MOTHER OF GAIUS CAESAR AUGUSTUS
Rev. A carpentum drawn by two mules. THE SENATE AND PEOPLE
OF ROME TO THE MEMORY OF AGRIPPINA

[179] *Small. 124*; cf. Dio 59.3.7
Aureus, 37-8, Lugdunum

Obv. Head of Gaius, bare. GAIUS CAESAR AUGUSTUS GERMANI-
CUS, PONTIFEX MAXIMUS, WITH TRIBUNICIAN POWER,
CONSUL
Rev. Head of Tiberius, radiate, with a star on either side.

[180] *Small. 125;* cf. Tac. *Ann*. 6.45.2; Suet. *Tib* 47;
Cal. 21
Sestertius, 37-8, Rome

Obv. Piety seated resting her arm on a small standing figure. GAIUS
CAESAR AUGUSTUS GERMANICUS, PONTIFEX MAXIMUS,
WITH TRIBUNICIAN POWER, PIETY
Rev. Gaius sacrificing before the temple of the divine Augustus. TO
THE DIVINE AUGUSTUS, BY DECREE OF THE SENATE

[181] *Small. 127*
Didyma,Caria

Imperator Gaius Caesar Germanicus, the divine Augustus, son of
Germanicus; his first temple-officers, in the high-priesthood of Gnaeus
Vergilius Capito, of the temple of Gaius Caesar at Miletus for the first
time, of Asia for the third, and when Tiberius Julius Demetrius was
lawgiver, son of Menogenes, high-priest for the second time and temple-
warden of the temple at Miletus, and when Protomachus, the son of
Glyco, the Julian, was chief temple-officer and *sebastoneos* and *sebas-
tologos*,[1] made this dedication from their own resources [a list of 13
names follows] , friends of Augustus, names written in order fixed by lot.
1. Temple offices.

[182] *Small. 34*; cf. Suet. *Cal*. 43-8; Dio 59.21.1-3
Koula (Lydia)

(Below a statue of a fighting cavalryman)
To Gaius Germanicus Imperator Caesar all the public place has

been dedicated.
(Below a female statue)
Germany.

[183] *Small. 35*
Copper quadrans, 1st Jan-17th March, AD 40, Rome

Obv. The letters S.C. (By decree of the Senate) on either side of a
liberty-cap. GAIUS CAESAR AUGUSTUS, GREAT-GRANDSON
OF THE DIVINE AUGUSTUS.
Rev. The letters R.C.C. (½% tax remitted)[1] in the centre. PONTIFEX
MAXIMUS, IN HIS THIRD YEAR OF TRIBUNICIAN POWER,
FATHER OF HIS COUNTRY, CONSUL FOR THE THIRD TIME.

1. Gaius abolished the ½% tax on auction sales in Italy; cf. Suet. *Cal*. 16.3; Dio
59.9.6.

[184] P. Cavuoto, *MGR*, 4, no. 3
Before 37, Telesia, Samnium

To Tiberius Caesar, son of Drusus Caesar, grandson of Tiberius Caesar
Augustus, by decree of the decurions.

[185] *Small. 88*
Rome, probably mausoleum of Augustus

Tiberius Caesar, son of Drusus Caesar, lies here.

[186] *Small. 89*
Pergamum

Julia, daughter of Drusus Caesar, under the supervision of Hypsaeus,
son of Metrodorus, and Diogenes, son of Choreus.

[187] *Small. 85; cf. Suet. Cal.* 15.1
(a) Rome, mausoleum of Augustus
Bones of Nero Caesar, son of Germanicus Caesar, grandson of the
divine Augustus, priest of Augustus, quaestor.

(b) Dupondius, 37-8, Rome
Obv. BY DECREE OF THE SENATE in the centre. GAIUS CAESAR

AUGUSTUS GERMANICUS, PONTIFEX MAXIMUS, WITH TRI-
BUNICIAN POWER
Rev. Gaius's two brothers on horseback. NERO AND DRUSUS CAESAR

[188] *Small. 86*
Sestertius, 37-8, Rome; cf. Suet. *Cal*. 15.3; 24

Obv. Head of Gaius, laureate. GAIUS CAESAR AUGUSTUS GER-
MANICUS, PONTIFEX MAXIMUS, WITH TRIBUNICIAN POWER
Rev. Gaius's three sisters, depicted as Security, Concord and Fortune.
AGRIPPINA, DRUSILLA, JULIA, BY DECREE OF THE SENATE

[189] *Small. 5*
Fragment of Arval Acta, AD 38

On 23rd Sept., for the consecration of Drusilla, in the new temple of
the divine Augustus,[1] ... the college of the Arval brethren ... to
succeed ... of Drusilla ... the divine Drusilla ...
1. Cf. Suet. *Tib*. 74.

[190] *Small. 128*
(a) Tibur
To the divine Drusilla, a dedication; Gaius Rubellius Blandus, son of
Gaius, quaestor of the divine Augustus, tribune of the plebs, praetor,
consul, proconsul, pontifex.

(b) Mytilene
To Nero and Drusus and Agrippina and Drusilla, the New Aphrodite,
the siblings of the imperator Gaius Caesar.

[191] *Small. 87*
Rome, probably the mausoleum of Augustus

Livilla, wife of Marcus Vinicius, daughter of Germanicus Caesar, lies
here.

[192] J. M. Reynolds, *PCPhS,* 26 (1980) pp. 80-1, nos. 13-15
Aphrodisias, Caria. Probably part of an imperial group

(1) Agrippina, daughter of Marcus Agrippa, wife of Germanicus
Caesar, wife of Gaius Imperator Augustus Caesar.

(2) Germanicus Caesar, son of Tiberius Augustus.
(3) Marcus Lepidus.[1]
1. Cf. Dio 59.22.6-7. Husband of Drusilla from 38 till his death in 39.

[193] *Small. 90*
37-40, Pola, Histria

To Tiberius Claudius Nero Germanicus, son of Drusus Germanicus, augur, *sodalis Augustalis*, Titian *sodalis*, consul.

[194] *Small. 36*; cf. Suet. *Claud.* 10; Dio 60.1
(a) Aureus, 41-2, Rome
Obv. Head of Claudius, laureate. TIBERIUS CLAUDIUS CAESAR AUGUSTUS, PONTIFEX MAXIMUS, WITH TRIBUNICIAN POWER
Rev. Praetorian camp, with soldier standing on guard. IMPERATOR RECEIVED.

(b) Aureus, 41-2, Rome
Obv. Same as (a).
Rev. Claudius in a toga clasping hands with a soldier. PRAETORIANS RECEIVED.

[195] Josephus, *Jewish Antiquities*, 19.248-73 (with omissions)
The aftermath of Gaius' assassination:

The consuls convened the Senate in the temple of Jupiter Victor. It was still night. Some senators who were hiding in the city dithered when they received the summons. Others had removed themselves to their private estates, anticipating the result and rejecting the advent of liberty, for they preferred to spend their lives free from the dangers of slavery and the burden of toil rather than gain the dignity of their fathers and risk losing their lives. Nevertheless, up to 100 senators assembled. While they were discussing the matter in hand, a shout was suddenly raised by the soldiers loyal to them, calling upon the Senate to choose an emperor and not destroy the empire through a republic. The senators voiced their agreement that the government should be by one man, not a plurality, but said that they must ensure that it be conferred on a man who was right for such pre-eminence. The position of the senators was thus much more uncomfortable through the loss of their much-vaunted liberty and through fear of

Claudius. However, there were those who had designs upon the principate by virtue of the dignity of their family and their marital connections.

Marcus Vinicius had a claim through his nobility and his marriage to Gaius's sister Julia; he was eager to take control of affairs, but was blocked by the consuls who raised a string of pretexts. Valerius Asiaticus who had similar aspirations was blocked by Vinicianus, one of the assassins of Gaius. There would have been unparalleled slaughter if those with designs upon the principate had been allowed to array their forces against Claudius. In particular, there were gladiators in significant numbers and the soldiers of the watch in the city and the oarsmen who were streaming into the camp. The consequence was that those who aspired to power stood aside, some to spare the city, others through fear for their lives ... [The soldiers support Claudius against the Senate and thus make its position untenable] ... Meanwhile, in the camp, there was an inrush of people come to pay their respects to Claudius. One of the consuls, Quintus Pomponius, was particularly guilty in the eyes of the soldiers because he had convened the Senate in the name of liberty. They set upon him, swords drawn, and would have done away with him if Claudius had not intervened. Having rescued him from danger, Claudius gave the consul a seat beside him, but he did not receive those senators who accompanied Quintus with the same honour. Some were struck and pushed away as they tried to greet him. Aponius went away, wounded; all were in danger. King Agrippa went to Claudius and advised him to take a more lenient attitude, for if the Senate came to harm there would be no others to rule. Claudius followed his advice and convened the Senate on the Palatine. Claudius was borne through the city with an escort of soldiers who inflicted considerable suffering upon the populace. Of Gaius's assassins, Chaerea and Sabinus came out more into the open, but they were prevented from attending by the written orders of Pollio, whom Claudius had shortly before chosen as praetorian prefect. When Claudius reached the Palatine he brought together his companions and put the fate of Chaerea to the vote. They considered his action to have been splendid, but they censured his disloyalty in carrying it out and thought it right that he be punished so as to deter future emulators. He was therefore led off to execution, together with Lupus and other Romans. . .

A few days later, when they were making offerings to the dead, the people of Rome brought offerings to their relatives and honoured Chaerea with portions placed on his pyre, calling upon him to be mild and not angry at the ingratitude shown towards him. Such was the end that befell Chaerea. In Sabinus's case, Claudius not only absolved him of guilt, but let him keep the office he held. But Sabinus considered it wrong to be wanting in loyalty to his fellow conspirators. He killed himself by falling on his sword until the hilt met the wound.

[196] *Small. 37*
Copper as, 41, Rome

Obv. Head of Claudius, bare. TIBERIUS CLAUDIUS CAESAR AUGUSTUS, PONTIFEX MAXIMUS, WITH TRIBUNICIAN POWER, IMPERATOR.

Rev. Liberty holding a liberty-cap. AUGUSTAN LIBERTY, BY DECREE OF THE SENATE.

[197] *Small. 91*
Quadrans, 41, Lugdunum; cf. Suet. *Claud.* 2

Obv. Head of Claudius, laureate. TIBERIUS CLAUDIUS CAESAR AUGUSTUS, PONTIFEX MAXIMUS, WITH TRIBUNICIAN POWER, IMPERATOR

Rev. The altar of Rome and Augustus at Lugdunum. ROME AND AUGUSTUS

[198] *Small. 93*
Sestertius, 41, Rome

Obv. Head of Claudius, laureate. TIBERIUS CLAUDIUS CAESAR AUGUSTUS, PONTIFEX MAXIMUS, WITH TRIBUNICIAN POWER, IMPERATOR (Countermarked APPROVED BY NERO CAESAR AUGUSTUS)

Rev. Within an oak-wreath BY DECREE OF THE SENATE FOR CITIZENS SAVED

[199] *Small. 13 (part)*
Excerpt from the Arval acta, 43-8

... January, a dedication to Jupiter, since Tiberius Claudius Caesar Augustus Germanicus has been called father of his country: on the Capitol, to Jupiter a male ox, to Juno a cow, to Minerva a cow, to Felicity a cow, to the divine Augustus a male ox, to the divine Augusta a cow. Present were Gaius Caecina Largus, Lucius Vitellius, Paullus Fabius Persicus, Taurus Statilius Corvinus, Gaius Piso, Marcus Silanus, Lucius Silanus, Magnus Pompeius, . . .

[200] *Small. 38*
Aureus, 41-2, Rome

Obv. Head of Claudius, laureate. TIBERIUS CLAUDIUS CAESAR AUGUSTUS, PONTIFEX MAXIMUS, WITH TRIBUNICIAN POWER.

Rev. A winged figure holding a caduceus; a snake in the foreground, TO AUGUSTAN PEACE.

[201] *Small. 39*
Aureus, 41-2, Rome

Obv. Head of Claudius laureate. TIBERIUS CLAUDIUS CAESAR AUGUSTUS, PONTIFEX MAXIMUS, WITH TRIBUNICIAN POWER.

Rev. Seated female figure holding her right hand to her face. TO THE CONSTANCY OF AUGUSTUS.

[202] *Small. 40*
Quadrans, 41, Rome

Obv. A hand holding a pair of scales with the letters P.N.R.[1] beneath. TIBERIUS CLAUDIUS CAESAR AUGUSTUS.

Rev. S.C.[2] in the centre. PONTIFEX MAXIMUS, WITH TRIBUNICIAN POWER, IMPERATOR, CONSUL DESIGNATE FOR THE SECOND TIME.

1. Probably means 'The weight of coins restored'.   2. 'By decree of the Senate'.

[203] *Small. 41*
Denarius, 41-2, Rome; cf. Dio 60.8.7

Obv. Head of Claudius laureate. TIBERIUS CLAUDIUS CAESAR AUGUSTUS, PONTIFEX MAXIMUS, WITH TRIBUNICIAN POWER.

Rev. Triumphal arch surmounted by an equestrian statue between two trophies. OVER THE GERMANS.

[204] *Small. 42*

Silver coin, Lycia; cf. Suet. *Claud.* 25.3; Dio 60.17.3

Obv. Head of Claudius, laureate. TIBERIUS CLAUDIUS CAESAR AUGUSTUS

Rev. Lyre. GERMANICUS IMPERATOR; THE LYCIANS.

[205] *Small. 95*

Aureus, 41-5; cf. Suet. *Claud.* 1.3; 11.2

Obv. Head of Claudius's father, Nero Drusus, laureate. NERO CLAUDIUS DRUSUS GERMANICUS IMPERATOR

Rev. Triumphal arch surmounted by an equestrian statue between two trophies; on the architrave OVER THE GERMANS

[206] *Small. 96*

Aureus, 41-5, Rome; cf. Suet. *Claud.* 11.2

Obv. Bust of Claudius's mother, Antonia, wearing a wreath of corn-ears. ANTONIA AUGUSTA

Rev. Two lighted torches bound together with a ribbon. PRIESTESS OF THE DIVINE AUGUSTUS

[207] *Small. 429*

Lead tessera, Rome

Obv. Bust of Antonia. ANTONIA

Rev. FROM THE LIBERALITY OF TIBERIUS CLAUDIUS CAESAR AUGUSTUS

[208] *Small. 97*

As, 42 or later; cf. Suet. *Claud.* 11.2

Obv. Head of Germanicus, bare. GERMANICUS CAESAR, SON OF TIBERIUS AUGUSTUS, GRANDSON OF THE DIVINE AUGUSTUS

Rev. BY DECREE OF THE SENATE in the centre. TIBERIUS CLAUDIUS CAESAR AUGUSTUS GERMANICUS, PONTIFEX MAXIMUS, WITH TRIBUNICIAN POWER, IMPERATOR, FATHER OF HIS COUNTRY

[209] *Small. 98*: cf. Suet. *Claud*. 27.2

(a) tetradrachm, first half 41, Alexandria

Obv. Head of Claudius, laureate. TIBERIUS CLAUDIUS CEASAR
AUGUSTUS GERMANICUS IMPERATOR. YEAR 1

Rev. Messallina standing holding corn ears and statuettes, MESSAL-
LINA WIFE OF CAESAR AUGUSTUS

(b) sestertius, 41, Rome

Obv. Head of Claudius, laureate. TIBERIUS CLAUDIUS CAESAR
AUGUSTUS, PONTIFEX MAXIMUS, WITH TRIBUNICIAN
POWER, IMPERATOR

Rev. Hope. AUGUSTAN HOPE, BY DECREE OF THE SENATE.

[210] *Small. 43*

(a) Aureus, 46-7, Rome; cf. Dio 60.22.1

Obv. Head of Claudius, laureate. TIBERIUS CLAUDIUS CAESAR
AUGUSTUS, PONTIFEX MAXIMUS, IN HIS SIXTH YEAR OF
TRIBUNICIAN POWER, IMPERATOR TEN TIMES.

Rev. Triumphal arch surmounted by an equestrian statue between two
trophies; on the architrave; OVER THE BRITONS.

(b) 51-2, Rome in the Campus Martius, probably from Claudius's
triumphal arch on the Via Flaminia

To Tiberius Claudius Caesar Augustus Germanicus, son of Drusus,
pontifex maximus, in his 11th year of tribunician power, consul 5
times, imperator 22 times, censor, father of his country; the Senate
and People of Rome, because he has received the surrender of 11 kings
of the Britons, conquered without any loss, and has been the first to
bring under the command of the Roman People barbarian peoples
beyond the Ocean.

[211] V. Saladino, *ZPE*, 39 (1980) no. 24

Rusellae, Etruria, AD 45. Perhaps the base of a statue of Victory

In fulfilment of a vow, for the safety and the return and the British
victory of Tiberius Claudius Caesar Augustus Germanicus, pontifex
maximus, in his fifth year of tribunician power, imperator ten times,
father of his country, consul designate for the fourth time; Aulus
Vicirius Proculus, priest of Augustus, military tribune, fulfilled his
vow for the British victory.

[212] F. Bücheler and A. Risee (eds.), *Anthologia Latina*, i² (1894) nos. 419 and 423

(a)   A land never despoiled by Ausonian triumphs
Struck by your thunderbolt, Caesar, lay prostrate
And Ocean observes your altars beyond himself;
The boundary of the earth was not the boundary of the empire.

(b)   Distant Tiber used to bound your realms, Romulus;
This was your boundary, religious Numa.
And your power, Divine One, consecrated in your sky,
Stood this side of farthest Ocean.
But now Ocean flows between twin worlds:
What once was a limit of the empire is now part of it.

[213] K. T. Erim, *Britannia*, 13 (1982) pp. 277-81
Aphrodisias, Caria, base of a panel depicting Claudius's conquest of a personified Britannia

(To the left) Tiberius Claudius Caesar.
(To the right) Britannia.

[214] *Small. 44*
49, cippus, Rome; cf. Tac. *Ann.* 12.23-4; cf. M. Griffin, *Seneca* (1978) pp. 401-6

Tiberius Claudius Caesar Augustus Germanicus, son of Drusus, pontifex maximus, in his 9th year of tribunician power, imperator 16 times, consul 4 times, censor, father of his country, having expanded the boundaries of the Roman People, has extended and delimited the *pomerium*.

(On the top) *Pomerium*
(On the side) 8

[215] Aulus Gellius, *Attic Nights*, 13.14 (in part)

The augurs of the Roman People who wrote the books *On Auspices* defined the nature of the *pomerium* as follows: 'The *pomerium* is the area inside the designated countryside, around the circuit of the whole city behind the walls, delimited by fixed lines, which marks the boundary of city auspices.' In fact the most ancient *pomerium*,

which was instituted by Romulus, was delimited by the foothills
of the Palatine. But that *pomerium* was extended several times as the
state expanded and it came to embrace many high hills. In fact the
right of extending the *pomerium* belonged to he who had contributed
to the growth of the Roman People by the capture of land from enemies ...   ... in the past the Aventine was outside the *pomerium*,
as I have said; subsequently, it was included by the divine Claudius
and regarded as inside the *pomerium*.

[216] *Small. 45*
51-2, Cyzicus, on a triumphal arch. Date is restored and uncertain

To the divine Augustus Caesar, to Tiberius Augustus, son of the divine
Augustus, imperator, to Tiberius Claudius Caesar Augustus Germanicus,
son of Drusus, pontifex maximus, in his 11th year of tribunician power,
consul 5 times, imperator 22 times, father of his country, champion of
liberty, conqueror of 11 kings of Britain; the Roman citizens of Cyzicus
and the Cyzicenes set up this arch, under the supervision of ...

[217] *Small. 99*
(a) 47-8, Rome
For the safety of Tiberius Claudius Caesar Augustus Germanicus,
pontifex maximus, in his seventh year of tribunician power, consul
four times, imperator 15 times, father of his country, censor, and
of Valeria Messallina wife of Augustus[1] and their children; in fulfilment of a vow, Gaius Julius Postumus, son of Sextus, of the tribe
Cornelia, prefect of Egypt of Tiberius Claudius Caesar Augustus Germanicus, from 16 lbs of gold.

1. Deleted, see Tac. *Ann*. 11.38.4.

(b) didrachm, Caesarea, Cappadocia
Obv. Bust of Messallina. MESSALLINA, WIFE OF AUGUSTUS
Rev. One male and two female figures standing. BRITANNICUS,
    OCTAVIA, ANTONIA.

[218] *Small. 100*
Rome, Campus Martius, probably accompanying statues of members
of Claudius's family surmounting his triumphal arch.

(1) To Germanicus Caesar, son of Tiberius Augustus, grandson of
    the divine Augustus, great-grandson of the divine Julius, augur,

priest of Augustus, consul twice, imperator twice.

(2) To Antonia Augusta, wife of Drusus, priestess of the divine Augustus, mother of Tiberius Claudius Caesar Augustus, father of his country

(3) To Julia Augusta Agrippina,[1] daughter of Germanicus Caesar, wife of Tiberius Claudius Caesar Augustus, father of his country

(4) To Nero Claudius Caesar Drusus Germanicus, son of Augustus, pontifex, augur, one of the 15 for the performance of sacred rites, one of the 7 for feasts, consul designate, princeps of the youth.

(5) To . . . Octavia, daughter of Tiberius Claudius Caesar Augustus, father of his country.

1. Cf. Tac. *Ann.* 12.58.1.

[219] *Small. 101*
Ilium

To Tiberius Claudius Caesar Augustus Germanicus and Julia Augusta Agrippina and their children and the Senate and Athena Ilias and the People, Tiberius Claudius Philocles, son of . . ., and his wife, Claudia Parmenis, daughter of Parmenio, dedicated the stoa and its contents, provided from their own resources.

(Below statues of the children)

(1) Octavia, daughter of Augustus.

(2) Antonia, daughter of Augustus.

(3) Tiberius Claudius Britannicus, son of Augustus

(4) Nero, son of Caesar Augustus; the Council and People honoured the kinsman of the city.[1]

1. Cf. Tac. *Ann.* 12.58.1; Suet. *Claud.* 25.3; *Nero* 7.2.

[220] *Small. 102*; cf. Tac. *Ann.* 12.26.1; 42.3

(a) tetradrachm, 50-1, Ephesus

Obv. Head of Claudius, laureate. TIBERIUS CLAUDIUS CAESAR AUGUSTUS, PONTIFEX MAXIMUS, IN HIS TENTH YEAR OF TRIBUNICIAN POWER, IMPERATOR 18 TIMES.

(b) sestertius, 50-4, Rome

Obv. Bust of Agrippina the Younger. AGRIPPINA AUGUSTA, DAUGHTER OF GERMANICUS, WIFE OF CAESAR AUGUSTUS

Rev. A carpentum drawn by two mules.

[221] *Small. 103*
Probably from Pompeii

To Tiberius Claudius Nero Caesar, son of Tiberius Claudius Caesar Augustus Germanicus, father of his country, by decree of the decurions.

[222] *Small. 104*; cf. Tac. *Ann.* 12.41.2
(a) Aureus, 51-4, Rome
Obv. Bust of Nero, bare-headed. NERO CLAUDIUS CAESAR DRUSUS GERMANICUS, PRINCEPS OF THE YOUTH
Rev. Simpulum, lituus, tripod and patera. CHOSEN SUPERNUMERARY PRIEST IN ALL THE COLLEGES, BY DECREE OF THE SENATE

(b) Aureus, 51-4, Rome
Obv. Bust of Nero, bare-headed. TO NERO CLAUDIUS DRUSUS GERMANICUS, CONSUL DESIGNATE
Rev. A spear and shield, on which is written EQUESTRIAN ORDER TO THE PRINCEPS OF THE YOUTH.

[223] *Small. 105*
(a) Copper coin, Hippo Diarrhytus, Africa
Obv. Bust of Britannicus, laureate. TIBERIUS CLAUDIUS CAESAR BRITANNICUS, BY DECREE OF THE DECURIONS, THE COLONY OF HIPPO
Rev. Bust of Nero, laureate. NERO CLAUDIUS CAESAR DRUSUS GERMANICUS

(b) sestertius, 53-4 (?), probably Moesia
Obv. Bust of Britannicus, bare-headed. TIBERIUS CLAUDIUS CAESAR BRITANNICUS, SON OF AUGUSTUS
Rev. Mars. BY DECREE OF THE SENATE

[224] *Small. 129*
Dupondius, 41-2 (?), Rome; cf. Suet. *Claud.* 11.2

Obv. Head of Augustus, radiate. THE DIVINE AUGUSTUS, BY DECREE OF THE SENATE
Rev. Livia seated, wearing a wreath of corn-ears. THE DIVINE AUGUSTA

[225] *Small. 130*
tetradrachm, Ephesus

Obv. Head of Claudius, bare. TIBERIUS CLAUDIUS CAESAR AUGUS-
TUS
Rev. The temple of Rome and Augustus, with an armed figure (Claud-
ius ?) standing inside, being crowned by a female figure. ROME
AND AUGUSTUS on the entablature. THE LEAGUE OF ASIA.

[226] *Small. 131*
1st Aug. 45 (?), Rome

To Tiberius Caesar Augustus Germanicus, son of Drusus, pontifex
maximus and to the master Lares of the decuria and to the greater
camp Augustan college, the decurions of this year have given at their
own expense a marbled shrine; that is, . . . Julianus, slave of Augustus,
attendant, Marcus Livius Tanais, freedman of a freedman of Augusta
. . . Attalus . . . Tiberius Claudius Soterichus and Tiberius Julius
Olympicus, who was the first decurion to become . . . Dedicated on
1st August in the consulship of Gnaeus Hosidius Geta and Titus Flavius
Sabinus.

[227] *Small. 132*
Fragments of the records of the Sodales Augustales Claudiales (cf.
Tac. *Ann*. 1.54. 1-2)

(a) 64-6, Bovillae (?)
. . . Gaius Laecanius Bassus, the father, and . . . Silanus, in year 51.
   In the consulship of Marcus Julius Vestinus Atticus and Aulus
Licinius Nerva Silanus Firmus Passidienus, Marcus Pompeius Silvanus,
Publius Cornelius Scipio and Gaius Memmius Regulus, for the second
time, in year 52.
   In the consulship of Gaius Luccius Telesinus and Gaius Suetonius
Paullinus . . .

(b) 51 and 68, Rome
Decuria 27
Adlected into the number by decree of the Senate was Nero Claudius
Caesar Germanicus, son of Augustus, in the consulship of Tiberius
Claudius Caesar Augustus Germanicus, for the fifth time, and Servius
Cornelius Orfitus, year 804 after the foundation of Rome.
   Gaius Rutilius Gallicus was co-opted, in the consulship of Publius

Galerius Trachalus and Tiberius Catius Silius Italicus, year 821 after the foundation of Rome.

[228] *Small. 133*
Thasos

The people honoured Paramonus, son of Nicades, who has piously been priest to Tiberius Claudius Caesar Augustus Germanicus and to Imperator Caesar, the divine Augustus, and who has conducted his magistracy with equanimity, justice and beneficence and who practises medicine to the well-being of all.

[229] *Small. 134*
Aezani, Phrygia

[Beginning is lost] ... of the games ... organiser for the second time of the games of Augustus Claudius, who has also established quinquennial games of the new Augusti, altar-sharers, from his own resources, and temple-officer of Zeus for life and of Tiberius Claudius Caesar Augustus Germanicus, the imperator, divine saviour and benefactor, for life and of Tiberius Claudius Caesar Britannicus, god manifest, to the festival-officers and the priest of Hermes in charge of the public ..., greetings.

Having learned of my energy with regard to the Augustan family and my service to the country in every way, for this the people of the Aezanitans has given me first the priesthood of the great gods, altar-sharers, Augusti and, second, that of Augusta Pronoia too, having called ... what, on account of approval conferred ...

[230] *Small. 135*
52-3, Cys, Caria

Tiberius Claudius Caesar Germanicus Imperator Divine Augustus, pontifex maximus, in his 12th year of tribunician power, consul 5 times, imperator 26 times, father of his country.

Euphanes, son of Charinus, a Rhodian, the present *stephanephorus* and priest of the divine Augustus and of the founder of the city, Zeus the Liberator, and being also gymnasiarch and having furnished oil and having washed the baths, and in the same year also being market-officer and having made it possible during his magistracy for goods to be sold in the market below cost price, having lowered prices, and having offered sacrifices to the gods and to the Augusti for the endurance and health of their house in eternity, and having made other expenditures from his own resources and especially monetary offers for the common benefit of the citizens, and having been crowned by the council of the Rhodians for his piety to Augustus with a gold crown and statue and the dedication of a silver mask, and having been honoured by the people of the Cyites with the greatest honours permitted by law for his piety towards Augustus and his unsurpassed energy towards the citizens, has dedicated from his own resources this statue of the saviour and benefactor of all mankind, as has his wife Ammias, daughter of Jason, a Rhodian and their children, Phanias and Charinus and Artemo and Menias, the children of Eratophanes, Rhodians, out of piety and benevolence to the gods and the people of the Cyites.

[231] *Small. 136*
Arneae, Lycia

Valeria Messalina, wife of Imperator Tiberius Claudius Caesar Augustus; the people and council of the Arneates.

Tiberius Claudius Caesar Britannicus, son of Imperator Tiberius Claudius Caesar Augustus; the people of the Arneates.

Tiberius Claudius Caesar Augustus Germanicus, god manifest, saviour of our people, the council and people of the Arneates has honoured with the foremost honours.

[232] *Small. 137*
Athens

Tiberius Claudius Caesar Augustus Germanicus, imperator, Apollo the Ancestor; the priest of him and his family for life and military general for the third time, Dionysodorus, son of Sophocles, of Sunium, has honoured the saviour and benefactor of himself and his whole house. Eubulides of the Piraeus made it.

[233] *Small. 138*
Acmonia, Phrygia

To Tiberius Claudius Caesar Britannicus, son of New Zeus Claudius Caesar Augustus.

[234] *Small. 139*
Bronze coin, Ephesus

Obv. Heads of Claudius and Agrippina the younger, facing each other.
MARRIAGE OF GODS
Rev. Statue of Artemis. EPHESIAN

[235] *Small. 47*
17th Nov. 54, draft of a proclamation of Nero's accession, Egypt

The Caesar owed to his ancestors, god manifest, has gone to them, while the imperator expected and hoped for by the world has been proclaimed. On account of this we should all wear garlands and sacrifice oxen to show thanks to the gods. Year 1 of Nero Claudius Caesar Augustus Germanicus, 21st of the month New Augustus.

[236] *Small. 106*
Aureus, 54, Rome

Obv. Busts of Nero and Agrippina the Younger facing each other, both bare-headed. AGRIPPINA AUGUSTA, WIFE OF THE DIVINE CLAUDIUS, MOTHER OF NERO CAESAR
Rev. BY DECREE OF THE SENATE within an oak-wreath. TO NERO CLAUDIUS CAESAR AUGUSTUS GERMANICUS IMPERATOR, WITH TRIBUNICIAN POWER.

[237] Seneca, *On Clemency*, 1.1.1-5 and 1.26.5
(a) I have undertaken, Nero Caesar, to write on clemency, so that I may do the job of a mirror, so to speak, and reflect you to yourself as one who will reach the greatest pleasure of all. For, though the true benefit of good deeds is to have done them and though there is no fit pay for virtues apart from virtues themselves, it is a pleasure to contemplate and inspect a good conscience and then to cast one's eyes upon this massive multitude, discordant, seditious and unruly, poised to gallop to disaster, that of others as well as itself, if it should break its yoke, and at the same time to say to oneself, 'Have I of all mortals found favour and been chosen to do the job of the gods on earth? I am the arbiter of life and death for the peoples; the nature of each man's lot and status rests in my hands; what Fortune wants to give to each mortal, she proclaims through my mouth; from our reply peoples and cities conceive reasons for joy; no part of the world

at all flourishes unless it is at my wish and under my auspices; these many thousands of swords, which my peace has sheathed, will be drawn at my nod; which nations are completely annihilated, which moved, which granted liberty, which be robbed of liberty, which kings must become slaves and whose head must be bound with the royal insignia, which cities fall, which rise, is within my jurisdiction. With everything so well within my grasp, anger has not driven me to unjust punishments, nor has youthful rashness, nor human temerity and contumacy, which has often twisted patience from even the most tranquil hearts, nor that glorying in the demonstration of power through terrors, awful, but common in great empires. With me the sword is hidden, sheathed in fact, and I am utterly sparing of the lowest blood; with me everyone who has nothing but the name of man finds favour. I keep severity hidden, but I keep clemency to the fore; I watch myself as if I was to answer to the laws which I have summoned into the light from decay and darkness. I am moved by the youth of one, the old age of another; I have pardoned one for his dignity, another for his humility; when I have found no grounds for pity, I have been merciful on my own account. Today, if the immortal gods should make me answer to them, I am in a position to reckon the human race.'

You can boldly make this claim, Caesar, that all that has come into your good faith and guardianship is held safe, that nothing has been taken from the state by you either forcibly or covertly. You have aspired to the rarest praise and that granted to no previous *princeps* – blamelessness . . .

(b) To give safety to many and to recall them to life from the very brink of death and to earn the civic crown through clemency – that is happiness. No ornament of the eminence of the *princeps* is more worthy or more beautiful than that crown for citizens saved – not enemy arms stripped from the conquered, not a chariot bloody with barbarian gore, not spoils won in war. This is divine power, to save life in mobs and states; but to kill many and indiscriminately is the power of conflagration and collapse.

[238] Calpurnius Siculus, *Eclogue*, 1.33-64

I, heaven-born Faunus, guardian of hills and woods,
Prophesy to the peoples this, the future. My pleasure is
To carve joyous verses on the sacred tree, fate revealing.
Rejoice especially, you, o wood-dwellers;

You rejoice my peoples. All the herd may wander,
Its guard untroubled and the shepherd may omit
To close the night-time pens with ashen hurdle;
Yet no predator may turn his craft upon the folds
Or, bridles loose, drive off the beasts.
The golden age is reborn with untroubled peace
And at last kindly Themis has returned to earth from squalour
And decay and blessed ages follow the young man,
Who won his cause with his maternal Julians.
While a god himself rules the peoples, impious Bellona
Will let her hands be bound behind her and, stripped
Of weapons, will cast her mad bite upon her own entrails
And the civil wars which of late she spread throughout the
World, she will wage with herself; now Rome will mourn
No Philippi and will lead no triumphs, a captive;
All wars will be quelled in the dungeon of Tartarus;
They will plunge their heads in darkness and fear the light.
Brilliant peace will be here; brilliant not only in face,
As she often was, when free from war declared, from
Far-off foe subdued, but, with prowling arms,
Spread public discord with silent steel.
Clemency has expelled every vice of false peace
And has broken the swords of insanity.
No funereal procession of a senate enchained
Will tire executioners at work, now will the
Unhappy House count a few senators, the dungeon full.
Full peace will be here, who, ignorant of the drawn sword,
Will restore a second Saturnian reign to Latium . . .

[239] Pseudo-Seneca, *Octavia*, 438-44

NERO
Carry out your orders; send a man to bring me
The severed heads of a dead Plautus and Sulla.

PREFECT
I shall not delay; I'm going straight to the camp.

SENECA
It's wrong to decide rashly against relatives.

NERO
The man without fear may easily be just.

SENECA
A great cure for fear is clemency.

NERO
To wipe out the enemy is the general's greatest virtue.

SENECA
To save citizens is a greater virtue for the father of his country.

[240] *Small. 107*
Aureus, 55, Rome

Obv. Jugate busts of Nero and Agrippina the Younger, both bare-headed. NERO CLAUDIUS CAESAR AUGUSTUS GERMANI-CUS, SON OF A GOD, IMPERATOR, WITH TRIBUNICIAN POWER, CONSUL
Rev. Two figures seated in a chariot drawn by elephants. BY DECREE OF THE SENATE, AGRIPPINA AUGUSTA, WIFE OF THE DIVINE CLAUDIUS, MOTHER OF NERO CAESAR

[241] *Small. 108*
Rome

To Tiberius Claudius Caesar Britannicus, brother of Nero Claudius Caesar.

[242] *Small. 109*
Aureus, 55-6, Rome

Obv. Head of Nero, bare. NERO CAESAR AUGUSTUS IMPERATOR
Rev. BY DECREE OF THE SENATE within an oak-wreath. PONTI-FEX MAXIMUS, IN HIS SECOND YEAR OF TRIBUNICIAN POWER, FATHER OF HIS COUNTRY

[243] *Small. 49*
Aureus, AD 60-1, Rome

Obv. Head of Nero, bare. NERO CAESAR AUGUSTUS IMPERATOR
Rev. Virtue in military dress with weapons. PONTIFEX MAXIMUS, IN HIS 7TH YEAR OF TRIBUNICIAN POWER, CONSUL 4 TIMES, FATHER OF HIS COUNTRY, BY DECREE OF THE SENATE.

[244] *Small. 50*
Neronian didrachm, Caesarea (Cappadocia)

Obv. Head of Nero, laureate. NERO CLAUDIUS CAESAR AUGUS-
TUS GERMANICUS, SON OF THE DIVINE CLAUDIUS
Rev. Victory holding a wreath and a palm-branch. ARMENIA

[245] *Small. 51*
(a) Miletopolis, near Cyzicus, bilingual
Legion 6 Ferrata which wintered in Greater Armenia under Gnaeus
Domitius Corbulo, propraetorian legate of Nero Caesar Augustus ...
to ... Asper, son of Publius, of the tribe Scaptia, chief centurion,
as a mark of its esteem.

(b) 64-5, Armenia
Nero Claudius Caesar Augustus Germanicus, imperator, pontifex
maximus, in his 11th year of tribunician power, consul 4 times, imperator 9 times, father of his country, Gnaeus Domitius Corbulo being
propraetorian legate of Augustus, Titus Aurelius Fulvus being legate
of Augustus of legion 3 Gallica.

[246] *Small. 52*
64-6, as from Lugdunum and Rome

Obv. Head of Nero bare. NERO CLAUDIUS CAESAR AUGUSTUS
GERMANICUS, PONTIFEX MAXIMUS, WITH TRIBUNICIAN
POWER, IMPERATOR, FATHER OF HIS COUNTRY.
Rev. Shield inscribed S.P.Q.R. held by Victory. BY DECREE OF
THE SENATE.

[247] *Small. 53*
64-5, Rome; cf. Suet. *Nero* 13.2

Obv. Bust of Nero, laureate. NERO CLAUDIUS CAESAR AUGUSTUS,
IMPERATOR, IN HIS 11TH YEAR OF TRIBUNICIAN POWER,
FATHER OF HIS COUNTRY
Rev. Temple of Janus, showing one front with door closed. WITH
PEACE OBTAINED BY LAND AND SEA HE CLOSED JANUS
BY DECREE OF THE SENATE

[248] *Small. 54*
64-6, sestertius, Rome

Obv. Head of Nero, laureate. NERO CLAUDIUS CAESAR AUGUSTUS GERMANICUS, PONTIFEX MAXIMUS, WITH TRIBUNICIAN POWER, IMPERATOR, FATHER OF HIS COUNTRY

Rev. A triumphal arch surmounted by Victory, Peace and a chariot in which the emperor is riding; there are soldiers at either end of the architrave and Mars in a niche to the left of the arch. BY DECREE OF THE SENATE.

[249] *Small. 55*
As, 64-6, Lugdunum

Obv. Head of Nero, bare. NERO CLAUDIUS CAESAR AUGUSTUS GERMANICUS, PONTIFEX MAXIMUS, WITH TRIBUNICIAN POWER, IMPERATOR, FATHER OF HIS COUNTRY (Countermarked SPQR)

Rev. The front wall of a rectangular enclosure with a central door and sculptured panels at either side. ALTAR OF PEACE BY DECREE OF THE SENATE.

[250] *Small. 26 (part)*
Excerpt from Arval acta, AD 66

Under the same consuls ... under the mastership of Imperator Nero Claudius Caesar Augustus for the second time, father of his country, the deputy-master, Marcus Aponius Saturninus, in the name of the college of Arval brethren, sacrificed ... for the laurel of Imperator Nero Claudius Caesar Augustus Germanicus in the temple of the divine Augustus; to the new divine Augustus a male ox, to the divine Augusta a cow, to the divine Claudius a male ox, to the divine Claudia the virgin a cow, to the divine Poppaea Augusta a cow, to the Genius of Imperator Nero Claudius Caesar Augustus Germanicus a bull, to Juno Messallina a cow

[251] J. M. Reynolds, *ZPE*, 43 (1981) p. 324, no. 10
Aphrodisias, Caria

(a) Nero[1] Claudius Drusus[2] Caesar Augustus Germanicus
(b) Armenia

1. Erased.　　2. Part of Nero's name through his adoption; seldom used after his accession.

[252] *Small. 116*
Sestertius, 66-7, Rome; cf. Suet. *Nero* 13.2

Obv. Head of Nero, laureate. IMPERATOR NERO CLAUDIUS CAE-
SAR AUGUSTUS GERMANICUS, PONTIFEX MAXIMUS, IN HIS
13th YEAR OF TRIBUNICIAN POWER, FATHER OF HIS COUN-
TRY.
Rev. Rome, seated on a breastplate with spear, shield and helmet.
ROME, BY DECREE OF THE SENATE.

[253] *Small. 56*
64-6, sestertius, Rome; cf. Tac. *Ann.* 13.31.2; Suet. *Nero* 21.1; Dio
61.18.1

Obv. Head of Nero laureate. NERO CLAUDIUS CAESAR AUGUSTUS
GERMANICUS, PONTIFEX MAXIMUS, WITH TRIBUNICIAN
POWER, IMPERATOR, FATHER OF HIS COUNTRY.
Rev. Nero seated on a platform from which an attendant hands some-
thing to a citizen accompanied by a child; Minerva and Liberality
are behind. FIRST LARGESSE GIVEN TO THE PEOPLE BY
DECREE OF THE SENATE

[254] *Small. 57*
64-6, semis, Rome; cf. Tac. *Ann.* 14.20-1; 16. 4-5

Obv. Head of Nero, laureate. NERO CAESAR AUGUSTUS IMPERA-
TOR
Rev. Urn and wreath on gaming table. QUINQUENNIAL CONTEST
ESTABLISHED AT ROME BY DECREE OF THE SENATE

[255] *Small. 58*
64-8, aureus, Rome; cf. Tac. *Ann.* 15.41; *Hist.* 1.43

Obv. Head of Nero, laureate. NERO CAESAR AUGUSTUS
Rev. Circular temple with six columns, with a statue of Vesta between
the middle columns. VESTA

[256] *Small. 59*
Aureus, 64-8, Rome

Obv. Head of Nero, laureate. NERO CAESAR AUGUSTUS

Rev. Jupiter enthroned holding a thunderbolt and long sceptre.
JUPITER THE GUARDIAN

[257] *Small. 60*
Aureus, 64-8, Rome; cf. Tac. *Ann*. 15.74

Obv. Head of Nero laureate. NERO CAESAR AUGUSTUS
Rev. Safety enthroned holding a patera. SAFETY

[258] *Small. 61*
Dupondius, 64-6, Lugdunum

Obv. Head of Nero, radiate. NERO CLAUDIUS CAESAR AUGUSTUS
GERMANICUS, PONTIFEX MAXIMUS, WITH TRIBUNICIAN
POWER, IMPERATOR, FATHER OF HIS COUNTRY
Rev. Security enthroned. SECURITY OF AUGUSTUS, BY DECREE
OF THE SENATE.

[259] *Small. 25 (part)*
Excerpt from Arval acta, heavily restored: AD 66

Under the same consuls ... under the mastership of Nero Claudius
Caesar Augustus, for a second time, father of his country, Marcus
Aponius Saturninus, deputy-master, in the name of the college of
Arval brethren, offered prayers on the Capitol for the discovery of
the plots of sinners: to Jupiter a male ox, to Juno a cow, to Minerva
a cow, to Mars a bull, to Providence a cow ... and on the same day
to the Genius of the most sacred princeps a bull ... a cow, to Honour
a cow, to Eternity of the empire a cow ... Members of the college
present were Marcus Aponius Saturninus, deputy-master, ... Quintus
Tillius Sassius, Lucius Salvius Otho Titianus ...

[260] *Small. 26 (part)*
Excerpt from Arval acta, heavily restored, AD 66; cf. Suet.
Nero 36.1

In the consulship of Marcus Arruntius ... and Marcus Vettius Bolanus
... the sacrifice was offered ... as the Arval brethren had vowed for
the discovery of the plots of sinners, under the mastership of Imperator
Nero Claudius Caesar Augustus for the second time, father of his
country, the deputy-master, Marcus Aponius Saturninus, in the name

of the college of Arval brethren, sacrificed on the Capitol: to Jupiter a male ox, to Juno a cow, to Minerva a cow ... to Providence a cow, to Mars a bull ... Members of the college present were Marcus Aponius Saturninus, deputy-master ...

[261] *Small. 64*
67, Acraephia, Boeotia, edict and speech of Nero, followed by a decree of Acraephia. Cf. Suet. *Nero* 24

Imperator Caesar proclaims:

Since I wish to reward most noble Greece for its good will and piety towards me, I order that as many as possible from this province attend at Corinth on November 29th.

When crowds had gathered in convention, he delivered the following address:

Men of Greece, I bestow upon you an unexpected gift — though anything may be anticipated from my generosity — a gift of such a size that you were incapable of asking for it. All you Greeks who inhabit Achaea and what until now was the Peloponnese, receive freedom and immunity from taxation, something you have not all had even in your most prosperous times, for you have been slaves either to foreigners or to each other. I wish that I might have bestowed this gift when Greece was at her peak, so that more might enjoy my beneficence. For this reason I hold the times to blame for having reduced the size of my beneficence. But, as it is, I bestow beneficence upon you not out of pity but out of good will and I reward your gods, whose constant care for me on land and sea I have enjoyed, because they have made it possible for me to bestow such great benefactions. For other principes have conferred freedom on cities, but only Nero[1] has done so even on a province.

The high-priest of the Augusti for life and of Nero Claudius Caesar Augustus, Epaminondas, son of Epaminondas, proclaimed (submitted by him for prior consideration to the council and people):

Since the lord of the entire world, Nero, pontifex maximus, in his 13th year of tribunician power, father of his country, New Sun that has shone on the Greeks, has decided to bestow beneficence upon Greece and has rewarded and shown piety towards our gods, who have stood by him everywhere for his care and safety; since he, Nero, Zeus the Liberator, the one and only greatest imperator of our times, friend of the Greeks, has bestowed the eternal indigenous, native freedom that had formerly been taken from the Greeks, he has shown his favour, he has brought back the autonomy and freedom of the past and to this great and unexpected gift has added immunity from taxation, quite complete, which none of the previous Augusti gave us. For all these reasons it has been decided by the magistrates and councillors and people to worship him at the existing altar dedicated to Zeus the Saviour, and to inscribe upon it 'To Zeus the Liberator, Nero, forever' and to erect statues of Nero Zeus the Liberator and the goddess Augusta Messallina in the temple of Ptoian Apollo to share it with our ancestral gods, so that, when these things have been done, our city may be seen to have poured out every honour and piety upon the house of the lord Augustus Nero; it has also been decided to inscribe the decree on a column set beside Zeus the Saviour in the market-place and on the temple of Ptoian Apollo.

1. Name erased.

[262] *Small. 62*
Bronze coin, Corinth

Obv. Head of Nero, radiate. NERO CAESAR AUGUSTUS IMPERATOR

Rev. Galley. PUBLIUS MEMMIUS CLEANDER BEING DUUMVIR QUINQUENNALIS AT CORINTH, THE ADVENT OF AUGUSTUS

[263] *Small. 63*
Tetradrachms, 66-7, Alexandria; cf. Suet. *Nero* 23-4; Dio 63.8ff.

Obv. Bust of Nero, radiate. NERO CLAUDIUS CAESAR AUGUSTUS GERMANICUS IMPERATOR YEAR 13

There are a variety of reverses:

(a) Bust of Olympian Zeus. OE OLYMPIAN ZEUS
(b) Bust of Zeus with aegis and parsley crown. NEMEAN ZEUS
(c) Bust of Poseidon with a trident. ISTHMIAN POSEIDON
(d) Bust of Apollo with a quiver. PYTHIAN APOLLO
(e) Bust of Apollo with a quiver. ACTIAN APOLLO

[264] Philostratus, *Life of Apollonius of Tyana*, 4.24

When Apollonius was at the Isthmus and the sea roared around Lechaeum[1] he said, 'This neck of land will be cut, but not, rather.' He thus predicted the cutting of the Isthmus shortly after, that planned by Nero seven years later. For Nero had left his palace and come to

Greece to submit himself to the orders of the heralds at the Olympic and Pythian Games; and he also won at the Isthmus. His victories were won with the harp and among the heralds; and he won in the tragedies at Olympia. It is said that he then set about the cutting of the isthmus, making it a thoroughfare for ships and connecting the Aegean and Adriatic, so that every ship would not sail beyond Cape Malea, but many of them might pass through the breach, short-cutting the circuitous route. But Apollonius's prediction came to pass. Digging started from Lechaeum and progressed some four stades, but it is said that Nero stopped it; some say that Egyptian philosophers told him that the sea above Lechaeum would pour over and wipe Aegina off the map, others that he was afraid of revolutionary bids for power.

1. Port of Corinth.

[265] *Small. 65*
Epidaurus

Achaeans and Boeotians and Phocians and Euboeans and Locrians and Dorians honour Titus Statilius Timocrates, who has been their secretary, for his virtue. Since Titus Statilius Timocrates, a man of account and of the first rank, has conducted himself most nobly in government in a life he has lived in an upright and remarkable fashion and since, chosen to be secretary after the restoration of freedom to us, in times of the most burdensome and difficult circumstances, he has magnanimously undertaken labours and services too large for one man and too many for one year; through these he often and excellently guided us and established firmly the conditions of freedom that were still wavering. For all these reasons the Panachaean council has decided to give thanks to the man and to set up bronze statues of him at the sites of the Panachaean festivals and in the precinct of Amarius and at Epidaurus in the temple of Asclepius, bearing the inscription: 'Achaeans and Boeotians and Phocians and Euboeans and Locrians and Dorians honoured Titus Statilius Timocrates, who has been their secretary, for his virtue.'

[266] *Small. 66*
Aureus, 66-8, Corinth (?)

Obv. Head of Nero, laureate. IMPERATOR NERO CAESAR AUGUSTUS

Rev. Jupiter enthroned holding a thunderbolt and long sceptre. JUPITER THE LIBERATOR

[267] *Small. 68*
Silver shekel with Hebrew legends struck by the Jewish rebels, 66-7

Obv. Chalice. SHEKEL OF ISRAEL. YEAR ONE
Rev. Three pomegranates on a stem. HOLY JERUSALEM

[268] *Small. 69*
Denarius, 66-8, Rome

Obv. Head of Nero, laureate. IMPERATOR NERO CAESAR AUGUS-
TUS, FATHER OF HIS COUNTRY
Rev. Legionary eagle between two standards.

[269] *Small. 110*
(a) tetradrachm, 56-8, Alexandria
Obv. Bust of Nero laureate. NERO CLAUDIUS CAESAR AUGUS-
TUS GERMANICUS IMPERATOR
Rev. Bust of Octavia. OCTAVIA, WIFE OF AUGUSTUS, YEAR 3

(b) Samos, temple of Hera
The people erected this statue of Claudia Octavia, the wife of Augustus
Nero Claudius Drusus Caesar Germanicus Imperator, and dedicated
it to Hera.

[270] *Small. 111*
(a) tetradrachm, 62-3, Alexandria
Obv. Head of Nero, radiate. NERO CLAUDIUS CAESAR AUGUSTUS
GERMANICUS IMPERATOR
Rev. Bust of Poppaea Sabina with a star. POPPAEA, WIFE OF AUGUS-
TUS YEAR 9

(b) tetradrachm, 63-4, Alexandria; cf. Tac. *Ann*. 15.23. 1
Obv. Bust of Poppaea Sabina. POPPAEA AUGUSTA
Rev. Eagle, Year 10

[271] *Small. 112*
Amisus, Pontus, 63-5

Nero Claudius Caesar Augustus Germanicus, Augusta Poppaea, Tiberius
Claudius Britannicus; the people, through the agency of Lucius Jutius
Potitus and his fellow-magistrates.

[272] *Small. 113*
Aureus, 64-8, Rome

Obv. Head of Nero, laureate. NERO CAESAR AUGUSTUS
Rev. Nero radiate, holding a patera and sceptre, with his wife, holding
   a patera and horn of plenty. AUGUSTUS, AUGUSTA

[273] *Small. 114*
Bronze coin, 66-8, Syria; cf. Suet. *Nero* 35.1; *Otho* 10.2

Obv. Head of Nero radiate. NERO CLAUDIUS CAESAR AUGUSTUS
   GERMANICUS
Rev. Security, seated, holding a long sceptre. MESSALLINA, WIFE
   OF AUGUSTUS

[274] *Small. 115*
67-8, Gerasa, Decapolis

With good fortune. Year 130. For the safety of the Augusti, Sarapio,
son of Apollonius, son of Demetrius ... of Nero Claudius Caesar,
has given for the building of a banquetting-hall and doors ... thousand,
four hundred drachmas, in piety.

[275] Pseudo-Seneca, *Octavia*, 899-913
OCTAVIA [cf. 239]
Where are you dragging me? What exile
Does tyrant or queen[1] command,
If, broken and beaten by all I've
Suffered yet, she restores my life?
But, if poised to swell my griefs
With death, why does she, in cruelty,
Grudge me death in my homeland?
But now there is no hope of safety –
A wretch, I see my brother's[2] ship.
Carried on that ship, once his mother's[3]
Note, and now driven from his bedroom, I,
Sister, wretch am to be carried.
Piety now lacks all divinity and
There are no gods; the world is ruled by
Grim Fury.
1. Nero and Poppaea.   2. Britannicus.   3. Agrippina.

[276] *Small. 140*
Aureus, 54-5 (?); cf. Tac. *Ann.* 12.69.4; *Apocolocyntosis*

Obv. Head of Claudius, laureate. THE DIVINE CLAUDIUS AUGUSTUS
Rev. Triumphal chariot. BY DECREE OF THE SENATE.

[277] *Small. 141*
Bronze coin, Cyme

Obv. Head of Nero, laureate. DIVINE NERO. OF THE CYMAEANS.
Rev. Bust of Agrippina the younger. THE DIVINE AGRIPPINA.

[278] *Small. 142*
60-1, Salamis, Cyprus

To Imperator Nero Claudius Caesar Augustus Germanicus, in his 7th year of tribunician power, imperator 7 times, consul 4 times, father of his country . . . dedicated this to his own god and saviour from his own resources.

[279] *Small. 143*
As, 64-6, Rome

Obv. Head of Nero, radiate. NERO CLAUDIUS CAESAR AUGUSTUS GERMANICUS, PONTIFEX MAXIMUS, WITH TRIBUNICIAN POWER, IMPERATOR, FATHER OF HIS COUNTRY.
Rev. Genius holding a horn of plenty and sacrificing over an altar. TO THE GENIUS OF AUGUSTUS, BY DECREE OF THE SENATE

[280] *Small. 144*
As, 64-6, Rome

Obv. Head of Nero, radiate. NERO CLAUDIUS CAESAR AUGUSTUS GERMANICUS
Rev. Apollo the Harpist. PONTIFEX MAXIMUS, WITH TRIBUNICIAN POWER, IMPERATOR, FATHER OF HIS COUNTRY.

[281] *Small. 145*
Athens

To Imperator Nero Caesar Augustus, New Apollo.

[282] *Small. 146*
Sagalassus, Pamphylia

To New Sun, Nero Tiberius Claudius Caesar Germanicus, Tiberius Claudius Darius and his sons have made this dedication.

[283] J. M. Reynolds, *ZPE*, 43 (1981) p. 324, no. 9
Aphrodisias, Caria

(a) Nero Claudius Drusus Caesar Augustus.
(b) Sun.

[284] *Small. 147*
Cos

Gaius Stertinius Xenophon, benefactor of his country and priest for life, has dedicated this to Asclepius Caesar, good god.

[285] *Small. 148*
Bronze coin, Corinth or Patrae (?)

Obv. Circular temple, with female figure standing inside. DIVINE
     CLAUDIA, DAUGHTER OF NERO
Rev. Two columns, representing a temple, with a woman seated between holding a horn of plenty. DIVINE POPPAEA AUGUSTA

[286] *Small. 26 (part)*
Excerpt from the Arval acta, AD 66

In the same consulship, 12th Oct., in the mastership of Imperator Nero Claudius Caesar Augustus, for the second time, father of his country, the deputy-master, Marcus Aponius Saturninus, sacrificed in the name of the college of Arval brethren in the new temple for the Augustalia: to the divine Augustus a male ox, to the divine Augusta a cow, to the divine Claudius a male ox, to the divine Claudia, the virgin, a cow, to the divine Poppaea Augusta a cow. Present in the college were Marcus Aponius Saturninus, deputy-master, Gaius Vipstanus Apronianus . . .

[287] *Small. 149*
66-7, Luna, Etruria

To the divine Poppaea Augusta, wife of Imperator Nero Caesar Augustus, Lucius Titinius Glaucus Lucretianus, son of Lucius, of the tribe Galeria, priest of Rome and Augustus, duumvir for the fourth time, patron of the colony, *sevir* of Roman equites, *curio*, prefect of engineers under a consul, military tribune of legion 22 Primigenia, prefect of the Balearic islands in place of a legate, military tribune of legion 6 Victrix, in fulfilment of a vow for the safety of Imperator Nero, which he had made on the Balearics in the year in which Aulus Licinius Nerva was consul[1] and the duumvirs were Lucius Saufeius Vegetus and Quintus Aburius Nepos, when he wanted to set this up, having been granted his prayer, he set it up to Jupiter, Juno, Minerva, Felicity of Rome, and the divine Augustus.

To Imperator Nero Claudius Caesar Augustus Germanicus, son of the divine Claudius, grandson of Germanicus Caesar, great-grandson of the divine Augustus, pontifex maximus, in his 13th year of tribunician power, imperator 11 times, consul 4 times, Lucius Titinius Glaucus Lucretianus, son of Lucius, of the tribe Galeria [the inscription continues as in the first paragraph].

1. In AD 65, with Marcus Vestinus Atticus, whose name is probably omitted because Nero had ordered his death in that year as a Pisonian conspirator, Tac. *Ann*. 15. 68-9.

[288] *Small. 70*
Coins struck by Vindex in Gaul

(a) Denarius
Obv. Victory holding a wreath and a palm. SAFETY OF THE HUMAN RACE
Rev. SENATE AND PEOPLE OF ROME within an oak-wreath

(b) Aureus
Obv. Bust of Mars. MARS THE AVENGER
Rev. Two standards with a legionary eagle and an altar between them. STANDARDS OF THE ROMAN PEOPLE

(c) Denarius
Obv. Bust of Hercules. HERCULES THE CHAMPION[1]
Rev. A female figure with a wreath and horn of plenty. AS THE FORTUNE OF THE ROMAN PEOPLE FLOURISHES

1. Especially the champion of liberty (*adsertor*).

(d) Denarius
Obv. Bust of Rome, helmeted. ROME RESTORED
Rev. Jupiter seated holding a sceptre and thunderbolt. JUPITER THE LIBERATOR

[289] *Small. 71*
Near Milan

To Jupiter Optimus Maximus, for the safety and victory of Lucius Verginius Rufus, Pylades, estate-man, has fulfilled his vow.

[290] *Small. 72*
Denarii of 68 from Spain

(a) Obv. Male bust with horn of plenty behind. TO THE GENIUS
    OF THE ROMAN PEOPLE
Rev. Mars. TO MARS THE AVENGER

(b) Obv. Bust of Liberty. LIBERTY OF THE ROMAN PEOPLE
Rev. A liberty cap with a dagger either side, pointing downwards.
    RESTORED

(c) Obv. Busts of Spain and Gaul facing each other, a small Victory
    between; a horn of plenty below Spain, an oblong shield below
    Gaul. CONCORD OF THE SPAINS AND GAULS.
Rev. Victory in a chariot. VICTORY OF THE ROMAN PEOPLE

[291] *Small. 73*
Denarius, 68, Carthage (?)

Obv. Head of Macer, bare. LUCIUS CLODIUS MACER BY DECREE
    OF THE SENATE
Rev. A galley. PROPRAETOR OF AFRICA

[292] *Small. 74*
Denarius, 68, Carthage (?)

Obv. Bust of Spain with two javelins, a shield and two corn-ears.
    SPAIN BY DECREE OF THE SENATE
Rev. A shield lying on two spears. THE SENATE AND PEOPLE OF
    ROME.

[293] *EJ 364*
Law on the power of Vespasian. Cf. P. A. Brunt, *JRS*, 67 (1977)
pp. 95-116

[Beginning is lost] ... And that he be permitted to make a ... or
treaty with whoever he wishes, just as the divine Augustus, Tiberius
Julius Caesar Augustus and Tiberius Claudius Caesar Augustus Germanicus were permitted.

    And that he be permitted to convene the Senate, to bring a matter
before it, to refer a matter back to it and to make decrees of the
Senate through a motion and division, just as the divine Augustus,
Tiberius Julius Caesar Augustus and Tiberius Claudius Caesar Augustus
Germanicus were permitted.

And that, when the Senate meets by his will or authority or order or mandate or in his presence, the legality of all matters be maintained and preserved, just as if the meeting had been declared or convened by statute.

And that those candidates for magistracy, power, imperium or the charge of anything whom he has commended to the Senate and people of Rome and to whom he has given and promised his electoral support be accorded extraordinary treatment in any elections.

And that he be permitted to carry forward and advance the boundary of the pomerium when he considers it in the interests of the state, just as Tiberius Claudius Caesar Augustus Germanicus was permitted.

And that whatever he considers to be to the advantage of the state and in accord with the majesty of matters divine and human, private and public, the right and power be his to do it, just as it belonged to the divine Augustus, Tiberius Julius Caesar Augustus and Tiberius Claudius Caesar Augustus Germanicus.

And that those laws or plebiscites in which it is written that the divine Augustus or Tiberius Julius Caesar Augustus or Tiberius Claudius Caesar Augustus Germanicus be exempted, from those laws or plebiscites Imperator Caesar Vespasianus be exempted; and that whatever, under any law or bill, the divine Augustus or Tiberius Julius Caesar Augustus or Tiberius Claudius Caesar Augustus Germanicus might do, Imperator Caesar Vespasianus Augustus be permitted to do it.

And that, whatever prior to the passage of this law has been done, performed, decreed or ordered by Imperator Caesar Vespasianus Augustus or by anyone under his order or mandate, these things be just as lawful as if done by order of the people or plebs.

Sanction:

If anyone because of this law has acted or shall act in contravention of laws, bills, plebiscites or decrees of the Senate, or if he does not do what a law, bill, plebiscite or decree of the Senate obliges him to do, it is not to be held against him as an offence nor must he pay anything to the people for this reason, nor is an action or judgement to be brought against him for this reason, nor is anyone to allow a case to be pleaded before him for this reason.

2 THE IMPERIAL HOUSEHOLD

[294] *EJ 143*

Smyrna; cf. G. W. Bowersock, *Augustus and the Greek World* (1965) p. 123

Marcus Artorius Asclepiades, doctor of divine Caesar Augustus; the council and people of the Smyrnaeans honoured him as their hero, due to his great learning.

[295] *EJ 144*

Smyrna, bilingual

Tiberius Claudius, freedman of Tiberius Claudius Thrasyllus, to Tiberius Caesar Augustus and Augusta, wife of Caesar Augustus, his mother.

[296] *EJ 145*

Funeral urn, Rome

Of Tiberius Claudius Melito, son of Athenodorus, of the tribe Quirina, doctor of Germanicus.

[297] *CIL 6.8909*

Rome

Thyrius Celadianus, slave of Tiberius Caesar Augustus, eye-doctor, dutiful to his parents, lived 30 years, is buried here in perpetuity.

[298] *CIL 6. 4458*
Rome

Hygia, freedwoman of Marcella,[1] midwife.

1. Daughter of Octavia and Gaius Claudius Marcellus.

[299] *EJ 146*
Urbinum, Italy

Tiberius Julius Latinus, son of . . . Julius Leonidas, tutor of the Caesars, military tribune of legion 4 Scythica, lived 37 years.

[300] *EJ 147*
Rome

Gaius Julius Niceros Vedianus, freedman of the divine Augustus, orderly of Germanicus Caesar in his consulship[1] and of Calvisius Sabinus in his consulship;[2] Julia Helice, daughter of Lucius, lived 20 years.

    Gaius Julius Amaranthus, freedman of Augustus, for himself and Julia Clarie, freedwoman of Gaius, and Julia Mercatilla, freedwoman of Gaius, my darling. Julia Euheteria, mother of Helice.

1. AD 12 or 18.
2. AD 26.

[301] *EJ 148*
Probably 37, Philippi

[Beginning is lost] . . . Tiberius Caesar, son of the divine Augustus, grandson of the divine Julius, and Drusus Caesar, son of Tiberius Augustus, grandson of the divine Augustus, great-grandson of the divine Julius, in his second year of tribunician power; Cadmus Atimetus Martialis, freedman of Gaius Julius Augustus, had this monument built at his own expense.

[302] *EJ 149*
Rome

Gaius Octavius Auctus, freedman of Octavia, sister of Augustus, records-clerk; Viccia Gnome, freedwoman of Gaius, his wife.

[303] *EJ 150*
Rome

Marcus Julius Cnismus, freedman of Augusta, for himself and his wife, Livia Helpis, freedwoman of Marcus, and Secundus and Julia Acte, freedwoman of Augusta, and Aegle, freedwoman of Tiberius Caesar Augustus, and for their freedman, freedwoman and descendants.

[304] *EJ 151*
Rome

Quintus Fabius Cytisus, freedman of Africanus, quaestorian agent of the treasury, tribunician records-clerk, quaestorian records-clerk of the three decuries.[1] Gaius Calpetanus Cryphius, freedman of Gaius, agent of the sacred chickens,[2] first husband of Culicina. Lucius Nymphidius Philomelus, freedman of Lucius, quaestorian records-clerk of the three decuries, dutiful and faithful brother of Cytisus. Gaius Proculeius Heracleo, freedman of Gaius, father of Culicina. Proculeia Stibas, mother of Culicina and of Livia Culicina, freedwoman of the divine Augusta. Plasidiena Agrestina, daughter of Lucius, wife of Calpetanus Livianus, chief-centurion.

1. Cf. A. H. M. Jones, *Augustus* (1970) p. 137.   2. Cf. Suet. *Tib.* 2.2.

[305] *CIL 6. 8848*
Rome

Antigonus, slave of Drusus Caesar, first feeder of the birds, made this for his wife.

[306] *CIL 6. 4001*
Rome

Anthus, slave of Livia, footman.

[307] *CIL 6. 4008*
Rome

Heracla, freedwoman of Augusta, painter.

[308] *CIL 6. 4045*
Rome

Galene, slavewoman of Livia, anointress.

[309] *CIL 6. 4035*
Rome

Agrypnus Maecenatianus, slave of Caesar Augustus, in charge of statues.

[310] *CIL 6. 8753*
Rome

Eros Cornificianus, slave of Caesar Augustus, cook.

[311] *EJ 152*
Rome

(a) Marcus Vipsanius Zoticus, freedman of Marcus, curator of the burial club three times, gave urn 14 for himself and for Vipsania Stibas, freedwoman of Marcus, club-member.
(b) Vipsania Acume, freedwoman of the Marci, wife of Zoticus, slave of Marcus Agrippa, in charge of the monuments of Marcus Agrippa.

[312] *EJ 153*
Rome, sarcophagus

For Antemus, freedman of Tiberius Caesar Augustus, appointed accounts-orderly by Augustus.

[313] *EJ 154*
Rome

Julia Glycera, freedwoman of Bola, woman of Dardanus Archelaianus, slave of Tiberius Caesar Augustus and Augusta, lived 37 years, in life their darling.

[314] *EJ 155*
Rome

Tiberius Julius Medates, freedman of Tiberius Julius Augustus, made this for himself and Julia Pryne, his wife, poultryman.

[315] *EJ 156*
Rome

(a) To Tiberius Julius Diogenes Rhoemetalcianus.
(b) Of Tiberius Julius Faustus. Of Vipsania Urbana. Urns which were of Diogenes Rhoemetalcianus.

[316] *EJ 157*
43, Rome

To the genius of Coetus Herodianus, taster of the divine Augustus and afterwards also bailiff in the Gardens of Sallust, died 5th August, in the consulship of Marcus Cocceius Nerva and Gaius Vibius Rufinus. Julia Prima for her patron.

[317] *EJ 158*
Rome; cf. B. M. Levick, *Tiberius the Politician* (1976) p. 134

To Musicus Scurranus, slave of Tiberius Caesar Augustus, steward of the Gallic fiscus of the province of Lugdunensis, from his own slaves who were with him when he died at Rome; to one well-deserving:

Venustus, business	Agathopus, doctor	Facilis, attendant
Decimianus, outgoings	Epaphra, silver	Anthus, silver
Dicaeus, manservant	Primio, wardrobe	Hedylus, bedchamber
Mutatus, manservant	Communis, bedchamber	Firmus, cook
Creticus, manservant	Pothus, attendant	Secunda
	Tiasus, cook	

[318] *EJ 159*
Rome

Diocles Germanicianus, servant of Tiberius Caesar, of Galatian nationality, lived 35 years.

[319] *EJ 160*
Aquitania

To Zmaragdus, bailiff, quaestor, master, by decree of the decurions of the slave-gang of Tiberius Caesar operating in the mines.

[320] *EJ 161*

Bronze plaque on a lamp, 11, Samnium

In the consulship of Titus Statilius Taurus and Manius Aemilius Lepidus, Tricunda, slave of Tiberius Claudius Nero, bailiff, master, dedicates with glad heart the lamp and its adornments to Bellona, 13th June, Ligures Baebiani.

[321] *CIL 6.5188*

Rome

Alexander Pylaemenianus, slave of Gaius Caesar Augustus Germanicus, officer of the Greek library of the temple of Apollo, lived 30 years.

[322] *Small. 172*

Rome

To the departed spirit of Tiberius Claudius Saturninus, freedman of Augustus, procurator of the 5% tax on inheritances in the province of Achaea; Saturnina, his wife, made this.

[323] *Small. 173*

Ostia (?), circular bronze plaque

Of Claudius Optatus, freedman of Augustus, procurator of the port of Ostia.

[324] *Small 174* with G. Rickman *Corn-Supply of Ancient Rome* (1980) pp. 215-16

Rome

Tiberius Claudius Januarius, freedman of Augustus, curator, from the Minucia on day 14, from gate 42, and Avonia Tyche, his wife, Pituaniani, built the terraces at their own expense . . .

[325] *Small. 175*

Rome

Of Tiberius Claudius Scirtus, freedman of Augustus, procurator of the library; Vettia Tyche, wife of Scirtus.

[326] *Small. 176*
Rome

Tiberius Claudius Marcellinus, procurator of Augustus in charge of the patrimony.

[327] *Small. 177*
Capena, Etruria

To the departed spirit of Tiberius Claudius Daus, freedman of Augustus, accounts-clerk of the patrimony of the Caesars. He lived 59 years. Servilia Aphro to her dearest husband.

[328] *Small. 178*
(a) Rome
Diadumenus, freedman of Augustus, in charge of accounts, to Anicetus, freedman.

(b) 12th Jan. 65, graffito on a tunnel wall near Naples
Macrinus, steward of Diadumenus Antoninianus, freedman procurator of Augustus, walked here in the consulship of Nerva and Vestinus, 12th January.

[329] *Small. 179*
(a) Florence
Of Domitia Phyllis, dearest wife of Domitius Lemnus, procurator of Germanicus Caesar.

(b) Rome
To Lemnus, freedman of Augustus, procurator of the patrimony and inheritances, and to Domitia Phyllis; Lucius Domitius Lemnus made this.

[330] *Small. 180*
Rome

Of Tiberius Claudius Avitus, freedman of Augustus, invitations-officer, and of Titus Aelius Theodotus, freedman of Augustus, judicial-assistant, and of Scetasia, slave of Octavia; Antonia Rhodine, their mother, made this for her dearest children.

[331] *Small. 181*
Rome

To the departed spirit; Lucia Pelagia lived 25 years, 9 months, 14 days. Thyrsus Halys, slave of Tiberius Claudius Caesar Augustus Germanicus, steward, for his most virtuous concubine, well-deserving of him, and for himself.

[332] *Small. 182*
Rome

To Tiberius Julius Xanthus, freedman of Augustus, accountant of Tiberius Caesar and the divine Claudius and sub-prefect of the fleet at Alexandria; Atellia Prisca, his wife, and Lamyrus, his freedman, his heirs. He lived for 90 years.

[333] *Small. 183*
Rome

Tiberius Claudius Lemnius, freedman of the divine Claudius Augustus, literary-officer.

[334] *Small. 184*
Tibur

Gaius Julius Samius, freedman of Augustus, procurator, attendant of the divine Claudius and Nero Augustus, his patrons.

[335] *Small. 185*
Rome

To the departed spirit; Tiberius Claudius Philius, freedman of the divine Claudius, secretary and foreman of the slaves of the bed-chamber, procurator of the pedagogues of Nero Augustus.

[336] *Small. 186*
Rome

To the departed spirit; Tiberius Claudius Dipterus, freedman of the divine Claudius, clothes-maker of Caesar in charge of theatrical costume. Claudia Lycoris made this for her husband and herself and her family.

[337] *CIL 6.8952*
Rome

Amoenus, slave of Messallina, wife of Tiberius Claudius Caesar, in charge of ornaments.

[338] *Small. 187*
Rome

To the departed spirit; to Claudia Lachne, freedwoman of Antonia, Philippus Rustianus, public slave of the shrine of the divine Augustus, made this for his dearest woman and himself.

[339] *Small. 188*
Rome

To Claudia Phthonge, nurse of Britannicus; Aphnius, slave of Caesar Augustus, correspondence-secretary, to his concubine who has deserved the best from him.

[340] *Small. 189*
Rome

Celadus, slave of the son of Tiberius Claudius Caesar, lived 25 years, dear to his family.

[341] *Small. 190*
Rome

Claudia Peloris, freedwoman of Octavia, daughter of the divine Claudius, and Tiberius Claudius Eutychus, freedman of Augustus, procurator of the Augusti,[1] for their sisters and freedmen and freedwomen and their descendants have left building-plans of the precinct and monument.
1. Building-plans are depicted here.

[342] *Small. 191*
Rome

To the departed spirit; to Helius, freedman of Acte, freedwoman of Augustus, of the bed-chamber.

[343] *ILS 7386*
Rome

To the departed spirit of Phoebus, freedman of Acte, freedwoman of Augustus, procurator of finances, Demetrius and Pensata for the best of parents.

[344] *ILS 7396*
Rome

To Thelycus, freedman of Acte, freedwoman of Augustus, attendant, lived 20 years.

[345] *ILS 7409*
Rome

To the departed spirit, a dedication; to Claudius Felix, eunuch, freedman of Acte, freedwoman of Augustus, lived 50 years, gladly to a well-deserving patron.

[346] *CIL 6.8693*
Rome

To Demetria, slave of Acte, freedwoman of Augustus, reciter of Greek, lived 35 years; Trophimus, slave of the bedchamber, to his well-deserving fellow slave; to the departed spirit.

[347] *CIL 6.8767*
Rome

(a) To the departed spirit; to Claudius Storax, freedman of Acte, secretary of the bedchamber, lived 60 years; set up to a well-deserving father.

(b) To the departed spirit; to Moschis, freedwoman of Acte; set up to a well-deserving mother. Claudius Storax and Glyptus.

[348] *CIL 6.9002b*
Rome

To the departed spirit; to Stephanus, pastry-cook of our Acte, lived 24 years. Saturninus, his sister's son, consecrated this.

[349] *Small. 192*
Arna, Umbria

Polytimus, steward of Poppaea Augusta, wife of Nero Caesar Augustus, has fulfilled his vow to Fortune.

[350] Statius, *Silvae*, 3.3.59-110. Cf. P. R. C. Weaver, *Familia Caesaris* (1972) pp. 179-95
Part of a poem addressed to Claudius Etruscus in consolation for the death of his father, who is not named. Details are given of the dead man's career in the imperial bureaucracy. Written under Domitian (AD 81-96).

But you were not brought to Latium from barbarian shores;
Smyrna was your native soil and you drank the venerable
Spring of Meles and Hermus' waters, where Lydian Bacchus
Dips and restores his horns with gilded mud.
Then came a joyful career and, with various roles in order,
Your honour grew; and ever to walk near divinities, ever
To tend Caesar's side and be privy to the holy secrets
Of gods was your lot. Tiberius' court was first opened
To you, your face hardly changing with early manhood –
Here your excellent versatility overcame your years and
Liberty came, unasked; nor did the next heir,
Though cruel and driven by Furies, expel you.
His frail companion even to the frosty North,
You endured the tyrant terrible in word and aspect,
A monster to his people, as trainers of the terrifying
Spirits of beasts who order their jaws to give up hands
Swallowed, blood already tasted, and that they live without prey.
Claudius, old, but not yet consigned to the starry sky,
Raised you to positions most high, but deserved,
And passed you to the keeping of his remote nephew.
What god-fearing man is permitted to serve as many temples,
As many altars? The winged Arcadian is the messenger of
Highest Jupiter; Juno is mistress of the rain-bringing
Thaumantian;[1] Triton stands swift to obey Neptune's orders;
You have duly borne the yokes of leaders so often changed,
Unharmed and happy in your dinghy on every sea.
    And it was now that a pillar of light entered your house
And Fortune at full pace; now was entrusted to you alone

The administration of sacred wealth and the riches gained
Among all the peoples and the revenues of the great world.
Whatever Spain throws out of its gold-bearing mines,
What gleams in a Dalmatian mountain, what is collected
In African harvests, whatever is threshed on the floor of
The sultry Nile, and what a diver gathers in the eastern sea
And the nurtured flocks of Spartan Galaesus,
Clear snows and Massylian wood and the honour of Indian
Ivory. Everything was entrusted to the order of one servant,
What north wind, what the wild east wind, what the cloudy south
Wind brings — you might more swiftly count the winter rains
And the wood foliage. He is both watchful and wise
And swift to calculate what the Roman javelin needs every day,
What the tribes, what the temples, what the tall
Aqueducts, what the sea defences,
Or the far-extended chains of roads;
What gold gleams on the high ceilings of the lord,
What mass of metal melts on the fire to be shaped into the
Faces of gods, what legend rings out on the fire of Italian Money.
Then there was little rest for you; pleasure was shut out
Of your mind. There were small meals and your cares were never
Drowned in deep wine; but the joys of wedlock were in your heart
And bound your mind with marital beds and linked festal marriage
And produced clients loyal to the lord . . .[2]

1. Mercury and Iris respectively.
2. Statius proceeds to tell us that the dead man's wife, Etrusca, was of noble birth, her brother becoming consul under Domitian. The dead man was made an eques by Vespasian.

[351] *CIL 6.8833*
Rome; cf. Suet. *Galba* 15.2

To the ashes of Atreia Procula, daughter of Lucius, his most virtuous concubine, well-deserving of him; Hyginus, procurator, slave and steward of Halotus, freedman of Augustus, made this.

3 SENATORS

[352] *EJ 187*

After 22 BC, near Caieta, Latium, mausoleum; cf. Suet. *Aug.* 29.5; Hor. *Od.* 1.7

Lucius Munatius Plancus, son of Lucius, grandson of Lucius, great-grandson of Lucius, consul, censor, imperator twice, one of the 7 for feasts, triumphed over the Raetians, built the temple of Saturn from booty, divided lands in Italy at Beneventum, in Gaul settled two colonies, Lugdunum and Raurica.

[353] *EJ 190*
Athens

The people honoured Marcus Licinius Crassus, son of Marcus, proconsul and imperator, for his virtue and good-will.

[354] *ILS 97*
6/5 BC, Ephesus, bilingual

Imperator Caesar Augustus, son of a god, consul for the twelfth time, in his 18th year of tribunician power, had the temple of Artemis and the Augusteum walled out of the sacred funds of the goddess, in the proconsulship of Gaius Asinius Gallus,[1] under the supervision of Sextus Lartidius, legate.

1. Erased but legible on the Latin version: see Tac. *Ann.* 6.23; cf. 1.12.

[355] *EJ 192*
Near Rome

To Gnaeus Baebius Tampilus Vala Numonianus, son of Gnaeus, quaestor, praetor, proconsul, triumvir for the casting and striking of bronze, silver and gold, husband.

[356] *EJ 193*
Aquileia

Gaius Appuleius Tappo, son of Marcus, praetor, aedile, tribune of the plebs, quaestor, judge of the capital court.

[357] *EJ 194*
Rome

Gaius Papirius Carbo, son of Gaius, of the tribe Clustumina, military tribune, one of the 26, propraetorian quaestor; Antullia, daughter of Quintus, his wife.

[358] *EJ 195*
Rome

To Publius Numicius Pica Caesianus, prefect of cavalry, one of the 6,[1] propraetorian quaestor of the province of Asia, tribune of the plebs; the province of Asia.

To Publius Numicius Pica Caesianus, prefect of cavalry, one of the 6,[1] propraetorian quaestor of the province of Asia, tribune of the plebs; Publius Cornelius Rufinus, Gaius Autronius Carus, Lucius Pomponius Aeschines, Sextus Aufidius Euhodus, Quintus Cassidienus Nedymus, Titus Manlius Inventus, Gaius Valerius Albanus and Sextus Aufidius Primigenius, to their patron.

1. Cf. Suet. *Aug.* 38.2.

[359] *EJ 196*
Rome

Quintus Propertius, son of Quintus, of the tribe Fabia. Gaius Propertius Postumus, son of Quintus, grandson of Titus, of the tribe Fabia, triumvir for executions, and in the following year protriumvir for executions,[1] quaestor, as praetor designate by decree of the Senate curator of roads, as praetor by decree of the Senate he administered justice in the place of the curule aediles, proconsul.

1. See T.P. Wiseman, *New Men in the Roman Senate* (1971) pp. 180-1.

[360] *EJ 197*
Histonium; cf. T. P.Wiseman, *New Men in the Roman Senate* (1971) p. 180

Publius Paquius Scaeva, son of Scaeva and Flavia, grandson of Consus and Didia, great-grandson of Barbus and Dirutia, quaestor, one of the 10 for the settlement of disputes by decree of the Senate after his quaestorship, one of the 4 for executions by decree of the Senate after his quaestorship and his membership of the 4 for the settlement of disputes, tribune of the plebs, curule aedile, court judge, praetor of the treasury, governed the province of Cyprus as proconsul, curator of the roads outside the city of Rome by decree of the Senate for five years, proconsul for the second time, outside the lot, by authority of Augustus Caesar, and sent to organise the state of the province of Cyprus for the future, fetial, cousin and also husband of Flavia, daughter of Consus, granddaughter of Scapula, great-granddaughter of Barbus, buried together with her.

Flavia, daughter of Consus and Sinnia, granddaughter of Scapula and Sinnia, great-granddaughter of Barbus and Dirutia, cousin and also wife of Publius Paquius Scaeva, son of Scaeva, grandson of Consus, great-grandson of Barbus, buried together with him.

[361] *EJ 198*
Forum Clodii, Etruria

To Gnaeus Pullius Pollio ... fetial, quaestor, one of the 10 for the settlement of disputes by decree of the Senate, tribune of the plebs, praetor of the treasury, proconsul of the province of Narbonensis ... of Imperator Caesar Augustus in Gallia Comata and likewise in Aquitania, sent to Athens as legate by Imperator Caesar Augustus ... duumvir quinquennalis; the Claudienses of the Claudian prefecture to their patron.

[362] *EJ 199*
Tibur. The identification of this man is disputed: R. Syme, *Vestigia*, 17 (1973) pp. 585-601

[Beginning is lost] ... king; when it had been brought into the power of Imperator Caesar Augustus and the Roman people, the Senate decreed two thanksgivings to the immortal gods for successful achievements and triumphal ornaments to the victor himself; as proconsul he held the province of Asia; as propraetorian legate of divine Augustus for a second time he held Syria and Phoenice ...

[363] J. M. Reynolds, *Aphrodisias and Rome* (1982) no. 45
Aphrodisias, Caria

(a) Marcus Vinicius the proconsul;[1] the people honoured its benefactor.
(b) Publius Vinicius the proconsul;[2] the people honoured its benefactor.

1. Identity uncertain, probably proconsul of Asia under Augustus.   2. Consul AD 2 and proconsul of Asia shortly after.

[364] *EJ 200*
Near Tibur

Marcus Plautius Silvanus, son of Marcus, grandson of Aulus, consul,[1] one of the 7 for feasts. To this man the Senate decreed triumphal ornaments for successful achievements in Illyricum. Lartia, daughter of Gnaeus, his wife. Aulus Plautius Urgulanius, son of Marcus, lived 9 years.

1. 2 BC.

[365] *EJ 201*
Attalea, Pamphylia

Marcus Plautius Silvanus, propraetorian legate of Imperator Caesar Augustus; the people and the resident Romans honoured their patron and benefactor.

[366] *EJ 378*
(a) Athens

The council of the Areopagus honoured Sextus Aelius Catus, legate of Caesar Augustus and proconsul of Macedonia, for his virtue and good-will.

(b) Callatis

The people dedicated this to Publius Vinicius, legate and propraetor, the patron and benefactor of the city of the Callatians.

[367] *EJ 202*
Athens; first part in Latin, second part in Greek.

To Lucius Aquillius Florus Turcianus Gallus, son of Gaius, of the tribe Pomptina, one of the 10 for the settlement of disputes, military tribune of legion 9 Macedonica, quaestor of Imperator Caesar Augustus, proquaestor of the province of Cyprus, tribune of the plebs, praetor, proconsul of Achaea.

The council of the Areopagus and the council of the 600 and the people honoured Lucius Aquillius Florus Turcianus Gallus, proconsul, for his good-will towards the city. When the priestess was Hipposthenis, the daughter of Nicocles, of the Piraeus.

[368] *EJ 203*
Tenos

The people honoured Publius Quinctilius Varus, quaestor of Imperator Caesar, divine Augustus, patron and benefactor; to the gods.

[369] *EJ 204*
New Carthage

To Publius Silius, propraetorian legate, patron; the colonists.

[370] *EJ 205*
Paelignian Superaequum

To Quintus Varius Geminus, son of Quintus, legate of divine Augustus for two years, proconsul, praetor, tribune of the plebs, quaestor, inquiry-judge, prefect for the distribution of grain, one of the 10 for the settlement of disputes, curator for the supervision of sacred buildings and public monuments. He was the first of all the Paelignians to become a senator and to hold those offices. The Superaequans at public expense to their patron.

[371] (a) *ILS 894*
Aesernia, Italy

To Sextus Appuleius, son of Sextus,[1] imperator, consul,[2] augur.

1. See T. P. Wiseman *New Men in the Roman Senate* (1971) p. 213. 2. 29 BC.

(b) *OGIS 461*
Pergamum

The people of the Cotiaeans[1] honoured Sextus Appuleius, proconsul and benefactor.

1. Cotiaeum was a city in Phrygia Epictetus.

(c) *OGIS 462*
Pergamum

The people honoured Octavia, sister of Caesar and mother of Sextus Appuleius.

(d) J. M. Reynolds, *Aphrodisias and Rome* (1982) no. 44
Aphrodisias, Caria

The people honoured Sextus Appuleius, the proconsul.

[372] *EJ 206*
Luna

To Sextus Appuleius, son of Sextus, grandson of Sextus, great-grandson of Sextus, of the tribe Galeria, born of Fabia Numantina,[1] the last in his family.

1. Possibly the lady at Tac. *Ann.* 4.22. This is the son of the Sex. Appuleius of *RG* 8.4, himself the son of Sex. Appuleius, the consul of 29 BC (above).

[373] *EJ 207*
Treia, Picenum

To Manius Vibius Balbinus, son of Manius, of the tribe Velia, military tribune, prefect of engineers, prefect of cavalry, quaestor, plebeian aedile, praetor of the treasury, legate of divine Augustus and Tiberius Caesar Augustus, proconsul of the province of Narbonensis.

[374] *EJ 208*
Epidaurus, Dalmatia

To Publius Cornelius Dolabella, consul,[1] one of the 7 for feasts, Titian *sodalis*, propraetorian legate of divine Augustus and Tiberius Caesar Augustus; the states of the upper province of Illyricum.[2]

1. AD 10.   2. See J. J. Wilkes, *Dalmatia* (1969) p. 82.

[375] *EJ 209*
Ipsus, Asia

To ... Favonius, consul, proconsul of Asia, one of the 15 for the performance of sacred rites, *sodalis Augustalis*, triumvir for the review of the equestrian centuries with censorial power,[1] legate of divine Augustus and Tiberius Caesar Augustus ...

1. Cf. Suet. *Aug.* 37.1 with J. Carter *ad loc.*

[376] Crinagoras, *Planudean Anthology*, 40; cf. Hor. *Od.* 2.2; Tac. *Ann*, 3.30

> Your neighbours should be not only three Fortunes,[1]
> Crispus, for the sake of your deep, rich heart,
> But all the fortunes of everyone; what is enough
> For one so devoted to the boundless prosperity of friends?
> And now may one greater than the Fortunes make you greater —
> Caesar: what fortune prospers without him?

1. Three temples of Fortune lay close to the Gardens of Sallust at Rome.

[377] Antipater of Thessalonica, *Palatine Anthology*, 9.428; cf. Dio 54.34; Tac. *Ann.* 6.10

> To you, despoiler of Thrace, Thessalonica,
> Mother of all Macedonia, sent me.
> I sing of Bessian Ares made subject to you;
> I have brought to bear all I know of warfare;
> Heed me as would a god and hear my prayer:
> What ear is too busy for the Muses?

[378] *ILS 939*
Mt Eryx, Sicily; cf. Tac. *Ann.* 3.21; 4.23

Lucius Apronius Caesianus, son of Lucius, one of the 7 for feasts, dedicates . . . to Venus of Eryx:

> He, sent by his father, proconsul of Libya,
> Victor in wars as Moor enemy fell,
> Who presented to you the lucky sword
> And the image of his father, Apronius, leader's son,
> Leader himself, victor in fair fight.
> For the dedication and, likewise, resumption of the praetexta,
> This garment, duly sought by his father and given by Caesar,
> As a boy he left for you, goddess, one of the 7.

> Of the gods . . .
> Mutual . . .
> The son of Apronius, greater in deed than name,
> Since he put to flight the Gaetulian tribes,
> Erected the image of his dear father, goddess,

Kindly parent of the Aeneadae, as your just reward,
And the arms he wielded; by his shield shattered with blows,
What virtue is revealed! His sword stands reddened by the enemy,
By slaughter worn, and the trophy is crowned by his spear,
Which the wild barbarian took full in the face and fell.

No monument is more venerated by both than this,
Which father and son have dedicated to you:
They have jointly ensured the dedication of the image of Caesar:
There was a contest of dutifulness — in each was the greatest.

Under the supervision of Lucius Apronius, freedman of Lucius.

[379] *EJ 209c*
Bronze coin, 22-3, Thapsus; cf. Tac. *Ann*. 3.32; 35

Obv. Head of Tiberius. TIBERIUS CAESAR AUGUSTUS, SON OF DIVINE AUGUSTUS, IMPERATOR 8 TIMES, CONSUL 4.
Rev. Livia, seated, as Vestal. BY PERMISSION OF QUINTUS JUNIUS BLAESUS, PROCONSUL FOR TWO YEARS. SUPERVISOR PUBLIUS GAVIUS CASCA. COLONIA PIA JULIA.

[380] *AE (1961) no. 107*
Oea, Tripolitania; cf. Tac. *Ann*. 3.47; 69

To Augustan Victory; Publius Cornelius Dolabella, consul, one of the 7 for feasts, sodalis Titiensis, proconsul, Tacfarinas having been killed, set this up.

[381] *EJ 210*
Brixia, Cisalpine Gaul; cf. Tac. *Ann*. 3.74; 4.23

To Publius Cornelius Lentulus Scipio, consul,[1] praetor of the treasury, legate of Tiberius Caesar Augustus of legion 9 Hispana, priest, fetial, by decree of the decurions.
1. AD 24.

[382] *EJ 211*
Brixia, Cisalpine Gaul

To Gaius Pontius Paelignus, son of Gaius, military tribune of legion

10 Gemina, quaestor, curator of public places for two years, curule aedile, propraetorian legate for two years by decree of the Senate and by authority of Tiberius Caesar; the decurions.

[383] *EJ 212*
Rome

Quintus Caerellius, son of Quintus, of the tribe Quirina, triumvir for executions, propraetorian quaestor, tribune of the plebs, propraetorian legate for three years, prefect for the distribution of grain by decree of the Senate, legate of Tiberius Caesar Augustus, proconsul, in accordance with his will.

To Quintus Caerellius, son of Marcus, of the tribe Quirina, his father, military tribune, quaestor, tribune of the plebs, praetor, legate of Marcus Antonius, proconsul.

[384] *EJ 213*
Allifae, Samnium; cf. B. M. Levick, *Tiberius the Politician* (1976) p. 96; T. P. Wiseman, *New Men in the Roman Senate* (1971) p. 134

[Beginning is lost] ... curator of roads[1] ... quaestor, tribune of the plebs, praetor, propraetorian legate of Imperator Caesar Augustus for two years, by commendation of Tiberius Caesar Augustus appointed consul by the Senate, patron.

1. Uncertain.

[385] *EJ 214*
Tibur

To the memory of Torquatus Novellius Atticus, son of Publius, one of the 10 for the settlement of disputes, military tribune of legion 1, tribune of detachments of four legions − 1,5,20 and 21 −, quaestor, aedile, praetor of the centumviral court, curator of public places, legate for the conduct of the census and levy and proconsul of the province of Narbonensis, at the end of his term in which office he died in his 44th year at Forum Julii.

[386] *EJ 215*
Rome, Forum; cf. B. M. Levick, *Tiberius the Politician* (1976) p. 86

For the safety of Tiberius Caesar Augustus, pontifex maximus, best and most just princeps, in fulfilment of a vow; Gaius Fulvius . . . proconsul, praetor, prefect for the distribution of grain by decree of the Senate, propraetorian legate . . . propraetorian quaestor, military tribune of legion 9 Hispana; to Concord. 5 pounds of gold, 23 pounds of silver.

[387] *EJ 216*
Rome; cf. Tac. *Ann.* 6.15; Suet. *Cal.* 24.1

To Lucius Cassius Longinus, consul,[1] one of the 15 for the performance of sacred rites, propraetorian legate of Tiberius Caesar Augustus; the Sextani Arelatenses to their patron.
1. AD 30.

[388] *EJ 217*
Ruscino, Narbonensis; cf. Tac. *Ann.* 14.47

To Publius Memmius Regulus, son of Publius, quaestor of Tiberius Caesar, praetor, consul,[1] one of the 7 for feasts, *sodalis Augustalis*, Arval brother, legate of Caesar Augustus, patron.
1. AD 31.

[389] *EJ 218 = Small.* 225
Delphi; cf. Suet. *Galba* 8

Publius Memmius Regulus, son of Publius, consul, propraetorian legate of the Augusti, priest in three priestly colleges, proconsul of Asia, and his son.

[390] C. Letta and S. D'Amato, *Epigrafia della regione dei Marsi* (1975) no. 55
Marruvium, Italy. Perhaps the father of the husband of Julia

To Gaius Rubellius Blandus, son of Lucius, of the tribe Camilia.

[391] *EJ 218a*
35-6 , Lepcis Magna; cf. Tac. *Ann.* 6.27

To Tiberius Caesar Augustus, son of divine Augustus, grandson of divine Julius, pontifex maximus, consul 5 times, imperator 8 times, in his 37th year of tribunician power; Gaius Rubellius Blandus, quaestor of divine Augustus, tribune of the plebs, praetor, consul,[1] proconsul, priest, patron, from the revenues from the lands which he restored to the Lepticani had all the main roads of the state of Lepcis paved with stone. Marcus Etrilius Lupercus, propraetorian legate, patron, auctioned the contracts for the work.

1. AD 18.

[392] *IRT 269*
Lepcis Magna

To Ceres Augusta, a dedication.
Gaius Rubellius Blandus, consul, priest, proconsul, dedicated this. Suphunibal, adorner of her country, wife of Annobal Ruso, had it made at her own expense.

[393] *ILS 1954*
Rome, Via Appia; cf. Tac. *Ann*. 3.30

To Lucius Volusius Elainus, assistant to the censor, priest of the Genius of our Lucius; Volusia Syntyche.

[394] J. M. Reynolds *JRS*, 61 (1971) pp. 142-3; (a) = *EJ 367*
Near Lucus Feroniae, Etruria, in the villa of the Volusii

(a) To Lucius Volusius Saturninus, son of Lucius, grandson of Quintus, consul,[1] augur, sodalis Augustalis, sodalis Titius, proconsul of Asia, legate of the divine Augustus, propraetorian legate of Tiberius Caesar Augustus in Dalmatia, with triumphal ornaments. He was prefect of the city and died in his very prefecture, in his 93rd year of age. The Senate decreed on the instigation of Nero Claudius Augustus Germanicus that he be buried with a public funeral, court appearances likewise postponed for the sake of his obsequies, likewise that statues be set up for him: triumphal statues − one of bronze in the Forum of Augustus, two of marble in the new temple of the divine Augustus −, consular statues − one in the temple of the divine Julius, a second on the Palatine within the Triple Gate, a third in the space of Apollo in sight of the Senate House −, an augural statue in the Regia, an equestrian statue close by the Rostra and a statue seated on a curule chair by the Theatre of Marcellus in the portico of the Lentuli.

1. In AD 3.

(b) To Quintus Volusius Saturninus, son of Lucius, grandson of Lucius, consul,[1] sodalis Augustalis, sodalis Titius, Arval brother, legate of Caesar for the census-receipts of the province of Belgica.

1. AD 56

[395] *Small. 221*
Bronze coin, Pergamum (?)

Obv. Drusus and Germanicus, togate and laureate, seated, one holding a lituus. DRUSUS AND GERMANICUS CAESAR, NEW BROTHER-LOVING GODS

Rev. The words OF THE LEAGUE OF ASIA within a wreath. TO GAIUS ASINIUS POLLIO

[396] *Small. 222*
Bronze coin, Smyrna

Obv. Head of Gaius, laureate. GAIUS CAESAR GERMANICUS, UNDER AVIOLA

Rev. Drusilla as Persephone, seated, holding a poppy-head and corn-ears. DRUSILLA, OF THE SMYRNAEANS, MENOPHANES

[397] *Small. 223*
Atina, Latium

To Titus Helvius Basila, son of Titus, aedile, praetor, proconsul, legate of Caesar Augustus, who bequeathed to the citizens of Atina 40,000 sesterces so that grain and, after, 1,000 sesterces each might be given to their children when they come of age. Set up by Procula, his daughter.

[398] *Small. 224*
Rome

Marcus Licinius Crassus Frugi, son of Marcus, of the tribe Menenia, pontifex, urban praetor, consul, legate of Tiberius Claudius Caesar Augustus Germanicus in Mauretania[1] . . .

1. Or, possibly, Macedonia.

[399] *Small. 226*
(a) Olympia

Aulus Didius Gallus, legate of Tiberius Claudius Caesar Augustus

Germanicus, with triumphal ornaments, one of the 15 for the performance of sacred rites, proconsul of Asia and of Sicily and of . . . prefect of cavalry, companion and legate of the imperator in Britain . . .

(b) Athens
. . . prefect of cavalry . . . companion and legate in Britain, legate of Caesar, legate of the divine Claudius, legate of Augustus, propraetorian legate in the province of Moesia, propraetorian legate in the province of Britain . . .

[400] *Small. 227*
Near Tibur, by the mausoleum of the Plautii

Publius Plautius Pulcher, son of a triumphalis,[1] augur, triumvir for the casting and striking of bronze, silver and gold, quaestor of Tiberius Caesar Augustus in his fifth consulship,[2] tribune of the plebs, praetor of the treasury, companion of Drusus, son of Germanicus, uncle of Drusus, son of Tiberius Claudius Caesar Augustus, and adlected among the patricians in the censorship of the latter, chosen curator for the paving of roads in the neighbourhood by authority of Tiberius Claudius Caesar Augustus Germanicus, proconsul of the province of Sicily.

Vibia, daughter of Marsus, born of Laelia, wife of Pulcher.

1. His father had received triumphal ornaments.   2. AD 31.

[401] *Small. 228*
After 74, Tibur, by the mausoleum of the Plautii.

To Tiberius Plautius Silvanus Aelianus, son of Marcus, of the tribe Aniensis, pontifex, sodalis Augustalis, triumvir for the casting and striking of bronze, silver and gold, quaestor of Tiberius Caesar, legate of legion 5 in Germany, urban praetor, legate and companion of Claudius Caesar in Britain, consul,[1] proconsul of Asia, propraetorian legate of Moesia, where he brought across more than 100,000 of the number of Transdanubians for the payment of taxes, together with their wives and children and leaders or kings; he stopped a movement of Sarmatians that was starting, although he had sent a great part of his army to the expedition into Armenia; kings previously unknown or hostile to the Roman people he brought across to the bank he protected so that they might pay reverence to the Roman standards; he returned to the kings of the Bastarnae and Roxolani their sons, to those of the Dacians, their brothers, captured or seized from enemies; from some of them he received hostages; by these actions he confirmed and advanced the peace of the province, the king of the Scythians having also been removed from the siege of Chersonesus, beyond the Borysthenes. He was the first to assist the corn-supply of the Roman people with a great quantity of wheat from that province. When he was recalled from his legateship in Spain to the urban prefecture, the Senate honoured him in the course of his prefecture with triumphal ornaments, on the motion of Imperator Caesar Augustus Vespasianus, in the words of his speech written below:

'His governorship of Moesia was such that the conferral of the honour of triumphal ornaments upon him ought not to have been left for me, except in that during the delay he won a greater title as prefect of the city.'

This man, in that same urban prefecture, Imperator Caesar Augustus Vespasianus made consul for a second time.

1. AD 45.

[402] *Small. 229*
Casinum, Latium

To Gaius Ummidius Durmius Quadratus, son of Gaius, of the tribe Teretina, consul, one of the 15 for the performance of sacred rites, legate of Tiberius Caesar Augustus in the province of Lusitania, legate of the divine Claudius in Illyricum and of the same and Nero Caesar Augustus in Syria, proconsul of the province of Cyprus, quaestor of the divine Augustus and Tiberius Caesar Augustus, curule aedile, praetor of the treasury, one of the 15 for the settlement of disputes, curator of the public records, prefect for the distribution of grain, by decree of the Senate.

[403] *Small. 230*
Bronze coin, Docimeium, Phrygia.

Obv. Head of Claudius, laureate. CLAUDIUS CAESAR.
Rev. Cybele between two lions. IN THE PROCONSULATE OF COR-
BULO. OF THE DOCIMEIANS.

[404] *Small. 231*
(a) Cyaneae, Lycia
Quintus Veranius, son of Quintus, triumvir for the striking of coinage, tribune of legion 4 Scythica, quaestor of Tiberius and Gaius Augustus, tribune . . .

(b) Cibyra, Phrygia
[Beginning is lost] ... the people honoured Quintus Veranius, propraetorian legate of Tiberius Claudius Caesar Augustus Germanicus, having taken care of the august works in accordance with the instructions of his appointer, Tiberius Claudius Caesar Augustus, the founder of the city, and of the august Senate ...

(c) Near Rome, the last part of the tomb-inscription of Quintus Veranius
[Beginning is lost] ... was governor of the province of Lycia and Pamphylia for a period of five years, reduced ... into the power of Tiberius Claudius Caesar Augustus Germanicus and took by siege and destroyed the stronghold of the Cietae of Tracheia; by the mandate and letter of the Senate and people of Rome and of Tiberius Claudius Caesar Augustus Germanicus ... in the state of Cibyra ... he completed the repair of the city-walls which had been interrupted and abandoned ... he pacified ... Because of this, consul designate at the instigation of Tiberius Claudius Augustus Germanicus, in his consulship by the nomination ... made augur ... he was adlected into the number of patricians; by the judgement of Tiberius Claudius Caesar Augustus Germanicus, the equestrian order and the Roman people, with the assent of the Senate, gave to him the care of sacred buildings and public works and places. He was put in charge of the *ludi maximi* by the princeps Augustus, of whose liberality he was a servant ... of the province of Britain,[1] where he died. Verania, daughter of Quintus Veranius, lived 6 years, 10 months.

1. Cf. Tac. *Ann.* 14.29.1; *Agr.* 14.3.

[405] *Small. 232*
Arretium, Etruria

To Lucius (?) Martius Macer, son of Lucius, of the tribe Pomptina, military tribune of legion 2, one of the 4 for the care of roads, quaestor, curule aedile, praetor, propraetorian legate of Tiberius Claudius Caesar Augustus in the province of Moesia of legion 4 Scythica and legion 5 Macedonica, proconsul of the province of Achaea without recourse to lots, by decree of the decurions, at public expense.

[406] *Small. 233*
Rome

To Titus (?) Domitius Decidius, son of Titus, of the tribe Voltinia, triumvir for executions chosen by Tiberius Claudius Caesar Augustus

Germanicus, who was the first quaestor in charge of the treasury for a three year period without recourse to lots, praetor.

[407] *Small. 234*
Suasa, Umbria

To Lucius Coiedius Candidus, son of Lucius, of the tribe Aniensis, military tribune of the legion 8 Augusta, triumvir for executions, quaestor of Tiberius Claudius Caesar Augustus Germanicus, quaestor of the treasury of Saturn, curator of the public records. This man, returned from military service, Tiberius Claudius Caesar Augustus presented with military gifts – a gold crown, a turreted crown, an earthwork crown, a headless spear – since he had had him amongst his quaestors, and in the same year ordered him to be quaestor of the treasury of Saturn. At public expense.

[408] *Small. 235*
Rome

Gnaeus Pompeius Magnus, son of Crassus, of the tribe Menenia, pontifex, quaestor of Tiberius Claudius Caesar Augustus Germanicus, his father-in-law.

[409] *ILS 240*
Rome, AD 69 (?); cf. Tac. *Hist*. 1.48

To the departed spirit of Lucius Calpurnius Piso Frugi Licinianus, one of the 15 for the performance of sacred rites and of Verania Gemina, daughter of Quintus Veranius, consul, augur, wife of Piso Frugi.[1]

1. For her father, see no. 404.

[410] *Small. 236*
Tusculum

Lucius Junius Silanus Torquatus, son of Marcus, grandson of Marcus, honoured at age 18 with triumphal ornaments,[1] quaestor, praetor for cases between citizens and foreigners, son-in-law of Tiberius Claudius Caesar Augustus.

1. Tac. *Ann*. 12.3.

[411] *Small. 237*
Velitrae, Latium

To Marcus Julius Romulus, son of . . ., of the tribe Voltinia, proconsul without drawing lots of the province of Macedonia, propraetorian legate of the province of Cyprus, prefect for the distribution of grain by decree of the Senate, propraetorian legate for the second time of the province of Asia, praetor, legate of the divine Claudius of legion 15 Apollinaris, adlected tribune of the plebs by the divine Claudius, sevir of Roman equites, with the public horse . . . military tribune.

[412] *Small. 238*
Nicaea, Bithynia, bronze coin

Obv. Jugate busts of Nero, laureate, and Agrippina. NERO CAESAR AUGUSTUS, AGRIPPINA AUGUSTA

Rev. Dionysus, standing on an elephant's head. OF THE NICAEANS, UNDER ATTIUS LACO, PROCONSUL

[413] *Small. 239*
Bronze coin, Nicaea, Bithynia

Obv. Head of Nero, bare. NERO CLAUDIUS CAESAR AUGUSTUS

Rev. OF THE NICAEANS and a lighted altar inscribed OF PATRON, MARCUS TARQUITIUS PRISCUS, PROCONSUL

[414] *Small. 240*
Bronze coin, Ephesus

Obv. Jugate busts of Nero, laureate, and Poppaea. NERO, POPPAEA

Rev. Stag. OF THE EPHESIANS, AVIOLA BEING PROCONSUL, AECHMOCLES

[415] *Small. 241*
Narona, Dalmatia

To Aulus Ducenius Geminus, consul, one of the 15 for the performance of sacred rites, sodalis Augustalis, curator of public taxes,[1] propraetorian legate, patron.

1. Cf. Tac. *Ann.* 15. 18.

[416] S. Dušanić, *Germania*, 56 (1978) pp. 461-75

65, found in Pannonia near the Danube, relating to three cohorts of Upper Germany. Military diploma.

Nero Claudius Caesar Augustus Germanicus, son of the divine Claudius, grandson of Germanicus Caesar, great-grandson of Tiberius Caesar Augustus, great-great-grandson of the divine Augustus, pontifex maximus, in his 11th year of tribunician power, imperator nine times, father of his country, consul four times, has given to the infantry and cavalry who serve in the three cohorts which are called (1) 1st and (2) 2nd Thracians and (3) 7th Breucians and are in Germany under Publius Sulpicius Scribonius Proculus, who had served 25 years each or more, their names being written below, to these men themselves, to their children and descendants he has given citizenship and conubium with the wives they had on receipt of citizenship or, if they were bachelors, with the wives they married afterwards, provided that one man had one wife.

17th June, in the consulship of Aulus Licinius Nerva Silianus and Publius Pasidienus Firmus.

To an infantryman of the 7th Breucian cohort, which is commanded by Gaius Numisius Maximus, son of Gaius, of the tribe Velina, Liccaius, son of Liccaius, a Breucian.

Copied and authenticated from the bronze tablet which is posted at Rome on the Capitol in front of the military treasury on the base of the monument of the Claudii Marcelli.

Of Gaius Marcius Nobilis, from Emona, of Sextus Teius Niceros, from Aquileia, of Gaius Caecina Hermes, from Aquileia, of Titus Picatus Carpus, from Aquileia, of Lucius Hostilius Blaesus, from Emona, of Marcus Trebonius Hyginus, from Aquileia, of Lucius Annius Potens, from Aquileia.

[417] *AE (1969/70) no. 443*

66, Colonia Agrippinensis, Lower Germany

Imperator Nero Caesar Augustus, son of the divine Claudius, grandson of Germanicus Caesar, great-grandson of Tiberius Caesar Augustus, great-great-grandson of the divine Augustus, pontifex maximus, in his 12th year of tribunician power, imperator ten times, consul four times, father of his country, Publius Sulpicius Scribonius Rufus being propraetorian legate of Augustus, legion 15 Primigenia.

[418] *Small. 242*

(a) Cyprus

To Apollo Hylates; to Titus Clodius Eprius Marcellus, quaestor, tribune of the plebs, praetor, legate of legion 14 Gemina of Gaius Caesar Augustus, propraetorian legate of Lycia of Tiberius Claudius Caesar Germanicus and Nero Claudius Caesar Germanicus, proconsul of Cyprus, Aristocles, son of Aristocles, in his honour.

(b) Near Capua

To Titus Clodius Eprius Marcellus, son of Marcus, of the tribe Falerna, consul twice, augur, curio maximus, sodalis Augustalis, peregrine praetor, proconsul of Asia for three years, the province of Cyprus.

[419] *Small. 243*

(a) Oenoanda, Lycia

Gaius Licinius Mucianus, propraetorian legate of Nero Claudius Caesar Augustus Germanicus; Hermaeus, son of Silleus, born the son of Diogenes, honours his benefactor.

(b) Attaleia, Pamphylia

Gaius Licinius Mucianus, propraetorian legate of Nero Claudius Caesar Augustus Germanicus . . .

[420] *Small. 244*

70 or 71 (?), Ephesus

To Gaius Rutilius Gallicus, son of Gaius, of the tribe Stellatina, military tribune of legion 13 Gemina, quaestor, curule aedile, legate of the divine Claudius of legion 15 Apollinaris, praetor, legate of the Galatian province, sodalis Augustalis, consul designate; Marcus Aemilius Pius, son of Marcus, of the tribe Palatina, prefect of the 1st. Bosporan cohort and the 1st Spanish cohort, to his legate.

[421] *Small. 245*

Andros

(a) The people honoured Publius Glitius Gallus, its patron and benefactor, for his virtue.

(b) The people honoured Egnatia Maximilla, its benefactress, for her virtue.

[422] *Small. 246*
Sentinum, Umbria

Marcus Cocceius Nerva, son of Marcus, consul, augur, sodalis Augustalis
... city, sevir of squadron ... of Roman equites, Palatine salian,
honoured with triumphal ornaments,[1] patron of the municipality ...
collapsed with age ...

1. Cf. Tac. *Ann.* 15.72. Nerva was later emperor, 96-98.

[423] *EJ 219*
Rome; cf. Suet. *Aug.* 66; Tac. *Ann.* 3.30; Hor. *Od.* 3.29; *Sat.* 1.6;
Sen. *Ep.* 114

Of the freedmen and freedwomen of Gaius Maecenas, son of Lucius,
of the tribe Pomptina, and for their descendants and those who have
contributed or shall contribute to its care.

[424] *EJ 374*; but cf. *JRS*, 61 (1971) p. 146
Late 30 BC (?), from Egypt. In bronze letters fixed to an obelisk,
which was later brought to Rome and re-used by Gaius, who dedicated
it to his predecessors

By order of Imperator Caesar, son of a god, Gaius Cornelius Gallus,
son of Gnaeus, prefect of engineers of Caesar, son of a god, built the
Forum Julium.[1]

1. In Alexandria.

Re-used (= *Small. 306*) as:

To divine Caesar Augustus, son of divine Julius, to Tiberius Caesar
Augustus, son of divine Augustus, a dedication.

[425] *EJ 21*
29 BC, Philae, Upper Egypt. In Greek and Latin; there is also an
Egyptian version, which is not a translation but a statement of the
victories in traditional Egyptian terms. See N.B. Millet, *Meroitic
Nubia* (1969) p. 12; W.Y. Adams, *Nubia; Corridor to Africa* (1977)
pp. 338-40. Cf. Suet. *Aug.* 66; Dio 53.23-4

Gaius Cornelius Gallus, son of Gnaeus, Roman eques, first prefect of
Alexandria and Egypt after the defeat of the kings by Caesar, son of
a god, put down the uprising of the Thebaid in 15 days, in which he
defeated the enemy, having won two pitched battles and taken five
cities by storm — Boresis, Coptus, Ceramice, Diospolis Magna and
Ophieion; the leaders of these uprisings were captured and our army

was led beyond the (first) cataract of the Nile, whither neither the arms of the Roman people nor those of the kings of Egypt had previously advanced; the Thebaid, a source of fear for all the kings alike, was subdued and envoys of the king of the Ethiopians were given audience at Philae and that king was received into protection, and a ruler of the Ethiopian Triakontaschoenus was established; he made this dedication to the ancestral gods and to Nile, his helper.

[426] R.D. Anderson, P.J. Parsons and R.G.M. Nisbet, *JRS*, 69 (1979) pp. 125-55

Poetry of Gallus. The date and reference is not clear. He might be looking foward to Octavian's victorious return to Rome in 29 BC, but it could be much earlier

> Then, Caesar, my fate will be sweet to me, when you
> Have become the greatest part of Roman history
> And I read of the temples of many gods
> Enriched upon your return, decorated with your trophies.

[427] *POxy 2820* with N. Lewis, *GRBS*, 16 (1975) pp. 295-303

The preparations of Aelius Gallus for his Arabian campaign?
[The beginning is lost] . . . summoned . . . to defect and on account of this made a more than sufficient quantity of weapons and he refitted Cleopatra's fleet, which, as might be expected, had been neglected after her death, and he posted garrisons at the entrances to the country and set in readiness everything needed for war, so that . . . considering the Egyptians around Thebes to be more warlike than their fellows, he first encouraged them to volunteer for the expedition, but when they did not come forward he resorted to a draft . . .

[428] *EJ 368* with P.A. Brunt, *ZPE*, 13 (1974) pp. 161-85; cf. T.D. Barnes, *JRS*, 64 (1974) pp. 25-6

Alexandria Troas, Troad

To Gaius Fabricius Tuscus, son of Gaius, of the tribe Aniensis, duumvir, augur, prefect of the Apulan cohort and of the works which have been executed in the colony by order of Augustus, military tribune of legion 3 Cyrenaica for eight years, tribune of the levy of the free-born which Augustus and Tiberius Caesar carried out at Rome,[1] prefect of engineers for four years, prefect of cavalry of the praetorian squadron for four years, awarded the headless spear and gold crown by Germanicus Caesar, imperator, in the German war, by decree of the decurions.

1. AD 6.

[429] *EJ 219a*
Bronze coin, Tralles-Caesarea; cf. Tac. *Ann*. 1.10; 12.60; R. Syme, *Roman Papers*, (1979) pp. 518-29

Obv. Head of Publius Vedius Pollio. POLLIO, OF THE CAESAREANS.
Rev. Head of Zeus. MENANDER, SON OF PARRHASIUS.

[430] *IGR 4.215*
Ilium

The council and people honoured Publius Vedius Pollio.

[431] *CIL 9.1556*
Beneventum

Publius Vedius Pollio, son of Publius, built the shrine of Caesar for Imperator Caesar Augustus and the colony of Beneventum.

[432] Seneca, *On Anger*, 3.40

To rebuke an angry man is to incite him to still greater anger. Approach him with all sorts of blandishments — unless you are a personage so great that you can quell his anger in the way that the divine Augustus did when dining with Vedius Pollio.

One of Vedius' slaves had broken a crystal glass: Vedius ordered him to be seized and executed in an extraordinary fashion. He was to be thrown to the huge lampreys which Vedius kept in a pool. Is it not obvious to everyone that Vedius did this as a mark of high-living? It was savagery. The slave broke free and took refuge at Caesar's feet, begging only that he might die in some other way and not be eaten. Caesar was stirred by this fiendish cruelty and ordered that the slave be released and that all the crystal glasses be smashed before his eyes and the pool filled in. Thus, could Caesar rebuke his friend: he made good use of his power.

[433] *CIL 6.9535*
Rome; cf. R. Seager, *Tiberius* (1972) p. 179 n. 6

Liburnus, slave of Lucius Seius Strabo, manservant; Salvilla, his wife, made this.

[434] *EJ 221*
Aeclanum, Samnium, Italy

To Marcus Magius Maximus, son of Marcus, prefect of Egypt; the Tarraconenses.

[435] *EJ 222*
Verona; cf. Dio 58.9-12; 60.23

To Publius Graecinius Laco, son of Publius, of the tribe Publilia, with consular ornaments.

[436] *EJ 223*
Rome

Laco, prefect of the watch, 13.[1]

1. The meaning of this number is uncertain; perhaps Region 13 of Rome.

[437] *EJ 369* with *AE* (1971) no. 477
Caesarea Maritima, Palestine

On 1st July,[1] Marcus Pontius Pilatus, prefect of Judaea, dedicated the shrine of Tiberius.

1. On this date Tiberius was first awarded tribunician power, but the text is most uncertain at this point.

[438] *EJ 224*
Paelignian Superaequum

Quintus Octavius Sagitta, son of Lucius, grandson of Gaius, great-grandson of Lucius, of the tribe Sergia, duumvir quinquennalis 3 times, prefect of engineers, prefect of cavalry, military tribune chosen by the people, procurator of Caesar Augustus among the Vindelici and Raeti and in the Poenine Valley for four years and in the province of Spain for 10 years and in Syria for two years.

[439] *EJ 225 Small. 255*
Teate Marrucinorum, Italy. Silver bust of Tiberius

To Tiberius Caesar Augustus, son of the divine Augustus, pontifex maximus, in his 38th year of tribunician power, consul 5 times, in accordance with the will of Marcus Pulfennius, son of Sextus, of the tribe Arnensis, centurion of legion 6 Ferrata. Gaius Herennius Capito, son of Titus, of the tribe Arnensis, military tribune for three years, prefect of cavalry, prefect of veterans, procurator of Julia Augusta, procurator of Tiberius Caesar Augustus, procurator of Gaius Caesar Augustus Germanicus. 10 pounds of silver.

[440] *EJ 226*
Cos, temple of Asclepius

The people dedicated this statue of Gnaeus Capito, procurator of Tiberius Caesar Augustus, the god, for his virtue and good-will towards it.

[441] *EJ 227*
Ilium

The council and the people honoured Titus Valerius Proculus, procurator of Drusus Caesar, who purged the Hellespont of piracy and kept the city free from oppression in every way.

[442] *EJ 228*
Sestinum, Umbria

To Lucius Volusenus Clemens, son of Lucius, of the tribe Clustumina, military tribune, prefect of cavalry, prefect of the recruits of Gallia Narbonensis for ... received discharge from the divine Augustus. This man, when sent by Tiberius Caesar Augustus to administer justice in Egypt, died in the province of Aquitania.

[443] *EJ 229*
Aquinum, Latium

To Quintus Decius Saturninus, son of Quintus, grandson of Marcus, lesser priest at Rome, flute-player of the public rites of the Roman people, the Quirites, prefect of engineers of a consul for three years, curator of the Labican and Latin roads, military tribune, prefect of engineers for the administration of justice and the selection of jurors by lot in Asia, one of the 4 for the administration of justice at Verona, quaestor for two years, duumvir for the administration of justice, and again duumvir quinquennalis, prefect quinquennalis[1] of Tiberius Caesar Augustus, and again of Drusus Caesar, son of Tiberius, and for a third time of Nero Caesar, son of Germanicus, priest, flamen of Rome and divine Augustus in perpetuity by authority of Tiberius Caesar Augustus and by his permission chosen patron of the colony; at public expense, by decree of the decurions.

1. Cf. F.F. Abbott and A.C. Johnson, *Municipal Administration in the Roman Empire* (1926) p. 62.

[444] *EJ 230*
Hasta, Etruria

To Publius Vergilius Laurea, son of Publius, grandson of Publius, of the tribe Pollia, aedile, duumvir for the administration of justice, prefect of engineers, judge in the four decuries, one of the equites chosen for public and private cases, prefect of Drusus Caesar, son of Germanicus, duumvir quinquennalis; to Publius Vergilius Paullinus, son of Publius, grandson of Publius, of the tribe Pollia, holder of the public horse, judge in the four decuries, prefect of engineers, prefect of veteran cohort 2 ... the army ...

[445] *EJ 230a*
Rome

To the departed spirit, a dedication; to Gaius Caesius Niger, son of Quintus, of the tribe Teretina, in the first rank of admission, member of the four decuries, lesser *curio*.[1] Caesia Theoris, freedwoman of Gaius, for her patron and herself.

1. A priest.

[446] *EJ 231*
Unknown origin

Quintus Aemilius Secundus, son of Quintus, of the tribe Palatina, in the military service of the divine Augustus, under Publius Sulpicius Quirinius, legate of Caesar in Syria, decorated with honours, prefect of cohort 1 Augusta, prefect of naval cohort 2. I too, by order of

Quirinius, carried out a census of the state of Apamea of 117,000 male citizens; I too, sent by Quirinius against the Ituraeans on Mt. Lebanon, captured their fort; and, by accelerated promotion, prefect of engineers, I was transferred by the two consuls to the treasury; and in the colony I have been quaestor, aedile twice, duumvir twice and priest. Buried there are Quintus Aemilius Secundus, son of Quintus, of the tribe Palatina, and Aemilia Chia, freedwoman. This monument will pass to an heir no more.

[447] *EJ 232*
10, Egypt, Mt Claudius

Year 40 of Caesar, Pauni 1st, with good fortune. When Publius Juventius was tribune of the third legion and prefect of Berenice and chief superintendent of the mines of Zmaragdus and Bazius and Margaritus and all the mines of Egypt, he dedicated a temple at Ophiatis to Pan, greatest god; and Publius Juventius Agathopous, his freedman, was also his procurator and curator and the benefactor of all the mines of Egypt. The offering of Ptolemy, curator of the cohort of Florus of the century of Bassus, who also erected this.

[448] *EJ 232a*
13-4, Sardinia, milestone

Imperator Caesar Augustus, son of a god, father of his country, pontifex maximus, in his 36th year of tribunician power, in the governorship of Titus Pompeius Proculus, prolegate. 10 miles.

[449] *EJ 233*
Emona, Pannonia

Titus Junius Montanus, son of Decimus, of the tribe Aniensis, military tribune for six years, prefect of cavalry for 6 years, prefect of engineers for 2 years, prolegate for 2 years.

[450] *EJ 234*
Dyrrachium

To Lucius Titinus Sulpicianus, son of Lucius, of the tribe Aemilia, priest, produumviral prefect and duumvir quinquennalis, military tribune and prolegatery military tribune and prefect of Titus Statilius Taurus as quinquennalis,[1] father.

1. Cf. F.F. Abbott and A.C. Johnson, *Municipal Administration in the Roman Empire* (1926) p. 62.

[451] *EJ 235*
Lanuvium

Aulus Castricius, son of Myriotalentus, military tribune, prefect of cavalry and of the fleet, master of the college of Luperci and Capitolini and Mercuriales and Aventine Villagers, one of the 26 . . . for several . . . selections by lot . . . obtained . . .

[452] *EJ 236*
Luceria, amphitheatre

Marcus Vecilius Campus, son of Marcus, grandson of Lucius, prefect of engineers, military tribune, duumvir for the administration of justice, priest, had the amphitheatre built on his own private land and the surrounding enclosure at his own expense in honour of Imperator Caesar Augustus and the colony of Luceria.

[453] *EJ 237*
Formiae

To Lucius Arrius Salanus, prefect of Tiberius Caesar as quinquennalis, prefect of Nero and Drusus Caesar as quinquennalis designate, flute-player of the rites of the Roman people, aedile for three years, augur, interrex, military tribune of legion 3 Augusta and legion 10 Gemina, prefect of cavalry, prefect of camp, prefect of engineers. Oppia, his wife.

[454] *EJ 238*
Antioch near Pisidia

To Gaius Caristanius Fronto Caesianus Julius, son of Gaius, of the tribe Sergia, prefect of engineers, military tribune of legion 12 Fulminata, prefect of the Bosporan cohort, priest, prefect of Publius Sulpicius Quirinius, duumvir, prefect of Marcus Servilius, prefect . . .

[455] *EJ 239*
Near Aquileia

To Tiberius Julius Viator, son of Gaius, of the tribe Fabia, sub-prefect of the 3rd Lusitanian cohort, one of the 4 for the administration of justice, prefect of the Ubian cavalry cohort. To Erbonia Grata, his wife, daughter of Sextus. Gaius Julius Linus, freedman of Augustus, to his son and daughter-in-law.

[456] *EJ 240*
Rome

Gaius Pompeius Proculus, son of Gaius, of the tribe Teretina, military tribune of legion 18, prefect of engineers, one of the 6 of the equestrian centuries, is buried here.

[457] *EJ 241*
Alpine Valley, above Brixia

To Staius Vobenus, son of Edragassus, princeps of the Trumplini, prefect of the Trumplinian cohort under Gaius Vibius Pansa, propraetorian legate, likewise of the Vindelician, tax-exempt . . . of Caesar . . . and for his family. Messava, daughter of Vecus, his wife.

[458] *Small. 254 = EJ 370*
Alba Fucens

Quintus Naevius Cordus Sutorius Macro, son of Quintus, of the tribe Fabia, prefect of the watch, praetorian prefect of Tiberius Caesar Augustus, gave this in his will.

[459] *Small. 256*
Near Verona

To Quintus Caecilius Cisiacus Septicius Pica Caecilianus, procurator of the Augusti and prolegate of the province of Raetia and the Vindelici and the Poenine valley, augur, priest of the divine Augustus and Rome; Gaius Ligurius Asper, son of Lucius, of the tribe Voltinia, centurion of the 1st cohort of free-born Roman citizens.

[460] *Small. 257*
Pompeii

Spurius Turranius Proculus Gellianus, son of Lucius, grandson of Spurius, great-grandson of Lucius, of the tribe Fabia, prefect of engineers for two years, prefect of curators of the bed of the Tiber, propraetorian prefect for the administration of justice in the city of Lavinium, made father of the people of Laurentum for the striking of a treaty in accordance with the Sibylline books with the Roman people; of the sacred beginnings of the Roman people, Quirites, and

Latin name, which are observed among the Lavinii, priest of Jupiter, priest of Mars, Salian dancer, augur, pontifex, prefect of the Gaetulian cohort, military tribune of legion 10. Site given by decree of the decurions.

[461] *Small. 259*
Vasio, Narbonensis

The Vasian Vocontii to their patron, Sextus Afranius Burrus, son of Sextus, of the tribe Voltinia, military tribune, procurator of Augusta, procurator of Tiberius Caesar, procurator of the divine Claudius, praetorian prefect, with consular ornaments.

[462] *Small. 260*
Paradisus, Thrace

To Marcus Vettius Marcellus, procurator of Augustus, the strategi of Thrace:
  Tiberius Claudius Dinis, Tiberius Claudius Auluzenis, Tiberius Claudius Auluporis, Marcus Vettius Dinis,[1] Tiberius Claudius Dinicenthus, Tiberius Claudius Theopompus, Tiberius Claudius Rhoemetalces, son of Bithycenthus, Tiberius Claudius Rhoemetalces, son of Apollonius, Tiberius Claudius Bithys, Tiberius Claudius Zycolaeses, Tiberius Claudius Cardenthes ... [22 more names follow, all but 10 with the nomenclature of a Roman citizen, as the above; the 10 non-citizens are listed after those who seem to be citizens].
1. Inscribed over an erasure.

[463] *ILS 1377*
Teate Marrucinorum

Marcus Vettius Marcellus, procurator of the Augusti, and Helvidia Priscilla, daughter of Gaius, wife of Marcellus, made this at their own expense.

[464] Pliny the Elder, *Natural History*, 2.199

And our age has known a portent no less marvellous, in the last year of Nero's principate — as I have set out in my history of the man —, when meadows and olive-groves in the territory of the Marrucini crossed an intervening public highway and changed places, this being on the estate of Vettius Marcellus, a Roman eques acting as procurator of the property of Nero.

[465] *Small. 261a*

Ephesus

To Tiberius Claudius Balbillus, son of . . . , of the tribe Quirina, . . . of the temples of the divine Augustus and . . . and of the groves and of all holy places at Alexandria and in the whole of Egypt and head of the museum and officer of the Alexandrian library and high-priest and officer of Alexandrian Hermes for . . . years and officer of embassies and replies in Greek[1] of Caesar Augustus, the divine Claudius, and military tribune of legion 20 and prefect of engineers of the divine Claudius and awarded gifts by the divine Claudius in his triumph — a turreted crown and a banner and a headless spear . . .

1. Restored.

[466] *Small. 261b*

Ephesus

The council and the people honoured Tiberius Claudius Balbillus, the greatest procurator of Augustus, for his unremitting piety towards the goddess and his beneficence towards the city.

[467] *Small. 262*

Cos

[Beginning is lost] . . . Gaius Stertinius Xenophon, son of Heracleitus, of the tribe Cornelia, head doctor of the divine Augusti and officer of Greek replies, having served as tribune and having been prefect of engineers and having been honoured in the British triumph with a gold crown and a spear, son of the people, friend of Nero,[1] friend of Caesar, friend of Augustus, friend of the Romans, friend of his country, benefactor of his country, high-priest of the gods and priest for life of the Augusti and Asclepius and Hygia and Epione. When the sacred treasurers were Marcus Septicius Rufus, son of Marcus, and Ariston, son of Philocles, friends of Caesar.

1. Over an erasure of 'friend of Claudius' and subsequently erased in turn.

[468] *Small. 263*
Corinth

To Gaius Julius Laco, son of Gaius, of the tribe Fabia, procurator of Tiberius Claudius Caesar Augustus Germanicus, augur, president of the Isthmian and Caesarian Games, duumvir quinquennalis, curio, priest of Augustus; Cydichus, son of Simon, of Thisbe, to one well-deserving.

[469] *Small. 264*
Corinth

To Gaius Julius Spartiaticus, son of Laco, grandson of Eurycles, of the tribe Fabia, procurator of Caesar and Augusta Agrippina, military tribune, decorated with the public horse by the divine Claudius, flamen of the divine Julius, priest, duumvir quinquennalis twice, president of the Isthmian and Caesarian Augustan Games, high-priest of the Augustan house in perpetuity, first of the Achaeans, for his virtue and eager and most generous munificence towards the divine house and towards our colony; the tribesmen of the tribe Calpurnia to their patron.

[470] *Small. 265*
Iconium, Lycaonia

The people of the Claudiconians honoured Lucius Pupius Praeses, son of Lucius, of the tribe Sabatina, military tribune, prefect of cavalry of the Picentine squadron, procurator of Caesar for the banks of the Tiber, procurator of Tiberius Claudius Caesar Augustus Germanicus and Nero Claudius Caesar Augustus Germanicus of the Galatian province, its benefactor and founder.

[471] *Small. 266*
Bronze coin, Nicaea, Bithynia; cf. Tac. *Ann*. 12.21

Obv. Jugate busts of Nero, laureate, and Agrippina. NERO CAESAR AUGUSTUS, AGRIPPINA AUGUSTA
Rev. Dionysus, standing on an elephant's head. OF THE NICAEANS, UNDER JUNIUS CILO, PROCURATOR

[472] *Small. 267*
Antioch, near Pisidia

To . . . Proculus, of the tribe Sergia, augur, military tribune of legion 3 Cyrenaica, juridicus of Alexandria and Egypt, procurator of Nero Claudius Caesar Augustus Germanicus of the province of Cappadocia and Cilicia; cavalry-squadron Augusta Germanica established this.

[473] *Small. 268*
London; cf. Tac. *Ann.* 14.38

To the departed spirit of Gaius Julius Alpinus Classicianus, son of Gaius, of the tribe Fabia, . . . procurator of the province of Britain; Julia Pacata Indiana, daughter of Indus,[1] his wife, made this.

1. Cf. Tac. *Ann.* 3.42.3.

[474] *Small. 269*
Brigetio, Pannonia; cf. Tac. *Ann.* 15.72; *Hist.* 1.5

To Jupiter Optimus Maximus, Gaius Nymphidius Sabinus, prefect . . .

5 THE ARMED FORCES

[475] *EJ 242*
Venafrum

Lucius Ovinius Rufus, son of Lucius, of the tribe Teretina, first rank of the praetorian cohorts of divine Augustus, chief centurion of legion 14 Gemina, military tribune of urban cohort 11, military tribune of praetorian cohort ... prefect of engineers, duumvir, to Lucius Ovinius, son of Marcus, of the tribe Teretina, his father, to Marcus Ovinius Vopiscus, son of Lucius, of the tribe Teretina, his brother, to Allidia Rufa, daughter of Lucius, his mother, and to Pullia Prima, his wife.

[476] *EJ 243 = Small. 258*
Julium Carnicum, Venetia

To Gaius Baebius Atticus, son of Publius, of the tribe Claudia, duumvir for the administration of justice, chief centurion of legion 5 Macedonica, prefect of the states of Moesia and Treballia, prefect of the states in the Maritime Alps, military tribune of praetorian cohort 8, chief centurion a second time, procurator of Tiberius Claudius Caesar Augustus Germanicus in Noricum; the state of the Saevates and Laianci.

[477] *EJ 244*
Paeligni

To Sextus Pedius Lusianus Hirrutus, son of Sextus, of the tribe Aniensis, chief centurion of legion 21, prefect of the Raeti and Vindelici of the Poenine Valley and light-armed troops, one of the 4 for the administration of justice, prefect for five years of Germanicus Caesar for justice by decree of the Senate, and again for another five years. This man built the amphitheatre at his own expense. Marcus Dullius Gallus, son of Marcus.

[478] *EJ 245*
Venafrum

Lusia Paullina, daughter of Marcus, wife of Sextus Vettulenus Cerialis, for herself and Marcus Vergilius Gallus Lusius, son of Marcus, of the tribe Teretina, her father, chief centurion of legion 11, prefect of the cohort of Ubian infantry and cavalry, awarded two headless spears and gold crowns by the divine Augustus and Tiberius Caesar Augustus, prefect of engineers for three years, military tribune of the first cohort, idiologus in Egypt, duumvir twice, priest, and for Aulus Lusius Gallus, son of Aulus, of the tribe Teretina, her brother, military tribune of legion 22 Cyrenaica, prefect of cavalry.

[479] *EJ 246*
Venafrum

To Sextus Aulienus, son of Sextus, of the tribe Aniensis, chief centurion twice, military tribune, prefect of light-armed troops, camp-prefect of Imperator Caesar Augustus and Tiberius Caesar Augustus, prefect of the fleet, prefect of engineers, duumvir at Venafrum and Forum Julii, flamen Augustalis; Nedymus and Gamus, freedmen.

[480] *EJ 247*
Sora, Latium

To Lucius Firmus, son of Lucius, chief centurion, military tribune, one of the 4 for the administration of justice, upon the settlement of the colony the first priest; legion 4 Sorana, for his honour and virtue.

[481] *EJ 248*
Varia, near Tibur

Marcus Helvius Rufus Civica, son of Marcus, of the tribe Camilia, chief centurion, gave the baths to the townsmen and inhabitants.

[482] *EJ 249*
Near Praeneste

Sextus Julius Rufus, son of Sextus, of the tribe Pollia, evocatus of divine Augustus, prefect of the 1st Corsican cohort and the states of Barbaria in Sardinia.

[483] *EJ 250*
Rome

Gaius Petronius Varia, son of Gaius, of the tribe Falerna, scout of
Caesar. Hordionia Egiste, freedwoman of Titus, his wife.

[484] *EJ 251*
Rome

To the departed spirit; Quintus Caetronius Passer, son of Quintus, of
the tribe Publilia, soldier of praetorian cohort 3 for 18 years, discharged
from the two Geminae, for himself and Masuria Marcella, daughter of
Marcus.
  I lived as I wished, always poor enough, but honest;
  I have cheated no one, which gladdens my bones.
Frontage 11½ feet, 13½ feet back.

[485] *EJ 252*
Ostia

To . . . soldier of praetorian cohort 6; the Ostienses gave the burial
place and decreed that he should be buried with a public funeral since
he died while extinguishing a fire.
Frontage 12 feet, 25 feet back.

[486] *EJ 253*
Rome

Of Lucius Aufustius Rufinus, son of Lucius, of the tribe Subura, centurion of cohort 7 of the Roman watch, candidate of Tiberius Caesar,
and of Aufustia Superantia and of Aufustius and Aufustia Gemella,
urn 4. Lucius Aufustius Fusculus Maior, son of Lucius, of the tribe
Subura, and Lucius Aufustius Serenus, son of Lucius, of the tribe
Palatina, had the monument made in result of a legacy.

[487] *EJ 254*
Ateste

Marcus Billienus Actiacus, son of Marcus, of the tribe Romilia, of legion
11, the naval battle concluded, was settled in the colony and chosen as
decurion by his unit . . .

[488] *EJ 255*
Lower Moesia

Lucius Plinius, son of Sextus, of the tribe Fabia, from Trumplia, soldier of legion 20, 45 years of age, 17 years service, lies here. He instructed this to be made in his will. Secundus, freedman of Lucius Plinius and Publius Mestrius, made this.

[489] *EJ 256*
Nemausus, Gaul

Discharged soldier of Tiberius Caesar Augustus, son of divine Augustus, Titus Julius Festus served 25 years in legion 16, received 50 measures of grain and the use of the baths free in perpetuity, by decree of the decurions, and the space between the two towers, assigned through Publius Pusonius Peregrinus, one of the 4 and one of the 11.

[490] *EJ 257*
Near Salonae, Dalmatia

(a) Titus Ancharenus, son of Lucius, of the tribe Sergia, from Laranda, soldier of legion 7, 45 years of age, 23 years' service, lies here.

(b) Gnaeus Domitius, son of Gnaeus, of the tribe Velia, from Pessinus, 44 years of age, 25 years' service, veteran of legion 7, lies here. He ordered this to be made in his will.

[491] *EJ 258*
Near Burnum, Dalmatia

Aulus Sentius, son of Aulus, of the tribe Pomptina, from Arretium, veteran of legion 11, lies here; he ordered this to be made in his will. This man was killed on the borders of the Varvarini in a meadow by the River Titus, near Long Rock. His heir had this made, Quintus Calventius Vitalis, son of Lucius.

[492] *EJ 259*
Near Philippi

To Sextus Volcasius, son of Lucius, of the tribe Voltinia, of legion 28, from Pisa.

[493] *EJ 260 = Small. 279*
Simitthu, Africa

Lucius Flaminius, son of Decimus, of the tribe Arnensis, soldier of
legion 3 Augusta, of the century of Julius Longus, chosen in a levy
by Marcus Silanus, served 29 years on garrison-duty when he was killed
in the Philomusian range by the enemy in battle, lived dutifully 40
years, lies here.

[494] *EJ 261*
Coptos, Egypt; cf. *CAH*, X, p. 246

[Beginning is lost] . . .
Cohort 4
Century of Longus:
    Gaius Marcius, son of Marcus of the tribe Pollia, Alexandrian.
Century of Cattus:
    Lucius Longinus, son of Lucius, of the tribe Sergia, from Tavium.
Century of Vedius:
    Lucius Licinius, son of Lucius, of the tribe Pollia, Sebastopolitan.
Century of Servatus:
    Marcus Lollius, son of Marcus, of the tribe Pollia, from Ancyra.
Century of Caecilius:
    Gaius Cornelius, son of Gaius, of the tribe Pollia, from Ancyra.
Century of Aquila:
    Gaius Sossius, son of Gaius, of the tribe Pollia, Pompeiopolitan.

Cohort 4
Century of Etrius:
    Lucius Longinus, son of Lucius, of the tribe Pollia, from Ancyra.
Century of Vettius Rufus:
    Gaius Longinus, son of Gaius, of the tribe Pollia, Alexandrian.
Century of Castus:
    Marcus Cassius, son of Marcus, of the tribe Pollia, from Isinda.
Century of Gaius Mammius:
    Marcus Petronius, son of Marcus, of the tribe Pollia, Alexandrian.
Century of Publius Mammius:
    Gnaeus Otacilius, son of Gnaeus, of the tribe Pollia, from Ancyra.
Century Oeniana:
    Marcus Longinus, son of Marcus, of the tribe Pollia, from Etenna.

Cohort 5
Century of Publilius:
   Gaius Didius, son of Gaius, of the tribe Pollia, from Ancyra.
Century of Gavisidius:
   Gaius Helvius, son of Gaius, of the tribe Pollia, from Gangra.
Century Iustiana:
   Titus Antonius, son of Titus, of the tribe Sergia, from Tavium.
Century of Licinius Verus:
   Gaius Sentius, son of Gaius, of the tribe Sergia, from Tavium.
Century of Numerius:
   Gaius Julius, son of Gaius, of the tribe Pollia, Alexandrian.
Century Lucretiana:
   Lucius Julius, son of Lucius, of the tribe Galeria, from Lugdunum.

Cohort 5
Century of Caninius:
   Gaius Valerius, son of Gaius, of the tribe Pollia, from Ancyra.
Century of Marcus Cornelius:
   Marcus Julius, son of Marcus, of the tribe Pollia, Alexandrian.
Century of Maternus:
   Marcus Lollius, son of Marcus, of the tribe Pollia, from Ancyra.
Century Cliterniana:
   Sextus Lusius, son of Sextus, of the tribe Pollia, from Tavium.
Century of Clemens:
   Gaius Vibius, son of Gaius, of the tribe Aniensis, from Vercellae.
Century Gavisidiana:
   Gaius Aufidius, son of Gaius, of the tribe Pollia, from Ancyra.

Cohort 6
Century of Trebonius:
   Marcus Valerius, son of Marcus, of the tribe Pollia, from Side.
Century of Curtius:
   Gaius Valerius, son of Gaius, of the tribe Papiria, from Nicaea.
Century of Minius:
   Gaius Granius, son of Gaius, of the tribe Pollia, from Ancyra.
Century of Cotius:
   Gaius Valerius, son of Gaius, of the tribe Galeria, from Lugdunum.
Century of Curiatius:
   Gaius Trebius, son of Gaius, of the tribe Pupinia, from Paraetonium.
Century of Galba:
   Gaius Aufidius, son of Gaius, of the tribe Pollia, from camp.

Cohort 6
Century of Firmus:
  Gaius Spedius, son of Gaius, of the tribe Pollia, from Cyrene.
Century of Longus:
  Gaius Antonius, son of Gaius, of the tribe Pollia, Alexandrian.
Century of Flaccus:
  Publius Papirius, son of Publius, of the tribe Pollia, from Ancyra.
Century of Varus:
  Gaius Longinus, son of Gaius, of the tribe Pollia, from camp.
Century of Paccius:
  Publius Flavius, son of Publius, of the tribe Aniensis, from Paphos.
Century of Hordionius:
  Gaius Romanius, son of Gaius, of the tribe Fabia, from Berytus.

Cohort 7
[Large portion lost, including the names and units of soldiers of the 7th, 8th, 9th and 10th cohorts, followed by the names of five officers, one *duplicarius* and four *sesquiplicarii*.[1]] ... Makes a grand total of three cavalry squadrons, 5 officers, one *duplicarius*, four *sesquiplicarii*, 424 cavalrymen.

Cohort 7
[Large portion lost, including the names and units of soldiers of the 7th, 8th, 9th and 10th cohorts, followed by the names of six auxiliary cohorts, with the names of seven centurions.] ... 1st Theban cohort, whose commander is Sextus Pompeius Merula; centurion Gaius Terentius Maximus, centurion Gaius Julius Montanus, centurion Lucius Domitius Aper. Total: 3 centurions.

Makes a grand total of seven cohorts, ten centurions, 61 cavalrymen, 788 soldiers.

Through the aforementioned cisterns were built and dedicated: the cistern of Apollo on December 26th, at Compasus on August 1st, at Berenice on December 15th, at Myoshormus on January 13th. They built and repaired the camp.

1. A *duplicarius* was a soldier awarded twice normal rations; a *sesquiplicarius* 1½ times normal rations.

[495] *EJ 263*
Boundary stones, Cantabria

(a) Augustan boundary separating the lands of legion 4 and the land of the Juliobriges.

(b) Augustan boundary separating the lands of legion 4 and the land
of the Segisamones.

[496] *EJ 264*
29-30, boundary stone, Africa

Legion 3 Augusta drew boundaries in the third year of the proconsulate
of Gaius Vibius Marsus: to the right of the central line 70 plots, above
the axis 280 plots.

[497] *CIL 5.6786*
Eporedia, Cisalpine Gaul. A military surveyor. Date uncertain

Of the Claudian tribe, Lucius Aebutius Faustus, freedman of Lucius,
surveyor, sevir, made this in his lifetime for himself and Arria Aucta,
freedwoman of Quintus, his wife, and their family and Zepyre the
freedwoman.

[498] *EJ 265*
18-19, Iader, Dalmatia

Tiberius Caesar Augustus, son of divine Augustus, imperator, pontifex
maximus, in his 20th year of tribunician power, consul 3 times; legion
7 and legion 11, Publius Cornelius Dolabella being propraetorian legate.

[499] *EJ 266*
Salonae, Dalmatia

[Beginning is lost] ... road, which is 167 miles long, he built with
detachments of legion 7 and legion 11. Likewise, he opened up and
built the Via Gabiniana, from Salonae to Andetrium, through legion 7.

[500] *EJ 267*
33-4, Iron Gate, Danube, Upper Moesia

Tiberius Caesar Augustus, son of Augustus, being imperator, pontifex
maximus, in his 35th year of tribunician power; legion 4 Scythica and
legion 5 Macedonica.

[501] *EJ 268*
Strymon valley

Under Imperator Caesar Augustus, son of a god, and Lucius Tarius Rufus, propraetorian legate; legion 10 Fretensis built the bridge.

[502] *EJ 269*
Palmyra, temple of Bel. The text incorporates later additions

To Drusus Caesar, son of Tiberius Augustus, grandson of a god, to Tiberius Caesar Augustus, son of divine Augustus, grandson of divine Julius, to Germanicus Caesar, son of Tiberius Augustus, grandson of a god, imperatores; Minucius Rufus, son of Titus, of the tribe Horatia, legate of legion 10 Fretensis, set this up.

[503] *EJ 270*
Velitrae, bilingual

To Marcus Mindius Marcellus, son of Marcus, prefect of the fleet; the nauarchs and trierarchs in the service of Caesar to their patron.

[504] *EJ 271*
Near Tuder, Umbria

Gaius Edusius, son of Sextus, of the tribe Clustumina, born at Mevania, centurion of legion 41 of Augustus Caesar and centurion of the fleet, by his will.

[505] *EJ 272*
Misenum

To Gaius Julius Automatus, freedman of Caesar, trierarch; Julia Plusia, freedwoman of Gaius, his sister, made this, also for herself and her family.

[506] *EJ 273*
Naples

Tiberius Julius Diogenes, freedman of Augustus and Augusta, trierarch, for himself and Nigidia Eutychia, his wife, and his family. Nigidia Eutychia for Staberia Margarita, freedwoman of Gaius, her friend. This monument will not pass to an heir.

[507] *EJ 274*
Brundisium

Julia Cleopatra, also known as Lezbia, daughter of Gaius Julius Menoetes, of Syrian Antioch by Daphne, wife of Malchio, trierarch of Caesar in the trireme Triptolemus.

[508] *EJ 275*
Puteoli

Gaius Julius Dama, freedman of Malchio, freedman of Caesar Augustus, . . . for himself and Julia Tertia, his wedded wife . . . and his freedmen and freedwomen and their descendants . . . Frontage . . . feet, 50 ft back.

[509] *EJ 276*
Forum Julii

To Anthus, Livian trierarch of Caesar; Gaius Julius Jason had this made.

[510] *EJ 277*
Rome

To Tiberius Julius Hilarus, freedman of Augustus, Tiberian nauarch; Claudia Basilea to her husband.

[511] *EJ 361*
11-12, Nisyra, Lydia

Year 96,[1] the colonists of Nisyra honoured Gaius Aemilius Geminus, centurion of Caesar Augustus of legion 7, for his utter virtue and generosity on behalf of Marcus Antonius, their colonist.

1. Of the Sullan era.

[512] *Small. 276*
Sestertius, 37-8, Rome

Obv. Head of Gaius, laureate. GAIUS CAESAR AUGUSTUS GERMANICUS, PONTIFEX MAXIMUS, WITH TRIBUNICIAN POWER

Rev. Gaius standing on a platform addressing five soldiers, four carrying standards. ADDRESS OF THE COHORTS.

[513] *Small. 277*
28th April 39, Syene, Egypt

To Gaius Caesar Augustus Germanicus, great grandson of the divine
Augustus, grandson of Tiberius Caesar Augustus, son of Germanicus
Caesar, consul twice, with tribunician power, pontifex maximus,
imperator, father of his country, through Gaius Vitrasius Pollio, prefect
of Egypt, the cohort of Ituraeans which is commanded by Lucius
Eienus Saturninus, son of Lucius, of the tribe Falerna, in year 3 of
Gaius Caesar Augustus Germanicus, 28th April, m ndh 3.[1]

1. The meaning of these letters is not known.

[514] *Small. 278*
Carinola, Campania

To Tiberius Julius Italicus, son of Tiberius, of the tribe Falerna, centurion of legion 7 Macedonica, centurion of legion 15 Primigenia,
centurion of legion 13 Gemina, chief centurion . . . decurion . . .

[515] *Small. 280*
Near Praeneste; cf. Suet. *Claud.* 25

To . . . Varus, son of Publius, of the tribe Aniensis, prefect of engineers,
prefect of the German cohort, prefect of cavalry, military tribune of
legion 5; to . . . Varus, son of Publius, of the tribe Aniensis, quaestor,
praetor, priest, praetor quinquennalis of Capitulum Hernicorum, son
. . . made . . . and for himself.

[516] *Small. 281*
Antioch, near Pisidia

To Publius Anicius Maximus, son of Publius, of the tribe Sergia, prefect
of Gnaeus Domitius Ahenobarbus,[1] chief centurion of legion 12
Fulminata, camp-prefect of legion 2 Augusta in Britain, prefect of the
army in Egypt, awarded military gifts by the imperator for the expedi-

tion, honoured with an assault-crown and a headless spear for the British war; the city of Alexandria in Egypt established this.

1. Father of Nero, consul in AD 32.

[517] *Small. 282*
Augusta Taurinorum; cf. Tac. *Ann.* 15.50 ff.

To Gaius Gavius Silvanus, son of Lucius, of the tribe Stellatina, chief centurion of legion 8 Augusta, tribune of cohort 2 of the watch, tribune of urban cohort 13, tribune of praetorian cohort 12, awarded gifts by the divine Claudius in the British war, torcs, arm-bands, discs, a gold crown; the colony to its patron by decree of the decurions.

[518] *Small. 283*
66, Ariminum

To Marcus Vettius Valens, son of Marcus, of the tribe Aniensis, soldier of praetorian cohort 8, beneficiarius[1] of the praetorian prefect, awarded gifts in the British war, torcs, arm-bands, discs, ordered out by Augustus, awarded a gold crown, centurion of cohort 6 of the watch, centurion of messengers, centurion of urban cohort 16, centurion of praetorian cohort 2, driller of cavalry-scouts, headquarters first-officer of legion 13 Gemina from being scout-centurion, chief centurion of legion 6 Victrix, awarded gifts for successful achievements against the Astures, torcs, discs, arm-bands, tribune of cohort 5 of the watch, tribune of urban cohort 12, tribune of praetorian cohort 3, tribune of legion 14 Gemina Mars Victrix, procurator of Imperator Nero Caesar Augustus of the province of Lusitania, patron of the colony, scouts established this in the consulship of Lucius Luccius Telesinus and Gaius Suetonius Paulinus.

1. A soldier granted special privileges.

[519] *Small. 284 19(a)*

Mid-first century (?), Colchester. Tombstone with relief of a cavalry-man spearing a fallen barbarian

Longinus, son of Sdapezematygus, duplicarius[1] of the 1st. Thracian cavalry, from the district of Serdica, aged 40, with 15 years' service; his heirs had this made in accordance with his will. He lies here.

1. Soldier rewarded with double pay.

[520] *Small. 284(b)*

Mid-first century (?), Colchester. Tombstone with a relief of a centurion

Marcus Favonius Facilis, son of Marcus, of the tribe Pollia, centurion of legion 20; Verecundus and Novicius, his freedmen, set this up. He lies here.

[521] *Small. 285*

Castulo, Tarraconensis; cf. Tac. *Ann.* 12.63

To Quintus Cornelius Valerinus, son of Marcus, of the tribe Galeria, prefect of cavalry ... prefect of 15 detachments in Thrace, awarded statues and crowns by ... legion 5 Macedonica, by legion 8 Augusta, by the tribunes of senatorial and lesser rank and by the prefects of cohorts, ... and of cohort Servia Juvenalis ... , and to Titia Optata, daughter of Lucius, his wife; to this person the colony ...

[522] *Small. 286*

(a) Oescus, Moesia

Under Tiberius Claudius Caesar Augustus Germanicus, son of Drusus, pontifex maximus, with tribunician power, consul twice, legion 5 Macedonica to Lucius Martius Macer, son of Lucius, propraetorian legate of Augustus.

(b) 44, on the Danube, Moesia

Under Tiberius Claudius Caesar Augustus Germanicus, son of Drusus, pontifex maximus, in his fourth year of tribunician power, consul designate, imperator, legion 4 Scythica and legion 5 Macedonica in the charge of Martius Macer, propraetorian legate of Augustus.

[523] *Small. 287*
47-8, legionary camp, Vindonissa, Upper Germany

Under Tiberius Claudius Caesar Augustus Germanicus, imperator 12 times, pontifex maximus, in his 7th year of tribunician power, consul four times, father of his country, ... being propraetorian legate of Augustus, Marcus Senecio being legate of Augustus; legion 21 Rapax.

[524] *Small. 288*
52-4, legionary camp, Bonna, Lower Germany

Under Tiberius Claudius Caesar Augustus Germanicus, son of Drusus, pontifex maximus, in his ... year of tribunician power, imperator 27 times, consul 5 times, father of his country, ... being propraetorian legate of Augustus, ... being legate of Augustus; legion 1.

[525] *Small. 289*
Cos

Tiberius Claudius Cleonymus, son of Heracleitus, of the tribe Quirina, the brother of Gaius Stertinius Xenophon, having served in Germany as military tribune of legion 22 Primigenia, having twice been monarch[1] and having often acted as ambassador on behalf of his country to the Augusti; Claudia Phoebe honoured her husband and benefactor for his virtue and kindness.

1. The eponymous magistracy of Cos.

[526] *Small. 290*
Modicia, near Mediolanum

Gaius Sertorius Tertullus, son of Lucius, of the tribe Oufentina, veteran of legion 16, curator of Roman citizens at Moguntiacum ...

[527] *Small. 291*
Tergeste, Histria; cf. Tac. *Ann*. 13.30

Publius Palpellius Clodius Quirinalis, son of Publius, of the tribe Maecia, chief centurion of legion 20, military tribune of legion 7 Claudia pious and loyal, procurator of Augustus, prefect of the fleet, gave this.

[528] *Small. 292*
Sestertius, 64-6, Rome

Obv. Head of Nero, laureate. NERO CLAUDIUS CAESAR AUGUSTUS
GERMANICUS, e.g. PONTIFEX MAXIMUS, WITH TRIBUNICIAN
POWER, IMPERATOR, FATHER OF HIS COUNTRY
Rev. Nero standing on a platform with the praetorian prefect behind
him, addressing two soldiers with standards and one without.
ADDRESS OF THE COHORTS, BY DECREE OF THE SENATE

[529] *Small. 293*
Rome

Indus, bodyguard of Nero Claudius Caesar Augustus, in the decuria of
Secundus, by nation a Batavian, lived 36 years. He lies here. Set up by
Eumenes, his brother and heir, of the college of Germans.

[530] *Small. 294*
Near Rome, on the Via Nomentana

To Nymphodotus, freedman of Augustus, record-keeper; Statoria
Nephele to the best of husbands and the four Tiberii Julii — Julianus,
prefect of engineers, tribune of cohort 8 of volunteers in Dalmatia,
Justus, Probus and Pius — and Julia Statorina, and Julius Primianus,
son of Julianus, his grandson, to the best of fathers and a kindly one,
and for themselves and their descendants.

[531] *Small. 295*
11 Dec. 52, Stabiae, Campania

Tiberius Claudius Caesar Augustus Germanicus, pontifex maximus, in
his 12th year of tribunician power, imperator 27 times, father of his
country, censor, consul 5 times, has given to the trierarchs and oarsmen
who served in the fleet at Misenum under Tiberius Julius Optatus,
freedman of Augustus, and have been dismissed with an honourable
discharge, their names being written below, to these men themselves,
to their children and descendants he has given citizenship and conubium with the wives they had on receipt of citizenship or, if they
were bachelors, with the wives they married afterwards, provided that
one man had one wife.

11th December, in the consulship of Faustus Cornelius Sulla Felix
and Lucius Salvidienus Rufus Salvianus.

For common soldier Sparticus Dipscurtus, son of Diuzenus, a Bessian.

Copied and authenticated from the bronze tablet which is posted at Rome, on the Capitol, in the temple of the Good Faith of the Roman people on the right-hand side.

Of Lucius Mestius Priscus, son of Lucius, of the tribe Aemilia, from Dyrrachium, of Lucius Nutrius Venustus, from Dyrrachium, of Gaius Dyrrachinus Anthus, from Dyrrachium, of Gaius Sabinus Nedymus, from Dyrrachium, of Gaius Cornelius Ampliatus, from Dyrrachium, of Titus Pomponius Epaphroditus, from Dyrrachium, of Numerius Minius Hylas, from Thessalonica.

[532] *Small. 296*
2nd July 60, military diploma, Vindobona, Pannonia

Nero Claudius Caesar Augustus Germanicus, son of the divine Claudius, grandson of Germanicus Caesar, great-grandson of Tiberius Caesar Augustus, great-great-grandson of the divine Augustus, pontifex maximus, in his 7th year of tribunician power, imperator 7 times, consul 4 times, has given to the infantry and cavalry who served in the 7 cohorts which are called (1) 1st Astures and Callaeci and (2) 1st Spanish and (3) 1st Alpines and (4) 1st Lusitanians and (5) 2nd Alpines and (6) 2nd Spanish and (7) 5th Lucenses and Callaeci and are in Illyricum under Lucius Salvidienus Salvianus Rufus, who have each served 25 years or more, their names being written below, to these men themselves, to their children and descendants he has given citizenship and conubium with the wives they had on receipt of citizenship or, if they were bachelors, with the wives they married afterwards, provided that one man had one wife.

2nd July, in the consulship of Gnaeus Pedanius Salinator and Lucius Velleius Paterculus.

Of the 2nd Spanish cohort, which is commanded by Gaius Caesius Aper, the cavalryman Iantumarus Varcianus, son of Andedunes.

Copied and authenticated from the bronze tablet which is posted on the Capitol, on the left side of the holy-wagon building, on the outside.

[533] *Small. 297*
63, the prefect of Egypt and a military delegation, apparently an official version and the version of the soldiers

(a) Copy from a journal.
In the tenth year of Nero Claudius Caesar Augustus Germanicus, imperator, seventh of the month Augustus, in the Great Hall, on the platform; present at the council were Norbanus Ptolemy, administrator of justice and officer of the Idios Logos, Aquillius Quadratus and Tennius Vetus ... Atticus, Papirius Pastor and Baebius Juncinus, tribunes, Julius Lysimachus, Claudius Heracleides, finance-officer, Claudius Euctemon and Claudius Secundus.

On discharged soldiers, concerning the citizenship:

Tuscus: I have already told you that the status of each of you is neither similar nor the same: some of you are veterans from the legions, others from the cavalry, others from the cohorts and others from the navy, so that you do not have the same rights. I will see to this matter and I have written to the strategi of each nome to ensure that the award to each of you is completely protected according to the rights of each man ... I wrote ...

(b) Copy of an audience.
With regard to the legionaries. On the camp road by the temple of Isis. Tuscus the prefect gave this reply to us:

Don't blaspheme! No one is causing you trouble. Write down on tablets where you are each posted and I shall write to the strategi that no one should bother you.

On the fourth of the month of Augustus, we gave him the tablets at his headquarters and he said to us:

Have you given me them separately, separately?

And the legionaries replied:

We have given them separately.

On the 5th of the same month we greeted him by the Thorn Bush and he returned our greeting, and on the ... of the same month we greeted him in the Hall, as he sat on the tribunal. Tuscus said to us:

I told you in the camp and I tell you the same thing again now. The life of the legionaries is one thing, that of the cohorts another and that of the navy another still. Attend to your own duties, each of you, and look sharp.

[534] *Small. 298*
16th March 65, Thebes, Egypt, on the statue of Memnon

Aulus Instuleius Tenax, chief centurion of legion 12 Fulminata, and Gaius Valerius Priscus, centurion of legion 22, and Lucius Quintius Viator, decurion; we heard Memnon, year 11 of Nero, our imperator, 16th March, . . . hour.

6 THE IMPERIAL ADMINISTRATION

[535] *EJ 303* with *RDGE* no. 60
31 BC, letter of Octavian to Mylasa, Caria

Imperator Caesar, son of the divine Julius, consul designate for the third time, to the magistrates, council and people of the Mylasans, greetings. If you fare well, it would be well. I too am well with my army.

In the past too you sent embassies to me, before, concerning the fate that has befallen you, and now there have come before me the envoys Ouliades ... [gap of uncertain length] ... that ... fell ... of the enemy and the city was taken and that many captured citizens were lost, many murdered, some even burnt with the city, the barbarism of the enemy not even sparing the holiest shrines and temples. And they informed me also about the plundering of the countryside and the burning of homesteads, so that you met misfortune in every way. In regard to all this I knew that you had suffered these things and that you had earned honour and favour from the Romans ...

[536] *EJ 304*
Letter of Octavian to Gaius Norbanus Flaccus. Josephus, *Jewish Antiquities*, 16.166

Caesar to Norbanus Flaccus, greetings.

The Jews, however many there may be, who in accordance with their ancient practice are accustomed to collect sacred money and send it to Jerusalem, are to do this without hindrance.

[537] *EJ 305*
Letter of Gaius Norbanus Flaccus to Sardis. Josephus, *Jewish Antiquities*, 16.171

Gaius Norbanus Flaccus, proconsul, to the magistrates and council of the Sardians, greetings.

Caesar has written to me instructing me that the Jews, however many there may be, are not to be prevented from collecting money and sending it to Jerusalem in accordance with their ancestral custom. I have therefore written to you so that you may know that Caesar and I wish this to be done.

[538] *EJ 306*
Letter of Gaius Norbanus Flaccus to Ephesus. Philo, *Embassy to Gaius*, 315

Gaius Norbanus Flaccus, proconsul, to the magistrates of the Ephesians, greetings.

Caesar has written to me that the Jews, wherever they may be, are accustomed, in accordance with their own ancient practice, to gather and contribute money which they send to Jerusalem. It is his wish that they not be prevented from doing this. I have therefore written to you so that you may know that he orders this to be done.

[539] *EJ 307* with *RDGE*, no. 26
25 BC, senatorial decrees on a treaty with Mytilene

A
Decree of the Senate concerning the treaty. In the consulship of Imperator Caesar Augustus for the ninth time and of Marcus Silanus . . . by order of Marcus Silanus after senatorial decree . . . June in the Curia Julia. Present at the drafting were Paulus Aemilius Lepidus, son of Lucius, of the tribe Palatina, Gaius Asinius Pollio, son of Gnaeus . . . Lucius Sempronius Atratinus, son of Lucius, of the tribe Falerna, Marcus Terentius Varro, son of Marcus, of the tribe Papiria, Gaius Junius Silanus . . . Quintus Acutius, son of Quintus . . .

With regard to the statement of Marcus Silanus that a letter was sent to Imperator Caesar Augustus, his fellow consul, and a reply obtained, so that, if the Senate wishes that a treaty be concluded with the Mytilenaeans, the arrangement of the matter be entrusted to Silanus himself, on this matter the following was decreed:

That Marcus Silanus, consul, if he thinks fit, should arrange the conclusion of a treaty with the Mytilenaeans and whatever else seems to be in accord with the public interest and his own good faith. Decreed.

B
June 29th in . . . Present at the drafting were Gaius Norbanus Flaccus, son of Gaius . . . son of Appius, of the tribe Palatina . . . Censorinus . . . Marcus Valerius . . . son of Marcus . . . of the tribe Clustumina . . . Marcus Terentius Varro, son of Marcus, of the tribe Papiria, Gaius . . .

With regard to the statement of Marcus Silanus that he had fully obeyed the decree of the Senate given to him, that, if he should think fit, he should arrange for the conclusion of a treaty with the Mytilenaeans and whatever else might seem to be in accord with the public interest and his own good faith; that it remained to deal with the consequences of this matter; on this matter the following was decreed:

That Marcus Silanus, consul, if he thinks fit, should arrange that the treaty be sent to the Mytilenaeans, as settled, and that this and the decrees of the Senate issued on this matter should be inscribed . . . on a bronze tablet and set up in public. Decreed.

C

In the consulship of Imperator Caesar Augustus for the ninth time and of Marcus Silanus . . . [gap of about 30 lines] . . .

Let the people of the Mytilenaeans keep the power and the might which it has hitherto held, whatever is held with the best justice and best legal right.

Let the people of the Mytilenaeans not allow enemies of the Roman people to pass through its own territory with public approval so as to make war upon the Roman people or its subjects or its allies and let it not help them with weapons, money or ships.

Let the Roman people not allow the enemies of the people of the Mytilenaeans to pass through its own land and its own territory with public approval so as to make war upon the people of the Mytilenaeans or its subjects or its allies and let it not help them with weapons, money or ships.

If anyone should begin a war with the people of the Mytilenaeans or with the Roman people and the allies of the Roman people, let the Roman people help the people of the Mytilenaeans and the people of the Mytilenaeans the Roman people and the allies of the Roman people . . . and let it be firm.

Let there be peace for all time . . .

[540] *EJ 308*

Letter of Agrippa to the Gerusia of Argos

Of the gerontes.

Agrippa to the Argive gerontes, descendants of Danaus and Hypermestra, greetings.

I know because I have been told why your assembly has lasted and retained its ancient dignity; and I have restored to you many rights which had lapsed. And, for the future, I am eager to take care of you and the . . .

[541] *EJ 309*

Letter of Agrippa to Ephesus. Josephus, *Jewish Antiquities*, 16. 167-8

Agrippa to the magistrates, council and people of the Ephesians, greetings.

It is my wish that the Jews of Asia, in accordance with their ancestral custom, exercise the care and custody of the sacred money conveyed to the temple in Jerusalem. And that those who steal the sacred money of the Jews and flee to asylum be dragged out and handed over to the Jews under that law by which temple-robbers are dragged out. I have also written to Silanus, the praetor, that no one should force a Jew to agree to bail on the Sabbath.

[542] *EJ 310*

Letter of Agrippa to Cyrene. Josephus, *Jewish Antiquities*, 16. 169-70

Marcus Agrippa to the magistrates, council and people of the Cyrenians, greetings.

On behalf of the Jews of Cyrene Augustus has already written to the the praetor in Libya, Flavius, and to the other officials of the province that the sacred money should be sent to Jerusalem in accordance with their ancestral custom without hindrance. They have now come before me to complain that they are being threatened by certain informers and prevented from sending the money on the pretext of tax payments which are not due. I order that reparation be made to them, that they be in no way molested and that, in whatever cities the sacred money has been taken, those charged with those matters restore that money to the Jews there.

[543] *EJ 311*

7-6 BC and 4 BC, Cyrene. Edicts of Augustus and a decree of the Senate on extortion

A

Imperator Caesar Augustus, pontifex maximus, in his 17th year of tribunician power, imperator 14 times, proclaims:

Since I find that there are in total 215 Romans of every age in the province of Cyrene who have a census rating of 2,500 denarii or more, from which number jurors are drawn, and that within this number exist certain cliques; and since embassies from the cities of the province have complained that these cliques have acted oppressively against Greeks on capital charges, when the same people take it in turns to act as prosecutors and witnesses; and since I have myself learnt that innocent individuals have been oppressed in this way and have been consigned to the ultimate penalty, it is my view that, until the Senate deliberates on this matter or I myself come up with something better, the governors of the province of Crete and Cyrenaica will act well and properly if they appoint the same number of Greek jurors from the highest census groups in the province of Cyrene as of Romans, none being younger than 25, whether Greek or Roman, and none having a census rating and property (if there is a sufficient number of such men) of less than 7,500 denarii; or if on this system the number of jurors needed cannot be attained, let them appoint as jurors in capital cases men with half – and not less than half – this census rating.

And if a Greek is on trial, being permitted the right, on the day before the accuser begins his statement, to decide whether he wants the jury to be Roman or half Greek, and chooses that half the jurors be Greek, then balls are to be apportioned and inscribed with names. The names of the Romans are to be drawn from one urn, the names of the Greeks from the other, until 25 of each race have been selected: of these the prosecutor may, if he wishes, challenge one of each race, and the defendant may challenge a total of three, provided that these are neither all Romans or all Greeks. Then all those remaining are to be set aside for jury duty and are to cast their votes separately, the Romans in one urn, the Greeks in another. When the votes from both have been separately counted, the governor is to declare publicly the judgement of the majority of all the jurors.

Further, since, by and large, relatives of the deceased do not overlook illegal killings and leave them unavenged, and since it is probable that there will be no shortage of Greeks to accuse those responsible and to bring an action on behalf of dead relatives or fellow citizens, it is my view that governors of Crete and Cyrene will act correctly and properly if, in the province of Cyrene, they do not permit a Roman to bring an accusation against a Greek over the killing of a Greek man or woman, except in a case where a Greek honoured with Roman citizenship brings an action over the death of one of his relatives or fellow citizens.

B

Imperator Caesar Augustus, pontifex maximus, in his 17th year of tribunician power, proclaims:

There is no need for malice and censure to be directed against Publius Sextius Scaeva, over Aulus Stlaccius Maximus, son of Lucius, and Lucius Stlaccius Macedo, son of Lucius, and Publius Lacutanius Phileros, freedman of Publius, because he sent them to me from the province of Cyrenaica in chains when they declared that they knew something bearing on my safety and affairs of state and wanted to divulge it. In this matter, Sextius acted properly and responsibly. However, since they know nothing bearing on myself or affairs of state and since they have made it clear to me that they were mistaken and deluded in the statement they made in the province I have freed and dismissed them from custody. As for Aulus Stlaccius Maximus, whom Cyrenian envoys accuse of having removed statues from public places and amongst these one on whose base the city had inscribed my name, I am preventing him from leaving Rome without my permission until I have come to a decision on this matter.

C

Imperator Caesar Augustus, pontifex maximus, in his 17th year of tribunician power, proclaims:

I order that whoever has been honoured with Roman citizenship in the province of Cyrenaica is to perform liturgies in his full share with the body of Greeks, with the exception of those to whom immunity from taxation was granted together with the citizenship by law or decree of the Senate or by the decree of my father or myself. As for those to whom immunity from taxation has been granted, it is my wish that they should be exempt from taxation upon the property they possessed at the time of the grant but that they should pay taxes upon all subsequent acquisitions.

D

Imperator Caesar Augustus, pontifex maximus, in his 17th year of tribunician power, proclaims:

With regard to any disputes that may arise among Greeks in the province of Cyrenaica, excepting capital cases — in these the provincial governor must himself act and judge or appoint a panel of jurors, but in the rest of such affairs it is my wish that Greek jurors be appointed unless the person accused or under examination wishes to have a jury of Roman citizens. But, with regard to those granted Greek jurors by this, my decree, it is my wish that no juror be from that city to which the prosecutor or the examiner or the person accused or under examination belongs.

E

Imperator Caesar Augustus, pontifex maximus, in his 19th year of tribunician power, proclaims:

I have decided to send to the provinces the decree of the Senate passed in the consulship of Gaius Calvisius and Lucius Passienus when I was present and shared in the drafting, a decree pertaining to the security of the allies of the Roman people, so that it may be known to all those whom we protect; and I have decided to add to it my own preface, from which it will be clear to all the inhabitants of the provinces how much care we take, the Senate and I, that none of our subjects suffer any improper treatment or exaction.

Decree of the Senate:

With regard to the statement of Gaius Calvisius Sabinus and Lucius Passienus Rufus, consuls, concerning matters which Imperator Caesar Augustus, our princeps, in accordance with the decision of his advisers, chosen from the Senate by lot, wanted us to bring before the Senate, matters bearing upon the security of the allies of the Roman people, the Senate decreed:

Given that our ancestors legally established courts for the recovery of property in order that our allies when deprived of property might more easily be able to come and take possession of what had been wrongfully seized; and since by their very nature such courts have sometimes been most burdensome and disagreeable for the very people on whose account the measure was enacted — the provinces being a great distance away to drag witnesses who are poor people or, in some cases, frail through illness or old age — it is the wish of the Senate that if, subsequent to this senatorial decree, any among the allies wish to reclaim property exacted publicly or privately (provided that the accused is not already on a capital charge) they should make themselves known to one of the magistrates empowered to convene the Senate; the magistrate should bring them before the Senate as soon as possible and should appoint an advocate of their choice to speak for them in the Senate. No one should act as advocate against his will if he has been granted the legal privilege of refusing this public service.

In order that the case they bring before the Senate may be heard, the magistrate who gives them access to the Senate, on the same day, in the presence of at least 200 senators in the Senate, should choose by lot four men out of all those of consular rank either in Rome itself or within twenty miles of the city. In the same way, three men from all those of praetorian rank either in Rome itself or within twenty miles of the city. In the same way, two men from all the rest of those with senatorial rank or all those who have the right to give their opinion in the Senate who may then be in Rome or within a distance of twenty miles from the city. But he should not choose by lot any man aged seventy or older, or one holding a magistracy or office or one presiding in a court or one in charge of grain distribution or one prevented by illness from performing this public service, once any such man has sworn an oath before the Senate and produced three senators to swear to his incapacity; nor should he choose by lot anyone who is a relative or kin of the defendant so that under the Julian law on courts he cannot be compelled to give evidence as a witness in a public court against his will; nor should he choose by lot one whom the defendant swears before the Senate to be his personal enemy, provided that he does not disqualify more than three persons by so swearing. When nine men have been chosen by lot in this fashion, the magistrate who drew the lots is to see to it that within two days those seeking their property and the man from whom they seek it take turns at challenging those chosen until five remain. Should any of these jurors die before he has heard the case or should there be some other reason preventing him from acting as juror — provided that his excuse is accepted, five senators having sworn to it — then the magistrate, in the presence of the jurors and those seeking their property and the man from whom they seek it, is to choose by lot from those men of the same rank and who have held the same magistracies as the men being replaced, provided that the chosen replacement is not a man ineligible to serve in a case against the defendant by the terms of this decree of the Senate.

The chosen jurors are to hear the case and come to their decision only with regard to what the defendant is alleged to have taken publicly or privately and they are to order the return of no more than the amount of property which the plaintiffs show to have been taken from them, provided that the jurors make their decision within thirty days. Those persons required to decide and pronounce judgement in this matter are to be exempted from all public service, with the exception of public religious duties, until they have decided and have pronounced judgement.

And it is the wish of the Senate that the magistrate who chose the jurors by lot or, if he is unable, the ranking consul preside over this hearing and permit the calling of witnesses who are in Italy, provided that he does not allow the plaintiff on a private matter to call more than five and the plaintiff on a public matter to call more than ten. In the same way, it is the wish of the Senate that the jurors chosen under the terms of this decree declare their individual decisions openly and that the decision declared by the majority constitute the verdict.

[544] *EJ 365 = RDGE*, no. 61

A pronouncement of Augustus and Agrippa, 27 BC, and a letter of one Vinicius, proconsul of Asia, Cyme. Cf. P.A. Brunt and J.M. Moore (eds.), *Res Gestae Divi Augusti* (1967) p. 66

A

Imperator Caesar Augustus, son of a god, for the seventh time, and Marcus Agrippa, son of Lucius, consuls, proclaim:

If there are any public or sacred places in cities or in the territory of each city of the province and if there are or will be any dedications at these places, let no one remove them or buy them or receive them as a present from anybody. Whatever may be removed from there or bought or given as a present, let the governor of the province, whoever he may be, ensure that it is replaced in its public or sacred place in the city and let him not administer justice with regard to what has been immediately returned.

B

Lucius (?)[1] Vinicius sends greetings to the magistrates of Cyme.

Apollonides, son of Lucius, the Noracean, your fellow citizen, has come to me and pointed out that the temple of Liber Pater is in the possession, by virtue of a sale, of Lysias, son of Diogenes, the Tucallean, your fellow citizen, and since the worshippers wanted to restore the sacred property to the god in accordance with the order of Augustus Caesar, after paying the price written on the temple of Liber Pater by Lysias. It is my wish that you ensure, if this is indeed the situation, that Lysias receives the price stated on the temple and restores the temple to the god and that on the temple is inscribed: 'Restored by Imperator Caesar Augustus, son of a god.' However, if Lysias contests the claims of Apollonides, let him give . . .

1. An uncertain restoration.

[545] *EJ 312* with *RDGE*, no. 67

Latter half of 6 BC, letter of Augustus to Cnidus

Imperator Caesar Augustus, son of a god, pontifex maximus, consul designate for the twelfth time, in his 18th year of tribunician power, to the magistrates, council and people of the Cnidians, greetings.

Your envoys Dionysius, son of Dionysius, and Dionysius, son of Dionysius, son of Dionysius, came before me at Rome and, presenting the decree, laid an accusation against Eubulus, son of Anaxandridas, now deceased, and against his surviving wife, Tryphera, with regard to the death of Eubulus, son of Chrysippus. I instructed Asinius Gallus, my friend, to interrogate under torture those slaves involved in the charge and I discovered that Philinus, son of Chrysippus, went on three consecutive nights, arrogantly, to the house of Eubulus and Tryphera and laid siege to it, so to speak, and that on the third night his brother, Eubulus, joined in. The owners of the house, Eubulus and Tryphera, since they had no business with Philinus and since they were besieged by his attacks and could find no safety in their own house, ordered one of their slaves not to commit murder, as, perhaps, rage might have led a man to do with some justice, but rather to remove them by scattering excrement over them. The slave dropped the chamber-pot with the excrement, whether deliberately or by accident — he was persistent in his denial of intent; Eubulus fell beneath it, though it would have been more just if his brother had been the victim. I have sent you the very replies of the slaves.

I am rather surprised that the defendants were so afraid lest the slaves be interrogated in your city, unless it is the case that they thought you unsympathetic to their cause and contrarily hostile in your anger not with those deserving to suffer any fate — going to the house of others with arrogance and violence on three occasions and destroying the common safety of you all — but with those who have been unfortunate even in defending themselves, though they have committed no crime at all. Now you will act rightly in my eyes if you take heed of my opinion of this affair and acknowledge my letter in your public records. Farewell.

[546] *EJ 313*

Letter of Iullus Antonius to Ephesus. Josephus, *Jewish Antiquities*, 16. 172-3.

Iullus Antonius, proconsul . . . to the magistrates, council and people of the Ephesians, greetings.

While I was dispensing justice at Ephesus on February 13th, the Jews resident in Asia pointed out to me that Caesar Augustus and Agrippa permitted them to follow their own ways and customs and to make, without hindrance, the contributions which each of them makes by his own choice out of piety towards the divinity, coming together for its conveyance. And they asked that I should confirm my opinion in conformity to the statements of Augustus and Agrippa. Therefore it is my wish that you know that I share the desires of Augustus and Agrippa in permitting them to behave and act in accordance with their ancestral customs, without hindrance.

[547] *EJ 314*

Edict of Augustus. Josephus, *Jewish Antiquities*, 16. 162-5

Caesar Augustus, pontifex maximus, in his ... year of tribunician power, proclaims:

Since the Jewish nation has proved to be well-disposed to the Roman people, not only at the present time, but also in the past and especially at the time of my father, Imperator Caesar, – and their high-priest Hyrcanus too – I and my council have decided under oath, with the approval of the Roman people, that the Jews are to follow their own customs in accordance with their ancestral law, just as they did under Hyrcanus, high-priest of the highest god, and that their sacred money is to be inviolate and sent to Jerusalem and given over to the treasurers in Jerusalem; and that they are not to agree to bail on the Sabbath or after the ninth hour on the day of preparation before it. And that whoever is caught stealing their sacred books or sacred money from a synagogue or hall is to be deemed a temple-robber and his property confiscated to the Roman treasury. And I order that the decree made for me, for the piety I exhibit towards all mankind, and for Gaius Marcius Censorinus, together with this edict, be set up in the most conspicuous place assigned to me by the league of Asia at Ancyra. And if anyone contravenes the above he will pay an extreme penalty.

[548] *EJ 315*

3 BC, oath of Gangra, near Neapolis, Paphlagonia

From the twelfth consulship of Imperator Caesar Augustus, son of a god, being the third year of the province, March 8th at Gangra in the market-place; the oath sworn by the inhabitants of Paphlagonia and the Romans in business among them:

I swear by Zeus, Earth, Sun, all the gods and goddesses and by Augustus himself that I will support Caesar Augustus and his children and descendants throughout my lifetime in word and deed and thought, regarding their friends as my friends and considering their enemies to be my enemies; and that in their interests I shall spare neither body nor soul nor life nor children, but shall endure any danger in any way in their service. That whatever I may observe or hear spoken or plotted or done against them I shall report and shall be the enemy of he who so speaks or plots or does. That whoever they adjudge to be enemies I shall pursue and repel with arms and sword by land and sea.

If I should do anything contrary to this oath or not in conformity with what I have sworn, I call down complete and utter destruction upon myself and my body and soul and life and children and all my family and property in every generation of myself and my descendants. And may neither land nor sea receive the bodies of mine or my descendants and may they not give sustenance to them.

The same oath was sworn by all those in the land in the local temples of Augustus at the altars of Augustus. In the same way the Phazimonites who inhabit what is now called Neapolis all swore the oath in the temple of Augustus by the altar of Augustus.

[549] *EJ 316* with *RDGE*, no. 69

1 BC, Nysa-on-the-Maeander, Asia. A famous temple of Pluto and Kore, with a sacred cave, the Charonicum, lay on the road between Tralles and Nysa. It received special privileges from the Hellenistic kings: in the following text the Roman governor approves the restoration of documents containing these privileges and thus tacitly confirms them

[Beginning is lost] . . . the priest of Rome and Imperator Caesar Augustus being Heracleides, son of Heracleides, of Mastaura, the stephanephorus being Diomedes, son of Athenagoras, son of Diomedes, priest of Capitoline Zeus for life, Gorpiaeus 19th August 12th, in the consulship of Cossus Cornelius Lentulus and Lucius Piso, when the secretary of the people was Heliodorus, son of Maeandrius, son of Theodotus, priest of Tiberius Claudius Nero for life.

Artemidorus, son of Demetrius, son of Papa, one of the generals of the city, following his remit, restored to the archive the sacred documents concerning the gods and their inviolability and the receipt of suppliants and the immunity of the temple from taxation, after informing the proconsul, Gnaeus Lentulus Augur, and receiving the following letter:

In the year of Diomedes, son of Athenagoras, Daesius 17th, Gnaeus Lentulus Augur, proconsul, to the magistrates of the Nysaeans.

Artemidorus, son of Demetrius, son of Papa, has asked if it is necessary . . .

[550] *EJ 317* with *RDGE*, no. 70

About 4-5, letter of a proconsul to Chios

[Beginning is lost] . . . belonging to Staphylus . . . to the Chian envoys . . . when they read out a letter of Antistius Vetus, the proconsul before me, a most illustrious man. Following my general policy of honouring the writings of my proconsular predecessors, I considered it reasonable to adhere in particular to the letter of Vetus adduced with regard to this matter. Subsequently, however, I heard each side presenting its case in turn concerning the matter at issue and asked from each side more carefully drafted documents, as is my practice. When I received these and stopped at the relevant place, I found a very old (by its date) sealed copy of a senatorial decree issued in the second consulship of Lucius Sulla,[1] in which — when the Chians had testified to the degree of their vigorous support for Rome against Mithridates and the amount they had suffered at his hands — the Senate specifically confirmed that they might follow the laws and customs and rights which they possessed when they entered the friendship of Rome, in order that they should not be subject to any regulation whatsoever of magistrates or promagistrates and that those Romans residing among them should be subject to Chian laws. And a letter of Imperator Augustus, son of a god, consul for the eighth time,[2] writing to the Chians . . . concerning the freedom of the city . . .

1. 80 BC.
2. 26 BC.

[551] *EJ 105** = T.B. Mitford, *JRS*, 50 (1960) pp. 75-9
14, Palaepaphos, Cyprus. An oath of loyalty to Tiberius

By our Aphrodite of the Promontory and our Kore and our Apollo Hylates and our Apollo Cerynetes and our Saviour Dioscuri and Hestia Boulaea, shared on the island, and the ancestral gods and goddesses shared on the island and the descendant of Aphrodite, the Divine Augustus Caesar, and eternal Rome and all the other gods and goddesses.

We, ourselves and our descendants, swear that we shall heed and obey by land and sea and shall be loyal and reverent . . . Tiberius Caesar Augustus, son of Augustus, with his whole house, and shall have the same friends and enemies as they, and shall introduce a decree for sacred honours for, together with the other gods, Rome and Tiberius Caesar Augustus, son of Augustus . . . and to the sons of his blood alone and to no other at all . . .

[552] S. Mitchell, *JRS*, 66 (1976) pp. 106-31
About AD 14 (?), Pisidia, bilingual

Sextus Sotidius Strabo Libuscidianus, propraetorian legate of Tiberius Caesar Augustus, proclaims:

Of all things it is the most inequitable that I, through my edict, should restrict the practice which the Augusti — one the greatest god, the other the greatest princeps — have most carefully forbidden; namely that no one should use transport without paying for it. Nevertheless, since the licence of some people demands ready retribution, I have published a list of those things which in my judgement must be provided in each city and village; I shall uphold it or, if it is ignored, shall exact retribution not only by my power, but by the majesty of the best princeps, from whom I received . . . in my orders.

The people of Sagalassus should provide a service of ten waggons and the same number of mules for the needs of those passing through and should receive from users 10 asses for each waggon over each schoenus[1] and 4 asses for each mule over each schoenus; but if they prefer to provide donkeys, they should provide two donkeys at the same price as one mule. Or, if they prefer, for each mule and waggon they may pay those of another city or town who provide the service the amount which they would have received if they had provided the service themselves, so that they provide the same service. And they must provide transport as far as Cormasa and Conana.

But the right to use these will not belong to everyone, rather to the imperial procurator and his son, who are granted the use of up to 10 waggons or, in place of each waggon, 3 mules or, in place of each mule, 2 donkeys used at the same time and are to pay the price fixed by me. In addition, the right to use is granted to those on military service, both to those who have a warrant and to those on military service from other provinces who will pass through, in the following way; for a senator of the Roman people no more than 10 waggons or 3 mules for each waggon or 2 donkeys for each mule should be provided, the amount I have prescribed to be paid; for a Roman eques in the employ of the best princeps 3 waggons or 3 mules for each waggon or 2 donkeys for each mule should be provided by the same arrangement, but anyone who requires more should hire them on terms fixed by the hirer; for a centurion a waggon or 3 mules or 6 donkeys should be provided by the same arrangement.

For those who transport grain or anything of that nature either for their own profit or use I want nothing to be provided, nor for anyone for his baggage or that of his freedmen or slaves. Hospitality must be provided free of charge for all who are members of our staff, serving soldiers from other provinces, or freedmen and slaves of the best princeps and for their baggage, in such a way that they do not exact the other services, free of charge, from the unwilling.

1. A unit of distance: see Mitchell, pp. 121-2, for discussion.

[553] *EJ 318*
15, letter of Tiberius to Cos

Tiberius Caesar Augustus, son of the divine Augustus, in his 17th year of tribunician power, imperator 7 times, to the magistrates, council and people of the Coans, greetings.

Your envoys have given me your decree and the letters you gave them for me; I congratulate you on your disposition in my regard. In the past I have been disposed towards your city . . .

[554] *EJ 319*
Letter of Tiberius to Aezani, Phrygia

Letter of Tiberius Caesar brought from Bononia in Gaul. Tiberius Caesar to the council and people of the Aezanitans, greetings.

Since it was long ago that I learned of your piety and fellow-feeling towards me, I was very glad to receive now from your envoys the decree illustrating the goodwill of the city towards me. I shall therefore try as far as I am able to benefit you on every occasion on which you require assistance.

[555] *POxy 3020*
Letter of Augustus, dated 10-9 BC, reporting an audience given to an Alexandrian embassy, and an account of the proceedings of the embassy

A

Imperator Caesar Augustus, pontifex maximus, in his 14th year of tribunician power, imperator 12 times, to the people of the Alexandrians, greetings.

The envoys whom you sent came to me in Gaul and made your representations and in particular informed me of what seems ,to have troubled you in past years . . .

B

The spokesman: 'Caesar, unconquered hero, these are the envoys of the Alexandrians. We have divided the embassy . . . amongst ourselves . . . according to the competence of each of us . . . Theodorus on Egypt . . . on the Idios Logos . . . myself on the city . . . not to give a defence but to request your imperial intervention' . . .

[556] *EJ 379* (part 1 = *POxy 2435* verso) with A.K. Bowman, *JRS*, 66 (1976) p. 154
Probably first half of 13

Year 42 of Caesar, . . . 4th, ninth hour. Augustus held session in the temple of Apollo in the Roman library and gave audience to the envoys of the Alexandrians. In session with him were Tiberius Caesar and Drusus Caesar and Valerius Messalinus Corvinus, Gaius Ateius Capito . . . and Marcus Avidius Orgolanius . . . Alexander presented the decree and said:

'The city has sent me to offer to you . . . and to present the decrees . . . and of Livia . . . and of Tiberius Caesar . . . the envoys and between . . .; the victory.'

Augustus looked at it . . . 'Bless you: Bless you!' . . . and then Timoxenus the orator said:

'Such a . . . as you have granted . . . nothing . . . Lord Augustus, such a grant we ask you to make today to your Alexandrians. For we are here under the title of suppliants, but in truth our city is worshipping your most sacred Fortune with full enthusiasm . . .'

[557] *EJ 379* (part 2 = *POxy 2435* recto) with D.G. Weingärtner, *Die Agyptenreise des Germanicus* (1969) pp. 73-4. Germanicus in Alexandria; cf. Tac. *Ann.* 2.59-61; Suet. *Tib.* 52

The spokesman: I have given the imperator both the decrees.
The imperator: I have been sent by my father, men of Alexandria −
(the crowd shouted 'Hurrah, Lord! May you receive every blessing!')
The imperator: Since you have made so much of my addressing you, men of Alexandria, restrain yourselves until I have finished answering each of your enquiries and signify your approval then. I have been sent, as I said, by my father to regulate the overseas provinces. I have a most difficult assignment: first, because of the voyage and the separation from my father and grandmother and mother and siblings and children and relatives . . . the aforesaid assignment. I

have been separated from my relatives much . . . a new sea, in order, first, that I might for the first time see your city — (the crowd shouted 'Bless you!')

The imperator: I thought that it would be a most brilliant sight, in the first place because of your hero and founder, to whom a common debt is owed by those with the same aspirations, and in the second place, because of the benefactions of my grandfather, Augustus. It is my father's . . . as you should towards me. I am therefore silent — (the crowd shouted 'Bravo! May your life be longer!')

The imperator: on what is common knowledge, but I recall how I have found your greetings multiplied through being treasured in your hearts. For honorary decrees have been drafted by an assembly of a few men . . .

[558] *EJ 320* with J.H. Oliver, *RSA*, 1 (1971) pp. 229-30

A

Germanicus Caesar, son of Augustus, grandson of divine Augustus, proconsul, proclaims:

Since I now hear that, in connection with my visit, requisitions of boats and beasts are being made and billets for lodging seized by force and private persons terrorised, I have considered it necessary to make it plain that I want no boat or animal to be taken by anyone, unless it is by order of Baebius, my friend and secretary, nor billets to be seized. For, if it should be necessary, Baebius will distribute billets on a fair and just basis. And I order that pay be given for boats or teams requisitioned in accordance with my memorandum. It is my will that transgressors be brought before my secretary, who will either personally put a stop to injustice to private persons or will report to me. And I order those who seize animals they find moving about the city to be stopped, for this is an act of downright banditry.

B

Germanicus Caesar, son of Augustus, grandson of divine Augustus, proconsul, proclaims:

Your goodwill, which you always show whenever you see me, I welcome, but your invidious and god-like appellations I utterly reject. For these befit only the actual saviour and benefactor of the whole race of men, my father, and his mother, my grandmother. The acts imputed to me are additional workings of their divinity, so that, if you do not do as I say, you will force me to appear before you but seldom.

[559] *Ostrakon Louvre* 9004; Wilcken, *Chrest*. no. 413
19

Phatres, son of Psenthotes, has written an order to the bank in Diospolis Magna for the cost of wheat from the store-house ... for the visit of Germanicus Caesar ... base drachmas ... Year 5 of Tiberius Caesar Augustus, Tybi 30th Menodorus.

[560] *EJ 320a*
22-3, Egypt, near the Sphinx

Ninth year of Tiberius Caesar Augustus ... the men of Busiris in the Letopolite nome met and unanimously decreed this:

Since Gnaeus Pompeius Sabinus, our strategus, has always been energetically and generously disposed towards the inhabitants of the nome, and especially in advancing to the full the inhabitants of the village in his beneficence; and since in his judgements he always dispenses justice fairly, correctly and without bribery in accordance with the will of the most divine prefect Gaius Galerius; and since he handles work on dykes at the required times extremely carefully and impartially, labouring night and day until he has finished the job, with the result that the flatlands have been completely flooded and an exceptional crop produced; and since he has brought it about that produce is paid to those working on the dykes of the village exceeding past practice, in addition to their being free from slanders and accusations; and since, moreover, he farms out public positions with total propriety, with no force or menace, which is the greatest contribution to the prosperity and endurance of villages, and by paying what the village owed to other officers of the administration he keeps the farmers free from suspicion and liability, as is proper. Because of all this, we ourselves, wishing to repay him with honours, decided to honour the aforementioned Gnaeus Pompeius Sabinus, the strategus, with a stone column bearing this decree, to set it up in the most prominent place in the village, and also to present him with a copy, signed by as many people as possible, a copy which will be valid.

[561] *EJ 321*
Kierion, Thessaly

A

[Beginning is lost] . . . they are in dispute with each other not . . . asks that . . . secretly under oath . . . Metropolites deciding, your appointed officer . . . acting as arbiter, according to which . . . and of the decision . . . votes have been cast under oath: for the Kierians, 298, for the Metropolites, 31, spoiled, 5.

B

To Gaius Poppaeus Sabinus, legate of Tiberius Caesar . . . the secretary of the councillors sends the greatest greetings.

You wrote to us with regard to the boundary-dispute between the Kierians and the Metropolites that you thought it proper that it be decided by the councillors and those whom you indicated to me personally at Aedepsus. Rest assured that I went straight home and set the dispute before the assembled council of the Thessalians of Larissa, that of the month Thyus. When both parties had come together for the hearing and presented their cases, votes were cast secretly under oath: for the Kierians, 298, and for the Metropolites, 31, spoiled, 5. We thought it proper to write this letter. Farewell.

C

To Gaius Poppaeus Sabinus, legate of Tiberius Caesar . . . the strategus of the Thessalians sends greetings.

You wrote to me and to the councillors with regard to the boundary-dispute between the Kierians and the Metropolites that . . . sent the decision up to you. Note, then, that the councillors met in the month of Thyus and cast their votes secretly under oath: for the Kierians, 298, for the Metropolites, 31, spoiled, 5. We therefore thought it proper to write this, so that the decision might receive confirmation from you . . .

[562] *Small. 32*
May 11th 37, Aritium, Lusitania. Oath of loyalty

Gaius Ummidius Durmius Quadratus being propraetorian legate of Gaius Caesar Germanicus, imperator.

Oath of the Aritians.

On my conscience I will be the enemy of those whom I find to be the enemies of Gaius Caesar Germanicus and if anyone threatens or shall threaten danger to him and his safety I will not desist from the

pursuit of him until he has paid the penalty to Caesar in full; and I
will not hold myself or my children dearer than his safety and I will
regard those who may have a hostile attitude towards him as my
enemies. If I am deliberately acting falsely, now or in future, then may
Jupiter Optimus Maximus and divine Augustus and all the other
immortal gods deprive me of my country, my safety and all my
fortunes.

11th May in the old town of Aritium, in the consulship of Gnaeus
Acerronius Proculus and Gaius Petronius Pontius Nigrinus, in the
magistracy of Vegetus, son of Tallicus . . .

[563] *Small. 33*
37, Assus, Troad. Decree and oath of loyalty

In the consulship of Gnaeus Acerronius Proculus and Gaius Pontius
Petronius Nigrinus. Decree of the Assians by the will of the people:

Since the principate hoped and prayed for by all mankind, that of
Gaius Caesar Germanicus Augustus, has been announced, and since the
world has found no limit to its joy, and since the whole city and the
whole province has been eager to see the god because man's sweetest
era is now with us, the council and the Romans in business among us
and the people of the Assians have decided to organise an embassy of
the first and best Romans and Greeks to meet and congratulate him
and beg him to remember and care for the city, as he himself promised
when he came for the first time, with his father Germanicus, to the
province of our city.

Oath of the Assians.

We swear by Zeus the Saviour and divine Caesar Augustus and the
ancestral Holy Maiden that we will support Gaius Caesar Augustus
and his whole house and will adjudge as friends whoever he may choose
and as enemies whoever he may accuse. If we swear truly, may it be
well with us, but, if falsely, the opposite.

The envoys carried out their mission at their own expense. Gaius
Varius Castus, son of Gaius, of the tribe Voltinia, Hermophanes, son of
Zoilus, Ctetus, son of Pisistratus, Aechrion, son of Calliphanes,
Artemidorus, son of Philomusus, who also, having prayed for the safety
of Gaius Caesar Augustus Germanicus, sacrificed to Capitoline Zeus in
the name of the city.

[564] *Small. 361*
19th August 37, Acraephia, Boeotia; letter of Gaius

Imperator Augustus Caesar, descendant of the divine Augustus, grandson of Tiberius Caesar, pontifex maximus, with tribunician power, consul, to the league of Achaeans and Boeotians and Locrians and Phocians and Euboeans, greetings.

I have read the decree given to me by your envoys and have noted that you have spared no extravagance in your zeal and piety towards me, in that you have each personally offered sacrifice for my welfare and have joined in a common festival and have decreed the greatest honours you could; for all this I congratulate you and give my approval and, mindful of the brilliance of each of the Greek peoples from ancient times, I permit you to meet as a league. But as for the statues you decreed for me, set aside the greater part, if you would, and be satisfied with those to be set up at Olympia and Nemea and Delphi and the Isthmus, so that you ... and you burden yourselves with less costs. The envoys whose names are written below delivered the decree to me. Farewell. Head of the embassy ... [the names of the envoys follow in fragmentary lines].

Given on 19th August, in Rome.

[565] Philo, *Embassy to Gaius*, 352-7
Embassies from the Jews and Greeks of Alexandria gain audience with Gaius in their dispute over civil rights in Alexandria. Philo was one of the Jewish envoys

When we were brought before him, we bowed our heads to the ground as soon as we saw him, with every respect and caution, and we greeted him by the name of Augustus Imperator. But he replied with the sort of mildness and generosity that led us to lose hope of not only our case but also our lives. For with sneering viciousness he said, 'Are you the god-haters who think I am not a god – I who am acknowledged by all others as such, but not named by you?' With that he stretched out his hands to the sky and voiced an invocation which was impious to hear, let alone report verbatim. The envoys of the other side were immediately filled with huge joy, already confident of success because of Gaius' opening words to our embassy. They waved their arms, leapt about and called him by the names of all the gods. When he saw that Gaius was flattered by titles above human nature, the malevolent sycophant Isidorus said, 'You will hate these men and their compatriots still more, Master, when you learn their ill-will and impiety towards you.

For when everyone was offering sacrifices of thanksgiving for your safety, these people alone could not bear to sacrifice. And when I say "these" I include the other Jews.' We cried out as one man, 'Lord Gaius, we are being slandered. In fact we did sacrifice and sacrificed hecatombs. Nor did we splash the blood on the altar and take home the meat to feast and banquet, as some usually do, but we consigned the sacred offerings wholly to the flame − and three times, not once, already. The first time, when you succeeded to the leadership; the second time, when you escaped that grave sickness that afflicted the whole world with you; the third time, in the expectation of the German victory.' 'Alright, that's true', he said, 'you have sacrificed − but to another, albeit on my behalf. So what's the good of it? You have not sacrificed to me.'

[566] Josephus, *Jewish Antiquities*, 18. 261-3

Gaius was terribly indignant at being so ignored by the Jews alone and sent Petronius to Syria as his legate in succession to Vitellius. He had orders to enter Judaea with a large force and, if the Jews acquiesced, set up a statue of Gaius in the Temple of God; but if they resisted, he was to defeat them in battle and do this. Having taken over Syria, Petronius was keen to carry out Gaius' orders; after collecting as large a force as he could, he led two legions of the Roman army to Ptolemais in order to winter there and set about war in spring. He wrote of his intentions to Gaius, who praised his energy and told him not to slacken but to wage war strenuously against the disobedient. But many thousands of Jews came to Petronius at Ptolemais to ask him not to force them to illegality and the contravention of ancestral law.

[567] Josephus, *Jewish Antiquities*, 18. 300-1
Gaius's letter to Petronius after his intention had been changed by King Agrippa:

... Gaius agreed and wrote to Petronius, praising him for collecting his army and for writing to him on the subject, 'Now, then, if you have erected my statue, let it stand. But if you have not yet made the dedication, go to no further pains, but disband your army and set about the tasks for which I sent you in the first place.'

[568] *Small. 367*
Speech of Claudius to the Senate

[Beginning is lost] . . . it seems obnoxious that . . . be attached to the five decuries. Take care that you ensure that no one aged 24 (or less) be appointed assessor, for it is equitable, to my mind, that those judge cases of slavery and liberty who in the conduct of their own affairs may in no way use the protection of the *lex Laetoria*[1] . . . I think, conscript fathers, that I have often noticed — at other times, but especially at this time — the remarkable tricks of pleaders, who, when the indictment has been signed, with . . . [10 fragmentary lines] . . . that to hold the case be to the advantage of the plaintiff. In order that these tricks should not benefit malicious pleaders, if you agree, conscript fathers, let us decree that, even when a recess has been declared, a requirement that they reach a decision should be imposed upon those judges who have not completed commenced cases within the days for the transaction of business. I know that many stratagems will be available to those who conduct their cases monstrously, for which, I hope, we have devised remedies. In the meantime, it is sufficient to have precluded this stratagem, which is all too common among all who bring malicious lawsuits. For I cannot at all abide the tyranny of prosecutors who, when they have made their enemies defendants before an inquiring court, leave them hanging on the notice-board and, themselves, as if they had done nothing, go abroad, when the nature of things more than the laws holds the prosecutor as much as the defendant entangled and constrained.

This proposal is complemented by the airs and graces of prosecutors and defendants which prevent the behaviour of those who disdain to dress filthily and to grow beard and hair so as to make their case seem more pitiable from being to their disadvantage. But let them see what an advantage they can derive from these tools of pity given by nature.

And let us take away from prosecutors this unrestrained tyranny of theirs by giving the praetor the power of summoning the prosecutor when the period for his collecting evidence has expired; and if he does not appear or obtain excuse, the praetor should declare that the prosecutor seems to have brought the case deceitfully for the sake of calumny.

If these proposals find favour with you, conscript fathers, signify immediately, simply and in accordance with your own opinion; if they do not find favour, however, devise alternative remedies, but do so here in the temple, or, if you want, perhaps, to take time to consider the matter at greater leisure, take it, provided that, wherever you are convened, you remember that you are to speak your own opinions. For it becomes the dignity of this order very ill, conscript fathers, that here just one consul designate should speak his opinion drawn verbatim from the motion of the consuls and that the rest should speak one word 'Aye' and then, when they have disbanded, 'We spoke'.

1. Also known as the *lex Plaetoria*, this law is imperfectly understood, but related to the protection of minors, i.e. those not yet 25.

[569] *Small. 368*
46, near Tridentum, edict of Claudius

In the consulship of Marcus Junius Silanus and Quintus Sulpicius Camerinus, 15th March, at Baiae in the imperial residence, the edict of Tiberius Claudius Caesar Augustus Germanicus set out below was issued:

Tiberius Claudius Caesar Augustus Germanicus, pontifex maximus, in his 6th year of tribunician power, imperator 11 times, father of his country, consul designate for the fourth time, proclaims:

Since there exist old disputes, at issue even in the time of Tiberius Caesar, my uncle, who sent Pinarius Apollinaris to deal with them (as far as I recall these disputes were only between the Comenses and Bergalei); and since first in the persistent absence of my uncle, then too in the principate of Gaius, he did not report back since no report was demanded of him (not through any incompetence); and since, subsequently, Camurius Statutus informed me that some fields and pastures belong to me, I have sent Julius Planta, my friend and companion, to look at the present state of affairs and, with the greatest care and the assistance of my procurators, both those in the area and those elsewhere, to hold an enquiry and come to a decision; with regard to other matters, as shown to me in a report he compiled, I permit him to judge and make proclamation.

As to the matter of the status of the Anauni and Tulliasses and Sinduni and the fact that an informant is said to have shown that some of them have been assigned to the Tridentini and others not, although I am aware that this category of people does not have too strong an inherited claim to Roman citizenship, nevertheless, since they are said to be in possession of it through its long usurpation and since they are so integrated with the Tridentini that they could not be separated without serious damage to that splendid municipality, I permit them in my beneficence to retain the status they thought was theirs; I do this all the more readily because some of this category of people are said to have seen military service even in my praetorian guard, some indeed to have become officers too, and some are said to have been incorporated into the decuries at Rome and to have acted as jurors.

I confer this benefaction upon them in such a way that I order that whatever they did or performed either among themselves or with the Tridentini or with others as if Roman citizens, that this should be lawful and I permit them to keep the names they formerly held as if Roman citizens.

[570] *Small. 369*
48, Lugdunum, speech of Claudius; cf. Tac. *Ann.* 11. 23-5; M. Griffin, *CQ*, 32 (1982) pp. 404-18

[First line is fragmentary] . . . I deplore that first thought of all men, which, I foresee, will stand in my path first and foremost, lest you shy away, as if from the introduction of some revolutionary innovation; rather, think instead how many changes have occurred in this state and through how many forms and constitutions our state has been taken, from the very foundation of the city.

Once kings ruled this city; however, they did not pass it on to successors within their families. Members of other families and even foreigners came to the throne, as Numa, coming from the Sabines, succeeded Romulus; he was a neighbour certainly, but at that time he was a foreigner, as Tarquinius Priscus succeeded Ancus Marcius. Tarquinius, prevented from holding office in his own land, because of his impure blood – for he was the son of Demaratus of Corinth and his mother was from Tarquinium, a lady noble but poor, as she will have been if she needed to give her hand to such a husband – subsequently migrated to Rome and gained the throne. Between Tarquinius and his son or grandson (for even this is disputed among the sources) Servius Tullius intervened. If we follow Roman authorities, his mother was a prisoner of war, Ocresia; if we follow Etruscan authorities, he was once the most faithful companion of Caelius Vivenna and took part in all his adventures; subsequently, driven out by a change of fortune, he left Etruria with all the remnants of the army of Caelius and occupied the Caelian hill, naming it thus after his leader Caelius; Servius changed his name (for his name in Etruscan was Mastarna) and was called by the name I have used and he obtained the throne, to the very great advantage of the state. Then, after the ways of Tarquinius Superbus became hateful to our state – both his ways and those of his sons – people doubtless became disillusioned with the monarchy and the government of the state was transferred to the consuls, annual magistrates.

Why should I remind you now of the power of the dictatorship, mightier than consular power itself, instituted among our ancestors to be used in particularly harsh wars or in particularly difficult civil unrest? Or of the tribunes of the plebs, created to help the plebs? Why should I remind you now of the powers transferred from the consuls to the decemvirs and returned to the consuls after the rule of the decemvirs was ended? Why should I remind you now of the distribution of the consular power among several men and of the military tribunes with consular power, as they were known, six or eight of whom were created each year? Why should I remind you now of the offices shared finally with the plebs, not only political offices but religious offices too? If I were now to tell of the wars, whence our ancestors started and to where we have advanced, I should be afraid lest I appear excessively arrogant and to be seeking to boast of the glory of having advanced the empire beyond the Ocean. But let me rather leave that aside.

... can ... citizenship. It was certainly an innovation when the divine Augustus, my great-uncle, and my uncle Tiberius Caesar decided to admit to this Senate House the entire flower of colonies and municipalities everywhere — upright, wealthy men, of course. But, you may say, is an Italian senator not better than a provincial one for all that? When I come to deal with this part of my censorship, I shall then show you by my actions what I feel on this matter. No, I think that not even provincials should be excluded, if they can ornament the Senate House at all.

Take the most distinguished and flourishing colony of Vienna: how long has it been sending senators to the Senate House? From this colony comes an ornament of the equestrian order with few peers, Lucius Vestinus, my most cherished friend, whom I employ in my service to this day. I ask that his children may enjoy the first grade of priesthoods and thereafter, with the passage of years, progress, through increases in their dignity. I shall not utter the wicked name of that brigand[1] — and I hate that portent of the wrestling-ring — because he brought the consulship to his family before his colony had achieved the firm benefit of Roman citizenship. I may say the same about his brother and that wretched and ignoble fate, so that he could not be of use to you as a senator.

It is now time, Tiberius Caesar Germanicus, to reveal to the conscript fathers where your speech is leading: for now you have come to the farthest borders of Gallia Narbonensis.

Take all the young men whom I see before me; that they are senators should cause no more regret than Persicus feels — a most noble man and my friend — when he reads among the images of his ancestors the name of Allobrogicus. But if you agree that this is so, what more do you want than that I should point out to you that the land beyond tbe borders of the province of Narbonensis already sends you senators, since we do not regret the fact that we take members of our order from Lugdunum? It was with some timidity, conscript fathers, that I left the boundaries of provinces known and familiar to you, but I must now plead the case of Gallia Comata with some severity. If in this case anyone looks to the fact that they occupied the divine Julius in war for ten years, let him also take note of the hundred years of their constant good faith and loyalty, more than tested many times when we were in difficulties. They were the ones who gave my father Drusus the benefit of safe, internal peace and a secure rear when he was conquering Germany, although he was called to war while conducting a census, a practice then new and strange to the Gauls. How difficult this practice is for us, even now, although nothing more is demanded of us than that our resources be officially noted, we know through too great experience . . .

1. Probably Publius Valerius Asiaticus of Vienna; cf. Tac. *Ann.* 11. 1-3. Nothing is known of his brother.

[571] *Small. 370*

41, proclamation of the prefect of Egypt and letter of Claudius to the Alexandrians.

A

Lucius Aemilius Rectus proclaims:

Since, at the reading of the most sacred and beneficent letter to the city, the whole city could not attend on account of its size, I considered it necessary to publish the letter in order that, reading it individually, you may wonder at the greatness of our god Caesar and be grateful for his good will towards the city.

Year 2 of Tiberius Claudius Caesar Augustus Germanicus, imperator, 14th of the month New Augustus.

B

Tiberius Claudius Caesar Augustus Germanicus, imperator, pontifex maximus, with tribunician power, consul designate, to the city of the Alexandrians, greetings.

Tiberius Claudius Barbillus, Apollonius, son of Artemidorus, Chaeremon, son of Leonides, Marcus Julius Asclepiades, Gaius Julius Dionysius, Tiberius Claudius Phanius, Pasion, son of Potamon, Dionysius son of Sabbion, Tiberius Claudius Archibius, Apollonius, son of Ariston, Gaius Julius Apollonius, Hermaiscus, son of Apollonius, your envoys, gave the decree to me and told me much about the city, setting clearly before me your good will towards us, which, you may be sure, I have been storing up for a long time — you are naturally pious towards the Augusti, as I have long known, and especially keen and made keen with regard to my house: to cite the latest example and pass over the rest, the greatest witness to this is my brother Germanicus Caesar, who addressed you in markedly familiar terms. For this reason I was glad to accept the honours which you have conferred upon me, although I am not disposed to such things.

First, I allow you to celebrate my birthday as Augusta in the way you yourselves have chosen; I permit you to erect statues of myself and my family everywhere. I do this because I appreciate your eagerness to set up memorials of your piety towards my house all over the city. And, as for the two gold statues, that of the Claudian Augustan Peace — just as my most honoured friend Barbillus persistently urged when I refused because it seemed too arrogant — will be dedicated at Rome, while the other, in the manner you think appropriate, will be carried in procession on the named days of Alexandria; and a chair, decked out as you wish, is to be carried in procession with it. In permitting honours of this magnitude it would perhaps be foolish to refuse to designate a Claudian tribe and oppose the establishment of groves in all the nomes of Egypt. Therefore, I allow you this too. And if you also wish to erect equestrian statues of my procurator, Vitrasius Pollio, do so. And I permit the erection of four-horse chariots, which you wish to post at the entrances to your land — one at Taposiris, as it is called, in Libya, one at Pharos in Alexandria and a third at Pelusium in Egypt. But I decline the establishment of temples and a high-priest for me, because I do not wish to be arrogant towards the people of my own time and because I consider temples and the like to be privileges granted to the gods alone by every age.

With reference to the requests as to what you are keen to receive from me, this is my decision. To all those who have been ephebes down to my principate I securely confirm Alexandrian citizenship together with all the honours and favours bestowed by the city, with the exception of any interlopers of slave descent who have been ephebes. And I wish that all the other rights bestowed upon you by my predecessors in the principate and the kings and the prefects be no less secure, as the divine Augustus also made them secure.

As to the officials of the temple of the divine Augustus in Alexandria, I wish that they be chosen by lot, just as the officials of the temple of the same divine Augustus at Canopus are chosen by lot.

Concerning the holding of civic magistracies for a period of three years, you seem to me to have reached an entirely correct decision, for magistrates will carry out their term of office more judiciously through fear of being called to account for their evil rulings. As to the council, I cannot say what was your usual practice in the time of the kings of old, but you are well aware that it was not held in the time of the Augusti before me. As it is an innovation, now being proposed for the first time – an innovation which is not obviously to the advantage of the city and my interests – I have written to Aemilius Rectus to examine the proposition thoroughly and show me whether the institution should be organised and, if it should be convened, how this should be arranged.

As to the disturbances and civil strife in respect of the Jews (or rather, if I must speak the truth, the war) and who was responsible – though your envoys, Dionysius, son of Theon, in particular, argued their case energetically – I have decided not to conduct a detailed investigation, but I am storing up immutable anger against those who have started it again. And I tell you bluntly that if you do not put a stop to this disastrous stubborn anger against each other, I will be forced to show what it is like when a benevolent princeps is moved to justifiable anger. Therefore, I once again ask that Alexandrians behave gently and benevolently towards the Jews, who have long been inhabitants of the same city, and that they do not commit any sacrilege against Jewish customs relating to the worship of their god; rather, that they allow the Jews to follow the customs which were confirmed in the time of the divine Augustus and which I too confirmed after giving a thorough hearing to both sides. On the other hand, I order the Jews not to strive after anything more than they previously had and not to send – as if they lived in two cities – two embassies in future, something never previously done, and not to seek involvement in the games of the gymnasiarch or cosmete; to enjoy what is theirs and to rejoice in the superfluity of abundant benefits in a foreign city, not bringing in or admitting Jews coming from Syria or Egypt (a practice which I will be forced to view with notably great suspicion). And if they disobey, I will attack them in every way as the carriers of some world-wide plague. If both sides change their ways and are willing to live in mutual gentleness and benevolence, I for my part will exercise the greatest care for the city, a characteristic which I, in my house, have inherited from my forefathers. I testify for Barbillus, my companion, that he has always exercised the greatest care for you in his dealings with me — he has devoted all his energy on your behalf in the present matter too. I testify also for Tiberius Claudius Archibius, my companion. Farewell.

[572] Josephus, *Jewish Antiquities*, 19. 280-5
41. Claudius confirms the rights of the Jews of Alexandria

Tiberius Claudius Caesar Augustus Germanicus, with tribunician power, proclaims:

I have been aware from the first that the Jews in Alexandria called Alexandrians settled in the very earliest times with the Alexandrians and received equal citizenship from the kings, as has been made clear by the documents in their possession and the edicts; also, that after Alexandria had been brought under our rule by Augustus their rights were maintained by the prefects appointed at various times and there was no dispute over their rights; furthermore, that during Aquila's period at Alexandria, when the ethnarch of the Jews died, Augustus did not prevent the appointment of ethnarchs, since he wished that each of his subjects continue in their particular customs and not be compelled to transgress their ancestral worship. And since I am aware that the Alexandrians were roused against the Jews of their city in the time of Gaius Caesar, who in his great stupidity and madness humiliated the Jews because the Jewish people would not transgress their ancestral worship and address him as a god, it is my wish that the Jewish people lose none of its rights on account of the madness of Gaius, rather that they keep their old privileges, continuing in their particular customs, and I order both sides to exercise the greatest care, so that no disturbance occurs after the publication of my edict.

[573] Josephus, *Jewish Antiquities*, 19. 287-91
41. Claudius confirms Jewish rights throughout the empire

Tiberius Claudius Caesar Augustus Germanicus, pontifex maximus, with tribunician power, elected consul for the second time, proclaims:

King Agrippa and Herod, my dearest friends, have asked me to allow the Jews of the whole Roman empire to keep the same rights as the Jews of Alexandria. I most gladly agreed, not only to favour those who made this request, but also because in my view they deserve it by virtue of their good faith and friendship to the Romans, and especially because I consider that no city, not even a Greek one, should lose these rights, since they were guaranteed for them in the time of the divine Augustus. It is therefore proper that the Jews of all the world under our sway keep their ancestral customs without hindrance. And I call upon the Jews themselves to take advantage of this generosity of mine with greater propriety and not to regard the beliefs of other god-fearing peoples as of no account and to abide by their own laws.

It is my wish that the magistrates of the cities and colonies and municipalities, both inside and outside Italy, and kings and dynasts through their own envoys have this edict of mine inscribed and set up for not less than thirty days in a place where it can easily be read from the ground.

[574] *Small. 435*
4th August 41

Sarapio to our Heraclides, greetings. I sent you two other letters, one through Nedymus, one through Cronius the policeman. Then I got the letter from the Arab and read it and was distressed. Follow Ptollarion at all times. Perhaps he may make you solvent. Tell him, 'It's one thing for me, another for everybody else. I am a slave. I've sold you my goods for a talent too little. I don't know what my master will do to me. We've got a lot of creditors. Don't wipe us out.' Ask him every day. Perhaps he may take pity on you. If he doesn't, watch out for the Jews, as they all do. On the other hand, by following him, you may win him over. See if through Diodorus the document can be signed through the wife of the prefect. If you do your bit, you're not to blame. Generous greetings to Diodorus. Farewell. Greetings to Harpocration.

Year 1 of Tiberius Claudius Caesar Augustus Germanicus, imperator, 11th of the month Caesareus.

To Alexandria to the Augustan market-place, to the ... store, to Heraclides from Sarapio, son of ... , son of Sosipatrus. [This is the address, written on the back of the above letter.]

[575] *Small. 436*
41 or 53, hearing of two leaders of the Greek anti-Semites of Alexandria before Claudius

[The beginning is lost] ... Tarquinius, senator ... stood up ... to Caesar: 'You will disturb the whole world ... for the native land ...'

And Aviola, senator, stood up . . .: 'Man is . . . I therefore ask . . . this the once . . . if these men do not . . . to the council . . .' He sat down. Alexandrian envoys were called, and the imperator postponed their hearing to the next day. Year . . . of Tiberius Claudius Caesar Augustus . . . Pachon 5th.

Second day. Pachon 6th. Claudius Caesar Augustus gives a hearing to Isidorus, gymnasiarch of the city of the Alexandrians, against King Agrippa in the . . . gardens, 20 senators being in session with him, 16 of these being consulars, and in the presence of the women . . . that of Isidorus.

Isidorus spoke first: 'My lord Caesar, at your knees I beg you to hear from me the sufferings of my homeland.'

The imperator: 'I shall allot you this day.' All the senators in session with him indicated their assent, knowing what sort of man is Isidorus.

Claudius Caesar: 'Do not blaspheme against my friend. You have already destroyed two other friends of mine, Theon the exegete and Naevius the prefect.'

[Another papyrus fragment]
Isidorus: 'Balbillus speaks well, Lord Augustus, about your business. But I shall oppose your submissions in regard to the Jews, Agrippa. I accuse them of seeking to destabilise the whole world. It is necessary to conduct a detailed examination in judging the tribe. They are not of the same sort as the Alexandrians, but like the Egyptians in their ways. Are they not on a par with those who pay the poll-tax?'

Agrippa: 'Their rulers set a poll-tax on the Egyptians . . . No one did so on the Jews.'

Balbillus: 'See the extreme arrogance to which either his god or . . .'

[Another papyrus fragment]
Lampon to Isidorus: 'I have already contemplated my death.'

Claudius Caesar: 'You have killed many of my friends, Isidorus.'

Isidorus: 'I obeyed the king who was then in power. Tell me who you would like me to accuse and I will do it.'

Claudius Caesar: 'It's clear that you're the son of a musical tart, Isidorus.'

Isidorus: 'I am neither a slave nor the son of a musician, but gymnasiarch of the illustrious city of Alexandria. But you are the cast-off son of Salome the Jewess. And so . . .'

Lampon to Isidorus: 'What can we do except give in to a crazy king?'

Claudius Caesar: 'Those to whom I previously assigned the execution of Isidorus and Lampon . . .'

[576] *Small. 437*

2nd December 56. Berenice, Cyrenaica

Year 2 of Nero Claudius Caesar Drusus Germanicus, imperator, Choiach 6th, the synagogue of the Jews of Berenice decided to write up on a column of Parian marble the names of contributors to the restoration of the synagogue:

Zenio, son of Zoilus, archon, 10 drachmas; Isidorus, son of Dositheus, archon, 10 drachmas; Dositheus, son of Ammonius, archon, 10 drachmas; Pratis, son of Jonathan, archon, 10 drachmas; Carnedas, son of Cornelius, archon, 10 drachmas; Heraclides, son of Heraclides, archon, 10 drachmas; Thaliarchus, son of Dositheus, archon, 10 drachmas; Sosibius, son of Jason, archon, 10 drachmas; Pratomedes, son of Socrates, archon, 10 drachmas; Antigonus, son of Strato, archon, 10 drachmas; Cartisthenes, son of Archias, priest, 10 drachmas; Lysanias, son of Lysanias, 25 drachmas; Zenodorus, son of Theophilus, 28 drachmas; Marion, son of . . . , 25 drachmas; Alexandrus, son of Euphranor, 5 drachmas; Isidora, daughter of Serapio, 5 drachmas; Zosime, daughter of Terpolius, 5 drachmas; Polo, son of Dositheus, 5 drachmas.

[577] Josephus, *Jewish Antiquities*, 19. 303-11

42. The governor of Syria responds to disturbances between Greek and Jew at Dora

Publius Petronius, legate of Tiberius Claudius Caesar Augustus Germanicus, to the leading Dorians proclaims:

Some of your number have been so perverse and audacious as to disobey the published edict of Claudius Caesar Augustus Germanicus on allowing Jews to continue their ancestral customs; they have done quite the contrary in preventing the Jews from having a synagogue by moving into it a statue of Caesar; they are breaking the law not only in their conduct towards the Jews but also in their conduct towards the imperator, whose statue was better placed in his own temple than in that of another, and in a synagogue at that, for natural justice demands that each is lord of his own place, in accordance with the decree of Caesar. For it would be ludicrous to recall my decree after the edict of the imperator who permitted the Jews to follow their own customs and, at the same time, ordered them to join with the Greeks in the community.

Since these men have so audaciously contravened the edict of Augustus — for which their leading members are themselves angry and state that it was not done by their particular plan but by the mob, on impulse −, I have ordered them to be brought before me by Proclus Vitellius, the centurion, to account for their actions. And I advise the leading magistrates, if they do not wish it to appear that the crime was committed at their instigation, to point out the guilty men to the centurion, allowing no chance of riot or physical conflict: this, in my judgement, is what they seek by such behaviour. I myself and King Agrippa, my most honoured friend, are concerned above all else that the Jews should not take their chance, muster in the name of self-defence, and proceed to folly. And, so that you may be better informed of Augustus' mind on the whole matter, I have appended the edicts he had published in Alexandria. Though they seem to be known to all, my most honoured friend King Agrippa read them out at my tribunal when he pleaded that the Jews ought not to be deprived of what Augustus had given them. For the future, I call upon you to seek no excuse for riot or disturbance but each to keep your own particular customs.

[578] *Small. 371*
42, Thasos, letter of Claudius

Tiberius Claudius Caesar Germanicus, pontifex maximus, in his second year of tribunician power, consul designate for the third time, imperator, father of his country, to the magistrates, council and people of the Thasians, greetings.

With regard to what I have been told by the envoys you sent, I tell you that I accept all the . . . of your zeal and piety alike. But I decline the temple because I consider that to be the privilege of the gods alone, though I permit the other honours, which befit the best principes. And I confirm to you, in accordance with the decrees of the divine Augustus, everything which was an honour from him and which . . . of the . . . you have . . . and of the export of grain . . . careful . . . to the prefect. If nothing . . . in the province, I am writing so that . . . when these have been given to you, may show me. And as to the other matters, you may be quite sure that I am taking care of the city. Those who gave me the decree were . . . [a fragmentary list of names follows].

[579] *Small. 372* with *IGRR* 4.1608
41, Hypaepa, Lydia, dedication by the hymnodes of Asia, letter of
Claudius and decree of the league of Asia

A
[Beginning is lost] ... for the eternal endurance of Tiberius Claudius
Caesar Augustus Germanicus and his whole house, when the stephanephorus was Tiberius Claudius Tryphon, son of Asclepiodorus, of the
tribe Quirina, when the secretary of the people and temple-officer and
treasurer of the Augustan funds was Alexander, son of Apollonides.
The hymnodes made the dedication in accordance with the decree
passed at Pergamum by the holy synod, having inscribed on it the just
and benevolent gifts they have received from him. Hosius, son of
Apollonius ...

B
Tiberius Claudius Caesar Augustus Germanicus, imperator twice, pontifex maximus, with tribunician power, consul deisgnate for the second
time, proconsul, father of his country, to the holy synod of hymnodes,
greetings.
    Having read the decree ...

C
[Beginning is lost] ... the Greeks of Asia have decided, on the proposal
of Anaxagoras ... friend of Caesar, high-priest of Asia and president
of the games for life of divine Rome and divine Augustus Caesar, son of
a god, imperator and pontifex maximus, father of his country and of
the whole race of men.
    Since we must make clear each year our piety towards the Augustan
house, the hymnodes of all Asia, meeting at the ... on the most holy
birthday of Augustus Tiberius Caesar, are to perform an outstanding
act to the renown of the synod by hymning the Augustan house and
performing sacrifice to the Augustan gods and holding festivals and
feasts and ... all ...

[580] *Small. 373*
Letters of Claudius to the Dionysiac artists.

(a) 43
Tiberius Claudius Caesar Augustus Germanicus, pontifex maximus, in
his second year of tribunician power, consul for the third time, imperator four times, father of his country, to the Dionysiac conquering
victors of the empire and their company, greetings.

On the one hand, I permit you to erect images so that we may be shown piety with the appropriate honour; on the other, I confirm the rights and favours bestowed upon you by the divine Augustus. The envoys were Claudius ... Claudius Epagathus, Claudius Dionysius, Claudius Thamyris ... written in Rome in the consulship of Tiberius Claudius Caesar for the third time and Vitellius for the second time.

(b) 48-9, Miletus
Tiberius Claudius Caesar Augustus Germanicus, in his eighth year of tribunician power, consul for the fourth time, imperator 15 times, father of his country, censor, to the Dionysiac victors and artists, greetings.

I welcome the fact that you have remembered what I bestowed when I confirmed the rights given by the Augusti before me and the Senate and I will try to increase these since you are piously disposed towards my house. Marcus Valerius Junianus, a member of my household, presented this to me; him I also praised because he is well-disposed towards you. Farewell.

[581] *Small. 374*
Letters of Claudius to the travelling athletes

(a) 46
Tiberius Claudius Caesar Augustus Germanicus Sarmaticus, pontifex maximus, in his sixth year of tribunician power, consul designate for the fourth time, imperator 12 times, father of his country, to the guild of travelling athletes, greetings.

I was pleased to receive the gold crown you sent me for the British victory, a symbol encapsulating your piety towards me. The envoys were Tiberius Claudius Hermes, Tiberius Claudius Cyrus and Dio, son of Miccalus, of Antioch. Farewell.

(b) 47
Tiberius Claudius Caesar Augustus Germanicus Sarmaticus, pontifex maximus, in his seventh year of tribunician power, consul six times,[1] imperator 18 times,[1] father of his country, to the Heraclean guild of travelling athletes, greetings.

In two decrees given to me at the same time you kindly told me how Gaius Julius Antiochus, the king of Commagene, and Julius Polemo, the king of Pontus, men honoured by me and friends, acted energetically and benevolently towards you when they held the games established by them in my name. I have congratulated you for your generosity towards them and have recognised rather than been surprised at their good will towards myself and their benevolence in your regard. Those mentioned in the decrees were Diogenes, son of Miccalus, of Antioch, who was the high-priest nearest to the guild and whom I have thought deserving of Roman citizenship, together with his two daughters, Sandogenes . . . son of Miccalus, of Antioch. Farewell.

1. Errors for four and 12 or 13 respectively.

[582] *Small. 375*
49-50, Tegea, edict of Claudius

Tiberius Claudius Caesar Augustus Germanicus, pontifex maximus, in his ninth year of tribunician power, imperator 16 times, father of his country, proclaims:

Although I have often attempted to relieve not only the colonies and municipalities of Italy but also those of the provinces, likewise the states of each province, from the burdens of transport provision and although I thought I had found a sufficient number of remedies, it has nevertheless proved impossible to cope adequately with the evil of men . . . false . . .

[583] *Small. 376* with A. Plassart, *REG*, 80 (1967) pp. 372-84
52, Delphi, letter of Claudius; cf. *Acts* 18. 12-17; Tac. *Ann*. 15. 73.4

Tiberius Claudius Caesar Augustus Germanicus, pontifex maximus, in his 12th year of tribunician power, imperator 26 times, father of his country, consul 5 times, censor, to the city of the Delphians, greetings.

I have long been well-disposed towards the city of the Delphians . . . and favourable from the beginning, and I have always protected the worship of Pythian Apollo . . . and what is now said and those disputes among your citizens . . . as Lucius Junius Gallio, my friend and the proconsul of Achaea, wrote . . . For this reason I permit you to retain your former . . .

[584] *Small. 377 = EJ 322*
An imperial edict assigned to various emperors by scholars, particularly
Claudius. The identity of the emperor and the date are quite uncertain

Edict of Caesar.
It is my wish that any graves or tombs made in commemoration of
ancestors or children or relatives remain undisturbed forever. And if
anyone should accuse someone of having destroyed them or of having
in any other way cast out the buried or of having with evil trickery
moved them elsewhere as an offence against the buried or of having
removed tombstones or gravestones, I order that the accused be
brought to trial with the same regard for the commemoration of
mortals as for that of gods. For it will be much more necessary to
honour the buried. Let no one at all be allowed to disturb them. And
if anyone does so, it is my will that he be condemned to death for
tomb-desecration.

[585] *Small. 379* with G. Pugliese-Carratelli, *PP*, 30 (1975)
pp. 102-4
Cos, letter of Gnaeus Domitius Corbulo, proconsul of Asia

Gnaeus Domitius Corbulo, proconsul, to the magistrates, council and
people of the Coans, greetings.
I have often thought it necessary to present [to Augustus] those
accusations which in my opinion may be deemed worthy of the divine
judgement of Augustus and which are stipulated for provincial governors, set out in the *mandata*.[1] As for this case, from your decree . . .[2]
made an appeal to Augustus, and I perceived that he did this as an
abuse to the system. It is necessary, however, if an appeal is made to
Augustus, that I look into the case first. But if it is made to me, it is
sufficient for the present to take 2,500 denarii as surety, in accordance
with the edict issued by me on account of those who shirk trials. But
if in this regard it does not come about . . .

1. Instructions issued to provincial governors by the emperor; see Millar, *ERW*,
pp. 313-16.   2. The name of the appellant is missing.

[586] *Small. 380*
Ephesus, edict of the proconsul of Asia

Paullus Fabius Persicus, priest, sodalis Augustalis, Arval brother, quaestor of Imperator Tiberius Caesar Augustus, praetor . . . consul . . . proconsul of Asia, proclaimed, at the instigation of Tiberius Claudius Caesar Augustus Germanicus himself, an edict beneficial to the city of the Ephesians and the whole province, which he published at Ephesus and ordered to be inscribed on a column before March 28th:

While it is very much my own view, above all else, that magistrates in charge of provinces must perform the office entrusted to them with all steadfastness and good faith, in such a way that they give thought to the long-term good of the individual, of the whole province and of each city, and not only to that of his own year of office, for all that I freely acknowledge that I have been drawn to this view by the example of the greatest and most truly just princeps, who has taken the whole race of men into his personal care and, amongst his benefactions, one and all most welcome, has conferred this favour – he has restored to each person what is his own.

For this reason I have taken a decision which is burdensome but necessary for the most illustrious city of the Ephesians . . . [9 lines missing] . . . for many houses . . . have been destroyed by fire or have been reduced to a heap of rubble by collapse; and the temple of Artemis herself, the jewel of the whole province on account of the grandeur of the building and the antiquity of the cult of the goddess and because of the abundance of funds which have been restored to the goddess by Augustus, is being deprived of its own money which would have sufficed for the care and decoration of the dedications. For this money is being siphoned off to the corrupt ends of those who lead the league in the way that they consider to be to their own profit. For whenever rather good news comes from Rome they exploit it to their own profit: using the condition of the divine house as a veil, they sell priesthoods in the manner of a public auction and they call together men of every kind to buy them; then they do not choose those most suitable to have the appropriate crown placed on their heads. They allot to the priests as much of the revenues as they are willing to take, so that they may pocket as much as possible . . . [about 11 lines missing] . . . I consider it necessary that the city bear these expenses so that the most suitable man may be thought to deserve the honour from the people. It is my wish that the excessive burden be removed by this decree. Since I know the payment of the money to be difficult for the city or completely impossible, if it were forced to pay out now what they took from the purchasers, it is my wish that the city give the priests no more than 1% of the price then paid, in accordance with the arrangement of Vedius Pollio, which was confirmed by the divine Augustus. But it is not my wish that the priests give anything to the council or take anything back from it in turn. Likewise, all those free men who do the jobs of public slaves and burden the community with an excessive expense must be dismissed and replaced in their jobs by public slaves. Likewise, in respect of public slaves, it is my wish that any of those slaves said to buy the offspring of a casual aquaintance and dedicate them to the goddess so that their slaves may be kept at the expense of her funds should provide sustenance for their own slaves. Likewise, in respect of victors at the sacred games who are said to be priests of Artemis with regard to the prize-account, it is not my wish that they be kept by Artemis; rather, that they receive as much as decreed under the arrangement of Vedius Pollio. Likewise, it is my wish that no priest of Artemis or annual magistrate borrow money on behalf of the public, unless he is able to pay the loan from the income of that year. But if anyone should commit the revenue of the following year, it is my wish that the moneylender be permitted to exact from him the money loaned. Likewise, it is my wish that money bequeathed to the city or to some part or organisation of the citizens be used in accordance with the terms of the bequest and not diverted by the magistrates to other uses and expenses. Likewise, that no more than 4,500 denarii be expended on the quinquennial games, in accordance with the arrangement of Vedius Pollio.

Likewise, it is my wish that the hymnodes, upon whom no small part of the city's income is spent, be released from this role and that the ephebes, whose age and status and aptitude for learning equip them for such a service, perform this function without payment. However, in order that it should not appear that I have made this pronouncement with regard to all hymnodes everywhere, I exempt those who hymn the divine Augustus himself at Pergamum in the precinct dedicated by Asia whose first synod was not convened with pay, but voluntarily and without payment, for which reason the divine Augustus confirmed the benevolence thereafter decreed to them and their successors and ordered the money spent on them to be defrayed not by the Pergamenes alone, but by the whole of Asia, reckoning it such an expense as to be burdensome for one city. However, the city of the Ephesians, saved this expense once the service has been transferred to the ephebes, will have to ensure that the ephebes perform the role with care and due attention, as befits those who hymn the divine house.

And since the long-due divine honour has been conferred upon Julia Augusta by our most pious imperator Augustus, her hymnodes must be granted the same rights as those of the divine Augustus, since the Senate and divine Augustus — after she had been honoured with sacred laws before her immortality — considered her worthy of divinity and conferred it upon her.

Likewise, it is right for others to ratify the honours proposed by the person who went up to the rostrum, the first of which has been appended to this edict:

The Greeks of Asia have resolved, Alexander having proposed . . . the . . . on the rostrum . . . in Asia, when Gaius Julius . . . was high priest. A pious act . . .

[587] M. Wörrle in J. Borchhardt (ed.), *Myra, eine lykische Metropole* (1975) pp. 254-86
Myra, Lycia

Decree of Quintus Veranius, propraetorian legate of Tiberius Claudius Caesar Augustus.

Tryphon, public slave of the city of Tlos, has not been taught either by my edicts or threats or even by the punishment inflicted upon slaves who have committed like crimes, that he must not accept into the city archive documents of an official nature which contain interpolations and erasures. I led him to understand my feelings against people like him by having him flogged and I thus made it clear to him that if he again ignores my instruction about official documents, it will not be with a simple beating but by exacting the supreme penalty from him that I will make the rest of the public slaves forget their past sloppiness.

As for the man who brought Tryphon to justice, Apollonius, son of Diopeithes, from Patara, let him receive from the city of Tlos, through the present treasurers, 300 drachmas, for I have fixed that amount as the reward for those who have brought public slaves to justice.

Further, in order that those concerned with issuing official documents, too, — on account of whom my solicitude ordered an enquiry on this matter — should cease working against their own security, I declare that any official document, of whatever sort, shall from the present day be invalid if it is written on a palimpsest or contains interpolations or erasures, whether it be a contract or a bond, whether a covenant, whether an order, whether a notice, whether an account, whether a legal challenge, whether a declaration concerning a legal case, whether an endowment, whether a decision of arbitrators or jurors. And if, through such a document, a fixed period is arranged, anyone not following my instructions in drafting the agreement will undermine the public administration, for how can something not be regarded as untrustworthy, when it was open to doubt in its very deposition, after it has fallen prey to forgetfulness from the passage of too much time, since the rationale behind the introduction of interpolations and erasures will be lost to those who come to examine the documents.

Those public slaves who accept such documents will be punished no less.

Let the magistrates in office in the month of Artemision write up this decree throughout the entire province entrusted to my care.

[588] *Small. 381*
42, edict of the prefect of Egypt

Lucius Aemilius Rectus proclaims:

No one is to be permitted to press into service the inhabitants of the countryside or to demand supplies or any other gift without my warrant. Anyone holding my warrant is to take a sufficiency of necessities and pay their cost. If, however, any of the soldiers or sword-bearers or any other servant in the public employ is reported to have acted contrary to my command or to have used violence or to have used violence against any inhabitant of the countryside or to have collected money, I shall exact the severest retribution from him.

Year 2 of Tiberius Claudius Caesar Augustus, imperator, the 4th Germanicius.

[589] *Small. 382*
1st Feb. 49, El Khargeh Oasis, on the outer gateway of the temple of Hibis. An edict of the prefect of Egypt

I, Posidonius, strategus, have appended for you a copy of the letter sent by the lord prefect together with the appended ordinance, so that you may know to comply and do nothing contrary to his instructions. Year 9 of Tiberius Claudius Caesar Augustus Germanicus, imperator, Mechir 7th.

Vergilius Capito to Posidonius, strategus of Oasis, greetings. I have sent you a copy of the edict which I have posted up in the city.[1] I wish you, therefore, to post it up in a visible place both in the metropolis of the nome and in each village, in clear and legible letters, and to ensure that these instructions of mine are carried out.

Gnaeus Vergilius Capito proclaims:

For some time I have been hearing that certain unjust and unreasonable charges have been made by those who exploit their powers avariciously and shamelessly, and now I have learned of it particularly in the case of Libyans: that, with those in military service stealing without fear of retribution, property is consumed on the excuse that it is due for their expenses and entertainment − this is not the practice, nor should it be −, likewise, also, under the head of transport. I therefore order that those travelling through the nomes, infantry and cavalry and messengers and centurions and tribunes and all the rest, take nothing nor requisition transport, unless they have my warrant; and that those passing through receive only shelter, no one being permitted to exact anything beyond what Maximus prescribed.[2] And if anyone gives payment or accounts it as given and exacts it from the public purse, I shall exact from him ten times the amount which he exacted from the nome and to the person who laid information against him I shall give four times that amount out of the property of the convicted man. And the royal secretaries and the village-secretaries and the district-secretaries in each nome are to write of all expenditures by the nome on anything or improper exactions or anything else and to pass these accounts, within sixty days − those in the Thebaid within four months − to the audit department and they are also to send auditors to Basilides, the freedman of Caesar, head of the audit department, so that if anything has been illegally collected or exacted, I will put it right. Likewise, I wish to show . . . [a large fragmentary section is omitted] . . . Year 9 of Tiberius Claudius Caesar Augustus Germanicus, imperator, Choiach 11th.

1. Alexandria.   2. An earlier prefect of Egypt.

[590] *Small. 383*
54, edict of the prefect of Egypt

Lusius Geta to Claudius Lysanias, strategus of the Arsinoite nome, greetings.

Post the following edict in the appropriate places in the nome, so that all may know of my orders. Farewell.

Lucius Lusius Geta proclaims:

Since the priests of the Arsinoite nome of the god Socnopaeus came before me and stated that they are being forced to work the land, I release them. And if anyone is found to have acted or intended to act so as to make my decisions, once made, uncertain, he will be punished either by a fine or corporal punishment, in accordance with his deserts.

Year 14 of Tiberius Claudius Caesar Augustus, 10th Pharmouthi.

[591] *Small. 384*
Histria, Moesia. Letters of Claudian and Neronian legates

Letter of Sabinus.
Flavius Sabinus to the magistrates, council and people of the Histrians, greetings.

It will be the responsibility of Arruntius Flamma, the prefect, to ensure that your right over Peuce remains unimpaired. For I have written to him to that effect. I shall also talk with Aelianus, my successor, and I shall give you total support.

Another letter of the same Sabinus.
Flavius Sabinus, legate, to the magistrates, council and people of the Histrians, greetings.

Even if the tax of the Danube bank stretches as far as the sea and the city stands at such a distance from the mouths of the river, nevertheless, since your envoys have given confirmation and Asiaticus the prefect said that the income from pickling fish was almost the only income of the city, I considered it necessary that you keep, in accordance with your custom, the same freedom to fish at the mouth of Peuce and to take pinewood for individual use without tax liability. For with regard to the use of the wood you have undisputed boundaries and you can exploit it, all without being subject to tax.

Letter of Pomponius Pius.
Pomponius Pius to the magistrates, council and people of the Histrians, greetings.

Even from what was written to you by Flavius Sabinus and Aelianus, men most illustrious and most honoured by me, it was possible to grasp that weakness of your city requires careful thought. It is a particular concern of the most divine Caesar, who is indeed also our saviour, that the rights of cities should not only be preserved but also increased: he has therefore decided that the income from fishing by Peuce is to be higher, by the right by which your forefathers and fathers enjoyed these revenues uninterruptedly by the grace of the Augusti.

Letter of Plautius Aelianus.
Plautius Aelianus to the magistrates of the Histrians, greetings.

The envoys, Callistratus, son of Demetrius, and Meidias, son of Artemidorus, have given me your decree. You requested through your decree that a deputation be sent to offer thanks to our most honoured Sabinus, something which I would gladly have done simply on account of Sabinus himself. You also requested that I keep your rights over Peuce inviolate. For my part, so far am I from violating any of the rights you have long kept that I would actually be delighted to find a means by which it would be possible to enhance a city that is ancient and Greek and pious towards Augustus and pious towards us.

Letter of Tullius Geminus.
Tullius Geminus, legate and propraetor of Tiberius Claudius Caesar Augustus Germanicus, to the magistrates, council and people of the Histrians, greetings.

Your envoys, Demetrius, Eschrion, Otacus, Meidias, Dionysodorus, Hegesagoras, Aristagoras and ... met me at Tomi and gave me your decree and, after indicating your goodwill towards our Augustus, offered me congratulations on my health and presence, having presented the most energetic case on the matters which you instructed them. Having learnt, then, of the state of your city, about which they explained to me, I shall always try to be responsible for some benefit towards you. And having been schooled on the subject of Peuce and the delta by your envoys, I have thought it right that the boundaries of your forefathers be preserved.

[592] O. Montevecchi, *Aegyptus*, 50 (1970) pp. 5-33

Ptolemais Euergetis, Egypt. An imperial letter, probably of Nero, at the beginning of his reign

[The beginning is lost] ... and of the two items remaining, I decline the temple you offer on the grounds that this honour is rightly paid by men to gods alone and I return, though with thanks, the gold crown, as I do not wish to burden you at the beginning of my principate. But as for what you, the 6475, have been granted by the imperators before me, ... and, as for what is shared by you all and what belongs to each individual, to keep you inviolate and unmolested, as my divine father also wished; you so testifying, with regard to everything he conferred upon the city and the 6475, I welcome and accept.

The envoys were Aeacidas, son of Ptolemy, Antenor, son of ... , Nibytas, son of Nibytas, Polycrates, son of Didymus, ... Themison ...

[593] *Small. 385*
Cnossus, Crete

Nero Claudius Caesar Augustus Germanicus restored to Aesculapius five iugera, given by the divine Augustus, confirmed by the divine Claudius, for the Julian colony of noble Cnossus, through Publius Licinius Secundus, procurator.

[594] J.M. Reynolds, *LibAnt*, 8 (1971) pp. 47-9
53, Cyrenaica, bilingual

Tiberius Claudius Caesar Augustus Germanicus, pontifex maximus, in his 13th year of tribunician power, imperator 27 times, father of his country, censor, consul five times, through Lucius Acilius Strabo, his own legate, restored areas held by private persons to the Roman people.

[595] *Small. 386*
55, Cyrenaica, bilingual; cf. Tac. *Ann.* 14. 18.2-4

Nero Claudius Caesar Augustus Germanicus, son of the divine Claudius, grandson of Germanicus Caesar, great-grandson of Tiberius Caesar Augustus, great-great-grandson of the divine Augustus, pontifex maximus, with tribunician power, imperator, consul, through Lucius Acilius Strabo, his legate, restored land occupied by private persons to the Roman people.

[596] *Small. 387*
Pisidia

As the result of a letter of the divine Augustus Germanicus Caesar, Quintus Petronius Umber, legate and propraetor of Nero Claudius Caesar Augustus Germanicus, and Lucius Pupius Praeses, procurator of Nero Claudius Caesar Augustus Germanicus, drew boundaries; that on the right belongs to the Sagalassians, that on the left to the village of the Tymbrianassians of Nero Claudius Caesar Augustus Germanicus, in which is also a fifth of the Sagalassians.

[597] *Small. 388*
64-5, Gortyn, Crete

By authority of Nero Claudius Caesar Augustus Germanicus, pontifex maximus, in his 11th year of tribunician power, imperator, consul 4 times, father of his country, and by decree of the Senate, Lucius Turpilius Dexter, proconsul, restored the public domains of the Gortynians, most occupied by private persons, and drew boundaries.

[598] *Small. 389*
Near Corinium, Dalmatia

Boundaries drawn between the Neditae and the Corinienses, measurements made by order of Ducenius Geminus, legate, through Aulus Resius Maximus, centurion of legion 11, *princeps posterior*[1] of cohort 1, and Quintus Aebutius Liberalis, centurion of the same legion, *hastatus posterior*[1] of cohort 1.

1. Titles of centurions of legionary cohorts.

[599] *Small. 390*
Aezani, Phrygia

From Rome. Nero to Menophilus, greetings.

Menecles and Metrodorus, your sons, came to me and explained to me in full how you yourself have striven in my regard and the innovations you have made in the city concerning my honours. On account of this, it was in no ordinary fashion that I heard firm news of your goodwill towards me and your perpetual eagerness to devise something extra in my honour ... [3 fragmentary lines] ... may your energy on my account be without cost to you, who have already shown so much that you do not choose to spare your energy for the sake of your own resources. Menecles, your son, was also prepared to stay with me as long as I might wish ... [15 fragmentary lines follow].

[600] *Small. 391*
6th July 68. Edict of Tiberius Julius Alexander

Julius Demetrius, strategus of the Thebaid Oasis.

I have appended for you a copy of the edict sent me by the lord prefect Tiberius Julius Alexander, so that you may know and enjoy his beneficence. Year 2 of Lucius Livius Augustus Sulpicius Galba, imperator, Phaophi 1st, Julia Augusta.[1]

Tiberius Julius Alexander proclaims:

In giving every thought to the maintenance of the city in its proper state, enjoying the benefactions that it receives from the Augusti, and to the maintenance of Egypt in tranquillity, contributing eagerly to the corn-supply and the greatest good fortune of present times, not burdened by new and unjust exactions, indeed, almost since I entered the city, being called upon by small and large delegations, both from the well-off here and the country farmers, denouncing the most pressing abuses, I have not ceased, as far as possible, correcting urgent wrongs. In order that you may more confidently have every expectation of the Augustus that has shone upon us for the safety of the whole race of men, imperator Galba, expectations both of safety and joy, and in order that you may know that I have given thought to what helps you, I have set out strictly with regard to each of your requests what it is possible for me to decide and to do, but greater matters, requiring the might and greatness of the imperator, I will show to him in total truth, since the gods have reserved the safety of the world for this most sacred time.

I have recognised, first of all, the entire good sense of your petition to the effect that people who are unwilling should not be forcibly made to collect taxes or other estate payments, contrary to the usual practice of prefects, and that it has greatly harmed the administration that many people inexperienced in such administration have been forced to it, tax-collection having been imposed upon them. For that reason I myself have not made anyone collect taxes or rents, nor will I, for I know that it is to the advantage of the imperial fiscus that the influential should willingly and eagerly take part in administration. I am convinced that in future no one will make the unwilling collect taxes or rents, but will allocate these tasks to those who freely and willingly come forward, preferring to maintain the long-standing habit of former prefects than to imitate the sporadic injustice of someone.

Since some people, under cover of the public finances, have taken upon themselves the debts of others and have put some in prison or another form of detention, I have decided that this practice must be stopped for this very reason, so that debts are exacted from people's property, not their persons, conforming to the will of the divine Augustus; I order that no one, under cover of the public finances, should take upon himself debts due to others which he himself did not contract from the first and that no one at all confine free people in any form of detention, unless he be a criminal, nor to the prison, except those with debts to the imperial account.

Further, in order that the name of the public finances should not at public cost oppress contracts between people and that those who use the right to first payment in inappropriate cases should not undermine the common credit, I have made strict provisions about this too. For it has often been revealed to me that certain persons have already tried to set aside mortgages legally contracted and to call in issued loans from debtors by use of force and to cancel sales by taking the property of the purchasers on the grounds that these obligations were entered into with persons who had contracted with the fiscus for the collection of special levies, either with strategi or with officials or with others connected with the public account. I therefore order that if any imperial procurator or oeconomus here should have any suspicion of those engaged in public business, he should enter his name or post it up, so that no one will make a contract with such a man or he should place part of his property in the public record office against the debt. But if anyone, his name not entered nor his property taken, should lend money having contracted a legal mortgage or call in his loan in advance of time or purchase anything from anyone whose name is not entered or whose property has not been taken, he shall have no right of action. Dowries belonging to others and not the property of husbands the divine Augustus and the prefects ordered to be paid from the fiscus to wives, whose right to prior payment must be maintained.

I have also received petitions about tax-immunities and tax-remissions, in which the accounts of revenue are also included, from those of the opinion that they should be maintained in accordance with the concessionary letter of the divine Claudius to Postumus and who state that property sold by private persons was later found against in the period between the decision of Flaccus and the concession of the divine Claudius. Therefore, since both Balbillus and Vestinus made these concessions, I honour the decisions of both these prefects, since their decisions were in accord with the dispensation of the divine Claudius, that they be freed from the charges not yet exacted from them; it is evident that in future their rights to tax-immunity and tax-remissions will be protected.

As for property sold by Caesar's account in the interval, on which charges were adjudged, since Vestinus ordered that the proper taxes be paid, I too ordain, having freed them from the charges not yet exacted, that also in future only the proper taxes be paid. For it is unjust that those who have bought properties and paid the price for them should be required to pay rentals for private property as if they were state tenants.

And it is in conformity with the dispensations of the Augusti that native Alexandrians and those Alexandrians dwelling in the country area should be made to perform no country liturgy. You have often requested, and I ensure it, that no native Alexandrian be made to perform country liturgies.

It will also be my concern to appoint strategi after careful consideration, those appointed to hold the office for a period of three years.

And I order with total authority that, whenever a prefect finds innocent a man brought before him, that man is not to be subjected to further examination. If two prefects have reached the same judgement, the accountant who has brought the same case under examination again is to be punished. For he is doing nothing other than providing himself with a means for blackmail, so too other officials. Indeed many have sought to divest themselves of their private possessions rather than pay more than its worth because at each examination the same matters are presented for judgement.

And I make the same provisions with regard to matters brought before the idiologus, that if anything, after trial, is dismissed or shall be dismissed by the officer appointed by the idiologus, it will not again be possible for the same charge to be submitted to the prosecutor or for this charge to be brought to trial; otherwise, the person so doing will be punished without mercy. For there will be no end to denunciations if the same matters, once dismissed, are brought to trial again until a conviction is gained. And since the city has become all but uninhabitable on account of the mob of informers and every house has been thrown into confusion already, I strictly order that if any prosecutor of the idiologus brings a case in joint prosecution with another, that that man who has brought the accusation should be presented by him in court, so that the man should not be free from all risk. But if he brings three cases and does not prove them, he shall not be allowed to bring a prosecution again, but half his property should be forfeit. For it is most unjust that one who puts many others at risk over their property and status should be completely unaccountable. And I shall order with full authority that the regulations of the idiologus should stand, now that I have abolished innovations made in contravention of the dispensations of the Augusti. And I shall publish openly how I have exacted retribution from informers already condemned.

I am well aware that you are exercising great prudence for the maintenance of prosperity in Egypt, prudence which is burdening you. I have therefore abolished your liturgies as far as was possible. For farmers all over the country area have often come to me and demonstrated that they have been made to pay many new charges, not on account of wrongdoings, but on account of payments in kind and in money, though it is not permitted just anyone irresponsibly to introduce some total innovation. I have found that these condemnations and the like stretch not only over the Thebaid or the far-off nomes of the low country, but they have also affected the outskirts of the city, the so-called Alexandrian country and the Mareote nome. For this reason I order the strategi of each nome, if any farmers have been condemned in the previous five years to pay unprecedented charges, in all or many nomes or toparchies, they shall restore the previous conditions and discontinue these charges, and any case brought under examination I dismiss from the courts.

In the past I have also curbed the unrestricted power of the accountants because everyone complained against them for entering a great number of assessments on the grounds of analogy, with the result that they were making money and Egypt was being devastated. And now I instruct the same people to enter no assessment on the grounds of analogy, nor yet anything else at all without the decision of the prefect. And I order the strategi to accept nothing from the accountants without the warrant of the prefect. As for the other officials, if they should be discovered to have entered any assessment falsely or improperly, they will pay to private persons what they have demanded from them and they will pay an equal amount to the treasury.

Of the same brand of malpractice is so-called taxation by estimate, on the basis not of the actual rise of the Nile, but of a calculation from certain previous rises, whereas nothing seems more just than the actual truth. I wish to encourage men to farm with enthusiasm, in the knowledge that taxation will be on the basis of the actuality of the real rise and flooded land and not on the basis of the chicanery of assessments by estimate. And if anyone is convicted of having cheated in taxation, he will pay three times his deceit.

As for those who have been frightened by the rumour that the ancient land in the Alexandrian country and the Menelaite nome is to be surveyed, land to which the measurement rod has never been applied, let their concern achieve its ends. For no one has ever ventured this survey nor will anyone do so. For it is proper that the ancient right of the land should stand.

And I make the same provision with regard to accretions to this territory, so that no new tax is to be instituted.

With regard to your older depositions, still standing, in which . . .

they often achieved nothing more than the enrichment of officials and the oppression of people, I shall write to Caesar Augustus, imperator, with the other reports I am making to him, the only one able completely to eradicate such practices, he whose continual beneficence and care are the causes of the welfare of us all.

Year 1 of Lucius Livius Galba Caesar Augustus, imperator, Epeiph 12th.

1. 28 Sept 68.

[601] *Small. 392*
Sardinia, 18th March 69

Under Imperator Otho Caesar Augustus, consul, 18th March, copied and authenticated from the handled ledger of Lucius Helvius Agrippa, proconsul, produced by Gnaeus Egnatius Fuscus, quaestorian secretary, in which was written the following, on the fifth tablet, in chapters 8, 9 and 10.

March 13th, Lucius Helvius Agrippa, proconsul, having heard the case, pronounced:

Since it is in the public interest that judgements reached should stand and since on the case of the Patulcenses Marcus Juventius Rixa,[1] a most distinguished man, procurator of Augustus, has repeatedly pronounced, 'The borders of the Patulcenses are to be preserved as ordained in the bronze tablet by Marcus Metellus,'[2] and finally pronounced, 'My inclination is to punish the Galillenses who keep renewing the controversy and do not obey my decree, but in view of the clemency of the best and greatest princeps[3] I am content to advise them by edict to rest quiet and stand by the judgements reached and, before 1st October next, withdraw from the lands of the Patulcenses and give them vacant possession; but if they persist in contumacy I will take severe measures against the authors of the sedition.' And after that Caecilius Simplex, a most illustrious man, approached over the same matter by the Galillenses who stated that they would bring from the archive of the princeps a document bearing on the matter, pronounced, 'It is humane that a delay should be granted for proof', and he gave them a postponement of three months to 1st December and said that if no document was produced before that date, he would follow that document in the province.

I in turn, approached by the Galillenses with excuses for the nonproduction of the document, granted a postponement to 1st February next, and since I see that the delay is to the liking of those in possession,

I order that the Galillenses should leave the territory of the Campanian Patulcenses, which they have forcibly seized, before 1st April next. But if they fail to comply with this pronouncement, they should know that they will be guilty of prolonged contumacy and will be prone to the action that has often been publicised already.

In the advisory council were: Marcus Julius Romulus, propraetorian legate, Titus Atilius Sabinus, propraetorian quaestor [and 6 others]. Signatories: [10 names follow].

1. Proconsul, AD 67.   2. Proconsul, 114 BC.   3. Probably Nero.

[602] *EJ 162*
New Carthage

To King Juba, son of King Juba, grandson of King Hiempsal, great-grandson of King Gauda, great-great-great-grandson of King Massinissa, duumvir quinquennalis, patron; the colonists.

[603] *EJ 162a*
Silver coin, Mauretania

Obv. Head of Juba II. KING JUBA
Rev. Bust of Cleopatra Selene. QUEEN CLEOPATRA

[604] Crinagoras, *Palatine Anthology*, 9.235

Great neighbour-lands of the world, which the Nile
In spate separates from black Ethiopians,
You have shared your kings through marriage,
You have made one the peoples of Egypt and Libya.
May the royal children inherit from their parents in turn
Firm rule over both lands.

[605] *EJ 163*
29-30, Iol-Caesarea, Mauretania

For the safety of King Ptolemy, son of King Juba, in the tenth year of his reign, I, Antistia Galla, have freely and duly fulfilled my vow to Saturn, the victim having been received from Julia Vitalis, daughter of Respectus, of Rusguniae.

[606] *CIL 8.21093*
Iol-Caesarea, Mauretania

To Gaius Julius Montanus, freedman of King Ptolemy; Julia Prima, his wife, made this.

[607] *EJ 164*
Athens

The people honoured King Ptolemy, son of King Juba, descendant of King Ptolemy, for his virtue and good-will towards it.

[608] M.P. Speidel, *Ant. Afr.*, 14 (1979) pp. 121-2
Iol-Caesarea, Mauretania

(a) Jacentus, a bodyguard, lies here; made by his sons.
(b) Crestus, decurion of the bodyguards. Aule, his wife, set this up, as he deserved.
(c) Aebutius Rufus, soldier of the urban cohort, in the century of Oletanus, lived 31 years.

[609] *EJ 176*
Athens

The council and the people honoured Queen Glaphyra, daughter of King Archelaus, wife of King Juba, for her virtue.

[610] *EJ 175*
Athens

The people honoured the king of Cappadocia and Rough Cilicia, Archelaus Philopatris, for his virtue.

[611] *EJ 166*
9-8 BC, Segusio, Cottian Alps, arch

To Imperator Caesar Augustus, son of a god, pontifex maximus, in his 15th year of tribunician power, imperator 13 times, Marcus Julius Cottius, son of King Donnus, prefect of the following states:

Segovii, Segusini, Belaci, Caturiges, Medulli, Tebavii, Adanates, Savincates, Ecdinii, Veaminii, Venisami, Iemerii, Vesubianii, Quadiates and the states which have been under that prefect.

[612] *EJ 168*
Philippi

To Gaius Julius Rhoemetalces, king, son of King Rhescuporis; Marcus Acculeius, son of Marcus, of the tribe Voltinia, had this made for his well-deserving friend.

[613] *EJ 169*
Near Neapolis, Thrace

To Zeus the Highest, a thank-offering for Lord King of the Thracians Rhoemetalces, son of Cotys, and his children; Eutychus, superintendent of the mines, and all those under him.

[614] *EJ 170*
Panticapaeum

In the reign of Great King of Kings Asander Philorhomaeus, Saviour, and of Queen Dynamis, Pantaleon, nauarch, to Poseidon Saviour of Ships and Aphrodite Nauarchess.

[615] *EJ 171*
Phanagoreia

Imperator Caesar Augustus, son of a god, the ruler of land and all sea, her own saviour and benefactor; Queen Dynamis Philorhomaeus.

[616] *CIRB 978*
Phanagoreia

Livia, the wife of Augustus; Queen Dynamis Philorhomaeus honoured her benefactress.

[617] *EJ 172*
Panticapaeum

Great King Aspurgus Philorhomaeus, Philocaesar and Philorhomaeus, son of King Asandrochus, king of all the Bosporus, of Theodosia and Sindi and Maeti and Tarpeti and Toreti, Psesi and Tanaiti, conqueror of Scyths and Tauri; Menestratus, son of Menestratus, governor of the island, honoured his own saviour and benefactor.

[618] T.V. Blavatskaya, *SA* (1965) pp. 197-209
Gorgippia

King Aspurgus Philorhomaeus, to Pantaleon and Theangelus, greetings.

Since I am generously disposed towards the city of the Gorgippians and since I wish to give them their due reward for having thought fit to support me in many matters, above all by maintaining the greatest good order in accordance with my instructions at the time of my visit to Augustus, I decree that in future they should keep firm possession of property inherited, in accordance with the inheritance law of Eupator.

Post up notices, then, and display this decree for all to see, in accordance with my decision. Farewell. Year 312, Daesius 20th.

[619] *EJ 173*
Smyrna (?)

The people honoured Zeno, son of Queen Pythodoris Philometor and King Polemo, grandson through his mother of Antonia the benefactress.

[620] *EJ 177*
Anazarbus, Cilicia

Drusus Caesar, son of Tiberius Augustus, grandson of divine Augustus; Helenus, freedman of King Philopator.

[621] *EJ 178*
Athens

The people honoured King Herod Philorhomaeus, for his benefaction and good-will towards it.

[622] *EJ 179*
Delos

The people of the Athenians and the residents of the island honoured Herod,[1] son of King Herod, tetrarch, for his virtue and good-wil towards them ... when Apollonius, son of Apollonius, of Rhamnusia, was epimelete of the island.

1. = Antipas.

[623] *EJ 180*
Abila, Syria

For the safety of the lords Augusti and their whole house; Nymphaeus
... freedman of Lysanias the tetrarch, who built the road where there
was none and erected the temple and planted all the orchards around
it at his own expense for divine Cronus, lord, and ... Eusebia, his
wife.

[624] *EJ 181*
Silver coin, Armenia

Obv. Head of Augustus. OF DIVINE CAESAR, BENEFACTOR.
Rev. Head of Artavasdes III. OF GREAT KING ARTAVASDES.

[625] *EJ 182*
Didrachm, Caesarea, Cappadocia; cf. Tac. *Ann.* 2.56; R. Seager, *Tiberius*
(1972) p. 101n.2

Obv. Head of Germanicus. GERMANICUS CAESAR, SON OF
    TIBERIUS AUGUSTUS, CONSUL TWICE.
Rev. Germanicus crowning Artaxias. ARTAXIAS GERMANICUS.

[626] *EJ 183*
Rome; cf. *RG* 32.2

Seraspadanes, son of Phraates the Arsacid, king of kings, Parthian.
Rhodaspes, son of Phraates the Arsacid, king of kings, Parthian.

[627] *Small. 197* with J.E. Bogaers, *Britannia*, 10 (1979)
pp. 243-54

To Neptune and Minerva, for the welfare of the divine house, by
authority of Tiberius Claudius Cogidubnus, great king of Britain,
the college of engineers and its members gave this temple from their
own resources, ... son of Pudentinus, presenting the site.

[628] *Small. 198*
Silver coin, S.E. Britain

Obv. Head of Hercules in a lion-skin. CARATACUS.
Rev. An eagle standing on a serpent.

[629] *Small. 200*
(a) Bronze coin, Laconia
Obv. Head of Claudius, laureate. TIBERIUS CLAUDIUS CAESAR
Rev. The round caps of the Dioscuri. THE SPARTANS, UNDER IACO

(b) Taenarum, Laconia
The league of the Free Laconians honours Gaius Julius Laco, son of
Eurycles, its own benefactor. Supervised by Damarmenidas, a general.

[630] *Small. 201*
(a) Bronze coin of Rhoemetalces III of Thrace
Obv. Head of Gaius, laureate. TO GAIUS CAESAR AUGUSTUS.
Rev. Bust of Rhoemetalces. KING RHOEMETALCES.

(b) Maroneia, Thrace
The people honoured the king of the Thracians, Rhoemetalces, son of
   Cotys, the benefactor of the Bistones.

[631] *Small. 203(b)*
58, Panticapaeum, Bosporus

Imperator Nero Caesar Augustus, son of Claudius, consul three times,
in his fifth year of tribunician power, father of his country, his own
saviour and benefactor; Cotys, son of Aspurgus, king, friend of Caesar
and friend of the Romans, pious, high-priest of the Augusti for life,
dedicated this.

[632] *Small. 204*
67, Bosporus, deed of manumission

To highest God, all-powerful, blessed, in the reign of King Rhescuporis,
friend of Caesar and friend of the Romans, year 364, month of Daesius
. . . I, Neocles, son of Athenodorus, manumit in the sight of Zeus,
Earth and Sun . . . Athenodorus, son of Athenaeus, my father, having
given his agreement, on the understanding that they are not to be liable
to seizure and molestation by any heir of mine and that they are to
go wherever they wish by virtue of my valid instruction.

[633] *Small. 205*
Bronze coin of Antiochus IV of Commagene

Obv. Bust of Antiochus, wearing a diadem. GREAT KING ANTIOCHUS
EPIPHANES
Rev. A wreath around a scorpion and the words OF THE
COMMAGENIANS

[634] *Small. 206*
52-3, silver coin of Polemo II of Pontus

Obv. Head of Polemo II. OF KING POLEMO
Rev. Head of Claudius, laureate. YEAR 15

[635] Y. Meshorer, *Jewish coins of the Second Temple
Period* (1970) no. 93, reading not entirely certain

Obv. Agrippa I (?) sacrificing with patera at small altar, crowned by
two female figures, one each side. KING AGRIPPA, FRIEND OF
CAESAR
Rev. Clasped hands. FRIENDSHIP OF KING AGRIPPA WITH THE
SENATE AND PEOPLE OF ROME

[636] *Small. 210*
43, bronze coin of Herod of Chalcis

Obv. Head of Herod, wearing a diadem. KING HEROD FRIEND OF
CLAUDIUS
Rev. A laurel wreath round the words TO CLAUDIUS CAESAR
AUGUSTUS, YEAR 3

[637] *Small. 211*
(a) Bronze coin of Agrippa II, Neronias (= Caesarea Philippi)
Obv. Head of Nero, laureate. NERO CAESAR AUGUSTUS
Rev. A wreath around the words. UNDER KING AGRIPPA, NERONIAS

(b) Seeia, Arabia
Under Great King Agrippa, friend of Caesar, pious and friend of the
Romans, the son of Great King Agrippa, friend of Caesar, pious and
friend of the Romans, Aphareus the freedman and his son Agrippa
dedicated this.

[638] *Small. 212*
(a) Athens
The council of the Areopagus and the council of the 600 and the people honoured Julia Berenice, great queen, daughter of King Agrippa and descendant of great kings, benefactors of the city, through her providence, epimelete of the city being Tiberius Claudius Theogenes of Paeania.

(b) Berytus, in the forum, heavily restored
Queen Berenice, daughter of Great King Agrippa, and King Agrippa have completely rebuilt the temple, collapsed with age, which King Herod, their great-grandfather, had built, and adorned it with marbles and six columns.

[639] *Small. 213*
51, tetradrachm of Vologaeses I

Obv. Bust of Vologaeses, wearing a diadem
Rev. Vologaeses seated, receiving a diadem from a city Tyche. OF KING OF KINGS ARSACES EUERGETES DIKAIOS EPIPHANES PHILHELLENE. YEAR 362, HYPERBERETAEUS

[640] (a) *EJ 324*
Pompeii

To Marcus Holconius Rufus, son of Marcus, military tribune chosen by the people, duumvir for the administration of justice, for five years, quinquennalis twice, priest of Augustus Caesar, patron of the colony.

(b) *ILS 6362*
Pompeii

To Marcus Holconius Celer, duumvir for the administration of justice, quinquennalis designate, priest of Augustus.

(c) *ILS 5638*
Pompeii

The Marci Holconii, Rufus and Celer, built the arcade, platforms and theatre[1] at their own expense.

1. Where these three texts were found.

[641] *EJ 325*
Pompeii

Publius Stallius Agathon, attendant by decree of the decurions in the consulship of Imperator Caesar for the ninth time and Marcus Silanus,[1] reappointed in the consulship of Publius Alfenus and Publius Vinicius,[2] by order of Marcus Pomponius Marcellus and Lucius Valerius Flaccus, duumvirs for the administration of justice, and of Lucius Obellius Lucretianus and Aulus Perennius Merulinus, duumvirs for the care of roads and sacred and public buildings.

1. 25 BC.   2. AD 2.

[642] *EJ 326*
Pompeii, weighing-table with five cavities for specimen weights

Aulus Clodius Flaccus, son of Aulus, and Numerius Arcaeus Arellianus Celadus, son of Numerius, duumvirs for the administration of justice on the balancing of measures by decree of the decurions.

[643] *EJ 327*
Pompeii

(1) Clodia, daughter of Aulus, public priestess of Ceres by decree of the decurions.

(2) Lassia, daughter of Marcus, public priestess of Ceres by decree of the decurions.

(3) Aulus Clodius, son of Marcus, of the tribe Palatina, secretary, master of the fortunate suburban Augustan district.

(4) Aulus Clodius Flaccus, son of Aulus, duumvir for the administration of justice three times, quinquennalis, military tribune chosen by the people.

In his first duumvirate, at the festival of Apollo, in the forum, he put on a procession, bulls, bullfighters, running performers, three pairs of platform-fighters, boxing troupes and Greek boxers, spectacles with every act and every sort of pantomime and Pylades and 10,000 sesterces to the state for the duumvirate.

In his second duumvirate, as quinquennalis, at the festival of Apollo, in the forum, he put on a procession, bulls, bullfighters, running performers and troupes of boxers; on the next day, alone, at the spectacles he put on thirty pairs of athletes and five pairs of gladiators, and 35 pairs of gladiators and beast-hunts, bulls, bull-fighters, boars, bears and various other forms of beast-hunt with his colleague.

In his third duumvirate,[1] he provided spectacles with the first theatre-company, with acts added jointly with his colleague.

(5) Lucius Gellius Calvus, son of Lucius, of the tribe Menenia, decurion at Pompeii.

Clodia, daughter of Aulus, erected this monument at her own expense for herself and her family.

1. Other evidence puts this in AD 2.

[644] *EJ 328*
12 BC, Capua

To Jupiter Optimus Maximus, in the consulship of Publius Sulpicius Quirinius and Gaius Valgius, in the duumvirate of Sextus Pontidius Bassus and Marcus Junius Celer, in the aedileship of Sextus Helvius, son of Gaius, and Publius Titius Falernus, Publius Rammius Chrestus, freedman of Publius, navigator, to Jupiter Optimus Maximus (picture of a ship).

[645] *EJ 329*
Capua

Since ... the duumvirs, made a statement that ... it was proper to decorate the best of men with every honour, private and public; asked for their opinion on that matter, on that matter this decree has been made:

Since Lucius Antistius Campanus, after a complete military career, having won the esteem of the divine Caesar and the divine Augustus and having been settled by the latter in our colony, has exercised his munificence in private and public in such a way that he all but shared his patrimony with the state by personally bearing very many different expenses and he always seemed happier to spend his money on the public than to the benefit of himself and his family and he grew old in amassing the leading offices of state, so that even now he is involved in our greatest affairs; and since he has now succumbed in his endeavour,

which has proved valuable to the state but onerous for his years, the
conscript fathers have decided that the memory of a most worthy and
valuable citizen . . . be decorated with these honours; that he be borne
from the forum to his funeral pyre in a funeral contracted . . . and
approved by the duumvirs, one or both, and that the day appointed
for the funeral be postponed, so that nothing may prevent the people
from attending the funeral of the best and most munificent of men in
numbers as great as possible, and that a gilded statue . . . be erected
to him at public expense, with this . . . decree of the decurions
inscribed on it, in the place where Antistius Campanus, the best of
sons and the heir of his service and munificence, should choose . . .
also with the other statues, shields and gifts which he received . . . down
to his death and honours presented to him posthumously and that a
site be given at public expense which Lucius Antistius Campanus should
choose . . . beside the Via Appia . . .

[646] *EJ 330*
Near Formiae

Marcus Caelius Phileros, freedman of Marcus, orderly of Titus Sextius,
imperator in Africa, at Carthage aedile, prefect for the administration
of justice in the sale of quinquennial taxes in 83 settlements, built the
temple of Tellus at his own expense; duumvir at Clupea twice; at
Formiae Augustalis, adorned the temple of Neptune with varied stone-
work at his own expense. To Fresidia Flora, freedwoman of Numerius,
his wife, most obedient to her husband. To Octavius Antimachus,
freedman of Gaia, dear friend.

[647] *EJ 331*
Suessula, Campania

[Beginning is lost] . . . son of Caesar Augustus, Gaius Sallustius
Epagathicus, by virtue of his office as Augustalis; site granted by decree
of the decurions.

[648] *EJ 332*
Rufrae, Campania

To Marcus Volcius Sabinus, son of Marcus, military tribune, because he
brought the Aqua Julia here at his own expense; the townsmen of
Rufrae.

[649] *EJ 333*
26, Veii, decree of the town council

The 100 of the municipality of Augustan Veii, when they met at Rome in the temple of Venus Genetrix, decided unanimously − to be permitted by the authority of all until the decree is drafted − that to Gaius Julius Gelos, freedman of the divine Augustus, who has not only always assisted the municipality of Veii by his care and favour but has also sought to extol it by his expenditures and through his son, the honour most fitting is to be decreed: that he be counted in the number of Augustales just as if he held that office, and that he be permitted to sit among the Augustales on his own double-seat at all spectacles in the municipality and to take part among the 100 at all public dinners; and likewise it is decided that no tax of the municipality of Augustan Veii be exacted from him or his children.

Present were Gaius Scaevius Curiatius and Lucius Perperna Priscus, duumvirs, Marcus Flavius Rufus, quaestor, Titus Vettius Rufus, quaestor, Marcus Tarquitius Saturninus, Lucius Maecilius Scrupus, Lucius Favonius Lucanus, Gnaeus Octavius Sabinus, Titus Sempronius Gracchus, Publius Acuvius, son of Publius, of the tribe Tromentina, Gaius Veianius Maximus, Titus Tarquitius Rufus, Gaius Julius Merula. Passed in the consulship of Gaetulicus and Calvisius Sabinus.

[650] *EJ 334*
Falerii

In honour of Imperator Caesar Augustus, son of a god, pontifex maximus, father of his country and the municipality, the masters of the Augustales, Gaius Egnatius Glyco, freedman of Marcus, Gaius Egnatius Musicus, freedman of Gaius, Gaius Julius Isochrysus, freedman of Caesar, Quintus Floronius Princeps, freedman of Quintus, had the Via Augusta paved with stone from the Via Annia outside the gate to the temple of Ceres at their own expense for the games.

[651] *EJ 335*
Asculum

To the departed spirit; to Marcus Valerius Verna, freedman of the colonists, sevir Augustalis and Tiberialis. Januarius, steward of the colonists, who had been his treasurer. Likewise Vibia Primilla, his wife, for herself and their descendants.

[652] *EJ 336*
Iguvium

Gnaeus Satrius Rufus, son of Gnaeus, one of the 4 for the administration of justice, provided the basilicas with panelled ceilings, affixed iron to the roof beams, faced them with stone and enclosed them with a faced step:

In the name of the duumvirate: 6,000 sesterces
For the supply of the legions: 3,450 sesterces
For the restoration of the temple of Diana: 6,200 sesterces
For the games of the Victory of Caesar Augustus: 7,750 sesterces

[653] *EJ 337*
Umbria

To . . . son of Vibius, of the tribe Clustumina, father.
To . . . son of Tiberius, of the tribe Clustumina, brother.
To . . . mother.
. . . Clemens, son of Tiberius, of the tribe Pupinia, secretary to the 26, military tribune chosen by the people, duumvir for the administration of justice at Carsulae, during six days of the circus and six of the theatre, was the first to put on a gladiatorial show in the municipality.

[654] *EJ 338*
23-20 BC, Augusta Praetoria

To Imperator Caesar Augustus, son of a god, consul 11 times, imperator 8 times, with tribunician power; the Salassian inhabitants who joined in the colony in the beginning to their patron.

[655] *EJ 339*
Pola, arch

Lucius Sergius, son of Gaius, aedile, duumvir.
Salvia Postuma, wife of Sergius.
Lucius Sergius Lepidus, son of Lucius, aedile, military tribune of
    legion 29.
Gnaeus Sergius, son of Gaius, aedile, duumvir quinquennalis.
Salvia Postuma, wife of Sergius, at her own expense.

[656] *EJ 340*
Mediolanum Santonum, Gaul

To Gaius Julius Marinus, son of Gaius Julius Ricoveriugus, of the tribe Voltinia, first priest of Augustus, curator of Roman citizens, quaestor, vergobret; Julia Marina, his daughter, set this up.

[657] *EJ 341*
Lutetia Parisiorum, altar

Under Tiberius Caesar Augustus, to Jupiter Optimus Maximus the sailors of the Parisii set this up at public expense.

[658] *EJ 344*
32-3, near Membressa, Africa

To Tiberius Caesar Augustus, son of Augustus, pontifex maximus, consul five times, imperator 8 times, in his 34th year of tribunician power; Gaius Septumius Saturninus, son of Gaius, priest, made the four columns at his own expense, the supervisor being Lucius Lurius Rufus, son of Quintus.

[659] *EJ 345*
36-7, Thugga, Africa

To Imperator Tiberius Caesar Augustus, son of the divine Augustus, pontifex maximus, in his 38th year of tribunician power, consul 5 times; Lucius Manilius Bucco, son of Lucius, of the tribe Arnensis, duumvir, made this dedication. Lucius Postumius Chius, son of Gaius of the tribe Arnensis, patron of the community, in the name of himself and his sons, Firmus and Rufus, paved the forum and the area in front of the temple of Caesar and had the altar of Augustus, the temple of Saturn and the arch built at his own expense.

[660] *EJ 346*
1-2, architrave with Latin and Neo-Punic inscription, Lepcis Magna

Imperator Caesar Augustus, son of a god, being pontifex maximus, in his 24th year of tribunician power, consul 13 times, father of his country, Annobal Rufus, adorner of his country, lover of concord, priest, suffete, prefect of sacred rites, son of Himilco Tapapius, had this made at his own expense and also dedicated it.

[661] *EJ 347*
Salonae

To Lucius Anicius Paetina, son of Lucius, one of the 4 for the administration of justice, quinquennalis, prefect quinquennalis of Drusus Caesar Germanicus, prefect quinquennalis of Publius Dolabella, priest, flamen of Julia Augusta, prefect of engineers, the Pharian prefecture of Salonae.

[662] *EJ 347a*
Dalmatia; cf. J.J. Wilkes, *Dalmatia* (1969) p. 112

To divine Augustus and Tiberius Caesar, son of Augustus, a dedication; the veterans of the Scunasticus region to whom the colony of Narona gave land.

[663] *EJ 348*
Chersus, Dalmatian island

To Tiberius Caesar Augustus, son of Augustus, pontifex maximus, Gaius Aemilius Oea, son of Volso, and Lucius Fonteius Rufus, son of Quintus, the duumvirs, had the portico and senate-house made by decree of the decurions and approved them.

[664] *EJ 349*
Corinth

To Titus Manlius Juvencus, son of Titus, of the tribe Collina, aedile, prefect for the administration of justice, duumvir, priest, president of the Isthmian and Caesarian Games, the first to celebrate Caesarean Games before the Isthmian Games; the members of the Amphictyonic Council.

[665] *EJ 350*
Gytheum, Laconia, bilingual

Gaius Julius Eurycles, son of Lachares; the Roman citizens who live and conduct business in Laconia, for his beneficence.

[666] *EJ 351*
Asopus, Laconia

The city honoured Gaius Julius Eurycles, its benefactor, who provided olive-oil in perpetuity.

[667] *EJ 353*
Thyateira, Asia

The gymnasts of the third gymnasium honoured Gaius Julius Lepidus, son of Marcus, the high-priest of Asia and president of the games for life, in his fifth year as gymnasiarch, in the charge of Artemidorus, son of Artemidorus, secretary.

[668]
Three patronage agreements found near Brixia, presumably kept in a house of Silius Aviola there. All three relate to communities in Africa, where Aviola served in legion 3 Augusta.

(a) *ILS 6100*
27

In the consulship of Marcus Crassus Frugi and Lucius Calpurnius Frugi, 3rd February, the state of Themetra in Africa made guest-friendship with Gaius Silius Aviola, son of Gaius, of the tribe Fabia, and chose him, his children and his descendants as patron to themselves, their children and their descendants. Gaius Silius Aviola, son of Gaius, of the tribe Fabia, received the state of Themetra, their children and their descendants into the good faith and clientage of himself, his children and his descendants. By the agency of Banno, son of Himilis, suffete, and Azdrubal, son of Baisillex, and Iddibal, son of Bosthar, envoys.

(b) *ILS 6099a*
Probably 28

In the consulship of Lucius Silanus, flamen of Mars, and Gaius Vellaeus Tutor, 4th December, the state of Apisa Maius made guest-friendship with Gaius Silius Aviola, son of Gaius, of the tribe Fabia, military tribune of legion 3 Augusta, prefect of engineers, and chose him and his children and descendants as patron to themselves, their children and descendants. Gaius Silius Aviola, son of Gaius, of the tribe Fabia, military tribune of legion 3 Augusta, prefect of engineers, received the state of Apisa Maius and their children and descendants into the good faith of himself, his children and descendants, by the agency of Hasdrubal . . . Aris, Ioiapoi, Saepo and Chanaebo, envoys.

(c) *EJ 354*
Probably 28

In the consulship of Lucius Silanus, flamen of Mars, and Gaius Vellaeus Tutor, 5th December, the senate and people of Siagu,[1] made guest-friendship with Gaius Silius Aviola, son of Gaius, of the tribe Fabia, military tribune of legion 3 Augusta, prefect of engineers, and chose him and his descendants as patron to themselves and their descendants. Gaius Silius Aviola, son of Gaius, of the tribe Fabia, received them and their descendants into his good faith and clientage. By the agency of Celer, son of Imilcho Gulalsa, suffete.

1. In Africa.

[669] *EJ 355*
12 BC, Africa, patronage agreement

In the consulship of Publius Sulpicius Quirinius and Gaius Valgius, the senate and people of the stipendiary states in the community of Gurza made guest-friendship with Lucius Domitius Ahenobarbus, son of Gnaeus, grandson of Lucius, proconsul, and chose him and his descendants as patron to themselves and their descendants, and he received them and their descendants into his good faith and clientage. Ammicar, son of Milchato, of Cynasyne, Boncar, son of Azzrubal, of Aethogursa, Muthunbal, son of Sapho, of Uzita.

[670] *EJ 356a*
6, Emerita

In the consulship of Marcus Aemilius Lepidus and Lucius Arruntius, the Martian decurions and townsmen, hitherto the Ugienses, made guest-friendship with the colonists of Colonia Augusta Emerita for themselves, their children and their descendants. By agency of the envoys Publius Mummius Ursus, son of Publius, of the tribe Galeria, and Marcus Aemilius Fronto, son of Marcus, of the tribe Galeria.

[671] *EJ 358a*
31, Lusitania, private patronage agreement

In the consulship of Tiberius Caesar, for the fifth time, and Lucius Aelius Sejanus, 21st January.

Quintus Stertinius Bassus, son of Quintus, Quintus Stertinius Rufus, son of Quintus, and Lucius Stertinius Rufinus, son of Quintus, made guest-friendship with Lucius Fulcinius Trio, legate of Tiberius Caesar, and his children and descendants.

Lucius Fulcinius Trio, legate of Tiberius Caesar, received Quintus Stertinius Bassus, son of Quintus, Quintus Stertinius Rufus, son of Quintus, and Lucius Stertinius Rufinus, son of Quintus, and their children and descendants into the good faith and clientage of himself, his children and his descendants.

[672] *EJ 352*
Cyzicus

When Pausanias, son of Eumenes, was hipparch for the second time, in the month of Calamaion, the council and people resolved: Pausanias, son of Eumenes, of the tribe Aegicoreis, at the second assembly, under the presidency of Demetrius, put the motion:

Since Antonia Tryphaena, daughter of King Polemo and Queen Pythodoris, in her complete piety towards the eternal house of the greatest of gods, Tiberius Augustus Caesar, and his immortal principate, joined in the dedication to Athena Polias of his mother Augusta Nicephora; and since, when she accepted from the city the priesthood of Augusta at the festival of the Panathenaea conducted last year, she properly gave the Augusti in full, by the performance of many sacrifices, everything concordant with the worship of the gods, as is her practice, and exercised her innate generostiy towards locals and foreigners so that she was admired by visiting foreigners with approbation for her piety and holiness and love of fame; and since, in the following year, when, although she was away, all the rites were performed in full accordance with her piety, traders of the empire and foreigners come to the celebration, in their wish to dedicate a gilded shield bearing her image, came for this reason to the council and the people, arguing that they should be permitted to make the dedication, the council and people resolved:

That they be permitted to dedicate the shield in the temple of Polias and to inscribe on it: 'The businessmen of Asia, come to the

celebration and the festival conducted at Cyzicus for the Augusti and
Athena Polias, honoured Antonia Tryphaena, daughter of King Polemo
and Queen Pythodoris Philometor, priestess of Augusta Nicephora,
for her piety towards the house of the greatest of gods, Tiberius
Augustus Caesar, and for her reverence in all things and her beneficence
towards themselves.'

[673] *Small. 401*
37, Cyzicus

When Gaius Caesar was hipparch, 9th of the month Thargelion, the
people resolved: on the introduction of all the archons, secretary of
the council Aeolus, son of Aeolus, of the tribe Oenopis, at the second
assembly, under the presidency of Menophon, put the motion:

Since the new Sun, Gaius Caesar Augustus Germanicus, was willing
that kings too, the bodyguards of empire, should with their own rays
join in illumination, so that the greatness of his immortality might be
all the more hallowed in this too, the kings, even if they devoted
themselves entirely to that end, being incapable of equally reciprocating
the favour of such a god for the benefactions they have received. And
since he has restored the sons of Cotys, Rhoemetalces and Polemo
and Cotys, who have been his own companions, to the kingdoms due
to them by inheritance from their fathers and forefathers. And they,
enjoying the abundant fruits of immortal favour, are greater than those
of the past for the reason that the latter took the succession from their
fathers, whereas the former have become kings by the grace of Gaius
Caesar to join in ruling with such gods; and the favours of the gods
differ from human successions as does sun from night and the eternal
from mortal nature. Having therefore become greater than the great
and more marvellous than the illustrious, Rhoemetalces and Polemo
have come to our city to join in worshipping and celebrating with
their mother as she holds the games of the divine new Aphrodite,
Drusilla; they have come not simply as if to a friendly land, but as if
actually to their own native land, because their mother, Tryphaena,
who is both the daughter and mother of kings, regarding this as her
native land, sets here the hearth of her house and the good fortune
of her life, to find prosperity in the kingdoms of her children that
have not incurred divine wrath. And the people, most delighted at their
visit, with all zeal ordered the magistrates to deliver a decree of meeting
to them, through which they should give thanks before them to their
mother Tryphaena for the benefactions she has chosen to bestow upon

the city and should also make plain the attitude of the people towards them.

The people resolved that the kings Rhoemetalces and Polemo and Cotys and their mother Tryphaena should be praised and that upon their entrance the priests and priestesses, having opened the precincts and adorned the images of the gods, should pray for the eternal endurance of Gaius Caesar and for the welfare of the kings. And that all the Cyzicenes, indicating their good-will towards them, having met them with the archons and the stephanephori, should greet them and welcome them and urge them to regard the city as their own native land and to be the source of every benefit to it. And that to the meeting the ephebarch should bring all the ephebes and the paedonomus all the free boys. And that the decree is a matter of piety towards Augustus and honour towards the kings.

[674] *IGRR 4.147*
Cyzicus

To Isthmian Poseidon, a thank-offering, Antonia Tryphaena, wife of Cotys, daughter and mother of kings and herself a queen, having restored the long-blocked area of the channels and lagoon from her own resources and the perimeter at her own expense and that of her son, the king of Thrace, Rhoemetalces, and in the name of his brothers, the king of Pontus, Polemo, and Cotys.

[675] *Small. 402*
Bronze coin, Philadelphia, Lydia, which became Neocaesarea under Gaius.

Obv. Head of Gaius, laureate. GAIUS CAESAR GERMANICUS, OF THE NEOCAESAREANS.
Rev. Agrippina as Demeter (?), seated, holding a horn of plenty. ARTEMON, SON OF HERMOGENES

[676] *Small. 403*
Bronze coin, about 37, Patrae, Achaea

Obv. Bust of Money, wearing a diadem and veil. OF AUGUSTAN INDULGENCE, MONEY GAINED.
Rev. Male figure holding an eagle-tipped sceptre, standing in a chariot. TO CAESAR AUGUSTUS, THE COLONY OF AROE[1] AUGUSTA PATRAE

1. The ancient name of Patrae.

[677] *Small. 404*
41-2 (?), Lycosura, Arcadia

When the priest of the Mistress was, for the second time, Nicasippus, son of Philippus, and the epimeletes were Damyllus, son of Zeuxis, and Damocrates, son of Clitor, year 32, under Augustus.

Since Nicasippus, son of Philippus, being a good man and descended from forefathers who were fine and illustrious and who gave their due to the city of the Lycosurans and to the gods in advocacies and priest-hoods and the attendance of children upon Kore and in all other expenditures, energetically and generously – Nicasippus accepted the priesthood of the Mistress during an Olympic year when no one was willing to come forward and, when money had not accrued for the mysteries, he made payment to the fiscus from his own resources, and in the current year, when there was a dearth of crops, with the assent of the Lycosurans, he accepted the priesthood with Timasistrata, his wife, thinking more of the favour of the Lycosurans than of the cost to his resources, and in the rest of his conduct he behaves piously and justly towards both the gods and all mankind. For all these reasons the city of the Lycosurans resolved to set up images of him and of Timasistrata his wife in the temple, inscribed with the inscription:

'The city of the Lycosurans honoured Nicasippus, son of Philippus, and Timasistrata, daughter of Onasicritus, for their virtue'

and to urge them, maintaining the same stance in future, always to be responsible for some benefit to the gods and to the city of the Lycosurans, in the knowledge that the city is grateful and has never lapsed in the bestowal of gratitude. And let the epimeletes deposit the decree in writing in the archive at Megalopolis and let them inscribe it on a stone column and dedicate it in the temple of the Mistress, so that the benefaction of good men and the gratitude of the city to the deserving may be known to all mankind.

[678] *Small. 405*
42, Hippo Regius, Africa

When Tiberius Claudius Caesar Augustus Germanicus, son of Drusus, was pontifex maximus, in his second year of tribunician power, imperator 3 times, consul twice, father of his country, the Senate and people of Hippo Regius dedicated this, at public expense, to Quintus Marcius Barea, son of Gaius, consul, one of the 15 for the performance of sacred rites, fetial, proconsul for two years, patron.

Quintus Allius Maximus, propraetorian legate for two years, made this dedication to the patron.

[679] *Small. 406*
44-5, Ammaia, Lusitania

To Tiberius Claudius Caesar Augustus Germanicus, imperator 3 times, pontifex maximus, in his fourth year of tribunician power, consul 3 times, designate for a fourth, the state of Ammaia, in fulfilment of an annual vow, Lucius Calventius Vetus Carminius being legate of Tiberius Claudius Caesar Augustus, duumvirs being Proculus, son of Pisirus, and Omuncio, son of Cila.

[680] *Small. 407*
(a) 44, Volubilis, Mauretania
To Tiberius Claudius Caesar Augustus Germanicus, son of a god, pontifex maximus, in his fourth year of tribunician power, imperator 8 times, father of his country, the municipality of Volubilis, having sought and gained Roman citizenship and conubium and remission of works, given by the decree of the decurions. Marcus Fadius Celer Flavianus Maximus, procurator of Augustus, prolegate, made the dedication.

(b) After 54, Volubilis
To Marcus Valerius Severus, son of Bostar, of the tribe Galeria, aedile, suffete, duumvir, first flamen in his municipality, prefect of auxiliaries against Aedemon, who has been subdued by war; this man the ruling body of the municipality of Volubilis honoured for his services to the state and an embassy successfully accomplished, in which he sought and gained from the divine Claudius for his people Roman citizenship and conubium with foreign women, immunity for 10 years, local settlers and the property of citizens killed in war who have no surviving heirs.

Fabia Bira, daughter of Izelta, his wife, to her most indulgent husband, having held office, returned the cost and made the dedication at her own expense.

[681] *Small. 408*
Cibyra, Caria

The people honoured Quintus Veranius Philagrus, son of Troilus, of the tribe Clustumina, priest of Virtue for life, who has undertaken embassies four times, at no cost to the state, to the Augusti at Rome and presented major topics and acted as legal officer in many great public cases, whence sufficient money accrued for the foundation of the city,[1] and brought under control 107 public slaves and took possession of land,[2] and became priest of Caesar Augustus, and gave the city in due years a distribution of 54,000 Rhodian drachmas for the celebration of Caesarean games, and loans amounting to 100,000 Rhodian drachmas he bestowed upon those chosen by the people, and he broke a great conspiracy which was doing the greatest harm to the city. And, what were the most pressing presentations he made in his embassies, he asked Tiberius Claudius Caesar to remove Tiberius Nicephorus, who was exacting 3,000 denarii from the city each year and keeping it, and that the sale of grain should take place in the market-place, of 75 modii per iugum over the whole territory. For these reasons the city gave him the honours of a Brave.

1. After earthquake damage, Tiberius refounded Cibyra in AD 23.   2. Text is uncertain; it seems to refer to the re-possession of land illegally held.

[682] *Small. 409*
Bronze coin, Seleucia Sidera, Pisidia

Obv. Turreted bust of the city goddess. CLAUDIOSELEUCIA
Rev. Ram.

[683] *Small. 410*
(a) Bronze coin, Ptolemais, Phoenicia
Obv. Head of Nero, laureate. IMPERATOR NERO CLAUDIUS
    CAESAR AUGUSTUS GERMANICUS, PONTIFEX MAXIMUS,
    WITH TRIBUNICIAN POWER
Rev. Claudius ploughing with ox and cow; four standards behind on
    one of which 12 can be read. DIVINE CLAUDIUS, COLONIA
    CLAUDIA STAB[1] GERMANICA FORTUNATE
1. Meaning unknown.

(b) On a road near Ptolemais
To Imperator Nero Caesar, villages of the veteran colony of Ptolemais, New Village and Gedru.

[684] *Small. 412*

(a) Rhodes

(The beginning is lost) ... Euchares, son of Euchares, Mnasaeus, son of ... , son of Python, Aristogenes, son of Papus, ... , Pisarchus, son of Timasarchus, Polycharmus, son of Philo, ... the most desired answers have been conveyed to the city ... upon ... Antipater and Dionysius, sons of Artemidorus, has outstandingly conferred every honour ... the erection of statues, the council and people have resolved, this decree having been ratified, that their names be written up by the generals on a base of Rhodian granite in the precinct of the Sun for ... and Antipater, son of Artemidorus, and Dionysius, son of Artemidorus and ... – Cratidas, son of Pharnaces, Aleximbrotidas, son of Chrysippus ... , Damagoras, son of Damagoras, Moeragenes, son of Timodicus, Damocharis, son of Gorgias ... , Polycharmus, son of Philo, Eucles, son of Agesarchus, Euthreptidas, son of ... , who were sent to Tiberius Claudius Caesar Germanicus, imperator, ... , the ancestral constitution having been restored to the city and the laws by the ... of Nero Caesar and the men having invoked the goodwill towards the city ...

(b) 54, Rhodes

When Diogenes was priest, the board of magistrates were those with Menecles, the son of Archagoras, the secretary of the council was Nicasimachus, son of Diaphanes, the adopted son of Archedamus; the letter sent by Nero Claudius Caesar, Petageitnyus 27th.

Nero Claudius Caesar Augustus Germanicus, son of the divine Claudius, grandson of Tiberius Caesar Augustus and Germanicus Caesar, great-grandson of the divine Augustus, pontifex maximus, with tribunician power, imperator, to the magistrates, council and people of the Rhodians, greetings.

Your envoys, whom you sent me in your confusion over the letter falsely sent you in the name of the consuls, delivered the decree and with regard to the sacrifices told me that you instructed them to sacrifice for the health of my whole house and for my endurance in the principate to Jupiter Capitolinus, the god particularly honoured amongst us; and with regard to what you wrote to them as being at issue with the democracy of the city, they explained through Claudius Timostratus, the chief-envoy, who made your case before me in an energetic manner, a man to me particularly distinguished because of the renewal of his standing claims upon us and among you counted as one of the most illustrious. I, therefore, being from my earliest youth well-disposed towards your city ...

[685] *Palatine Anthology*, 9.178 (Antiphilus)

As once of the Sun, now of Caesar I, Rhodes, am
The island; and equal light I boast from both;
As my light was going out a new ray illumined me,
Sun, and excelling your brightness shone Nero.
How can I say to whom I owe more? One showed me
From the sea, the other saved me as I was sinking.[1]

1. This epigram might refer to Tiberius, not Nero. But cf. Tac. *Ann.* 12.58; Suet. *Claud.* 25; *Nero* 7.

[686] *Small. 413*
1st August 55, Hippo Regius, Africa

In the consulship of Nero Claudius Caesar Augustus Germanicus and Lucius Antistius Vetus, 1st. August, Quintus Julius Secundus, son of Quintus, of the tribe Quirina, propraetorian legate, made guest-friendship with the decurions and colonists in Colonia Julia Augusta Tupusuctu of legion 7 for himself and his children and descendants and received them in the protection of his patronage, through the agency of the legates Quintus Caecilius Firmanus, son of Quintus, of the tribe Palatina, and Marcus Pomponius Vindex, son of Marcus, of the tribe Quirina.

[688] *Small. 415*
Athens

Tiberius Claudius Herodes of Marathon, priest and high-priest of Nero Caesar Augustus for life, made this dedication to Dionysus the Liberator and Nero Claudius Caesar Augustus Germanicus and the council of the Areopagus and the council of the 600 and the people of the Athenians from his own resources, when Tiberius Claudius Novius was general of the hoplites for the seventh time.

[687] *Small. 414*
Athens

The council of the Areopagus and the council of the 600 and the people honoured Tiberius Claudius Novius, son of Philinus, general of the hoplites for the fourth time and priest of Delian Apollo for life and president of the great Augustan Panathenaea and the Augustan Caesarea and high-priest of Antonia Augusta, friend of Caesar and friend of his country, for his virtue. When Junia Megiste, wife of Zeno, of Sunium, was priestess. Made by Epagathus, son of Aristodemus, of Thriasia.

[688] *Small, 415*
Athens

Tiberius Claudius Herodes of Marathon, priest and high-priest of Nero Caesar Augustus for life, made this dedication to Dionysus the Liberator and Nero Claudius Caesar Augustus Germanicus and the council of the Areopagus and the council of the 600 and the people of the Athenians from his own resources, when Tiberius Claudius Novius was general of the hoplites for the seventh time.

[689] *Small. 416*
Bronze coin, Patrae, Achaea

Obv. Head of Nero, radiate. NERO CAESAR AUGUSTUS GERMANICUS
Rev. Genius of Patrae standing by an altar, holding a patera and horn of plenty. THE GENIUS OF COLONIA NERONIA PATRENSIS

[690] *Small. 417*
63-4, Palmyra

Nero Claudius Caesar Augustus Germanicus, son of the divine Claudius, grandson of Germanicus Caesar, great-grandson of Tiberius Caesar Augustus, great-great-grandson of the divine Augustus, pontifex maximus, in his tenth year of tribunician power, imperator nine times, consul four times, father of his country . . .

[691] *Small. 418*
Memphis, Egypt

With good fortune. Since Nero Claudius Caesar Augustus Germanicus, imperator, the good spirit of the world, in addition to all the other benefactions he has conferred upon Egypt, has exercised the most brilliant foresight by sending to us Tiberius Claudius Balbillus as prefect, and since, on account of the favours and benefactions of this man, Egypt is brimming with every good as she sees the gifts of the Nile increasing year by year and has now enjoyed the more the due rising of the Nile-god, it has been resolved by those of the village of Busiris in the Letopolite nome near the pyramids and by the district secretaries and village secretaries serving there to pass a decree and to erect a stone column in the precinct of the greatest god Sun

Harmachis, showing through the benefactions inscribed on it the benefaction he generated, from which all will know his fine goodness to
the whole of Egypt. For it is fitting that his god-like favours, inscribed
in sacred writing, be remembered for all time. For he came to us in
the nome and paid homage to the Sun Harmachis, custodian and
saviour, and delighted in the greatness and majesty of the pyramids;
and, having seen . . . a very great deal of sand on account of the length
of time . . . [the rest is fragmentary]

[692] *Small. 419*
August 60-August 61, Ptolemais Euergetis, Egypt

To Nero Claudius Caesar Augustus Germanicus, imperator, the saviour
and benefactor of the world; the city of Ptolemais through the 6470
and all those who were ephebes in year 2 of the divine Tiberius
Claudius Caesar Augustus Germanicus, imperator, in the prefecture of
Lucius Julius Vestinus, year 7 of Nero Claudius Caesar Augustus
Germanicus, imperator . . .

[693] *Small. 420*
Lycopolis, Egypt

To Caesar, the synod. For the good fortune of Nero Claudius Caesar
Augustus Germanicus, imperator, the synod of Lycopolitans and the
young men who have been ephebes . . .

SOCIETY AND ECONOMY

[694] Ulpian, *Rules*, 13-14
Lex Julia on the marriage of the orders, 18/17 BC

Under the lex Julia, senators and their children are forbidden to marry freedwomen who have themselves, or whose father or mother has, practised dramatic art; likewise, any that have sold their bodies. And other free-born males are forbidden to marry a procuress or a woman manumitted by a procuress or procurer or a woman caught in adultery or a woman condemned in a public court or one who has practised dramatic art; Mauricius adds also a woman condemned by the Senate.

To women the lex Julia gave a year's respite after the death of a husband, after divorce six months, while the lex Papia gave two years after the death of a husband, after a divorce eighteen months.

[695] Gaius, *Institutes*, 1.145
Lex Julia and Lex Papia Poppaea, 18/17 BC and AD 9

And so, if someone by his will has appointed a guardian for his son and daughter and both reach puberty, the son ceases to have the guardian, but the daughter remains in guardianship none the less; for it is only under the lex Julia and Papia Poppaea, by the right of children that women are freed from guardianship – with the exception of the Vestal virgins, that is, whom even the ancients wanted to be free in honour of their priesthood.

[696] Gaius, *Institutes*, 3.50
Lex Papia Poppaea, AD 9

But the lex Papia in the case of a free-born patroness distinguished with two children – and in that of a freedwoman patroness with three – has given that woman almost the same rights as the male patron possesses under the praetor's edict; to a free-born patroness distinguished with the right of three children the same rights are given as given to a male patron by the same law; to a freedwoman patroness, though, it has not given the same rights.

[697] *FIRA III.2*
AD 62. Wax tablet, Alexandria. Cf. J.A. Crook, *Law and Life of Rome* (1967) pp. 46-8

In the consulship of Publius Marius and Lucius Afinius Gallus, 23rd July, in year 8 of Nero Claudius Caesar Augustus Germanicus, on the 29th day of the month of Epeiph, at Alexandria by Egypt.

Copied and authenticated from the list of declarations of parenthood which is posted up in the Great Hall and which contains the following:

Lucius Julius Vestinus, prefect of Egypt, posted up the names of those who declared that children had been born to them in their households in accordance with the lex Papia Poppaea and Aelia Sentia, in the consulship of Publius Marius and Lucius Afinius Gallus, 18th July.

Lucius Valerius Crispus, son of Lucius, of the tribe Pollia, owner of 375,000 sesterces, reported the birth of a son, Lucius Valerius Crispus, son of Lucius, of the tribe Pollia, to Domitia Paulla, daughter of Lucius, on 29th June last, c.r.e.k.[1]

1. The meaning of these letters, found on most documents of this sort, is not known.

[698]
The lex Julia on the suppression of adultery, 18/17 BC

(a) *Digest*, 48.5.1 (Ulpian)
This law was introduced by the divine Augustus.

(b) *Digest*, 48.5.5 (Julian)
There is no doubt that I can bring my wife to trial on a charge of adultery committed in a previous marriage, as is clearly provided in the lex Julia on the suppression of adultery.

(c) *Digest*, 48.5.6 (Papinian)
The lex Julia applies only to free persons who have suffered adultery or debauchery.

(d) *Digest*, 48.5.12.13 (Papinian)
'I married a woman accused of adultery; when she was condemned I swiftly repudiated her. What I want to know is, am I considered to have been the cause of the separation?' He replied, 'Since you would be forbidden to keep such a wife by the lex Julia, you will not be considered to be the cause of the separation.'

(e) *Digest*, 48.5.16.6 (Ulpian)
The lex Julia on adultery specifically prohibits accusation by certain persons; for example, one less than 25 years of age, for one who is not yet of robust age is not considered a suitable accuser.

(f) *Digest*, 48.5.40 pr. (Papinian)
The decision of a provincial governor was that a woman had suffered assault; I replied that she was not liable under the lex Julia on adultery, though she was not allowed to report the matter to her husband, in order that her modesty might be protected.

(g) *Digest*, 4.4.37 (Tryphonimus)
But to come to the provisions of the lex Julia on the suppression of adultery, if a minor confesses his adultery he cannot escape the penalty for adultery. And, as I have stated, he cannot do so if he has committed any of those crimes which that same law punishes as adultery — if he has knowingly married a woman condemned for adultery, or if he has not divorced a wife caught in adultery, or if he profits from the adultery of his wife, or if he takes money for concealing debauchery, or if he makes his house available for the committing of debauchery or adultery therein; and there is no excuse on grounds of age against the provisions of the law for one who breaks the law while he invokes it.

(h) Justinian, *Institutes*, 4.18.3-4
Public cases are these: the lex Julia on treason, which directs its force against those who have engineered something against the imperator or the state — the penalty for this entails loss of life and the memory of the defendant is condemned after death. Likewise, the lex Julia on the suppression of adultery, which punishes with the sword not only those who pollute the marriages of others, but also those who dare to exercise unspeakable lust with males. Under this same lex Julia the crime of debauchery is also punished, when someone has debauched either a virgin or a widow living virtuously.

[699] *Digest*, 48.14.1 (Modestinus)
Lex Julia on bribery

Today this law is obsolete in Rome because the appointment of magistrates is a matter for the princeps, not popular favour.

But if in a municipality anyone should stand for a magistracy or priesthood and break this law, he suffers, by decree of the Senate, a fine of 100 aurei and infamy. If someone condemned under that law should obtain the conviction of another, he is restored to his previous position. He does not, however, get the money back. Likewise, anyone who institutes an improper exaction is included in this punishment, by decree of the Senate. And if any defendant or accuser enters the house of a judge, he is committing bribery under the judicial lex Julia, which means that he is ordered to pay 100 aurei to the fiscus.

[700] Justinian, *Institutes*, 4.18.11

In addition, public cases occur under the lex Julia on bribery and the lex Julia on extortion and the lex Julia on the corn supply and the lex Julia on the misappropriation of public funds.

[701] *Digest*, 48.12.2 pr. (Ulpian)
Lex Julia on the corn supply

Under the lex Julia on the corn supply a penalty is fixed against those who act or form an association to the detriment of the corn supply in order that the corn supply might be more expensive. In the same law it is stipulated that no one should delay a ship or a sailor or act with malice aforethought to detain them longer; and a penalty of 20 aurei is fixed.

[702] Leges Juliae on public and private cases
(a) *Digest*, 48.2.12.2 (Venuleius Saturninus)
In the lex Julia on private cases it is provided that no one can bring a charge against two people at the same time, unless it is for his own injuries.

(b) *Digest*, 43.16.1.2 (Ulpian)
That nothing should be taken by force is also provided in the Julian laws on public and private cases.

[703] Justinian, *Institutes*, 2.23.1
Trusts

It must be understood that, in early times, trusts had no legal force ... Later, for the first time, the divine Augustus, repeatedly stirred by favour to individuals or because someone was said to have been requested by the safety of himself or because of the gross perfidy of some people, ordered the consuls to interpose their authority.

[704] *ILS 4966*; cf. E.J. Jory, *Hermes*, 98 (1970) p. 251
Augustan period, Rome

To the departed spirit; for the college of bandsmen, who perform at public rites, whom the Senate permitted to meet, to be convened, to be assembled under the Julian law[1] by authority of Augustus, for the sake of the games.

1. Cf. Suet. *Aug.* 32.

[705] Aulus Gellius, *Attic Nights*, 2.24.14-15; cf. Suet. *Aug.* 34.1; Tac. *Ann.* 3.54

Finally, the Julian law came to the people in the principate of Caesar Augustus, under which 200 sesterces was the limit for expenditure on a dinner on ordinary days, 300 on the Kalends, Ides and Nones and certain other festal days, 1,000 at weddings and the subsequent celebrations.

Ateius Capito, in addition, states that there is an edict – I am not sure whether it was of the divine Augustus or of Tiberius Caesar – by which, in the context of days of various rites, expenditure on dinners was raised from 300 to 2,000 sesterces, so that by this limit at least the tide of seething luxury might be contained.

[706] Gaius, *Institutes*, 1.42-6
Lex Fufia Caninia, 2 BC

Moreover, under the lex Fufia Caninia a limitation has been set on the manumission of slaves by will. For he who has more than two but not more than ten slaves is permitted to manumit up to half of them; and he who has more than ten but not more than thirty is permitted to manumit up to a third of them. And he who has more than thirty but not more than 100 is granted power to manumit up to a quarter of them. Finally, he who has more than 100 but not more than 500 is permitted to manumit no more than a fifth of them. He who has more than 500 is not granted power to manumit any more; rather, the law prescribes that no one be permitted to manumit more than 100. The owner of only one or two slaves is not affected by this law and has unrestricted power of manumission. Nor does this law apply to anyone manumitting other than by will, and so those manumitting by the rod or by the census or among friends are free to manumit their entire body of slaves, unless, of course, some other cause restricts this freedom.

But what has been stated on the number of slaves to be manumitted by will should be understood in such a way that, where a half, third, fourth or fifth part may be freed, it is always permissible to manumit no fewer than possible under the preceding number, and this is provided in the law itself; for it would obviously be absurd if the master of ten slaves could manumit five, because he is allowed to manumit up to half of his number, while the owner of 12 slaves can manumit no more than four; but those with more than ten ... For if in a will liberty is granted slaves whose names are written in a circle, none will be free, since no order of manumission is established, because the lex Fufia Caninia nullifies attempts at fraud. Attempted frauds against this law are also nullified by special decrees of the Senate.

[707] Gaius, *Institutes*, 1.36-9. 18-9, 13-4
Lex Aelia Sentia, AD 4

It is not permitted that anyone so wishing may manumit. For when a man manumits in order to defraud his creditors or patron, his act is void, because the lex Aelia Sentia prevents the liberation. Likewise, by the same law, an owner younger than 20 years of age is not permitted to manumit, unless he does so by the rod and with proper cause for manumission proven before a council. And proper causes for manumission are, for example, when someone manumits his father or mother or pedagogue or foster-brother.

The requirement concerning the age of the slave was introduced by the lex Aelia Sentia. For that law did not allow slaves younger than 30 to become Roman citizens, unless they were freed by the rod and with proper cause for manumission proven before a council. And a proper cause for manumission is, for example, when someone manumits before a council his natural son, daughter, brother or sister, or his pupil or pedagogue, or a slave to be his procurator, or a slave girl he intends to marry.

And by the lex Aelia Sentia it is provided that slaves put in chains by their masters as a punishment, or who have been branded, or have been questioned under torture for wrongdoing and have been convicted in that wrongdoing, or have been consigned to fight in the arena with men or with beasts, or have been cast into gladiatorial school or into prison, and who have subsequently been manumitted either by the same master or by another, become free in the status enjoyed by surrendered foreigners. And those are called surrendered foreigners who once took up arms and fought against the Roman people and then surrendered unconditionally upon their defeat.

[708] Dionysius of Halicarnassus, *Roman Antiquities*, 4.24.4-6

Most slaves used to gain freedom at no cost as a reward for fine and good conduct. This was the best manner of manumission from masters. A few bought their freedom with sums amassed through proper, honest toil.

But this is not the situation today. Rather, affairs have come to such a state of chaos and glories of the city of Rome have become so ignoble and low that some buy freedom with the proceeds from robberies and burglaries and prostitution and every other crime and are immediately Romans. Others who have served their masters as accomplices and aides in poisonings and murders and crimes against the gods and the community receive this as a favour from them. And others are freed so that they may receive grain given by the state each month and any other benefit conferred by the leaders upon poor ctizens and take it to those who gave them freedom. Yet others are freed through the irresponsibility of their masters and the vain search for a reputation. I know of some who have granted freedom to all their slaves after their death so as to be called good corpses and so that at their funeral many may follow their biers with liberty caps on their heads. Some of these paraders, as one could hear from those who knew, had just left prison and were criminals who had committed crimes deserving ten thousand deaths. However, when they look at these scabs which can scarcely be removed from the city, most people are angry and condemn the custom, because it is wrong that an imperial city, aspiring to universal rule, should make citizens of men like this.

[709] *EJ 358*
Via Appia

Marcus Aurelius Zosimus, freedman of Cotta Maximus, attendant of his patron.

> Freedman I was, I admit; yet by my patron
> Ennobled my shade will be read.
> He gave me equestrian wealth, often generous;
> He told me to raise children for him to feed;
> He entrusted his business always to me, and he too
> Gave my daughters dowries, like their own father;
> And he advanced my Cottanus with the tribune's rank,

Which bravely he held in the army of Caesar.
What did Cotta not give? He who now in his sorrow
These verses too has given, to be seen on my tomb.

Aurelia Saturnia, wife of Zosimus.

[710] (a) Justinian, *Institutes*, 1.5.3
Lex Junia Norbana, 19 (?)

The status of freedman had previously been in three divisions, for those who were manumitted sometimes gained the greater and legal liberty and became Roman citizens, sometimes a lesser liberty and became Latins under the lex Junia Norbana, sometimes the lowest and became under the lex Aelia Sentia one of the dediticii.

(b) Gaius, *Institutes*, 3.55-7

Next, we consider the estates of Junian Latin freedmen. So that this area of law may be more plain we must recall what we have stated elsewhere, that those who are now called Junian Latins were once slaves by Quiritary law, but kept in a state of freedom by the support of the praetor; for this reason their property used to pass to their patrons in the manner of peculium; subsequently, by the lex Junia, all those whom the praetor kept in freedom began to be free and were called Junian Latins: Latins, because the law made them as free as if they were free-born Roman citizens who had been taken from the city of Rome and settled in Latin colonies and begun to be Latin colonists: Junians, because they had been made free by the lex Junia, even if they were not Roman citizens.

The author of the lex Junia, since he saw that in future by this legal fiction the property of deceased Junian Latins would not pass to their patrons, since of course they would die neither as slaves, whose property would pass to their patrons as peculium, nor as freedmen, whose estates would pass to their patrons by right of manumission, thought it necessary, so that the benefit conferred upon these people should not become a loss to their patrons, to provide that their estates would pass to their manumittors just as if the law had not been passed. Thus, by the right of peculium, one might say, the estates of Junian Latins pass to their manumittors under that law. In consequence there is a great difference between the rights set up by the lex Junia with regard to the estates of Junian Latins and those observed with regard to inheritance from Roman citizen freedmen.

[711] *Small. 365*
45(?) and 56, Herculaneum, decrees of the Senate

A

In the consulship of Gnaeus Hosidius Geta and Lucius Vagellius, 22nd September, decree of the Senate.

Since the providence of the best princeps has looked to the buildings of our city and of the whole of Italy in eternity, buildings to which he has given the benefit not only of his most august precept but also of his own example; and since it suits the good fortune of the present era to take proportionate care of both public and private buildings; and since all should abstain from the most bloody form of business and not introduce an inimical sight in peacetime through the demolition of town and country houses, it is the will of the Senate:

That if anyone in the course of business should buy any building so that by demolishing it he might gain more than what he paid for it, then he should deposit a sum of money double the price he paid for that property in the treasury; and that, even so, the matter should be referred to the Senate.

And since, likewise, it is no better to sell than to buy in a vicious manner, in order that vendors too may be constrained when they deliberately with malice aforethought sell in contravention of this, the will of the Senate, it is the will of the Senate that such sales are to have no force in law. Yet the Senate bears witness that this legislation does not apply to owners who, to inhabit their own property, make alterations to any parts of it, provided that this is not done in the course of business.

Passed. Present in the Senate were 383.

B

In the consulship of Quintus Volusius and Publius Cornelius, 2nd March, decree of the Senate.

Since Quintus Volusius and Publius Cornelius presented a statement concerning the request of the relatives of Alliatoria Celsilla and asked for the decision of the Senate on that matter, on that matter the Senate decided as follows:

Since in the decree of the Senate made in the consulship of Hosidius Geta and Lucius Vagellius, most illustrious men, on 22nd September, at the instigation of the divine Claudius, it is provided that no one should demolish a town or country house in order to make a profit for himself and that no one should sell or buy property in the course of business; and since a penalty has been laid down against the buyer who contravenes said decree of the Senate — viz. that the buyer be made to pay into the treasury twice the purchase price — and against the vendor — viz. that the sale should have no force in law —, while in the case of those who, to inhabit their own property, make alterations to any parts of it, there is no intervention, provided that they do not make alterations in the course of business.

And since the relatives of Alliatoria Celsilla, the wife of Atilius Lupercus, a most distinguished man, informed this order that her father, Alliatorius Celsus, had bought lands with buildings in the region of Mutina known as Poor Fields, where there used to be a market in former times, not now held for a number of years, and where the buildings were collapsing through their great age and, even repaired, would not be of use, since no one lives there and no one would move into empty and ruined buildings.

It is decided that no criminal fine or penalty is to be imposed on Celsilla if those buildings at issue before this order are demolished or if she sells them in the stated condition, whether separately or with the lands, so that the buyer may be permitted legally to destroy or remove them. For the future, however, that others be warned to abstain from a form of business so foul, especially in this era when it is more fitting that new buildings be started and all buildings decorated, so that the good fortune of the world may shine out, rather than through the demolition of buildings, to disfigure any part of Italy and maintain the neglect that has afflicted them all, so that it might be said to have been brought about by old age ... Passed. Present in the Senate were ...

[712] Gaius, *Institutes*, 1.32c

Likewise, under an edict of Claudius Latins gain the right of Roman citizenship if they build a sea-going vessel capable of carrying at least 10,000 modii of corn, and if that ship, or one substituted in its place, carries corn to Rome for six years.

[713] *Small. 364*

And we are not moved by the line that it is to the benefit of the son to have a *peculium*; in fact, it is more to the benefit of the father than the son, although in any event *peculium* looks to the son: consider the hypothesis that the property of his father was seized by the fiscus for debt, for his *peculium* is kept separate under the enactment of Claudius.

[714] *Small. 362*
Between 41 and 45, SC Ostorianum

In the decree of the Senate passed in the time of Claudius in the consulship of Publius Vellaeus Rufus and Publius Ostorius Scapula concerning
the assigning of freedmen the following is laid down:

If anyone, who had in his *potestas* two or more children born of
legal matrimony, had signified with regard to his freedman or freedwoman as to which of his children he wanted he or she to be the freedman or freedwoman of, then that son or daughter would be the sole
patron or patroness to that freedman when he who manumitted the
freedman or freedwoman — in his lifetime or by his will — had passed
away, just as if the freedman or freedwoman had gained freedom from
that son or daughter. And it was decreed that if that child had passed
away and had no children, all the rights of the other children of the
manumittor would be preserved, just as if that parent had signified
nothing with regard to that freedman or freedwoman.

[715] *Small. 363*
42, SC Largianum

Subsequently, in the consulship of Lupus and Largus, the Senate
decreed that the property of Latins should pass first to the person who
liberated them; next, to their children, according to proximity, unless
disinherited by name; then it passes under the ancient law to the
children of those who liberated them.

[716] *Digest* 45.8.2 (Modestinus)
47; cf. Suet. *Claud.* 25

By the edict of the divine Claudius liberty devolves upon a slave whom
his master has abandoned on account of his severe ill-health.

[717] *SC Claudianum*, 52; cf. Tac. *Ann.* 12.53
(a) Gaius *Inst.* 1.160
Capitis deminutio maxima occurs when someone loses citizenship and
liberty at the same time; this happens to those who have evaded the
census, people whom census regulations require to be sold. This
measure ... who against that law take up residence in the city of
Rome; likewise the women who under the SC Claudianum become the

slaves of those masters with whose slaves they have had intercourse, the masters being unwilling and giving warning.

(b) Gaius *Inst*. 1.84

Note that under the SC Claudianum a Roman citizen woman who had intercourse with another's slave with the consent of the master, could herself, through the agreement, remain free, but give birth to a slave; this is so because under that decree of the Senate it is ordained that what is agreed between that woman and the master of that slave has legal validity.

[718] *Digest* 16.1.2 (Ulpian)
46(?), SC Vellaeanum (or Velleianum)

Since Marcus Silanus and Vellaeus Tutor, consuls, presented a statement concerning the obligations of women who undertake liability for others; asked for their decision on that matter, they decreed on that matter as follows:

With regard to sureties and *mutuum* arrangements for others, in which women might have become involved. Although it seems that hitherto justice has been administered in such a way that under that head no claim is made from these women and no suit is brought against them, since it is not equitable that they perform male roles and that they be bound by obligations of that type, the Senate takes the view that persons before whom there is recourse to law on that matter will act rightly and properly if they see to it that the will of the Senate in that matter is sustained.

[719] *Small. 366*
25th August 56, SC Trebellianum

For a decree of the Senate was made in the time of Nero, on 25th August, in the consulship of Annaeus Seneca and Trebellius Maximus, the words of which are these:

Since it is most equitable in all trust-inheritances that, if lawsuits concerning the property are pending, those to whom the legal right and benefit have been transferred should undergo them, rather than that a man's good faith should endanger him; it is the will of the Senate that cases usually brought against heirs or by heirs should not be brought against those or by those who have restored what was committed to their good faith in the manner requested, but by those and against those to whom a trust has been restored in accordance with the will, in order that in future the last wishes of the dead should be strengthened.

[720] *EJ 357* with E. Wistrand, *The So-called Laudatio Turiae* (1976)

(Beginning is lost) . . . by the propriety of your behaviour . . . you remained . . . You were orphaned suddenly before our wedding day when both your parents were killed at once, alone in the countryside. It was very much through you – since I had gone to Macedonia and your sister's husband, Cluvius, to the province of Africa – that your parents' death did not remain unavenged. You did your duty with so much energy, making petitions and pursuing justice, that we could not have done more if we had been there to do it. This you share with that most virtuous woman your sister. While you were active in this case, when you had required the punishment of the guilty parties, you left your father's house to guard your reputation and immediately transferred to the house of my mother, where you awaited my return. Then you were both harassed so that your father's will, under which we were heirs, might be declared invalid on the grounds that he had made a *coemptio* with his wife.[1] That being so, you would have inevitably fallen together with all the possessions of your father, under the guardianship of those who were pursuing this argument; your sister would have been altogether disinherited, since she had been transferred into the power of Cluvius. Your attitude to this and the presence of mind with which you put up a fight are well known to me, despite my absence. You defended our common cause with the truth: that the will was not invalid so that we should both receive the inheritance instead of you alone taking possession of all the property. You were resolute that you would act in accordance with your father's provisions, so that you affirmed that if you did not have your way, you would divide the inheritance with your sister anyhow; that you would not enter the condition of legal guardianship, because there was no relevant legal right in your regard, for it could not be proved that your family belonged to any clan that could legally compel you to do it; for, even if your father's will were invalid, the fact would remain that those who presented the claim did not have that right, since they did not belong to the same clan. They bowed to your determination and did not press the matter further. In this way, you, on your own, carried the defence you had undertaken to a successful conclusion, the defence of your duty to your father, your devotion to your sister and your good faith to me.

Rare are such long marriages, ended by death, not broken by divorce; for we were so fortunate that it lasted till its forty-first year without animosity. Would that our partnership had changed through me, it being more just that I, the elder, yield to fate.

Why should I recall your domestic virtues — concern for your reputation, obedience, affability, sweetness, attention to wool-making, religion without superstition, modest dress, judicious appearance? Why should I recount your love for your relatives, your dutifulness towards your family, you who have exercised the same concern for my mother as for your own parents have seen to it that she enjoys the same quiet life as your relatives, you who possessed countless other virtues in common with all matrons who nurture a high reputation? These are your own virtues that I am asserting and very few women have fallen on such times that they have suffered and achieved the like; fortune has decreed that these be unusual for women.

We have conserved all the patrimony you received from your parents with shared diligence; for you were not interested in acquiring for yourself what you transferred entirely to me. We shared our duties in such a way that I exercised guardianship over your fortune, while you stood guard over mine. I say nothing of much under this head for fear that I might appropriate for myself a share of virtues which belong to you. Let it suffice that I have given this indication of your attitude.

You have shown your generosity both to very many friends and especially to your beloved family. One might praise by name other women in the same terms, but you have had only one at all equal ... your sister; for you brought up your female relatives worthy of such ... duties, with us in your own property. So that these girls might attain a situation worthy of your family, you provided them with dowries: when you had fixed these I and Gaius Cluvius agreed to bear the expense. We approved your generosity, but, in order that your patrimony should not suffer, we made our personal property available and gave our estates as dowries. I have not mentioned this for our glorification, but in order that it might be seen that we considered it a matter of honour to carry out those plans of yours, conceived in dutiful generosity.

I have decided to pass over your several other benefactions ... [several lines missing] ... You gave me the greatest help in my flight; you adorned my life with ornaments, when you gave me gold and jewellery stripped from your body; and then you enriched my absence with slaves, money and provisions, after cleverly deceiving enemy guards. You begged for my life in my absence — an attempt which your virtue led you to make. Conquered by your words the clemency of those against whom you deployed them was my defence; your plea was always uttered with firmness of mind.

Meanwhile, when a column of troops assembled by Milo, whose

house I had bought during his exile, sought to use the opportunities of civil war to break in and ravage, you successfully repelled it and defended our house . . . [about 12 lines missing] . . . that I was brought back home by him,[2] for, had you not kept something he might save in your care for my safety, he would have promised his assistance in vain. Thus I owe my life no less to your dutifulness than to Caesar.

Why should I now divulge our private and secret plans and our personal conversations? How I was saved by your advice when summoned by unexpected reports to face present and imminent dangers? How you did not allow me rashly to test the issue too boldly, but, when I took a more sensible view, you found me a safe hiding-place and you chose as your helpmates in your plans to save me your sister and her husband, Gaius Cluvius, all joined in danger? There would be no end to it if I were to try to go into detail. It is enough for me and for you that I hid safely.

For all that, I declare that the bitterest event of my life is your fate when I had returned home as a citizen through the beneficence and decision of the absent Caesar Augustus, when his colleague who was here, Marcus Lepidus, was accosted by you over my restoration and you threw yourself to the ground at his feet and were not only not raised up but were dragged away and hauled off forcibly like a slave; your body covered with bruises, your spirit quite undaunted, you admonished him with Caesar's edict and his congratulations for my restoration; even after you had heard the most insulting words and suffered cruel wounds, you openly persisted with your case, so that the author of my perils might be known. He soon suffered as a result of this affair. What could have been more effective than virtue such as this — to present Caesar with an opportunity for clemency and, while guarding my life, to brand the offensive cruelty of Lepidus with your outstanding endurance?

Why say more? Let us spare my speech which should and can be brief, lest in relating your very great deeds we speak less well than you deserve, when for the magnitude of your services to me I set before the eyes of all the commemoration of a life saved.

When the world had been pacified and the state restored, then peaceful and happy times came to us. We wanted children, which chance begrudged, for a time. If Fortune had seen fit to continue obedient as usual, what could either of us have wanted? Continuing otherwise, it put an end to hope. What you did for this reason and the steps you tried to take would perhaps be outstanding and remarkable in some women, but in your case were not particulary remarkable: comparing this with your other virtues, I pass over it.

Unsure of your fertility and grieved by my childlessness, lest by keeping you as my wife I should give up hope of having children and be unhappy in consequence, you talked of divorce. You said that you would hand over an empty house to the fertility of another with the intention of personally – in our known harmony – seeking out and providing a match worthy and fit for me; and you affirmed that you would treat future children as partly yours and as if they were yours; and that you would not divide our property, previously shared, but that it would remain under my control and, if I wished, under your management – that you would have nothing apart, nothing separate, that you would thereafter perform the duties and the role of a sister or mother-in-law.

I must say that I so flared up that I went out of my mind, that I was so astounded at your project that I scarcely regained my composure. That our separation could be envisaged before fate had so decreed, that your mind could conceive a reason why you should cease to be my wife in my lifetime when you had remained utterly faithful when I was an exile and all but dead!! What desire or need to have children could I have found so great as to make me set aside my good faith for the sake of it or exchange certainty for uncertainty?? But why go on? You stayed with me as my wife; the fact was that I could not have given in to you without disgrace to myself and unhappiness for us both. Yet what have you done more praiseworthy than, in your obedience to me, to exercise yourself so that, although I could not have children by you, I might nevertheless have them through you, so that, in your despair of bearing children, you might put at my disposal the fertility of another wife??

I wish that, if our lifetimes had permitted, our marriage had continued until, when I was carried for burial, the elder, as would have been more just, you administered the last rites, that I had passed away leaving you alive to be my daughter in place of my childlessness!! It was fated for you to be my precursor. You left me grief in my longing for you, but you did not leave me children to care for a wretched man. For my part I shall temper my feelings to accord with your decisions and I shall follow your advice. Let all your ideas and prescriptions take second place to your praiseworthiness, so that it may be my solace and stop me from pining too much for what I have consecrated to immortality for eternal remembrance.

I shall not lack for your attainments in life. Fortified by the thought of your reputation and taught by your example, may I stand up to Fortune, which has not robbed me of everything since it has allowed your memory to flourish through praise. But with you I have lost my state of tranquillity, you whom I regard as my look-out and front line against dangers — I am broken by the calamity and cannot keep my promise. Natural grief tears asunder the strength of my character; I am overcome by sorrow and do not stand my ground against either the grief or the fear that assail me; as I look back at my past fortunes and look with trepidation towards my future, my courage fails. Deprived of protection so mighty and of such a type, as I contemplate your reputation I do not seem to be equal to this endurance so much as to be destined to pine and grieve.

The conclusion of this speech will be that you deserved everything but that it was not my fate to give you everything. I have treated your last wishes as law; what more I can do, I shall do.

I pray that your departed spirit lets you rest and so watches over you.

1. The fictitious sale of a woman to a man by which she passed into his power at marriage.   2. = Augustus.

[721] *EJ 359*
Near Corfinium

[Beginning is lost] ... of ... Niger, for 39 years married to one husband, lived to her last day in the greatest concord, left three surviving children by him, a son who has held the highest municipal posts through the favours of Augustus Caesar, another who in the army of the same Caesar Augustus has held the highest posts of the equestrian rank and is now marked out for a higher rank, and a most virtuous daughter, married to a most upright man and, through her, two grandchildren ...

[722] *EJ 262*
5 BC. Contract with a wet-nurse

To Artemidorus, chief-judge, in charge of the circuit-judges and the other judges, from Marcus Sempronius, son of Marcus, of the tribe Aemilia, soldier of the 22nd legion, cohort ... and from Erotarion, the daughter of ... with as guardian and protector my kinsman, Lucius ..., son of Lucius ... Erotarion agrees that for 15 months from Phaophi of the present 26th year of Caesar she will nurse and suckle outside at her own home in the city, with her own milk, pure and untainted, the slave baby named Primus which Marcus placed with her from as long ago as Epeiph of last year, monthly pay for milk and nursing being ten drachmas and two cotyls of oil. [A long list of conditions follows.]

[723] *POxy 744 = SelPap105*
1 BC. Private letter involving possible exposure

Hilarion to Alis, his sister, very many greetings and to my lady Berous and Apollonarion.

Let me tell you that we are still in Alexandria. Don't worry. If they do go home, I shall remain. I ask you and beg you, take care of the child and as soon as we get pay I shall send up to you. If you have a child and it's a boy, so be it, but if it's a girl, throw it out. You said to Aphrodisias that I should not forget you — how could I forget you? So please don't worry. Year 29 of Caesar, Pauni 23rd.

[The address, on the reverse] From Hilarion. Deliver to Alis.

[724] M. Malavolta, *MGR*, 6, pp. 347-82 with B. Levick, *JRS*, 73 (1983) pp. 97-115
19, Larinum, Italy; cf. Tac. *Ann*. 2.85; Suet. *Tib*. 35

Decree of the Senate . . . on the Palatine, in the portico adjoining the temple of Apollo. Present at the drafting were Gaius Ateius Capito, son of Lucius, of the tribe Arniensis, Sextus Pomp . . . Octavius Fronto, son of Gaius, of the tribe Stellatina, Marcus Asinius Mamilianus, son of Curtius, of the tribe Arnesis, Gaius Gavius Macer, son of Gaius, of the tribe Publilia, quaestor, Aulus Didius . . .

Since Marcus Silanus and Lucius Norbanus Balbus, the consuls, stated that they had composed a memorandum, as specifically instructed, on matters pertaining to . . . to those who, contrary to the dignity of their order, disport themselves on stage or in a spectacle or hire out their services, as is proscribed in senatorial decrees made on that matter in previous years, using fraudulent evasion to the deminution of the majesty of the Senate; and since they asked for a decision on that matter, on that matter the Senate decided as follows:

That no one should put on stage the son, daughter, grandson, granddaughter, great-grandson or great-granddaughter of a senator or any man whose father or grandfather, whether paternal or maternal, or brother or any woman whose husband or father or grandfather, paternal or maternal, or brother had the right of sitting as the spectator in the equestrian seats; nor should anyone require them under contract to fight with beasts or to take the plumage of gladiators or to take up the wooden sword or otherwise to perform any service of that sort; and that if such persons should make themselves available, no one should hire them; and that no such persons should hire themselves out

— and under that head particular care is to be taken to ensure that those who have the right of sitting in the equestrian seats and, to make a mockery of the authority of that order, have deliberately sought to receive public ignominy or to be condemned on a charge involving infamy and have thereafter voluntarily resigned their equestrian seats and put themselves under contract or disported themselves on stage, do not persist with malice aforethought; and that none of the afore-mentioned persons should receive proper burial if they so act contrary to the dignity of their order, with the exception of any who have already appeared on stage or hired out their services in the arena or who is the son or daughter of an actor or a gladiator or a trainer or a producer.

And it was decreed that in the decree of the Senate which was passed on the motion of Manius Lepidus and Titus Statilius Taurus, the consuls[1] ... written ... that no free-born girl younger than 20 years of age and no free-born boy younger than 25 years of age should be permitted to put themselves under contract or hire out their services in the arena or on stage ... with the exception of anyone consigned ... by the divine Augustus or by Tiberius Caesar Augustus ... it is the will of the Senate that this be held good, with the exception of ...

1. They were consuls in 11.

[725] Seneca, *On Benefits*, 2.27.1-2; cf *Res. Gestae*, appendix 4; F. Millar, *The Emperor in the Roman World* (1977) pp. 297-8

Gnaeus Lentulus Augur,[1] an example of the greatest wealth, until his freedmen made him a poor man — this man who saw 400 million sesterces his own (I choose my words carefully: he did no more than see it) — was devoid of character and no less despicable in spirit. Although he was the greatest miser he was nevertheless quicker to give out money than words, so great was the poverty of his speech. This man owed his advancement entirely to the divine Augustus, to whom he had brought his poverty, labouring under the weight of nobility, whence, through Augustus, he became a leading man in the state in both wealth and influence. Despite all this, he habitually complained that Augustus had taken him away from his studies and that he had not gained as much as he had lost when he abandoned oratory. But in fact the divine Augustus, as well as other benefits, had conferred upon him this benefit — he had freed him from ridicule and wasted effort!

1. Consul in 14 BC. Cf. Tac. *Ann.* 4.29 and 44; Suet *Tib.* 49.

[726] Lucillius, *Palatine Anthology*, 9.572

'From the Muses of Helicon let us start to sing',
Wrote shepherds of Helicon, they say.
'Of wrath sing, goddess' and 'Of a man tell me, Muse',
Said Calliope in Homer's mouth.
I too must write a beginning, but what shall I write,
About to publish a second little book?
Muses of Olympus, daughters of Zeus, I would not have been saved,
If Nero Caesar had not given me money.

[727] N. Horsfall, *BICS*, 23 (1970) p. 88
17-13 BC (?), Rome. A college of poets?

Publius Cornelius Syrus, freedman of Publius, name-servant, master of
... herald in the treasury on the three panels, master of scribes and
poets ... made in the stone theatre, orderly of a consul and censor.

[728] *POxy 1453 = SelPap 2 no. 327*
Oath of temple lamplighters, Oxyrhynchus, 30-29 BC

Copy of an oath. We, Thonis, also known as Patoiphis, son of Thonis,
and Heraclides, son of Totoes, both lamplighters of the temple of
Sarapis the greatest god and of the temple of Isis nearby, and Paapis,
son of Thonis, and Petosiris, son of the aforementioned Patoiphis,
both lamplighters of the temple of Thoeris the greatest goddess in the
town of Oxyrhynchus, all four swear by Caesar, god and son of a god,
to Heliodorus, son of Heliodorus, and Heliodorus, son of Ptolemy,
superintendents of the temples of the Oxyrhynchite and Cynopolite
nomes, that we will attend to the lamps of the stipulated temples as
laid down and that we will supply the appropriate oil for the daily
lamps burning in the temples indicated from Thoth 1st to the 5th
intercalary day of Mesore in this the first year of Caesar punctually and
in accordance with what has been supplied up to the 22nd which is also
the 7th year; we are all sureties for each other with regard to the above,
all our property being collateral for our conduct in conformity with the
above. If we swear truly, may it go well for us; if falsely, the opposite.
Year 1 of Caesar ... Copy. I, Paapis, son of Thonis, have sworn and I
shall act as laid down. I, Thonis, son of Harpaesis, have written for him
at his request, since he is illiterate. I, Heraclides, have sworn and I shall
act as laid down. I, Petosiris, have sworn and shall act as laid down. I,
Horus, son of Totoeus, have written for him at his request, since he is
illiterate. I, Thonis, have sworn likewise, as laid down.

[729] *SelPap 2 no. 328*
Oath of floodgate guards, AD 25

Marepsemis, about 21 years old, with a scar on his left thigh. Pecheus, about 45 years old, with a scar on his left wrist. Sokonopis, about 40 years old, with a scar on a finger of his left hand. Phanesis, about 39 years old, with a scar on his left calf.

To Gaius Julius Philetus, superintendent of sowing in the Arsinoite nome, from Marepsemis, son of Marepsemis, also known as Katutis, and Pecheus, son of Psephis, guards of the priests' outlet to the west of the bridge, and from Sokonopis, son of Sokonopis, and Phanesis, son of Pastous, guards of the priests' outlet to the east. We four priests of Tebtunis in the division of Polemo, guards of the two afore-mentioned outlets, swear by Tiberius Caesar Augustus New Imperator, son of the divine Augustus, that we will each guard our respective outlet at no expense and that we will attend to it always so that no loss will result; but if we fail ... to supervise the outflow, we will be responsible for all consequent damage. If we swear truly, may it go well with us; if falsely, the opposite. Apion, public scribe of the village, wrote on their behalf, since they are illiterate. Year 11 of Tiberius Caesar Augustus, 16th of the month of Augustus. I, Marepsemis, son of Marepsemis, also known as Katutis, have joined in swearing the aforementioned oath and I shall guard and act as laid down. Year 1 of Tiberius Caesar Augustus, 16th of the month of Augustus.

[730] *SelPap 2 no. 329*
Oath of fishermen, AD 46

We, Heraclides, son of Tryphon, secretary of the fishermen of the shore of Berenicis Thesmophori, and Harmieus, son of Anoubas, Papis, son of Onnophris, Panomieus, son of Akes, Sekoneus, son of Patunis, Anchorimphis, son of Orseus, Harpagathes, son of Nilus, Panomieus, son of Harmais, Neeches, son of Opis, Patunis, son of Orseus, Orseus, son of Orseus, Patunis, son of Satabous, Pelous, son of Patunis, the thirteen elders of the fishermen of the villages of Narmouthis and Berenicis Thesmophori, swear, all fourteen, to the agents of Sarapio, son of Ptolemy, nomarch and supervisor of the revenues and supervisor of the assessment of the Arsinoite nome, by Tiberius Claudius Caesar Augustus Germanicus, imperator, that we have not been and will never be involved in fishing or trawling or casting nets to catch the likenesses of the divine oxyrhynchi and lepidoti,[1] in accordance with the public contract made by us and the other fishermen. If we swear truly, may it go well with us; if falsely, the opposite. Year 6 of Tiberius Claudius Caesar Augustus Germanicus Imperator, 22nd Pharmouthi.

1. Sacred fish, regarded as likenesses of the gods in their form.

[731] *FIRA 3. no. 46*
47, Tebtunis, Egypt. Agreement among the salt-merchants of Tebtunis

Year 7 of Tiberius Claudius Caesar Augustus Germanicus, imperator, 25th of the month Caesareus.

Having met together, the undersigned men, salt-merchants resident at Tebtunis, have decided by general agreement to appoint a good man from their number as both supervisor and collector of public taxes in the coming eighth year of Tiberius Claudius Caesar Augustus Germanicus, imperator, — Apynchis, son of Orseus, collecting all public taxes of the same trade in the same coming year; and they decided that all should sell salt in the same way in the aforementioned village of Tebtunis and that Orseus has won by lot the sole right to sell gypsum in the aforementioned village of Tebtunis and adjacent villages, for which he is to pay, in addition to the portion of public taxes falling upon him, a further 66 silver drachmas; likewise that the same Orseus has won by lot Kerkesis, the sole right to sell salt there, for which he is likewise to pay a further 8 silver drachmas. And that Harmeusis, also called Belles, son of Harmeusis, has won by lot the sole right to sell salt and gypsum in the village of Tristomou, also called Boukolou, for which he is to pay, in addition to the portion of public taxes falling upon him, a further 5 silver drachmas. The condition is that they are to sell the good salt at 2½ obols, the light at 2 obols and the lighter at 1½ obols by our measure or that of the warehouse. And if anyone should sell at rates lower than these, let that man be fined 8 silver drachmas for the common fund and 8 for the public treasury; and if anyone is found to have sold to a trader more than a stater of salt, let that man be fined 8 silver drachmas for the common fund and 8 for the public treasury; and if a trader seeks to buy more than 4 drachmas of salt, all must sell to him jointly; and if anyone should bring in gypsum and seek to sell it outside, he must place it with Orseus, son of Harmeusis, until he takes it outside and sells it. The condition is that they each drink every month on the 25th one jar of beer . . . in the village one drachma, outside 4 drachmas, in the metropolis 8 drachmas. But should anyone not render his accounts and not fulfil any public duty or claims lodged against him, the said Apynchis will have the

power to arrest him in the street and in the houses and in the countryside and to hand him over to the head ... [fragments of 5 names
follow; one might be Apynchis].

[732] *Small. 430*
43-4, Moguntiacum

To Tiberius Claudius Caesar Augustus Germanicus, pontifex maximus,
in his third year of tribunician power, imperator four times, father of
his country, consul three times, the Roman citizen businessmen in
wallet-manufacture, Gaius Vibius Rufinus being propraetorian legate.

[733] Pliny the Elder, *Natural History*, 6.101; cf. A.H.M. Jones, *The Roman Economy* (1974) p. 144

It is appropriate to set out the entire route from Egypt [to India],
now for the first time definitely known. It is an important subject:
in no year does India drain off less than 50 million sesterces from our
empire, sending back goods which are sold at 100 times their cost price.

[734] Strabo 17 p. 798

In the past less than twenty ships risked the voyage across the Red Sea
to pass beyond its mouth. But now great fleets are despatched as far
as India and the extremities of Ethiopia and from these places the most
valuable cargo is carried to Egypt and thence sent on to other places.
In this way duties are collected twice, on both imports and exports;
on goods of high value the taxes are also high. In fact Egypt enjoys
monopolies, since, by and large, Alexandria is the sole recipient of such
goods and sells them on to the outside world.

[735] (a) *EJ 360a*
March, 2 BC, Coptos-Berenice road, Egypt

Gaius Numidius Eros was here in year 28 of Caesar, returning from
India, in the month Phamenoth.

(b) *EJ 360b*
6, same place, bilingual

I, Lysa, slave of Publius Annius Plocamus, came here in year 35 of
Caesar, 5th July.

[736] Strabo 4 pp. 200-1

However, in the present day, some of the rulers there[1] have won the friendship of Caesar Augustus through embassies and diplomacy, have placed dedications on the Capitol and have made the whole island friendly to the Romans. They submit to heavy duties upon their exports to Gaul and their imports from there (these imports consist of ivory bangles and necklaces and amber jewellery and glassware and other trinkets of that sort), with the result that there is no need to occupy the island: at least one legion plus cavalry would be needed to exact taxes from them and the cost of the troops would cancel the money raised: duties would have to be reduced if direct taxation was introduced and, at the same time, the application of force would involve risks.

1. In Britain.

[737] A. Wilhelm, *JOAI,* 17 (1914) pp. 1-120 with K. Hopkins, *JRS,* 70 (1980) p. 121 n.59
Messene, S. Greece. Date uncertain, probably AD 35-44.

(a) In the priesthood of Agathus, sixth month, decrees:

A

Since Aristocles, the secretary of the councillors, presented the assessment of the 8-obol tax and submitted a statement with regard to the monies accruing from it – and how those monies have each been put towards the demands and that they have been used for no other purpose than this; and since, with regard to the monies outstanding under the special tax, he balanced the accounts in the theatre before the populace and in the presence of Vibius, the praetor; and since he saw to the exaction, as far as possible, of the sums outstanding to the city, just as the councillors themselves all thought right in order that the demand be fulfilled and that there should be no borrowing or shortfall with regard to these special taxes.

   All the councillors therefore recognised his application and honesty and, together with Vibius, the praetor, resolved that he be honoured with a bronze image; and Vibius, the praetor, granted him in person, in the presence of the citizens, the right to wear a gold ring; and the councillors themselves conferred the same honour upon him, in addition to the image; and the crowd declared, 'Good luck to Aristocles, the secretary of the councillors in receiving the honours'.

When he had received these honours the councillors decided that Aristocles should be congratulated for the application and honesty with which he has conducted himself in the public affairs of the city, both in this matter and in all his other services to the city; and that the honours conferred upon him, both by the councillors and by the praetor, should remain in perpetuity; and that he should be permitted to erect the image in front of the office of the secretary of the councillors and to inscribe upon its base, 'The city honoured Aristocles, son of Callicrates, being secretary of the councillors, for the virtue and goodwill which he consistently displayed towards it.' And let the cost of the image and the base be met from the public revenues and let Aristocles himself be supervisor of the image and the base.

B

Since Aristocles, secretary of the councillors, having assumed the office entrusted to him by the magistrates and councillors, immediately looked to the protection of the city and its inhabitants, within the limits of his office. And since, first, he saw to it that all city-business was written up on a wall for all to see each day by those administering any city-business, setting good men an example of just and honest administration. And since, in his wish to put his honesty totally beyond doubt in the minds of all citizens, he did not engage in the administration of monies, either in his own person or in partnership with other persons, but rather appointed good men as tax-collectors for each liturgy and financial office; and since everything was set in order for the city at a time when demands great and numerous were being made. And since he has acted in the interests of the city in ways many and large through the governors, sometimes in the city, sometimes as an envoy. And since, by receiving both governors and many other Romans as his guests, he spends his private resources in the interests of the city. And since he has concerned himself with the just and equitable administration of the rest of the affairs of the inhabitants of the city, showing himself worthy of the offices entrusted to him by the city, for his good conduct in which he was honoured with images by the city; and since, in recognition of his conduct with regard to the above, Memmius, the proconsul, and Vibius, the praetor, each granted him the right to wear gold; and since, likewise, the councillors, with everyone declaring in one voice that appropriate honours must be given to Aristocles for all the above. And since all the citizens resolved that a statue and two inscribed images should be given in his honour. And since it is proper to congratulate men who are good and patriotic and act responsibly in complete equitability in the public service and to honour them with appropriate honours.

The council and the people therefore resolved that Aristocles, son of Callicrates, the secretary of the councillors, should be congratulated for his responsibility and honesty in public affairs and for his equitability and propriety towards the citizens and, likewise, for his actions in the interests of the city in ways numerous and large . . .

(b) Assessment of:	Talents	Minae	Staters	Drachmas	Obols	½ obols	Chalkoi
Cresphontis	122	30	1	–	8	1	–
Daïphontis	106	56	5	–	8	–	–
Aristomachis	249	4	20	–	10	–	–
Hyllis	149	15	–	–	1	–	–
Cleodaïa	261	50	1	–	4	–	10
Foreigners, including the Romans assessed in the tribe							
	129	11	22	1	–	–	–
Total	1018	32	1	–	8	–	10

Craftsmen not included in the tribes: grand total of their property assessed as:

	31	49	15	–	10	–	–
Olympic victors	4	15	13	–	9	–	–

Romans not assessed under Damon and those covered by special treaties, not including the amendment of the assessment under review:

	118	21	22	–	7	–	–

Amended assessment fixed under review as prescribed, not including cases undecided up to the tenth month:

	73	25	12	–	11	–	–

Those not assessed who are liable to special taxation; total used:

	7	50	25	–	–	–	–
Total	1256	5	16	–	10	–	10

Omitted are those given the same assessment under Damon:

	2	34	–	–	–	–	–

Assessment of Hippice and Calliste, the lands of Thalon, including the amended assessment:

	8	37	21	–	8	–	–

Automeia, property of Nemerius for which Damon had been assessed:

	2	50	–	–	–	–	–
Total	14	1	21	–	8	–	–

Residue, from which the special eight-obol tax must be drawn:

	1242	4	30	–	2	–	10

	Denarii	Obols	Chalkoi
Resulting special eight-obol tax:	99,365	2	–
Amount of this received up to the thirtieth day of the seventh month as written up on the wall by the collectors:	83,574	–	1 Trichalkon
Residue outstanding	15,797	5	9
Amount of this due from those on military service:	411	–	6
Deceased free persons	487	–	6
Craftsmen performing public services	89	2	6
Slave oarsmen	82	5	–
Included in the amount ouustanding are taxes due from			
Cresphontis	1870	4	–
Daïphontis	1158	3	6
Aristomachis	2202	5	–
Hyllis	2177	4	6
Cleodaïa	1480	5	6
Foreigners	3752	–	–
Those not assessed	97	2	–
Romans and those covered by special treaties:	1424	–	–
Those exempted from the payment of special taxes and Olympic victors	1349	5	–

[738] *EJ 191*

Near Rome; cf. Tac. *Ann.* 4.6 with A.H.M. Jones, *The Roman Economy* (1974) p. 181

To ... Fonteius, son of Quintus, quaestor, the tax-collectors of Africa.

[739] *Small. 431*

43-4, Rome

To Tiberius Claudius Caesar Augustus Germanicus, son of Drusus, pontifex maximus, in his third year of tribunician power, consul three times, imperator 5 times, father of his country, the company members engaged in the 5% liberty tax and the 4% sales tax.

[740] *Small. 432*

September, 58, Palmyra

Lucius Spedius Chrysanthus made this in his lifetime for himself and his people, year 369, in the month Gorpiaeus. [An Aramaic translation follows, describing him as a publican.]

[741] *Small. 438*
About 50. Petition to the strategus of Oxyrhynchus

To Tiberius Claudius Pasion, strategus, from Sarapio, son of Theon, weaver of the city of Oxyrhynchus, resident in Gymnasium square quarter.

Apollophanes, become collector of the weavers' tax in the first year of Tiberius Claudius Caesar Augustus Germanicus, imperator, using great force, seized a linen cloak I was wearing, worth 8 drachmas; and he exacted from me a further 4 drachmas and 2 drachmas a month in the six months from the month of New Augustus in the ninth year of Tiberius Claudius Caesar Augustus Germanicus, imperator, to Pharmouthi; in total 24 drachmas. I therefore request that you take action against him as you think fit. Farewell.

[742] *Small. 439*
Petition from tax-collectors to the prefect of Egypt

To Tiberius Claudius Balbillus, from Nemesion, collector of the poll-tax of Philadelphia [the names of 5 other poll-tax collectors of different villages follow], the six collectors of the poll-tax of the aforesaid villages of the Heraclides division of the Arsinoite nome.

The previously numerous population of the aforesaid villages has now declined to a few, because some have migrated through poverty, while others have died without heirs; therefore, there is a danger that we shall abandon the collectorship. Turning to you for these reasons, with a view to not abandoning the collectorship, we ask you, the saviour and benefactor of all, to write, if you think fit, to the strategus of the nome, Asianus, to protect us from molestation and wait for your decision at the assize of the upper nome, so that we may receive your beneficence. Farewell.

[743] (a) *ILS 2923*
Tarentum. Probably the agricultural writer

To Lucius Junius Moderatus Columella, son of Lucius, of the tribe Galeria, military tribune of legion 6 Ferrata.

(b) Columella, *On Agriculture*, 1. pref. 20

And so in this Latium and Saturnian land, where the gods taught their progeny about the crops of the fields, we now contract out at auction, so that from provinces across the sea grain may be brought to us to prevent us suffering famine, and we lay down vintages from the Cyclades islands and regions of Baetica and Gaul. No wonder, since the common opinion is now publicly held and confirmed that farming is a sordid occupation and a business requiring no instruction or precept.

[744] C. Giordano, *RendNap*, 41 (1966) no. 3

Pompeii. An agreement of bail, *vadimonium*: each party promises to appear in court at a certain time, on pain of an agreed monetary penalty. The text survives on a wax tablet

Bail arranged with Trypho, son of Potamo, an Alexandrian for 23rd March at Rome in the Forum of Augustus before the triumphal statue of Gnaeus Sentius Saturninus at the fifth hour; Gaius Sulpicius Cinnamus called for a promise of 3,000 sesterces, . . . made the promise.

[745] Seneca, *Letters*, 77. 1-4

Unexpectedly, today, Alexandrian ships appeared within sight, those which are usually sent ahead and announce the arrival of a fleet behind them; they call them 'mail-boats' — a welcome sight in Campania. A vast mob stood on the docks of Puteoli and spotted the Alexandrians from the configuration of their sails, despite the great mob of ships. They alone use their top-sails then in the way that all ships do in the open sea: nothing helps them cut through the water as much as their top-sails; that is what drives the ships on most . . .

In the midst of this turmoil, as everyone rushed to the water's edge, I took great pleasure in my leisure, because, while I was about to receive letters from my people, I was in no rush to find out the state of my affairs there or know what the ships brought; it is a long time since I either lost or gained anything.

[746] *POxy 2873*
Oct. 25th 62. Withdrawal from a lease concerning the Egyptian property of Seneca

Psenamounis, son of Psenamounis, grandson of Thonis, and Dionysius, son of Ptollis, son of Orthonoos, inhabitants of the village of Sesphtha, in the lower toparchy, to Tiberius Claudius Theon, lessee of the estate of Lucius Annaeus Seneca, greetings.

Since we are not able to farm the five aruras which we had in our own name in the lot of Diotimus on said estate, we are leaving as from the ninth year of Nero Claudius Caesar Augustus Germanicus Imperator so as not to be in any difficulties at all over the rents of the land. We therefore request that you assent to our leaving so that we may not be subject to false accusations. Farewell.

Ninth year of Nero Claudius Caesar Augustus Germanicus Imperator, Phaophi 28th.

[Second hand] I, Psenamounis, son of Psenamounis, am leaving the farm, as stated.

[Third hand] I, Dionysius, son of Ptollis, am leaving, as stated. The same date.

[747] J.A. Crook, *ZPE*, 29 (1978) pp. 234-6
Wax tablets, Pompeii

(a)   28th June 37
In the consulship of Gnaeus Acerronius Proculus and Gaius Petronius Pontius, 28th June, I, Gaius Novius Eunus, have written that I have received as a loan from Euenus Primianus, freedman of Tiberius Caesar Augustus, in his absence, through Hesucus, his slave, and owe to him 10,000 sesterces, which I shall repay to him when he asks; and Hesucus, slave of Euenus Primianus, freedman of Tiberius Caesar Augustus, sought assurance that those 10,000 sesterces mentioned above be properly and rightly given, and I, Gaius Novius Eunus, gave my assurance and, for those 10,000 sesterces, I gave as a pledge and security 7,000 modii, more or less, of Alexandrian wheat and 4,000 modii, more or less, of chick-peas, legumes and lentils in 200 sacks, all of which I have, deposited, in my hands, in the public Bassian warehouse of the Puteolans, which I declare and admit to be free from every outrage at my risk.

(b) 2nd July 37

In the consulship of Gaius Caesar Germanicus Augustus and Tiberius Claudius Nero Germanicus, 2nd July, I, Diognetus, slave of Gaius Novius Cypaerus, have written, by order of Cypaerus, my master, in his presence, that I have rented to Hesucus, slave of Tiberius Julius Euenus, freedman of Augustus, space 12 in the public Bassian warehouse, central part, of the Puteolans, where the Alexandrian wheat, which he received in pledge today from Gaius Novius Eunus, has been placed; likewise the area in the same warehouse, lower part, where he has, deposited, 200 sacks of legumes, which he received in pledge from the same Eunus, from 1st July, at one nummus per month.

[748] Pliny the Elder, *Natural History*, 18.35

If truth be told large estates have been the ruin of Italy and are now indeed the ruin of the provinces too. Six owners possessed half the province of Africa when the princeps Nero had them killed . . .

[749] *CIL 8.5383*
Africa

Januarius, estate-man, slave of Nero Caesar Augustus, lived thirty years, lies here.

[750] L. Gasperini, *MGR*, 3 pp. 178-9
Near Tarentum, very probably relating to Calvia Crispinilla; cf. Tac. *Hist*. 1.73; Dio 63.12.3

(a) Camulus, slave of Crispinilla, herdsman, lived 35 years, lies here.

(b) Quietus, slave of Crispinilla, herdsman. His concubine made this for one well-deserving. Lived 35 years.

[751] *ILS 8574 a-b*
Poetovio and elsewhere in the Adriatic. Stamps on amphorae of olive-oil

(a) Of Traulus[1] and Crispinilla.

(b) Of Calvia Crispinilla.

1. Crispinilla's husband; cf. Tac. *Ann*. 11.36.

[752] D. Colls *et al.*, *Gallia*, 33 (1975) pp. 61-94

On tin ingots from the wreck of a ship carrying oil from Baetica, found off Port-Vendres, near Perpignan

Lucius Valerius, freedman of Augusta,[1] records-secretary.

1. = Messallina.

[753] *PRyl 126*

AD 28-9. Petition to a strategus about damage to crops on an estate of Livia in Egypt

To . . . strategus of the Arsinoite nome, from Onnophris . . . inhabitant of Euhemeria in the division of Themistes, farmer on the estate of Julia Augusta of lands previously belonging to Gaius Julius Alexander.

In the present month . . . of the 15th year of Tiberius Caesar Augustus, Demas, son of Psaesis, living in the so-called farmstead of Dromeus, near the village, let his sheep and cattle into the lands of my mother which I farm; they grazed down two arurae of young wheat of mine and half an arura of barley, whence I suffered in result no slight loss. The accused is pasturing with Harpaesis, son of Heras. I therefore request that the accused be brought before you for subsequent punishment. Farewell.

Onnophris, aged 50 years, with a scar on the little finger of his left hand.

[754] Josephus, *Jewish Antiquities*, 18.31

. . . Salome the sister of King Herod passed away and bequeathed to Julia[1] both Jamneia and its whole area and Phasaelis, situated in the plain, and Archelais, where date-palms are planted in abundance and their produce is the best.

1. = Livia. Salome, her friend, died about AD 10.

[755] *PRyl 134*

AD 34. Petition to the chief of police concerning the theft of a pig

To Gaius Arrius Priscus, chief of police, from Anchorimphis, son of Anchorimphis, inhabitant of Euhemeria in the division of Themistes, farmer of the Germanician estate of Tiberius Caesar Augustus.

On the 6th of the present month of Pharmouthi, in the 20th year of Tiberius Caesar Augustus, there was stolen from me in the village by certain bandits a pregnant breeding-sow, tawny-skinned, worth 12 drachmas. I therefore request that you give written instructions for an inquiry into the matter. Farewell.

[756] *POxy 244*
AD 23. The transfer of cattle

To Chaeteas, strategus, from Cerinthus, slave of Antonia, wife of Drusus.

As I want to transfer from the Oxyrhynchite to the Cynopolite nome, for the sake of pastures, the 320 sheep and 160 goats and the consequent lambs and kids, which I have on the register in the Oxyrhynchite nome in the present ninth year of Tiberius Caesar Augustus, I am submitting the memorandum so that you may write to the strategus of the Cynopolite nome to register the indicated sheep . . .

[In another hand, in Latin with a Greek flavour.] I, Cerinthus, slave of Antonia, wife of Drusus, submitted this in year 9 of Tiberius Caesar Augustus, Mechir 8th.

[In a third hand, in Greek.] Chaereas to Hermias, strategus of the Cynopolite nome, very many greetings.

Cerinthus, slave of Antonia, wife of Drusus, has submitted a return to me: he wants . . .

[757] *PRyl 140*
AD 36. Petition to the chief of police concerning the theft of a pig

To Gaius Arrius Priscus, chief of police, from Aunes, son of Anchorimphis, inhabitant of Euhemeria, state-farmer – and I also farm the estate of Antonia, wife of Drusus.

On the 18th of the present month of New Augustus, in the 23rd year of Tiberius Caesar Augustus, there was stolen from me by certain bandits, at my very door, a tawny-skinned pig, worth 8 drachmas. I therefore request that you give written instructions for an inquiry into the matter. Farewell.

Aunes, aged 35 years, with a scar on his left thumb.

[758] *PRyl 141*
AD 37. Petition to a centurion concerning an assault

To Gaius Trebius Justus, centurion, from Petermouthis, son of Heracleus, inhabitant of Euhemeria, state farmer and tax collector – and I also farm the estate of Antonia, wife of Drusus.

On the second of the present month of Pachon, in the first year of Gaius Caesar Imperator, while I was talking to Papontos, son of Orsenouphis, and Apion, known as Capareis, who are shepherds, about damages owed me for the grazing-down done by their flocks, they gave me a serious beating and blatantly announced that they would not pay. And I also lost 40 drachmas which I had with me from the sale of opium, and my belt. I therefore request that I receive redress, so that the state may suffer no harm. Farewell.

[759] *PRyl 138*

AD 34. Petition to the chief of police concerning crop-damage and robbery on an imperial estate

To Gaius Arrius Priscus, chief of police, from Sotas, son of Maron, superintendent of the lands of the children of Tiberius and of Livia, wife of Drusus Caesar.

Orsenouphis, son of Heracleus, and Heracles, son of Ptollis, let their flocks into the newly-planted oliveyards of the said estate in the farmstead of Dromeus and they grazed down 200 olive plants, among those which previously belonged to Falcidius. And what is more, I caught this man when, at night, he sprang into the farmstead from an entrance-point and robbed me of a number of tools kept in the tower: 5 rakes, 6 hay-sickles and 16 measures of wool, as well as other stuff, and 200 drachmas that I was keeping on the farm to buy goods. I therefore request that the accused be brought before you so that I may get justice. Farewell.

Year 20 of Tiberius Caesar Augustus, 22nd Epeiph.

[760] *PRyl 148*

AD 40. Petition to the chief of police concerning the theft of anise

To Gaius Julius Pholus, chief of police, from Chaeremon, son of Acusilaus, superintendent of the estate of Gaius Caesar Imperator Augustus and that of Tiberius Claudius Germanicus, in the region of Euhemeria, in the division of Themistes.

On the night before the 18th of Pachon in the present 4th year of Gaius Caesar Imperator Augustus, certain people, bandit-fashion, broke into the store of anise which I keep on the settlement property and threshed out 20 loads, which came to 10 artabae of anise, so that I suffered no slight loss in result. I therefore request that you write to the archephodus of the village, so that he may inquire into this affair and send those responsible to you. Farewell.

I, Chaeremon, son of Acusilaus, presented the above petition. Year 4 of Gaius Caesar Imperator Augustus, Pachon 19th.

[761] *POxy 2837*
AD 50. Notification of death

To Heraclides, entrepreneur of the estate of lord Tiberius Claudius Caesar Augustus Germanicus Imperator, from Aline, daughter of Comon, with, as guardian, her brother, Dionysius, son of the said Comon.

My husband Mnesithes, son of Petesouchus, one of those enjoying the tax exemption of the aforementioned estate, who is registered in the quarter of the street of Sarapis, great god, died in the month of Caesareum in the present tenth year of Tiberius Claudius Caesar Augustus Germanicus Imperator. I therefore request that you register him in the category of like persons, as is proper, and I swear by Tiberius Claudius Caesar Augustus Germanicus Imperator that this is true.

[762] *Small. 440*
Probably Neronian. Petition to a strategus about an oil-factory

To Philoxenus, who was cosmetes, strategus of the Arsinoite nome, Themistus division, from Herieus, son of Satabous, of Socnopaei Nesus.

As far back as the 13th year of the divine Claudius[1] I leased from the former estate of Narcissus an oil-factory at a rent of 200 drachmas and three measures of oil. But, then, when those in charge did not give me iron-sockets or the other things needed for the press, I was forced to buy and install these at my own expense; and, likewise, a lever and mortars and the other essentials, again at my own expense, since they paid no attention to me. Therefore, since the factory was also delapidated and I was also forced to fit beams and supports and am compelled over a two-year period of not using the factory to pay the rent for it from my own resources, I ask, as I am no longer able to bear these costs, that you require those in charge not to molest me over the rent.

1. AD 53.

[763] *ILS 5682*
Coela, Thracian Chersonese

To the divinity of the Augustan house, Titus Claudius Faustus Reginus and Claudia Nais, wife of Faustus, built a bath for the populace and the estate of our Caesar at their own expense and they also channeled water for the needs of the bath and they consecrated it in the consulship of Nero Caesar Augustus and Antistius Vetus.[1]

1. 55. Augustus had inherited lands in the Thracian Chersonese from Agrippa (Dio 54.29.2). Nero's name has been erased from this text.

[764] *PRyl 171*
AD 56-7. A lease application

To Euschemon, agent of the estate of Tiberius Claudius Doryphorus,[1] formerly that of Narcissus, from Papus, son of Trypho, inhabitant of Heraclia in the division of Themistes, living in the farmstead of Antonia, wife of Drusus, through Psenhericus, a Persian of the Epigone.

I want to lease for four years from the coming third year of Nero Claudius Caesar Augustus Germanicus Imperator the ... around the said village ... in two parcels 27 aruras, in one parcel ... 7 aruras, and in the second parcel 20 aruras, the adjacent areas being on the south royal land ... on the north royal land on the lake-shore, on the west the lands of ... on the east the lands of the estate of Maecenas, on condition that I have received for the working and banking of the land ... silver drachmas per arura, not to be returned, I shall pay a total annual rent for the area resulting from the survey ... to include the one artaba of wheat per arura which I shall receive for seed-corn ...

1. Cf. Suet. *Nero* 29; Tac. *Ann*. 14.65.

[765] *FIRA III 128a and c*; cf. J.A. Crook, *Law and Life of Rome* (1967) p. 220
(a) 15, Pompeii

520 sesterces for the sale of the mule to Marcus Pomponius Nico, freedman of Marcus, which sum Marcus Cerrinius Euphrates is declared to have made the object of a stipulatory contract with Lucius Caecilius Felix.

All that sum which is stated above, Marcus Cerrinius Euphrates, freedman of Marcus, declared that he received from Philadelphus, slave of Caecilius Felix.

Transacted at Pompeii, 28th May, in the consulship of Drusus Caesar and Gaius Norbanus Flaccus.

(b) 54, Pompeii

1,985 sesterces, which sum was under stipulatory contract with Lucius Caecilius Jucundus for the auction of the box plantation of Gaius Julius Onesimus for 15th July next, less fee, Gaius Julius Onesimus declared that he received from Marcus Fabius Agathinus in the name of Lucius Caecilius Jucundus.

Transacted at Pompeii, 10th May, in the consulship of Manius Acilius Aviola and Marcus Asinius Marcellus.

[766] J.A. Crook, *ZPE*, 29 (1978) pp. 233-4
Wax tablet, Pompeii, 5th Oct. 51

In the consulship of Tiberius Claudius Caesar, for the fifth time, and Lucius Calventius Vetus, 5th October, at Puteoli in the forum, in the Sextian portico of Augustus, on the rectangular column, a notice was affixed, on which was written what follows:

The man Felix, the man Carus, the man Januarius, the woman Primigenia, the woman Primigenia, the younger, and the boy Ampliatus, which chattels Marcus Egnatius Suavis was said to have given to Gaius Sulpicius Cinnamus by mancipation for one sesterce on transaction of fiducia for a debt of 23 sesterces, will be offered for sale on 14th October next at Puteoli in the forum in front of the Caesonian porch; the pledge became forfeit from 15th September.

[Suavis has defaulted on the loan he borrowed from Cinnamus; Cinnamus therefore announces the auction of the slaves which Suavis had given as security for the loan.]

[767] *Small. 433*
Wax tablets, Herculaneum; cf. J.A. Crook *Law and Life of Rome* (1967)

(a) 2nd September 60 (?)
In the consulship of Gaius Velleius Paterculus and Marcus Manilius Vopiscus, 2nd September.

I, Quintus Junius Theophilus, have written that I have given an undertaking to Aulus Tetteius Severus that from the Blandian estate that he may harvest, exploit, take away and carry off all the produce of his part, and that for the wine-jars a shed be guaranteed until 13th August next and undamaged seals, and that he may take away, carry off, lead away and auction off from there all his property and slaves and flocks, as permitted.

Aulus Tetteius Severus sought assurance that everything written above be done and guaranteed; I, Quintus Junius Theophilus, gave my assurance. Transacted at Herculaneum. [Names of witnesses follow.]

(b) 8th May 63
[The beginning is lost; it was probably a declaration by Primus about his purchase of a slave] . . . it is guaranteed that this man is healthy and free from theft and charges of injurious conduct, and that if anyone should evict that man or any share in him to the detriment of the lawful holding, use and possession of Lucius Cominius Primus or his heir, then the simple and proper price is to be duly paid; Lucius Cominius Primus sought assurance that these things be duly guaranteed in the usual way; Publius Cornelius Poppaeus gave his assurance. Transacted in Pompeii in the Arrian potteries of Poppaea Augusta, 8th May, in the consulship of Gaius Memmius Regulus and Lucius Verginius Rufus. [The names of witnesses follow.]

[768] *EJ 30*
17 BC, Rome. Senatorial decrees on the Secular Games

A
23rd May, in the Julian Precinct . . . present at the drafting were . . . Aemilius Lepidus, Lucius Cestius, Lucius Petronius Rufus . . .

Since Gaius Silanus, the consul, stated that Secular Games are to be held in the present year, after some years, by Imperator Caesar Augustus and Marcus Agrippa,with tribunician power, and that because religion demands that there be as many spectators as possible and also because no one will witness such a spectacle a second time, it seems proper that, on the days of said games, those not yet married be permitted to attend without fear of punishment; and since he asked the Senate what it wished to be done in this matter, in this matter the following was decreed:

That, since said games have been instituted for the sake of religion and since no mortal is allowed to see them more than once[1] . . . those who are liable under the law on the marriage of the orders may be permitted to watch, without fear of punishment, the games which the masters of the 15 for the performance of sacred rites are to present.

B
On the same day, in the same place, the same were present at the drafting and a decree of the Senate was made.

Since Gaius Silanus, the consul, stated that, in the interest of the preservation of the memory of such great divine benevolence, a record of the Secular Games should be inscribed on a pillar of bronze and a pillar of marble and that both should be erected for the future remembrance of the celebration in the place where the games are to be held; and since he asked the Senate what it wished to be done in this matter, in this matter the following was decreed:

That one or both of the consuls, for the future remembrance of the celebration, should erect a pillar of bronze and another of marble, on which a record of said games has been inscribed, in said place and that the same men should contract out for the work and instruct the praetors in charge of the treasury to pay the contractors the amount for which they contracted.

1. Because the Secular Games were only to be held once every 110 years (*saeculum*).

[769] *ILS 5050, including EJ 31 and 32*
17 BC, Rome, Campus Martius. This is no doubt the inscribed record envisaged in the preceding document

[The beginning is lost] . . . On the following night, in the Campus, by the Tiber, Imperator Caesar Augustus sacrificed to the divine Moerae 9 she-lambs, offered whole, in the Greek manner, and, in the same manner, 9 she-goats and he prayed as follows:

Moerae, as it is written in your regard in those books, that each and everything may prosper for the Roman people, the Quirites, a sacrifice of 9 she-lambs and 9 she-goats should be offered to you, I beseech you and pray that you increase the empire and majesty of the Roman people, the Quirites, at war and at home and that you always protect the Latin name; that you bestow upon the Roman people, the Quirites, eternal safety, victory and health; and that you favour the Roman people, the Quirites, and the legions of the Roman people and keep safe the state of the Roman people, the Quirites; and that you be well-disposed and propitious to the Roman people, the Quirites, the college of 15, myself, my family, my household, and that you accept this sacrifice of 9 she-lambs and 9 she-goats duly made. For these reasons be honoured by this sacrificial she-lamb and, now and in future, be well-disposed and propitious to the Roman people, the Quirites, the college of the 15, myself, my family, my household.

The sacrifice completed, performances were begun at night on stage, where there was no theatre and no seats set out, and 110 married citizen women, instructed by the 15, held a *sellisternium*, with two chairs set out for Juno and Diana.

1st June on the Capitol, Imperator Caesar Augustus duly sacrificed a bull to Jupiter Optimus Maximus; in the same place Marcus Agrippa sacrificed another. And they prayed as follows:

Jupiter Optimus Maximus, as it is written in your regard in those books, that each and every thing may prosper for the Roman people, the Quirites, a sacrifice of this fine bull should be made to you, I beseech you and pray, the rest as above.

Present at the *atalla* were Caesar, Agrippa, Scaevola, Sentius, Asinius Gallus and Rebilus.

Then Latin performances were begun in the wooden theatre which was erected in the Campus, by the Tiber, and in the same way mothers of households held *sellisternia* and the performances which were started at night were not interrupted; and an edict was published.

The 15 for the performance of sacred rites proclaim: Since there is an established tradition with, moreover, ample precedent that the mourning-period for married citizen women be reduced whenever there is rightful cause for public rejoicing, and since the reintroduction and diligent observation of this tradition, at a time of rites and games so traditionally religious, seems appropriate both to the worship of the gods and to the commemoration of their cult, we have decided that it is our duty to instruct women by edict to reduce their period of mourning.

At night, by the Tiber, Imperator Caesar Augustus offered sacrifice to the divine Ilithyiae with 9 barley-cakes, 9 round-cakes and 9 pill-cakes, and prayed as follows:

Ilithyia, as it is written in your regard in those books, that each and every thing may prosper for the Roman people, the Quirites, a sacrifice of 9 round-cakes, 9 barley-cakes and 9 pill-cakes should be made to you, I beseech you and pray, the rest as above.

2nd June, on the Capitol, Imperator Caesar Augustus sacrificed a cow to Juno the Queen; in the same place Marcus Agrippa sacrificed another; and he prayed as follows:

Juno the Queen, as is written in your regard in those books, that each and every thing may prosper for the Roman people, the Quirites, a sacrifice of this fine cow should be made to you, I beseech you and pray, the rest as above.

Then 110 wedded mothers of households, instructed by ... spoke as follows:

Juno the Queen, whatever may prosper for the Roman people, the

Quirites, ... the wedded mothers of households, on bended knees ... you that ... you increase the ... majesty of the Roman people, the Quirites, at war and at home, and that you always protect the Latin name; that you bestow upon the Roman people, the Quirites, eternal safety, victory and health; and that you favour the Roman people, the Quirites, and keep safe the legions of the Roman people, the Quirites, and the state of the Roman people, the Quirites; and that you be well-disposed and propitious to the Roman people, the Quirites, the 15 for the performance of sacred rites, to us ... This we, 110 wedded mothers of households of the Roman people, on bended knees, beseech you and pray.

Present at the *atalla* were ...

Performances were staged, as on the previous day ...

By night, by the Tiber, Imperator Caesar Augustus sacrificed a pregnant sow to Mother Earth and prayed as follows:

Mother Earth, as it is written in your regard in those books, that each and every thing may prosper for the Roman people, the Quirites, that a sacrifice of a pregnant sow should be duly ... made to you, I beseech you and pray, the rest as above.

The married citizen women held *sellisternia* in the same way as on the previous day.

3rd June, on the Palatine, Imperator Caesar Augustus and Marcus Agrippa made sacrifice to Apollo and Diana with 9 barley-cakes, 9 round-cakes and 9 pill-cakes and they prayed as follows:

Apollo, as it is written in your regard in those books, that each and every thing may prosper for the Roman people, the Quirites, that a sacrifice should be made to you with 9 round-cakes, 9 barley-cakes and 9 pill-cakes, I beseech you and pray, the rest as above.

Apollo, as I have prayed to you with offerings of round-cakes and proper prayer, for this reason be honoured by this offering of barley-cakes and, now and in future, be well-disposed and propitious.

The same for pill-cakes.

To Diana in the same words.

The sacrifice completed, 27 boys so instructed, who have both parents living, and the same number of girls sang the hymn; and in the same way on the Capitol.

Quintus Horatius Flaccus composed the hymn.

Present from the 15 were Imperator Caesar, Marcus Agrippa, Quintus Lepidus, Potitus Messalla, Gaius Stolo, Gaius Scaevola, Gaius Sosius, Gaius Norbanus, Marcus Cocceius, Marcus Lollius, Gaius Sentius, Marcus Strigo, Lucius   Arruntius, Gaius Asinius, Marcus

Marcellus, Decimus Laelius, Quintus Tubero, Gaius Rebilus and Messalla Messallinus.

Stage performances concluded ... next to the place where sacrifice had been made on previous nights and a theatre and stage had been erected, turning-posts were set out and chariots raced and Potitus Messalla set off acrobats on horseback.

An edict was published, as follows:

The 15 for the performance of sacred rites proclaim: To the traditional games we have added seven days of games at our own expense. On 5th June we present Latin performances in the wooden theatre by the Tiber at the second hour, Greek actors in the theatre of Pompey at the third hour, Greek Dionysiac artists in the theatre situated in the Circus Flaminius at the fourth hour.

A day's interval, which was 4th June ...

5th June ... performances were presented in the wooden theatre ..., Greek actors in the theatre of Pompey, Greek Dionysiac artists in the theatre situated in the Circus Flaminius.

10th June, an edict was published, as follows:

The 15 for the performance of sacred rites proclaim:

On 12th June we will give a beast-hunt in ... and we will present circus games ...

12th June, a procession ... boys ... Marcus Agrippa set off the chariots ...

All this was performed by the 15 for the performance of sacred rites: Imperator Caesar Augustus, Marcus Agrippa ... Gnaeus Pompeius, Gaius Stolo, Gaius ... Marcus Marcellus ...

[770] *Zosimus 2.5*
Sibylline Oracle concerning the Secular Games

> But whenever the longest mortal lifetime passes,
> Travelling in a cycle of 110 years,
> Remember, Roman, and if perchance you yourself forget,
> Remember all these things: to sacrifice to the immortal
> Gods in the Campus by the endless stream of Tiber,
> Where narrowest, when night has come upon earth,
> Sun having hidden his light. There make sacred
> Sacrifice to the Moerae, creators of all, she-lambs and she-goats,
> Black, and, for the Ilithyiae, win over
> The child-bearers with sacrifices, as is right. Again, for Earth,
> May a black sow be offered, pregnant with piglets.

And let all-white bulls be led to the altar of Zeus
By day, not by night. For to the heavenly gods
Daytime sacrifice belongs: thus you too make sacrifice.
The fine body of a heifer let Hera's
Temple receive from you. And Phoebus Apollo,
Who is also called Helius, let him receive the same
Offerings, the son of Leto. And may Latin paeans,
Sung by youths and maidens, fill the temples
Of the immortals. And, separately, may the maidens have their chorus
And, separately, the male offspring, boys, but all with
Parents alive, with which their tree is still in flower.
And the women yoked in wedlock, on that day,
On their knees by Hera's renowned altar, let them
Beseech the deity. And cleanse all
Men and women, especially the females.
And let all bring from home what it is right for
Mortals to offer from the first-fruits of their resources.
Propitiations for the gracious deities and the blessed
Children of Heaven. Let all these things lie in store,
Until for females and men in their places,
You remember whence to provide them. Let there be, in days
And nights continuous, by altars worthy of gods,
Thronged festival. May seriousness mix with laughter.
Keep these things always in your heart and remember,
And all the land of Italy and all that of the Latins will
Always wear your yoke on its neck, beneath your sceptres.

[771] Horace, *Secular Hymn*
This is the hymn mentioned in the record of the Secular Games

O Phoebus and Diana, mistress of the woods, bright glory of the
  heavens,
Ever worshipped and ever to be worshipped,
Grant our prayers on this sacred occasion,

When the Sibylline verses have told that
Chosen maidens and chaste youths should hymn
The gods benign to the seven hills.

O kindly Sun, you who bring and take the day with shining chariot,
And are born again, another and the same,
May you behold nothing greater than the city of Rome.

O Ilithyia, duly gracious to timely birth,
Watch over mothers,
Whether you prefer the name Lucina or Genitalis.

Goddess, bring forth the young and
Bless the senators' decrees on the marriage of women
And marital law, fruitful in new offspring,

That the fixed cycle of 110 years
May bring again songs and games, thronged,
Thrice in bright day and thrice in welcome night.

And you, Fates, true in your prophesies, once uttered —
And may the fixed bound of events confirm them —
Join now to our propitious past a prosperous future.

May the earth, productive in crops and herds,
Give Ceres a corn-ear crown,
May Jupiter's breezes and wholesome rains nurture her product.

Phoebus, your weapons set aside, gracious and benign,
Heed the boys that beseech you.
Heed, Moon, crescent queen of the stars, the girls.

If Rome is your creation and the Trojan bands
That reached the Tuscan shore in safety,
A remnant, changing home and city at your command,

Which righteous Aeneas, last hope of his country,
Led in safety through burning Troy to freedom,
Destined to produce more than was abandoned,

Then, gods, bestow virtuous habits on the pliant youth,
Bestow, gods, rest on the peaceful aged,
To the people of Romulus give wealth, peace and every glory.

And may you answer the prayers, offered with white cattle,
Offered by the great descendant of Anchises and Venus,
Conqueror of the ferocious, merciful to the defeated.

Now the Parthian fears our forces, mighty by land and sea, and
   Alban axes.
Now Scythians and Indians, lately proud,
Send us their envoys.

Now Good Faith, Peace, Honour and old-fashioned Propriety
And neglected Virtue are encouraged to return
And blessed Plenty, her horn brim-full.

Phoebus, the prophet, adorned with gleaming bow,
Dear to the Muses, who by his healing skill
Relieves the body's weary limbs —

May Phoebus, if he looks with favour on the altars of the Palatine,
Prolong the Roman state and blessed Latium
Into another cycle and an ever better age.

And may Diana, to whom belong the Aventine and Algidus,
Heed the prayers of the 15
And lend a friendly ear to the entreaties of the boys.

That these are the feelings of Jupiter and all the gods
We cherish the good and confident hope,
We, the chorus, trained to hymn the praises of Phoebus and Diana.

[772] *EJ 33*
Aureus, Rome

Obv. Herald. AUGUSTUS, SON OF A GOD, SECULAR GAMES.
Rev. Head of Iulus (?). MARCUS SANQUINIUS, TRIUMVIR.

[773] *EJ 41*
4 BC, Rome, Forum; cf. *RG* 19.2

Dedicated to the public Lares; Imperator Caesar Augustus, pontifex
maximus, in his 19th year of tribunician power, from the fund which
the people awarded him on January 1st in his absence, in the consulship of Gaius Calvisius Sabinus and Lucius Passienus Rufus.

[774] *ILS 9337*
17 or later, Rome. Record of auguries. Cf.Suet.*Aug*.31.4; Tac.*Ann*.12.23

Auguries.
The greatest, through which the safety of the Roman people is sought,
which was held in the consulship of Lucius Aelius Lamia and Marcus
Servilius and in the consulship of Lucius Pomponius Flaccus and Gaius
Caelius.[1]

1. AD 3 and 17 respectively. The inscription proceeds to record lesser auguries
held in AD 1, 2, 8, 12 and 17.

[775] *CIL 6.141* with A. Audollent, *Defixionum Tabellae* (1904) p. 195 no. 138.
Rome

Danae, the new slave girl of Capito, have this sacrifice offered and consume Danae. You have Eutychia, the wife of Soterichus.

[776] *Small. 156*
3rd April 42. On the wall of the eastern temple at Tentyris, Egypt. Below a relief showing Claudius offering a garland to two Egyptian deities, Khonsou and Seb

For the peace and concord of Tiberius Claudius Caesar Augustus Germanicus, imperator, the above gods, in the prefecture of Lucius Aemilius Rectus, when Tiberius Julius Alexander was epistrategus and Arius, son of Arius, strategus, in year 2 of Tiberius Claudius Caesar Augustus Germanicus, imperator, Pharmouthi 8th Augusta.

[777] *Small. 157*
30th Jan. 49, Egypt

On behalf of Tiberius Claudius Caesar Augustus Germanicus, imperator, . . . , son of Paesis, priest of Dog-Head, the greatest god, built this precinct out of piety. Year 9, Mecheir 5th, for the good.

[778] *Small. 158*
7th July 61; over the main gate of the temple at Caranis, Egypt

For Nero Claudius Caesar Augustus Germanicus, imperator, and his whole house to Pnepheros and Petesouchus, the greatest gods, when Julius Vestinus was the most mighty prefect. Year 7 of the sacred[1] Claudius Caesar Augustus Germanicus, imperator, Epeiph 13th.

1. Inscribed over the erased name Nero.

[779] *Small. 159*
Near Vetera, Lower Germany

[Between two laurels] To Mars Camulus, a dedication for the safety of Nero[1] Claudius Caesar Augustus Germanicus, imperator, the citizens of the Remi who have established the temple. [On the back, within an oak-wreath] For citizens saved.

1. Tiberius is carved over the erased name of Nero in another hand.

[780] *Small. 160*

(a) Moguntiacum, on the base of a column bearing a statue of Jupiter
To Jupiter Optimus Maximus for the safety of Nero Claudius Caesar
Augustus, imperator, the inhabitants of the canabae by public decree,
when Publius Sulpicius Scribonius Proculus was propraetorian legate
of Augustus, under the supervision and at the expense of Quintus
Julius Priscus and Quintus Julius Auctus.
[On the side] Samus and Severus, sons of Venicarus, were the sculptors.

(b) On an adjacent altar
To Jupiter Optimus Maximus, Quintus Julius Priscus and Quintus
Julius Auctus.

[781] *Small. 161*
56-7, Cyrene

For the victory and safety of Nero Claudius Caesar and his whole
house, to Apollo the Disembarker, Marcus Antonius Gemellus from the
funds of Apollo.

[782] *Small. 162*
57-8, Cyrene

To Iatrus and Iaso, for the victory and safety of Nero Claudius Caesar
Augustus Drusus Germanicus, imperator, and his whole house, the
priests of Apollo provided the statues from the funds of Apollo in the
priesthood of Tiberius Claudius Apollonius, son of Priscus.

[783] *EJ 362*
15, Rome

In the consulship of Drusus Caesar and Gaius Norbanus Flaccus,
Menander, slave of Gaius Cominius Macer and Gaius Cornelius Crispus,
won the chariot race at the Games of Mars, put on by the consuls,
with the horses Basiliscus and Rusticus; and at the Games of the
Victory of Caesar, put on by Publius Cornelius Scipio and Quintus
Pompeius Macer, the praetors, with the horses Hister and Corax.

[784] *Small. 48*
Graffiti from Pompeii; cf. Tac. *Ann.* 14.17

(a) Good luck to the Puteolans, good luck to all the Nucerians [in another hand] and the hook for the Pompeians and Pithecusans.
(b) Bad luck to the Nucerians.

[785] *Small. 434*
Graffiti from Pompeii

(a) 24th May, the imperator. It was the day of the Sun.
(b) 18th May, Augustus the consul has come.
(c) Fight, Ganges, Caesar is watching you.
(d) Myrtilus, may Caesar be lucky for you.

[786] *Small. 411*; cf. Tac. *Ann.* 14.27.2-3; Suet. *Nero* 9 Cf. J.H. D'Arms, *Romans on the Bay of Naples* (1970) p. 98.
Graffiti from Pompeii

(a) By the lucky judgement of Augustus, Puteoli, Antium, Tegianum Pompeii – these are true colonies.
(b) To Colonia Claudia Neronensis Puteolana, luckily, written by Gaius Julius Speratus. Farewell, Speratus!

[787] *EJ 360*
Celeia, Noricum

Gaius Julius Vepo, awarded Roman citizenship individually and immunity from taxation by the divine Augustus, made this in his lifetime for himself and Boniata, daughter of Antonius, his wife, and his family.

[788] Vitruvius, *On Architecture*, Preface to Book 1

When, Imperator Caesar, your divine mind and spirit won power over the world and the citizens gloried in your triumph and victory, your virtue invincible, all enemies laid low, and when all the conquered peoples looked to your nod and the Roman people and Senate, freed from fear, was being guided by your very great thoughts and plans, I did not have the courage, at a time so very busy, to publish writings on architecture, unfolded with great deliberation, for I was afraid of intervening at an unsuitable time and obstructing your thoughts.

However, when I saw that you cared not only for the common life of all and the situation of the state but also for the good condition of public buildings, so that through you the city has not only been made greater by the addition of provinces, but the majesty of empire has also gained outstanding authority through the public buildings, I then decided that I should lose no time in publishing, at the first opportunity, this work on this subject for you – all the more so because it was by your father that I was first accorded recognition on the subject and because I was devoted to his virtue. And since the council of heavenly ones have dedicated a place to him in the home of immortality and transferred the empire of your father to your power, that same devotion of mine, true to his memory, has found favour with you.

And so, with Marcus Aurelius and Publius Minidius, I was put in charge of the provision of *ballistae* and *scorpiones* and the repair of other artillery and, with them, received my due, as you, who first gave me this surveyorship, confirmed on the recommendation of your sister.

Since, therefore, I have been bound by that act of beneficence, which means that to my dying day I have no fear of poverty, I begin to write this to you, for I have observed that you have built and are now building a great deal and that in future you will care for both public and private buildings in such a way that they will be remembered by subsequent generations as proportionate to the greatness of your achievements. I have composed detailed prescriptions so that, by attending to them, you can personally understand the nature of past and future constructions. For in these books I have disclosed all the skills of the art.

[789] *EJ 278*
11 BC, senatorial decrees concerning aqueducts

A
Since Quintus Aelius Tubero and Paulus Fabius Maximus, the consuls, presented a statement concerning the appointment of those who have been nominated by Caesar Augustus with the approval of the Senate as the curators of the public aqueducts; asked for their decision on that matter, on that matter they decided as follows:

It is the will of this order that those in charge of the public aqueducts, when their duties take them outside the city, have two lictors each and three public slaves each, one architect each and the same number of secretaries, clerks, assistants and heralds as have those who distribute grain to the plebs. But when in the performance of these same duties they do anything inside the city, that they use the same staff, with the exception of the lictors. And that the curators of aqueducts bring to the treasury, within ten days after the decree of the Senate has been made, the servants that they are permitted to use under this decree of the Senate; and to those so brought the praetors of the treasury should give and grant pay and food for a year, as much as the prefects for the distribution of grain usually give and confer; and they should be permitted to draw that money without prejudice to themselves. And that, with regard to the tablets, paper and other things which the curators need for their performance of their duties, Quintus Aelius and Paulus Fabius, the consuls, both or one of them, if they so decide, should contract out for their provision in consultation with the praetors in charge of the treasury. And likewise, since the curators of roads and grain perform their public duty in a quarter of the year, that the curators of aqueducts should be available for private and public lawsuits.

B

Since Quintus Aelius Tubero and Paulus Fabius Maximus, the consuls, made a statement concerning the number of public fountains which are in the city and inside buildings conjoining the city, fountains which Marcus Agrippa built; asked for their decision, they decided on that matter as follows:

That the Senate does not wish to increase or diminish the number of public fountains reported to exist at present by those charged by the Senate with the task of inspecting the public aqueducts and determining the number of public fountains. And likewise, it is the will of the Senate that the curators of aqueducts whom Caesar Augustus has nominated on the authority of the Senate see to it that the public fountains pour forth water for the use of the people as unremittingly as possible all day and night.

C

Since Quintus Aelius Tubero and Paulus Fabius Maximus, the consuls, made a statement that certain private persons were tapping water from the public conduits; asked for their decision on that matter, on that matter they decided as follows:

That no private person be permitted to tap water from the public conduits and that all those who have the right to draw water draw it from the reservoirs and that the curators of the aqueducts point out places within the city where private persons may properly create reservoirs, from which to draw the water which they had received from the public reservoir through the curators of aqueducts. And that none of those granted public water should have the right to attach a pipe larger than a *quinaria*[1] within fifty feet of that reservoir.

1. A pipe which could carry several thousand gallons per day.

D

Since Quintus Aelius Tubero and Paulus Fabius Maximus, the consuls, made a statement that it must be decided by what right those granted water drew it inside the city and outside the city; asked for their decision on that matter, on that matter they decided as follows:

That the grant of water stand as long as the same owners hold that ground for which they had received water, excepting water given for the use of bath-houses or in the name of Augustus.

E

Since Quintus Aelius Tubero and Paulus Fabius Maximus, the consuls, made a statement concerning the repair of the conduits, channels and arches of aqueducts Julia, Marcia, Appia, Tepula and Anio; asked for their decision on that matter, on that matter they decided as follows:

That when those conduits, channels and arches are repaired – those which Augustus Caesar promised the Senate that he would repair at his own expense – the earth, clay, stones, earthenware, sand, wood and the other materials needed for the task be given up, removed, taken and carried off from the lands of private persons, whence each item may most conveniently be removed, taken and carried without injury to private persons, the cost being assessed by the arbitration of an upright man; and that, in order to carry off all those items and for the sake of the repair of those structures, paths and access remain open and be given through the lands of private persons without injury to them, as often as it may be necessary.

F

Since Quintus Aelius Tubero and Paulus Fabius Maximus, the consuls, made a statement that the courses of the aqueducts which come into the city have been blocked with monuments and buildings and planted with trees; asked for their decision on that matter, on that matter they decided as follows:

When it comes to the repair of conduits and channels, so that a space may be left clear around them and nothing placed in them which might impede the water and damage the public structures, it is decided that 15 feet should be left clear on either side of springs and arches and walls outside the city and that five feet be left empty on either side of underground conduits and channels inside the city and buildings adjoining the city, in such a way that it be permitted henceforth to place no monument or building in those places nor plant trees; whatever trees are now within that space should be uprooted, with the exception of any adjoining a country house or incorporated in buildings. If anyone should act against these regulations, the penalty for each offence is to be 10,000 sesterces, of which half should be given as a reward to the accuser whose endeavour was most responsible for obtaining conviction of the transgressor of this decree of the Senate, but the other half should be paid into the treasury; and on that matter the curators of aqueducts should judge and reach a decision.

[790] *EJ 279*
Quinctian law on aqueducts, 9 BC

Titus Quinctius Crispinus, the consul, on his own initiative duly put the question to the people and the people duly gave its vote in the Forum before the Rostra of the temple of Divine Julius on June 30th. The tribe Sergia led the voting. For his tribe Sextus Vibidius Virro, son of Lucius, was first to vote.

Whoever after the promulgation of this law deliberately, with malice aforethought, should pierce, break, have pierced or broken or do worse to conduits, channels, arches, pipes, tubes, reservoirs or cisterns of the public waters brought into the city so as to impede those waters or part thereof from passing, falling, flowing, coming, being brought into the city of Rome or so as to impede them from rising, being distributed, separated or poured into reservoirs and cisterns in the city of Rome and where there are or will be buildings conjoining the city, in those gardens, estates, places, whose owners, possessors and users have been or will be given or granted water — whoever should so act, that man is to pay a fine of 100,000 sesterces to the Roman people; and he who thus does any of these things with malice aforethought is to be obliged to mend, repair, restore, build, erect, root out and demolish it without malice aforethought; and whoever is or will be curator of aqueducts — or, if there is no curator of aqueducts, then that praetor who administers justice between citizens and peregrines — he is to use compulsion and coercion with fines and sureties; and that curator, or, if there is no curator, then that praetor under that title is to have the right and power of compulsion, coercion, fixing of fines or taking of sureties. If a slave should do any of those things, his master is to pay a fine of 100,000 sesterces to the people. If any place around the conduits, channels, arches, pipes, tubes, reservoirs or cisterns of the public waters, which are or will be brought to the city of Rome, is or will be enclosed, no one is to block, build, fence off, fix, erect, place, locate, plough or sow in that place subsequent to this law, nor is anyone to introduce anything into it, except for the purpose of building or replacing those structures, which will be permitted and necessary under this law. Whoever would do anything against those measures, the same statute, law and procedure is to apply, in each and every particular, as applies or should apply if that man had broken or pierced a conduit or channel contrary to this law. This law does nothing to impede the right to pasture, cut grass or hay and gather briar in that place. The curators of the aqueducts, at present and in future, are to act so that, in that place which is enclosed around springs and arches and walls and conduits and channels, trees, vines, brambles, briars, banks, fences, willows and reed-beds are removed, cut out, dug out and uprooted, as they wish it properly done; and under that title they are to be able to take sureties, fix fines and exercise coercion and they are to be permitted to do it without personal prejudice, and they are to have the right and power. This law does nothing to impede the retention of vines and trees incorporated in country houses, buildings and walls, and walls in the case of which the curators of aqueducts have allowed their owners exception from demolition after hearing the case and on which the names of the curators who gave their permission have been inscribed or carved. This law does nothing to impede those who are or will be permitted to take and draw water from those springs, conduits, channels and arches, quite apart from those permitted to use wheel, tapping-pipe or machine, provided that no well or new breach is made.

[791] *EJ 280*
Boundary stones near Rome, separating aqueducts and adjacent lands from other lands: they were regularly placed 240 feet apart

(a) The Julia, Tepula and Marcia; Imperator Caesar Augustus, son of a god, by decree of the Senate, 103,240 feet.
(b) The Marcia; Imperator Caesar Augustus, son of a god, by decree of the Senate, 1152,240 feet.
(c) The Julia; Imperator Caesar Augustus, son of a god, by decree of the Senate, 302,240 feet.

[792] *EJ 281*
5-4 BC, Rome, on the Aqua Marcia

Imperator Caesar Augustus, son of a god, pontifex maximus, consul 12 times, in his 19th year of tribunician power, imperator 14 times, repaired the conduits of all the aqueducts.

[793] *EJ 282*
Between 18 and 11 BC, near Venafrum: edict of Augustus on the aqueduct there

Edict of Imperator Caesar Augustus . . . [about six lines missing] . . . in the name of the Venafrans . . . it should be right and permitted. As to those conduits, channels, sluices, springs and . . . made, built or constructed above or below the water-level for the purpose of aqueduct erection or repair, or any other construction built above or below the water-level for the purpose of the erection or repair of that aqueduct, it is ordered that whichever of these things has been built, it is to continue in the same state and in the same state be rebuilt, replaced, restored, refurbished once and more often; pipes, culverts, vessels are to be put in place, an aperture made, and anything else necessary for the erection of the aqueduct is to be done. At the same time, as to that stretch of land in the estate which is or is said to be that of Quintus Sirinius, son of Lucius, of the tribe Teretina, and on the estate which is or is said to be that of Lucius Pompeius Sulla, son of Marcus, of the tribe Teretina, fenced-off by a wall, through which place or under which place conduits of that aqueduct pass, let neither that wall nor any part of that wall be demolished or removed, except for the purpose of repairing or inspecting a channel; and let there be no private obstacle to the passage, flow or conveyance of that water . . .

It is ordered that to the right and left of that conduit and of those structures erected for the conveyance of water, eight feet of land be left empty, through which place it should be right and permitted for the Venafrans or those acting in the name of the Venafrans . . . to pass for the purpose of building or rebuilding the aqueduct or structures pertaining to that aqueduct, provided that this is done without malice aforethought. And it should be right and permitted for them to convey, bring, carry whatever is necessary for the purpose of this building or rebuilding, by the shortest possible route, and to deposit whatever is removed from there in the eight feet to the right and left, as equally as possible, provided that a promissory oath is made for any consequent damage.

It is ordered that the Venafran colonists should have jurisdiction and power over all this so arranged provided that no owner of any field or place through which that water usually passes, flows or is conveyed, is denied access as a result of this work; and provided that he is no less able to pass, transfer or traverse directly from one part of his land to another; and provided that no one through whose land the water is conveyed is permitted to damage, tap or divert the aqueduct or hinder the direct conveyance and flow of the water to the town of the Venafrans.

As to the water which passes, flows, is conveyed to the town of the Venafrans, it is ordered that jurisdiction and power to distribute and apportion that water for the purpose of sale or to impose and constitute a tax on that subject be vested in the duumvir or duumvirs appointed in that colony by decree of the majority of decurions, provided that that decree is made when at least two-thirds of the decurions are present; and that he should have jurisdiction and authority to regulate the matter by a decree of the decurions made in the manner prescribed above. This obtains provided that the water so distributed and apportioned or concerning which such a decree is made is not conveyed in any way other than by lead pipes up to fifty feet from the main course; and provided that those pipes and the main course are only placed and situated underground, which ground is to be treated as the course of a public road, way or boundary; and provided that the water is not conducted through a private place whose owner is unwilling. And it is ordered that any regulation, which the duumvirs appointed by decree of the decurions in the manner prescribed above should enact for the protection of the water and for the protection of the conveyance or use of the water, should be firm and ratified . . . [about 11 lines missing] . . . Venafran . . . which to a colonist or inhabitant . . . it is ordered that the person entrusted with the matter by decree of the decurions in the manner stipulated above, when bringing a lawsuit, the judge of disputes between citizens and peregrines should grant a recuperatory action for 10,000 sesterces in each matter, and up to ten witnesses may be called, provided that the complainant and the defendant are permitted to reject recuperators as will be their right and privilege under the law passed concerning private lawsuits.

[794] *EJ 283*
Two boundary stones with identical inscriptions, near the aqueduct of Venafrum

By order of Imperator Caesar Augustus, around the channel built for the conveyance of water, eight feet of land to right and left has been left empty.

[795] *EJ 284*
Between 21 and 30, Nicopolis, Syria

Tiberius Caesar Augustus, imperator, son of divine Augustus, grandson of divine Julius, pontifex maximus, consul four times, with tribunician power, had the Aqua Augusta brought to Nicopolis under the supervision of Gnaeus Saturninus, legate of Caesar Augustus.

[796] *EJ 285*
10-11, Alexandria, bilingual

Imperator Caesar Augustus, son of a god, pontifex maximus, brought in the River Sebaste from Schedia from the 25th milestone to flow throughout the city due to himself, the prefect of Egypt being Gaius Julius Aquila, year 40 of Caesar.

[797] *EJ 286*
27 BC, Ariminum, arch

The Senate and people of Rome to Imperator Caesar Augustus, son of a god, imperator seven times, consul seven times, designate for an eighth, the Via Flaminia and the other most frequented roads of Italy having been built through his initiative and expense.

[798] *EJ 287*
Denarius, 16 BC, Rome

Obv. Head of Augustus. AUGUSTUS, IN HIS 7TH YEAR OF TRIBUNICIAN POWER.

Rev. Boundary stone inscribed: THE SENATE AND PEOPLE OF ROME TO IMPERATOR CAESAR BECAUSE THE ROADS WERE BUILT OUT OF THE MONEY WHICH HE TRANSFERRED TO THE TREASURY. Outside the stone: LUCIUS VINICIUS, SON OF LUCIUS, TRIUMVIR.

[799] *EJ 288*
2-1 BC, near Bononia, milestone

Imperator Caesar Augustus, pontifex maximus, consul 13 times, in his 22nd year of tribunician power, had the Via Aemilia built from Ariminum to the River Trebia, 79.

[800] *EJ 289*
2 BC, Baetica, milestone

Imperator Caesar Augustus, son of a god, consul 13 times, in his 21st year of tribunician power, pontifex maximus, from the Baetis and Janus Augustus to the Ocean, 63.

[801] *EJ 290*
14, Africa, milestone

Imperator Caesar Augustus, in his 16th year of tribunician power. Asprenas, consul, proconsul, one of the 7 for feasts had the road built from the winter quarters at Tacape. Legion 3 Augusta, 1 . . .

[802] *EJ 291*
Lepcis Magna, milestone

By order of Imperator Tiberius Caesar Augustus, Lucius Aelius Lamia, proconsul, laid down this road from the town to the mediterranean, 44 miles.

[803] *EJ 292*
16-7, Salonae

5. Tiberius Caesar Augustus, son of divine Augustus, imperator, pontifex maximus, in his 18th year of tribunician power, consul twice, built the road from the colony of Salonae . . . streets . . . and he also built . . . to Ulcirus, the highest peak of the Ditiones, over a distance of 423 miles from Salonae, Publius Dolabella being propraetorian legate.

[804] *EJ 293*
19-20, Salonae

Tiberius Caesar Augustus, son of divine Augustus, imperator, pontifex maximus, in his 21st year of tribunician power, consul three times, built the road from the colony of Salonae to ... the fort of the Daesitiates over a distance of 156 miles and he also built a road from Salonae to the River ... which divides ... from ... 158 miles.

[805] *EJ 294*
6 BC, Comama, Pisidia; cf. B.M. Levick, *Roman Colonies in Southern Asia Minor* (1967) pp. 38-41

Imperator Caesar Augustus, son of a god, pontifex maximus, consul 11 times, designate for a twelfth, imperator 15 times, in his 18th year of tribunician power, built the Via Sebaste under the supervision of Cornutus Aquila, his propraetorian legate.

[806] *EJ 295*
Rome

Gaius Asinius Gallus, son of Gaius,[1] and Gaius Marcius Censorinus, son of Lucius, consuls,[2] drew boundaries by decree of the Senate, next boundary stone being 18½ feet in a straight line. The curators of river banks who first drew boundaries restored them by decree of the Senate.

1. Name erased.
2. 8 BC.

[807] *ILS 5924a*
7-6 BC, Rome

Imperator Caesar Augustus, son of a god, pontifex maximus, in his 17th year of tribunician power, drew boundaries by decree of the Senate, next boundary stone being 206 feet in a straight line. [On the back] Next boundary stone, 205 feet in a straight line.

[808] *EJ 297*
27-23 BC, Rome

(a) That land within the boundary stones in the direction of the Campus Caesar Augustus, having bought it back from private persons, made public property.

(b) That land within the boundary stones in the direction of the Campus is public property.

[809] *EJ 298*
Rome

Titus Quinctius Crispinus Valerianus, Gaius Calpetanus Statius Rufus, Gaius Pontius Paelignus, Gaius Petronius Umbrinus and Marcus Crassus Frugi, curators for the judgement of disputes over public places by decree of the Senate, after hearing the case, restored this from private to public possession.

[810] *Small. 307*
(a) Ostia = *EJ 296*
Gaius Antistius Vetus, son of Gaius, grandson of Gaius, Gaius Valerius Flaccus Tanyris (?), Publius Vergilius Pontianus, son of Marcus, Publius Catienus Sabinus, son of Publius, and Tiberius Vergilius Rufus, son of Tiberius, curators of the banks and bed of the Tiber by decree of the Senate drew boundaries . . . feet distant in a straight line.

(b) Rome, Campus Martius
Paullus Fabius Persicus, Gaius Eggius Marullus, Lucius Sergius Paullus, Gaius Obellius Rufus and Lucius Scribonius Libo, curators of the banks and bed of the Tiber, by authority of Tiberius Claudius Caesar Augustus Germanicus, their princeps, drew boundaries on the bank with boundary-stones set up from Trigarium to the bridge of Agrippa.

[811] *Small. 308*
(a) 44-5, Rome, on the Aqua Virgo
The Virgo; Tiberius Claudius Caesar Augustus Germanicus, son of Drusus, pontifex maximus, in his fourth year of tribunician power, consul 3 times, imperator 8 times, father of his country, 45,240 ft.

(b) 46, Rome, on the Aqua Virgo
Tiberius Claudius Caesar Augustus Germanicus, son of Drusus, pontifex maximus, in his fifth year of tribunician power, imperator 11 times, father of his country, consul designate for the fourth time, made new from the foundations and restored the arches of aqueduct Aqua Virgo disturbed by Gaius Caesar.[1]

1. In connection with the amphitheatre he began; cf. Suet. *Cal.* 21.

[812] *Small. 309*; cf. Tac. *Ann.* 11.13; Suet. *Claud.* 20
52-3, Rome on the Aqua Claudia, at the Praenestine Gate

Tiberius Claudius Caesar Augustus Germanicus, son of Drusus, pontifex maximus, in his 12th year of tribunician power, consul 5 times, imperator 27 times, father of his country, had brought into the city at his own expense the Aqua Claudia, from the springs which are called Caeruleus and Curtius, from milestone 45, likewise the Aqua Anio Nova from milestone 62.

[813] *Small. 310*
Rome

Here the channels of three aqueducts pass;[1] boundary-stones set up by order of Aulus Didius Gallus, Titus Rubrius Nepos, Marcus Cornelius Firmus, curators of the water supply.[2]

1. The Julia, Tepula and Marcia.   2. Gallus was curator; the other two seem to have been his assistants.

[814] *Small. 311*
47-8, Rome near the Tiber

Tiberius Claudius Caesar Augustus and Lucius Vitellius, son of Publius, restored to the state, after judicial inquiry, by due form of law, places which were in the possession of private persons through pillars and columns.

[815] *Small. 312*
(a) dupondius, 41, Rome
Obv. Head of Claudius, bare. TIBERIUS CLAUDIUS CAESAR AUGUSTUS, PONTIFEX MAXIMUS, WITH TRIBUNICIAN POWER, IMPERATOR
Rev. Ceres, enthroned, holding corn-ears and a long torch. CERES AUGUSTA, BY DECREE OF THE SENATE

(b) 46, near Ostia
Tiberius Claudius Caesar Augustus Germanicus, son of Drusus, pontifex maximus, in his sixth year of tribunician power, consul designate for the fourth time, imperator 12 times, father of his country, with ditches dug from the Tiber on account of the port project and extended into the sea, liberated the city from the danger of flooding.

[816] *Small. 313*

(a) Sestertius, 64-6, Rome

Obv. Head of Nero, laureate. NERO CLAUDIUS CAESAR AUGUSTUS GERMANICUS, PONTIFEX MAXIMUS, WITH TRIBUNICIAN POWER, IMPERATOR, FATHER OF HIS COUNTRY

Rev. The harbour at Ostia, represented by a pier, breakwaters and a lighthouse surmounted by a statue of Neptune; ships in the centre and a reclining figure of Neptune below. OF THE AUGUSTAN PORT OF OSTIA, BY DECREE OF THE SENATE

(b) Sestertius, 64-6, Rome

Obv. Head of Nero, laureate. NERO CLAUDIUS CAESAR AUGUSTUS GERMANICUS, PONTIFEX MAXIMUS, WITH TRIBUNICIAN POWER, IMPERATOR, FATHER OF HIS COUNTRY

Rev. Annona[1] standing, holding a horn of plenty; Ceres, seated, holding corn-ears and a torch; between them a modius on an altar, with the stern of a ship behind. ANNONA OF AUGUSTUS,[1] CERES, BY DECREE OF THE SENATE

1. The goddess Corn-Supply; cf. G. Rickman, *The Corn Supply of Ancient Rome* (1980) pp. 260-7.

[817] *Small. 314*

Dupondius, 64-6, Rome

Obv. Head of Nero, radiate. NERO CLAUDIUS CAESAR AUGUSTUS GERMANICUS, PONTIFEX MAXIMUS, WITH TRIBUNICIAN POWER, IMPERATOR, FATHER OF HIS COUNTRY

Rev. A large two-storey circular building with projecting wings. MARKET-HOUSE OF AUGUSTUS, BY DECREE OF THE SENATE

[818] *Small. 315*

42-3, Cyprus

Under Imperator Tiberius Claudius Caesar Augustus Germanicus, year 3, Titus Cominius Proculus, proconsul, and Titus Catienus Sabinus, legate and propraetor, brought in the water that flows from the spring in the Marshes ... [several lines missing] ... as quaestor he conducted his magistracy in the first year of the principate of Tiberius Claudius Caesar Augustus, imperator.

[819] *Small. 316*
47-8, Samos

Tiberius Claudius Caesar Augustus Germanicus, pontifex maximus, in his 7th year of tribunician power, imperator 15 times, consul 4 times, father of his country, censor, restored the temple of Liber Pater, collapsed through age and earthquake.

[820] *Small. 317*
49-50, lead pig, S. W. Britain

Tiberius Claudius Caesar Augustus, pontifex maximus, in his 9th year of tribunician power, imperator 16 times, over the Britons.

[821] *Small. 318*
52-4, Sardis, bilingual

Tiberius Claudius Caesar Augustus Germanicus, son of Drusus, pontifex maximus, in his ... year of tribunician power, consul 5 times, imperator 27 times, father of his country, brought an aqueduct from the spring to the city of the Sardians, Tiberius Claudius Apollophanes, son of Demetrius, of the tribe Quirina, supervising the work.

[822] *Small. 319*
57, Olisipo, Lusitania

To Nero Claudius Caesar Augustus Germanicus, son of the divine Claudius, grandson of Germanicus Caesar, great-grandson of Tiberius Caesar, great-great-grandson of the divine Augustus, pontifex maximus, in his third year of tribunician power, imperator three times, consul twice, designate for a third time, Gaius Heius Primus Cato, Augustalis in perpetuity ... Heia ... dedicated this.

[823] *Small. 320*
53-4, Lepcis Magna, Tripolitania

To Tiberius Claudius Caesar Augustus Germanicus, son of Drusus, pontifex maximus, in his 13th year of tribunician power, imperator 27 times, consul 5 times, censor, father of his country, Marcus Pompeius Silvanus,[1] consul, one of the 15 for the performance of sacred rites, proconsul, patron, made this dedication, Quintus Cassius

Gratus, praetor, proconsul of Crete and Cyrene, being propraetorian legate of Africa. The son of Gaius Anno, in the name of the son of Gaius Anno, his grandson, gave at his own expense the columns with their superstructure and the forum; Balitho Commodus, son of Anno Macer, adopted by will, had this made.

1. cf. Tac. *Ann*. 13.52.

[824] *Small. 321*
61-2, Lepcis Magna, Tripolitania

To Nero Claudius Caesar Augustus Germanicus, son of the divine Claudius, grandson of Germanicus, great-grandson of Tiberius Caesar, great-great-grandson of the divine Augustus, pontifex maximus, in his 8th year of tribunician power, imperator . . . times, consul 4 times, father of his country, Servius Cornelius Orfitus, son of Servius, of the tribe Lemonia, quaestor of the divine Claudius, urban praetor, consul, priest, sodalis Augustalis, proconsul, patron, made this dedication, Publius Silius Celer . . . being legate . . . columns and upper-columns and upper-doors in three . . . Ithymbal Sabinus, son of Arinis, priest of the divine Augustus, had these made while suffete and also, as curator of public money, . . . those porticoes . . .

[825] *Small. 328 = EJ 363a*
46

Tiberius Claudius Caesar Augustus Germanicus, pontifex maximus, in his sixth year of tribunician power, consul designate for the fourth time, imperator 11 times, father of his country, built the Via Claudia Augusta, which Drusus, his father, constructed after opening the Alps by war, from the River Po to the River Danube, a distance of 350 miles.

[826] *Small. 329*
47, cippus, Foruli, Sabinum

Tiberius Claudius Caesar Augustus Germanicus, son of Drusus, pontifex maximus, in his 7th year of tribunician power, consul 4 times, imperator 11 times, father of his country, censor designate, had the Via Claudia Nova paved from Foruli to the confluence of the Atternus and Tirinus, a distance of 47 miles, 192 paces.

[827] *Small. 330*
48-9, Teate Marrucinorum

Tiberius Claudius Caesar Augustus Germanicus, pontifex maximus, in his 8th year of tribunician power, imperator 16 times, consul 4 times, father of his country, censor, built the Via Claudia Valeria from Cerfennia to Ostia Aterni and also built 43 bridges.

[828] *Small. 331*
On a bridge on the Via Cassia, near Viterbo

Tiberius Claudius Caesar Augustus built this.

[829] *Small. 332*
Near Tergeste, Histria

This road, built by the agency of the centurion Atius in pursuance of the decision of Aulus Plautius, legate of Tiberius Claudius Caesar Augustus Germanicus, and later carried from the Rundictes to the borders of Gaius Laecanius Bassus, was restored by order of Tiberius Claudius Caesar Augustus Germanicus, imperator, by Lucius Rufellius Severus, chief centurion.

[830] *Small. 333*
39, milestone on the Via Augusta, Cordoba

Gaius Caesar Germanicus Augustus, son of Germanicus Caesar, grandson of Tiberius Augustus, great-grandson of the divine Augustus, great-great-grandson of the divine Julius, father of his country, consul twice, imperator, in his second year of tribunician power, pontifex maximus, from the Baetis and Augustan Janus to the Ocean, 62.

[831] *Small. 334*
39 or 40, milestone, near Santiago de Compostela

Gaius Caesar Augustus Germanicus, son of Germanicus Caesar, grandson of Tiberius Caesar Augustus, great-grandson of the divine Augustus, father of his country, pontifex maximus, in his fourth[1] year of tribunician power, consul twice,[1] . . . miles.

1. One of these figures is wrong.

[832] *Small. 335*
41, milestones on the Via Domitia, Narbonensis

(a) Between Nemausus and Arelate
Tiberius Claudius Caesar Augustus Germanicus, son of Drusus, pontifex maximus, with tribunician power, consul designate for the second time, imperator twice, repaired this.

(b) Between Nemausus and Narbo
Tiberius Claudius Caesar Augustus Germanicus, son of Drusus, pontifex maximus, with tribunician power, consul designate for the second time, imperator twice, repaired this, 85.

[833] *Small. 336*
43-4, milestone near Vienna on the Lugdunum-Arelate road

Tiberius Claudius Caesar Augustus Germanicus, son of Drusus, pontifex maximus, in his third year of tribunician power, imperator three times, consul three times, father of his country, 7.

[834] *Small. 337*
43-4, milestone on the Lugdunum-Genava road

Under Tiberius Claudius Caesar Augustus Germanicus, son of Drusus, pontifex maximus, in his third year of tribunician power, consul three times, imperator, father of his country, 119.

[835] *Small. 338*
43-4, milestone on the Cavillonum-Andemantunnum road, Lugdunensis

Tiberius Claudius Caesar Augustus Germanicus, son of Drusus, pontifex maximus, in his third year of tribunician power, imperator three times, father of his country, consul three times, designate for the fourth, from Andemantunnum 22 miles.

[836] *Small. 339*
45-6, milestone on the Lugdunum-Augustonemetum road

Tiberius Claudius Caesar Augustus Germanicus, son of Drusus, pontifex maximus, in his fifth year of tribunician power, imperator 11 times, father of his country, consul three times, designate for the fourth, from Augustonemetum 21 miles.

[837] *Small. 340*
44-5, milestone at Confluentes, on the Colonia Agrippina-Moguntiacum road

Tiberius Claudius Caesar Augustus Germanicus, son of Drusus, pontifex maximus, in his fourth year of tribunician power, imperator 8 times, consul designate for the fourth time, father of his country, from Moguntiacum 59 miles.

[838] *Small. 341*
44-5, milestone near Ilerda on the Osca-Barcino road, Tarraconensis

Tiberius Claudius Caesar Augustus Germanicus, pontifex maximus, in his fourth year of tribunician power, imperator 8 times, consul three times, father of his country, 238.

[839] *Small. 342*
50, milestone on the Emerita-Salmantica road, Lusitania

Tiberius Claudius Caesar Augustus Germanicus, son of Drusus, pontifex maximus, in his tenth year of tribunician power, consul 4 times, imperator 21 times, repaired the road.

[840] *Small. 343*
46, milestone on the Carrales-Turris road, Sardinia

27 miles from Turris; Tiberius Claudius Caesar Augustus Germanicus, pontifex maximus, in his sixth year of tribunician power, father of his country, imperator 11 times, consul designate for the fourth time, Lucius Aurelius Patroclus being prefect of the province of Sardinia.

[841] *Small. 344*
47-8, milestone on the Burnum-River Sana road, Dalmatia

Tiberius Claudius Caesar Augustus Germanicus, pontifex maximus, in his 7th year of tribunician power, imperator 14 times, consul 4 times, father of his country, censor, 36.

[842] *Small. 345*
45-6, first milestone on the Cyrene-Balagrae road

Tiberius Claudius Caesar Augustus Germanicus, pontifex maximus, in his fifth year of tribunician power, imperator 11 times, father of his country, consul 3 times, designate for the fourth, restored this in year . . . of Caernius Veiento, proconsul of Crete and Cyrene, 1.

[843] *Small. 346*
Hierapytna, Crete

Tiberius Claudius Caesar Augustus Germanicus repaired the roads and the footpaths through Gaius Paconius Agrippinus,[1] quaestor for the second year and fixer of boundaries.

1. Cf. Tac. *Ann.* 16.28ff.

[844] *Small. 347*
50, Attalea, Pamphylia, bilingual

Tiberius Claudius Caesar Augustus Germanicus, son of Drusus, pontifex maximus, in his tenth year of tribunician power, imperator 18 times, father of his country, consul designate for the fifth time, through Marcus Arruntius Aquila, his procurator, repaired the roads.

[845] *Small. 348*
Amastris, Pontus, bilingual

For the Augustan peace, in honour of Tiberius Claudius Germanicus Augustus, the perpetual priest of the divine Augustus, Gaius Julius Aquila,[1] prefect of engineers twice, transferred to the treasury by the consuls Aulus Gabinius Secundus and Taurus Statilius Corvinus,[2] cut the mountain and at his own expense built the road and its bed.

1. Cf. Tac. *Ann.* 12.15 and 21.
2. AD 45.

[846] *Small. 349*
58, near Prusa, Bithynia

Nero Claudius Caesar Augustus Germanicus, son of the divine Claudius, grandson of Germanicus Caesar, great-grandson of Tiberius Caesar Augustus, great-great-grandson of the divine Augustus, pontifex maximus, in his fourth year of tribunician power, imperator 5 times, consul

3 times, restored the road from Apamea to Nicaea, collapsed with age, and had it built through Gaius Julius Aquila, his procurator.

[847] *Small. 350*
56, milestone near Berytus, Syria

Nero Claudius Caesar Augustus Germanicus, in his second year of tribunician power, consul designate for the second time, built the road from Antioch to the new colony of Ptolemais of 234 miles, 47 miles, Gaius Ummidius Durmius Quadratus being propraetorian legate.

[848] *Small. 351*
61-2, near Philippopolis, Thrace

Nero Claudius Caesar Augustus Germanicus, son of the divine Claudius, grandson of Germanicus Caesar, great-grandson of Tiberius Caesar Augustus, great-great-grandson of the divine Augustus, pontifex maximus, in the 8th year of his tribunician power, imperator 8 times, consul 4 times, father of his country, ordered inns and rest-houses to be built along the military roads through Tiberius Julius Ustus, procurator of the province of Thrace.

[849] *Small. 352*
58, milestone on the Forum Julii-Aquae Sextiae road, Narbonensis

Nero Claudius Caesar Augustus Germanicus, son of the divine Claudius, grandson of Germanicus Caesar, great-grandson of Tiberius Caesar Augustus, great-great-grandson of the divine Augustus, pontifex maximus, in his fourth year of tribunician power, imperator four times, consul three times, father of his country, restored this.

INDEX OF PERSONAL NAMES

NB. Figures refer to the numbers of items in this collection. The names of some minor characters have been omitted, as have names mentioned in passing. Names are listed in their more familiar forms: M. Vipsanius Agrippa thus occurs as Agrippa, M. Vipsanius.

INDEX OF SOURCES

DATE DUE